The Wines of New Zealand

Rosemary George was lured into the wine trade in 1972 by a glass of the Wine Society's champagne and became one of the first women to pass the Master of Wine examinations in 1979. Her first book *The Wines and Chablis of the Yonne* won both the André Simon Award and the Glenfiddich Prize. She has since written several more books, including the very successful *French Country Wines* (for Faber) and *Lateral Wine Tasting*. She now works as a freelance wine writer and is a regular contributor to wine magazines in both Britain and the USA.

THE WINES OF
NEW ZEALAND

ROSEMARY GEORGE

To Nick

Hope this leads yr
to some good bottles

Rosemary

ff

faber and faber

LONDON · BOSTON

First published in 1996
by Faber and Faber Limited
3 Queen Square London WC1N 3AU

Phototypeset by Intype London Limited
Printed in England by Clays Ltd, St Ives plc

Cartography by Terralink NZ Ltd,
Licence PL 10003/1 Crown Right Reserved

A CIP catalogue record for this book
is available from the British Library

ISBN 0-571-17420-5

2 4 6 8 10 9 7 5 3

I would like to dedicate this book to Margaret Harvey, who first kindled my enthusiasm for New Zealand wine. I suspect that few members of the New Zealand wine industry realize the debt they owe to Margaret for her pioneering of New Zealand wine at a time when most of us this side of the world were totally ignorant of it. She paved the way for the explosion of interest in New Zealand wines, laying solid foundations and even now continues quietly and persistently to fight for the cause. Thank you, Margaret.

Contents

CONTENTS

List of Maps

Acknowledgements

Books about wine are ultimately books about people and thus it is all the members of the New Zealand wine industry, mentioned between the covers of this book, whom I must thank – for their friendly welcome and warm hospitality, their readiness to open bottles, share their thoughts and ideas, and discuss their plans and projects, aspirations and achievements. They each contributed in their own way and without them this book would never have happened.

Next, I must recognize other debts of gratitude. I owe enormous thanks to Rod MacKenzie and his organization, The New Zealand Way, which is funded principally by New Zealand industry in order to promote the image of New Zealand. One of the ways in which it does this is by sponsoring projects that will be seen to enhance New Zealand's international standing. Luckily for me, it deemed a book on New Zealand wine worthy of its attention and relieved me of the financial burden, not only of travelling twice to the other side of the world, but also contributed to my travelling expenses within New Zealand.

Vicky Bishop of the New Zealand Wine Guild here in London and Louise Hill, her counterpart in Auckland, simplified my life with their organization of the intricacies of my itinerary. Thanks to their efforts, I knew that all I had to do was get up each morning and someone would appear to take me to the first winery, and thus I was passed like a parcel, from winery to winery, around Hawke's Bay, Marlborough, and so on, with barely a hitch in the arrangements. It would have been quite impossible for me to have achieved the same efficient use of time from London.

Two friends read my manuscript and made constructive comments: Margaret Harvey of Fine Wines of New Zealand, based here in London, and John Comerford in Wellington, who, although not actively involved in the wine industry, has acted as chairman of the judging panel for the Air New Zealand Wine Awards for a number of years. I am immensely grateful for their comments, insights and encouragement, all of which helped to make this a much better book. Steve Smith from the Villa Maria Group also deserves special thanks for reading my viticulture chapter. As a complete novice on the subject who has never even picked grapes, I was very reassured to have his expert guidance.

I would also like to thank my great friends in Waimauku, Anne and Mike Minton, and their daughter Sarah, for providing a relaxed haven from the rigours of a day of winery visits on the several occasions that I stayed with them, not to mention meeting me and taking me to Auckland airport at anti-social hours.

Back home, I must thank Julian Jeffs for commissioning this book and thereby enabling me to spend more time in one of my favourite countries, and at Faber and Faber I would like to thank Belinda Matthews for her encouragement during the writing process. My husband too, Christopher Galleymore, deserves thanks not only for enduring my disappearances to the other side of the world, but also for living with a gestating book.

Author's Note

The first visit of a European to a vineyard in the southern hemisphere can be something of a shock as things are back to front down under.

You need to remember that a north-facing vineyard site is highly desirable as it receives the full warmth of the midday sun. South-facing slopes remain firmly in the shade.

Secondly, their spring is in our autumn. The vines break bud in September and October; the flowering takes place at the end of November, not in June; and the vintage in Gisborne may start in February and carry on until June in Central Otago.

New Zealanders tend to talk in acres, as we do, but official statistics use hectares. I have tried to reconcile the two, using a conversion factor of 2.471 acres to the hectare.

The other useful conversion figure is that £1 buys you approximately NZ$2.30 (New Zealand dollars).

- LONGVIEW ESTATE

- GOLDWATER
- PENINSULA
- STONYRIDGE
- TE MOTU

- OKAHU ESTATE

- TOTARA

- HERON'S FLIGHT
- THE ANTIPODEAN

- OHINEMURI

- DE REDCLIFFE

- MORTON ESTATE

- MILLS REEF

- ASPEN RIDGE
- RONGOPAI

Kaitaia
Waitangi
Kerikeri
Dargaville
2 Whangarei

Waikeke I.
Auckland
1.
Thames
Te Kauwhata
Hamilton
Tauranga
Whakatane

TASMAN SEA

Rotorua

Taupo

New Plymouth

Hawke's Bay
2. Gisborne

MAPPED AREAS
1. Auckland
2. Gisborne
3. Hawke's Bay
4. Martinborough
5. Nelson
6. Marlborough
7. Canterbury
8. Central Otago

Waiouru
3.
Napier
Hastings
- COVELL ESTATE

Wanganui
Palmerston North

Motueka
Nelson
Richmond
5.
6.
Blenheim

Masterton
4. Martinborough
Wellington

Westport

Greymouth
Hokitika
Kaikoura

7.
Christchurch

PACIFIC OCEAN

8.
Wanaka
Timaru
Queenstown
Arrowtown
Oamaru

0   100   200 km

Dunedin

Invercargill

Stewart Island

New Zealand

I

Introduction: Setting the scene

The rise of New Zealand wines in the last decade has been nothing short of meteoric. Ten years ago we could have been forgiven for asking, 'New Zealand? Do they make wine?' Abroad, New Zealand wines were quite unknown. On the British market, odd examples were just beginning to appear at tastings. They were not taken very seriously, but treated as a curiosity, with the same attitude applied to English and Welsh wines. Yet in an amazingly short time span, New Zealand has become a serious participant in the British wine market, more than holding its own alongside other New World countries, not to mention the old established wine regions of Europe.

The wine that converted most of us to the delights of New Zealand was Sauvignon Blanc. I am no exception. I can vividly remember arranging to meet another wine-writing friend for a drink in the Cork and Bottle, a London wine bar run by a New Zealander, Don Hewitson, who is always abreast of any new wines, whatever their provenance. This was some time in 1984. I was late, Aileen Hall was already installed with a bottle and I was greeted with the words, 'Don has just put this wonderful new New Zealand wine on his list. It's simply delicious and you've got to try it.' The wine was Montana's Marlborough Sauvignon. It was delicious and we had a second bottle.

Somehow, New Zealand had achieved the impossible. It had given us a completely new flavour, a taste that was quite unlike any other from anywhere else. Sauvignon from France, from the Loire Valley, was discreet and understated; in contrast, Sauvignon from New Zealand packed a punch of flavour. It was unique in that not only did it lack the subtlety of European wines, but it was also quite unlike any of the other upfront flavours coming out of the New World vineyards for the simple reason that those of New Zealand are significantly cooler than any in California, Australia, South America or South Africa.

Where these countries look for their cooler microclimates for grape growing, New Zealand looks for drier, warmer sites. This means that New Zealand is able to achieve the depth of flavours that are not possible in warmer countries. Why do English apples and strawberries taste better, or Tuscan olive oil? For the simple reason that they are grown on the climatic edge, where the fruit struggles to survive and therefore achieves a depth of flavour that is not dulled by too much sunshine. This is the reason why an Australian chose to plant a vineyard in Marlborough, so that he could produce Sauvignon Blanc with flavours that were impossible to achieve in Western Australia. The result was Cloudy Bay and another success story for New Zealand wine.

Gradually, during the second half of the 1980s, the range of New Zealand wines expanded. Margaret Harvey, a New Zealander and pharmacist turned wine merchant, was largely responsible for extending my acquaintance with the variety of wines New Zealand was producing. I came to realize that there were some fine Chardonnays too. I well remember a bottle of Babich Chardonnay enjoyed at the Miller Howe, which was the first time that my husband had ever drunk New Zealand wine. Some serious red wines began to appear at the annual New Zealand tastings, which had been started by Don Walker of the New Zealand Trade Office and had become an important fixture in the tasting calendar.

Then, in 1989, a great friend went back to New Zealand and a year later produced a baby daughter. 'It's time you came to see us,' she said. 'Come for the christening.' So the prospect of a god-daughter in New Zealand saw us on a flight to Auckland. This was my very first visit to the Antipodes and I was enchanted. Forget all the jokes about New Zealand being out of date and thirty years behind the times. That is simply not so. New Zealand may have a fundamental disadvantage in that it is a long way from anywhere, but that is part of its charm. Most New Zealanders have a completely different attitude towards the long air journeys, compared to Europeans who are accustomed to find themselves in a completely new environment and a different country after a mere couple of hours of flying time. Most New Zealanders are travellers and that includes much of the wine industry, who keep abreast with all the latest developments all over the world.

You will see equipment in a New Zealand wine cellar that is as modern and technically advanced as anything you might find in California, Australia, Bordeaux or Tuscany. Hastings in Hawke's Bay claims to have the highest per capita consumption of stainless steel in the world. The wine industry has benefited from the exacting hygiene standards of the dairy industry, with the expertise required for one readily being switched to the other. In the vineyard, too, New Zealand may have lagged behind, though no more than some other parts of the world, but they have caught up fast, cramming into twenty years what other countries have taken a century to achieve.

New Zealand winemakers have made wine in other parts of the world. There is a ready exchange with France and California. Some have played the role of flying winemaker in Eastern Europe and many have trained in Australia. As yet, New Zealand does not have an oenology course that is comparable to Roseworthy or even Wagga Wagga – the problem is that with a population of just over 3 million people, there simply isn't the demand – so many New Zealanders cross the Tasman for their training. This also means that many Australians, in turn, have crossed the 'ditch' in the other direction and settled in New Zealand, making their mark on the development of its wines. Kevin Judd, John Hancock, Jane Hunter and Larry McKenna are to name but a few, but they are all now committed to New Zealand as though it were their own.

So as well as acquiring a god-daughter, I spent three happy but intensive weeks exploring New Zealand vineyards from Central Otago to Auckland. My god-daughter's parents live, conveniently, in Waimauku. Their next-door neighbour has a small vineyard and makes wine for home consumption, rather than on a commercial scale, and Matua Valley is just down the road. On that and on successive visits, the Mintons provided a comfortable base for visiting the wineries of Kumeu, Huapai and Henderson. That first visit was in February 1991 and it was two days in Martinborough which really converted me to the delights of New Zealand Pinot Noir. Not only was New Zealand producing Sauvignon with a difference, but also Pinot Noir that could hold its own with red Burgundy – admittedly not with the greatest, but with the wines that you and I can afford. I often thought how much I would rather drink a Martinborough Vineyard or an Ata Rangi Pinot Noir than an indifferent village Pommard or Volnay.

I was also charmed by the enthusiasm and friendly hospitality of most of the winemakers I met. New Zealanders are very willing and ready to discuss their wines and they seem to welcome an outsider's opinion. Many of the vineyard settings are stunningly beautiful. The vineyards of Marlborough may lie on the flat Wairau Plain, but the backdrop of the Richmond Ranges is dramatic. Central Otago must have some of the most spectacular vineyard scenery in the world, with the lakeside vineyard of Rippon and the scraggy mountains overlooking the vineyards of Black Ridge and Gibbston Valley.

It was therefore with great eagerness that I accepted an invitation to return in November 1992 to participate in the judging of the Air New Zealand Wine Awards in Christchurch. It was an opportunity to see how things had changed in the short space of eighteen months, with more wineries developing in areas such as Nelson and Marlborough. The Pinot Noir was even better and there was a marked improvement in the Cabernet Sauvignons, as well as some stylish sparkling wines. And that was when the idea of this book was first kindled. I felt that the New Zealand wine industry had reached a stage in its development that deserved an outsider's look at it. It had come of age. People were no longer laughing at the idea of New Zealand wine, but enthusing about the latest Marlborough Sauvignon or Martinborough Pinot Noir. New Zealand had established its position on the British market and the interest was undoubtedly there. I hesitated for a couple of years while other projects intervened, then suddenly the moment was right.

I went back for two more intensive research trips, concentrating on the North Island in October 1994 and the South Island in February 1995, covering as many wineries as possible between Longview at Whangarei in Northland, down to Chard Farm and Gibbston Valley on the 45th parallel in Central Otago. Sadly, time did not allow me to visit New Zealand's northernmost vineyard at Kaitaia by the Ninety Mile Beach, but I travelled the rest of the country, hopping from region to region in the stomach-churning Metroliner aeroplanes. The differences between the various regions are considerable, for the distance is some thousand miles, which in European terms means London to Madrid, with an equally startling climatic variation from the warm humidity of Northland to the crispness of Central Otago. With the two exceptions of Central Otago and West Auckland, all the vineyards lie on the dry eastern seaboard of both islands. Central Otago is the one region to claim a continental climate. In contrast, the west coast, particularly of the South Island, is wet, registering record-breaking levels of rainfall in the forests around the glaciers of Franz Josef and Fox, and the declining number of vineyards outside Auckland do suffer from problems with humidity.

Each region has its own individuality and originality. Although Northland is where the very first vines were planted in New Zealand, it has not developed much as a viticultural region and the vineyards are somewhat scattered, without much cohesion as yet. Auckland forms the historical centre of the industry, for that is where many of the Dalmatian immigrants settled whose families developed what are now some of the leading wineries in the country. Nowadays, most of their wines are sourced from further south, but their cellars are still in Henderson, Kumeu or Huapai. Waiheke remains in splendid island isolation, establishing a reputation for serious Cabernet Sauvignon. In terms of scale it can never rival Hawke's Bay, home to some of New Zealand's oldest wineries dating back to the last century, and with a reputation for Cabernet Sauvignon and Chardonnay. Gisborne, on the easternmost part of the North Island, proudly proclaims itself to be the Chardonnay capital of the country, while over the last ten years Martinborough has gradually become synonymous with Pinot Noir.

Cross the Cook Strait to Nelson, which is a delightful small enclave set apart from the mainstream. Marlborough is the home of Sauvignon and a fast-expanding area for other varieties and new wineries. Canterbury, the area around Christchurch, shows most promise in the limestone hills of Waipara, while Central Otago is also growing apace, with a core of pioneering wineries proving the potential of the world's southernmost vineyards. In each area there is an underlying energy, resulting in new plantings with new wineries in the planning.

I have recorded the history and development of the industry since the first vines were planted by an Anglican missionary in 1819, recalling some of the colourful figures who had vineyards in the last century, as well as the chequered progress of the prohibitionists, and the switch from *vitis vinifera* varieties to hybrids and back again. A subsequent chapter covers some of the problems and preoccupations of the industry today.

There are exciting viticultural developments which have been responsible for the significant improvement in the quality of the wines, by bringing sunlight into the vines to enable the production of ripe grapes. The role of the key grape varieties and their vinification has also been examined, with a separate chapter on sparkling wine. The main body of the book comprises a survey of the different wine regions, describing the key threads of each region, and the strengths and weaknesses of as many wineries as possible – it was simply not possible to visit them all. I have also avoided precise tasting notes which are soon obsolete (or, worse still, marks out of 100), but have tried to give a broad idea of winery styles.

As it is, the face of the New Zealand wine industry is changing at breath-taking speed and, like so many wine books, this too will be out of date in its detail by the time it is published. It records the condition of the New Zealand wine industry at the end of August 1995. The broad themes will remain the same, with an overview of the main currents of development, but the details will change. New wineries will doubtless have produced their first wines in the 1996 vintage and maybe others will have disappeared.

The New Zealand wine industry is poised for great change. It has finally come of age, playing a serious role on the world market, with a firm place assured in the export market. It will never have a large share, but that is not its role. Not for New Zealand is the large-scale bulk production of easy-to-drink, unmemorable wine; instead, it can produce small quantities of wines with wonderful intense fruit at a sensible price. Gradually, it is moving away from Sauvignon. Chardonnay now exceeds Sauvignon in total plantings, but in the next few years numerous other grape varieties will become more important, such as Riesling, Pinot Gris and Pinot Blanc. Although Sauvignon will always fill a vital role in the market, it will cease to be synonymous with New Zealand.

When I was thinking about writing this book, I mentioned the idea to John Buck of Te Mata, whose reaction was that New Zealand should be put in its geographical context. Write a book on the wines of the Pacific Rim, he said, which would include Chile and California too, not to mention parts of Australia and even Japan. It was an exciting concept, but a daunting idea and, in any case, I really felt that New Zealand's wines deserved a book all to themselves. Too often they have been lumped together with their bigger but not more beautiful neighbours across the Tasman Sea. A book of their own is what they need, so that is what they have. They are unique among the wines of the New World and can stand alone on their own merits.

2
A Historical Perspective

The development of viticulture in New Zealand is a fascinating story. It ebbs and flows, enjoying moments of great energy and suffering times of decline. The very first vines were planted by missionaries and the Church played its part in the development of vineyards, as it has done in other parts of the world. More colourful characters – some substantial, some more fleeting – entered the stage, trying their best with some of the classic varieties of Europe, encouraged by a far-sighted wanderer whose work was undone by a puritanical streak of prohibitionism. *Vitis vinifera* varieties gave way to hybrids, fortified wines superseded table wines, and the vineyards were sustained by countless Dalmatian immigrants whose families still make their mark on the industry today. Then the tide turned again towards table wines, once again made from *vitis vinifera* varieties. The beginnings were hesitant, with tentative examples of Müller-Thurgau, then Sauvignon was discovered and the first vines were planted in Marlborough. The tide gathered momentum. Suddenly New Zealand realized, and the world realized too, that the wines from these two islands at the other end of the Pacific Ocean had wonderful flavours with an originality all of their own. New Zealand had entered the modern era of winemaking.

The first faltering beginnings of New Zealand viticulture depended on the Church, for it was a missionary who planted the very first vines. His name was Samuel Marsden and on his second visit to New Zealand, as Chief Chaplain to the government of New South Wales, he decided to make a settlement at Kerikeri in Northland. The site was chosen for convenience rather than its particular suitability for vines, and even today there is uncertainty over the potential of the area for viticulture. However, this did not

8

prevent Marsden from recording in his diary on 25 September 1819

> We had a small spot of land cleared and broken up in which I planted about a hundred grape vines of different kinds, brought from Port Jackson (in New South Wales). New Zealand promises to be very favourable to the vine as far as I can judge at present of the nature of the soil and climate.

Other early colonists followed Marsden's example. Lieutenant Thomas McDonnell planted vines at Hokianga, and William Powditch even further north at Whangaroa Harbour, so when Charles Darwin came to the Bay of Islands in 1835 on his voyage round the world in the *Beagle*, he recorded well-established grape-vines.

There is no record of these early grape growers actually making wine, though if they did not, one could wonder why they bothered to plant vines, especially a missionary who would need wine for the Eucharist. It was James Busby, who is widely regarded as the father of Australian viticulture, who takes the credit for the first recorded New Zealand wine. He was a Scot who emigrated to Australia in the 1820s, established a vineyard in the Hunter Valley, then came to New Zealand as the first British Resident in 1833. Before settling in New Zealand, he made a tour of the European vineyards and selected cuttings of many French and Spanish grape varieties for planting in New South Wales. Many were established in the Sydney Botanical Gardens, some in Busby's own vineyard in the Hunter Valley, and others he took with him to the Bay of Islands.

In 1836 Busby wrote to his brother, describing how 'the vines were planted out under the most favourable circumstances, just after a soaking rain. I think the majority of them are likely to survive.' This was in the Bay of Islands at Waitangi, a significant name in New Zealand history for the treaty that accorded land to the new settlers. Mention is made of Busby's wine being sold to the British soldiers, and the French explorer d'Urville tasted the wine, recording that he saw

> a trellis on which several flourishing vines were growing . . . with great pleasure I agreed to taste the product of the vineyard that I had just seen. I was given a light white wine, very sparkling and delicious to taste, which I enjoyed very much. Judging from

this sample, I have no doubt that vines will be grown extensively all over the sandy hills of these islands, and very soon New Zealand wine may be exported to the English possessions in India.

This was praise indeed and a prediction unfulfilled.

Although Busby's enthusiasm seemed boundless, his vines were not to survive. He records that they fell prey 'to the ravages of horses, sheep, cattle and pigs. The leaves are ripped off as soon as they come out.' You may wonder why the vines were not protected in some way, but a Tuscan wine grower today whose vineyard has been ravaged by rampaging wild boar would appreciate the problem. The final destruction came from British soldiers during clashes with the Maoris in 1845. After that, it seems that Busby turned his attention to land speculation and nothing more is heard of his viticultural activities. Happily, other settlers took up the challenge in his place.

Henry Petrie, a propagandist for the New Zealand Company which represented the interests of the early settlers, records taking vine cuttings from Sydney to a settlement in Port Nicholson. The vines appeared to flourish, but he admits to one distinct disadvantage: the English settlers knew nothing about vines. 'To cultivate them to any extent, we shall require French and German cultivators, to whom the most liberal encouragement should be given.' Indeed, French peasants did plant vines at Akaroa on Banks Peninsula outside Christchurch, and German settlers came to Nelson, but sadly neither vineyard survived.

Meanwhile, French Marist missionaries arrived in New Zealand led by Bishop Pompallier of Lyons, who was the first Catholic bishop of the South Pacific. He landed at Hokianga in 1838 in a ship that was carrying French vine cuttings. The missionaries established vines to supply their need for sacramental wines, as well as for wine and grapes for the table. From Hokianga, the Marist brothers went first briefly to Poverty Bay and then on to Hawke's Bay, where they established the first vineyard there in 1851. The Mission Vineyards flourish today as its successor.

The second half of the nineteenth century saw the establishment of several other vineyards that were to have a lasting effect. An Englishman, Charles Levet, who had been a Cambridgeshire coppersmith, planted vines at Kaipara Harbour and successfully exploited the commercial viability of growing grapes and making wine for over forty years, from 1863 to 1907. Dick Scott in *Winemakers of New Zealand* describes the gruelling task of clearing land and planting vines. Sadly, father and son died within two years of each other and the vineyard was abandoned.

A Spaniard, José Sole, anglicized to Josef Soler, made wine at Wanganui in the north from 1869 until his death in 1906 and established quite a reputation. A Masterton magistrate wrote to a friend in the 1880s: 'I have just had a case of Soler's Wanganui wine sent to me; it is quite equal to the best Australian and is a credit to the colony – the constantia is specially excellent.' Soler's wines won prizes at the Melbourne International Exhibition of 1880 and at the London Colonial and Indian Exhibition of 1886. His nephew, Anthony Vidal, carried on the family tradition, but chose the more suitable area of Hawke's Bay for his vineyard.

In 1897, an article in *The Farmer* entitled 'Successful Winemaking in Wanganui' said that Mr Soler has wines for the connoisseur, but added 'from a European point of view, not nine out of ten in the colonial community are good judges of wine . . . ' The article concluded: 'He has found out the kind of wine the colonial palate prefers and, as a businessman, he makes that wine. He does not theorize about educating the public as to what they ought to drink; he simply manufactures what they want to drink . . .' A later article in the same publication elaborated on the theme of colonial taste:

 . . . it is the strong-bodied kind that appears to have best hit the paying colonial taste. The natural uneducated British taste, when it calls for wine, craves something that is red and sweet and strong. Good wine of a lighter kind might be better for the average drinker, but the ascent to that better state of affairs seems long and slow. For our drinking as a beverage without meals, these light wines are advisable and would well vary and displace the tyrannous unvarying tea, tea, tea . .

Strong sweet wines – the so-called 'port' and 'sherries', 'Madeiras' and 'Marsalas' – were to remain the popular choice for nearly a century. It was only with the planting of Sauvignon in Marlborough that New Zealand table wine really came of age. But that is to jump several decades.

Meanwhile, the crowning success of Josef Soler's career came in 1906, the year in which he died, when, in a competition with overseas exhibitors, his wines received three gold medals out of a possible five at the Christchurch International Exhibition. Leading Australian winemakers protested at the result and a retrial was ordered, carried out by an expert acceptable to the Australians, and this time Soler's wines swept the board, taking all five medals.

Heinrich Breidecker was a German settler from the Rhine who also planted vines in the Hokianga district and produced wine from Isabella grapes for many years during the second half of the century. It was described as 'a good unadulterated wine' which sold for 10 shillings a gallon. Breidecker subsequently gave his name to a crossing of Müller-Thurgau and Seibel 7053, which enjoyed a limited popularity for a time.

There was a brief moment of government support for the fledgling industry when Sir George Grey became Prime Minister in 1877 and planned to establish a settlement of skilled wine growers at Hokianga. A block of 26,000 acres (10,117 hectares) was reserved for the purpose, with a view to bringing out winemakers from the South of France. However, the scheme failed to materialize and Grey lost the Premiership in 1879.

While Soler's vineyards flourished at Wanganui, others were planting, laying the viticultural foundations for areas such as Hawke's Bay and the Wairarapa that today enjoy a reputation for their wines. William Beetham planted vines in the Wairarapa, Henry Tiffen set up the Greenmeadows winery and Bernard Chambers planted the Te Mata vineyard in Hawke's Bay. Their stories are covered in more detail in the relevant regional chapters, but there was no doubt about the unprecedented popularity and success of New Zealand wines during the 1890s.

However, the success was not without its problems. Many of the early settlers of New Zealand were of British rather than European origin and sympathized with the sentiment of teetotalism. Alcohol provided a relief from the hardships of the pioneering life and drunkenness was common. The result was the formation in the 1860s of a large number of temperance societies which called for the total prohibition of all liquor. The very first temperance societies had concentrated on an abstention from spirits, but increasingly they became more vocal, campaigning against wine as well. Their first public victory was the Licensing Act of 1881, restricting the conditions under which new liquor licences could be granted. It was the first of the many restrictions which were gradually to escalate until the end of the Second World War. It is only in recent years that New Zealand has thrown off the legacy of temperance, or, more precisely, of narrow prohibitionism.

Yet at the same time it was recognized that viticulture was one of the new industries which could boost the country's economy. Romeo Bragato came from the northern Dalmatian coast, which at that time was part of the Austro-Hungarian Empire, but he is often described as an Italian as he trained at Conegliano in the Veneto – then, as now, one of Italy's most reputable schools of oenology. In 1895, Bragato was invited to New Zealand, on loan from the government of Victoria, to investigate the potential for viticulture and winemaking. He travelled the country extensively, examining vineyards and winemaking practices from Central Otago northwards, and wrote a detailed account which is often cited to substantiate a new area's potential for grape growing today. The big omission in his travels was Marlborough, but just about every other area was covered. A very favourable report was submitted to the Prime Minster, Richard Seddon, who consequently became a convinced supporter of the cause of the wine growers, for the reason that 'this colony had great capabilities in the matter of viticulture' and that 'he did believe that if (the settlers) had light wines available ... it would probably keep people from drinking something stronger'.

Bragato described both Hawke's Bay and the Wairarapa as 'pre-eminently suited' to viticulture. He believed the potential was enormous and encouraged the expansion of the industry, which led to a growth in planting from Central Otago to North Auckland. Powdery mildew or oidium had arrived in New Zealand in the mid-1870s, devastating vineyards in Northland. Phylloxera had also arrived with the European vine cuttings and it was Bragato who identified it and advised on its elimination, proposing the grafting of vines on to American rootstock. His advice was not always taken. However, the New Zealand government continued its interest in viticulture and offered Bragato the newly created post of Viticulturist and Head of the Viticultural Division of the Department of Agriculture in 1902.

A small area at Te Kauwhata in the Waikato had already been set aside by the government in 1898 as an experimental nursery. The site had been chosen not for its suitability for viticulture, but to show what could best be done with that type of land. Fruit trees had been planted as well as vines. The vines flourished, the fruit trees were removed and, under Bragato's direction, Te Kauwhata became the centre of instruction in winemaking and viticulture. He imported disease-resistant rootstock and in his handbook *Viticulture in New Zealand*, published in 1906, explained how to graft vines on to American rootstock. The European *vitis vinifera* varieties still dominated New Zealand viticulture at the time, with varieties such as 'Hermitage and Pineaus'. But sadly, Bragato's advice was never seriously followed and he became disenchanted with the government's ineptitude and stifling bureaucracy, as well as the growing threat of prohibition. He resigned and left New Zealand for Canada in 1909. A few years later he committed suicide in the aftermath of a domestic crisis.

Meanwhile, the turn of the century saw the beginning of the next significant influence in the development of New Zealand viticulture: the influx of immigrants from the Dalmatian coast. They came to work in the kauri gumfields of the north. Most originated from small farming villages where grapes were grown along with other crops, and wine was made for family consumption as part of everyday life. Not surprisingly, they began to do the same in New Zealand. The far north of the North Island is not the most suitable area for viticulture, although today there are those who are trying to disprove that theory. Gradually the immigrants saved money, enabling them to buy land, and shifted southwards, settling on pasture land just to the north of Auckland in the villages of Henderson, Huapai and Kumeu.

Life in the gumfields was tough, from the sheer hard slog of physical labour. The kauri tree is still part of the New Zealand landscape. It looks rather like a Douglas fir tree but, unlike a fir, produces very hard wood. Above all, kauri trees were valued for their resin, which was used for varnish and for waterproofing ships. Old kauri trees had survived in the swamplands of the north, some for as many as 40,000 years. The sap from the live trees solidified to look like amber and, as such, could be mined and was much valued. As an industry it entailed no production expenses, just the cost of the labour to mine it, and at the turn of the century kauri gum represented an important export commodity for New Zealand. The trade died with the advent of synthetics.

Many of the main wineries based around Auckland owe their origins to these early immigrants. Some arrived later in the century than others. Some have disappeared, but many survive: well-known names such as Babich, Nobilo, the Fredatoviches at Lincoln, the Brajkoviches at Kumeu River, Delegat and Selak, to name but a handful. The Dalmatians formed a very close community, inter-marrying and working with each other. The present incumbents in the wineries are usually the second or third generation. You have to admire the courage and tenacity of these early immigrants. Joe and Peter Babich talked about their father Josip who arrived in New Zealand in 1910 at the age of fourteen. He came to join an older brother in the gumfields who had arrived six years earlier and he never saw his parents again. The two brothers, Steve and Josip, saved enough money to buy some cheap bushland which they cleared to farm and grow the same crops that their parents had grown on the Dalmatian coast: tobacco, olive trees, figs, corn and, of course, vines. Their father's first licence was at Waiharara, twenty miles north of Kaitai, where he was growing vines in sub-tropical conditions. The main problem was that there was an insufficient difference between the seasons to give the vines a period of dormancy.

Josip Babich came to Henderson in 1919. The story goes that he lost the toss of a coin and paid £6 10s. per acre for his land, rather than £6 if he had won the toss. At the time the land was cheap, but by the 1950s it had become some of the most productive land around Auckland and was intensively cultivated for straw-berries in particular, as well as rearing poultry. From the fruit and egg bowl of Auckland, it has now become the house bowl as the urban sprawl has encroached.

Another important influence came from just one family, the Corbans, who arrived from the Lebanon at the turn of the century. Their enormous contribution to the wine industry has been recorded in Dick Scott's book *A Stake in the Country*. Bragato described the Mount Lebanon vineyards as 'the model vineyard of New Zealand and an object lesson to grape growers', while Scott wrote of the life of a very tight-knit family business and a close family unit, all working incredibly long hours. By the 1920s, Cor-bans had become the biggest winemakers in the country, with no significant competitors.

Meanwhile, the prohibitionists had won their first victories in 1908 when Masterton, in the Wairarapa and Eden, which is now part of Auckland, voted 'no licence'. This meant that the winemakers were allowed to produce their wines, but were denied the right to sell them. As a result, many were forced out of business. Corbans survived because the no-licence boundary ran along the railway line that marked the front boundary of their vineyard, thus providing a means of transport for their wines.

Things were not flourishing at Te Kauwhata either, with a move in the research away from viticulture to horticulture, and there were predictions of the ruin of the wine industry. J. O. Craike, the manager of the Te Mata vineyard, criticized the government for encouraging people to grow grapes and make wine, spending public money on developing the industry, when there was no prospect of a fair return for the labour and capital expended while it was fostering the threat of ruination by national prohibition. However, in 1911 the New Zealand Viticultural Association was formed to defend the vine growers against the prohibitionists. It called for the licensing of all winemakers and regular checks on winemaking practices, condemning at the same time the widespread adulteration of wine. The so-called Austrian wine, produced by the Dalmatian immigrants, was criticized by, among others, the Prime Minister W. F. Massey in 1914 as a 'degrading, demoralizing and sometimes maddening drink'. The Licensing Amendment Act of 1918 ensured that if national prohibition was passed, the industry would receive no financial compensation but would simply be forced to close down. New Zealand did indeed vote in favour of national prohibition in 1919, a year before the United States, but happily the subsequent vote of the returning servicemen who had enjoyed wine in Europe tipped the balance, so that New Zealand escaped prohibition. Support for the movement gradually declined with the example of its failure in the United States, but its spectre lingered on in the form of archaic licensing laws from which New Zealand has only recently escaped.

The 1920s and 1930s saw the expansion of the industry with the opening of several new wineries. In 1925 there were just 40 licensed winemakers, a drop from the 70 listed in 1913, but by 1932 the number had grown to 100. Friedrich Wohnsiedler, remembered in one of Montana's popular brands, established a vineyard in Poverty Bay in 1921. Tom McDonald bought land in Hawke's Bay in 1927, which is now part of Montana's Church Road complex, and in 1933 Glenvale, now Esk Valley, was founded by

Robert Bird. But despite the growth, not all was well in the industry.

A new organization, the Viticultural Association of New Zealand, was founded to solve some of the problems facing the industry. Wine adulteration was a common practice. There was the example of a customs officer visiting John Vella in 1926 and finding just four small rows of vines. When pressed, Mr Vella admitted that he had used raisins for making his wine, had blended it with other wine and labelled it as coming from the best of grapes. In the same year, Fred Sherwood was convicted of selling wine made from apple juice and coloured with dye.

Another significant problem was the condition of the vineyards. Many of the *vitis vinifera* vines were badly affected by virus and oidium was rampant. American rootstocks had been imported to combat phylloxera, but many of those were also virused. Some growers had decided not to graft the rootstock, but simply to plant the American vines which proved to have a greater resistance to oidium and rot. With the perpetual threat of prohibition, many growers had understandably opted for dual-purpose varieties which could be used for both table grapes and wine. The American Isabella vine acquired the name peculiar to New Zealand of Albany Surprise when it was grown on a property at Albany, outside Auckland, and produced fruit of surprisingly fine quality. It proved disease-resistant and produced good table grapes, but as wine, its taste left much to be desired. Assid Abraham Corban damned it as 'an ideal grape for a lazy grower'. I had the dubious privilege of trying some, made as a blush wine, on my first visit to New Zealand. It had the distinctive foxy taste of *vitis labrusca*. Despite its flavour deficiencies, it was still the most widely planted grape variety in the vine survey of 1960 and was to fall from favour only during the ensuing decade.

The 1920s also saw the arrival of the hybrids: the Seibels and Bacos. Their only virtue was their resistance to rot and oidium, combined with prolific yields. It seemed that flavour was very much a secondary consideration. *Vitis vinifera* varieties were simply ignored in most quarters and the Depression of the 1930s did nothing to help the industry. Many growers were in severe financial straits. As Tom McDonald put it, 'They were forced to sell the grapes to get the money to buy the sugar to make the wine.'

However, the government once more began to take interest in

the industry. A new viticultural inspector was appointed and Te Kauwhata was given funds to encourage the development of its research activity. Better still, the government raised duty on Australian and South African wines, giving domestic wines a distinct price advantage. Sales of imported wines fell and those of local wines increased dramatically. American servicemen who came to New Zealand on leave during the Second World War did much to boost the demand for New Zealand wine. The wartime demand for wine created an unprecedented boom in which quality was a secondary consideration. This was the period for adding water and sugar to the wine.

Politics in the industry reared its ugly head with contentions between large and small growers resulting in the formation of splinter-group organizations such as the New Zealand Wine Council and the Hawke's Bay Grape Winegrowers' Association. The internal dissensions were exacerbated by the contrasting fortunes of the large growers, represented by the New Zealand Wine Council and the small growers, mainly of Dalmatian origin, who formed the Viticultural Association. It was only when the Wine Institute was created in 1975 that these differences were finally resolved.

In 1948, wine became more easily available to the public with the creation of a licence allowing the growers to establish retail outlets, and, during the early 1950s, the government introduced various measures intended to help the industry. Separate licences were created for the manufacture of grape and fruit wines, and no company could hold both. The aim was to prevent adulteration. Then in 1955, the minimum quantity of wine that could be sold was reduced from two gallons to a quart for table wine and to half a gallon for fortified wines. Other measures increased the number of wine shops in the country. None the less, conditions still had the lingering taint of prohibition, with the notorious six o'clock swill when the bars closed. Peter Fredatovich remembered people drinking in the back rooms of a bar as though it were a private party, with a code of three rings on the bell for a customer, while one ring told you it was the police. It was illegal to sell wine on a Sunday or after 9 p.m. Restaurants were not licensed until 1960. People drank beer in the pubs and wine at home, but you were considered a little odd if you drank wine as it was still not really part of the country's social culture. Even today, dry areas remain around Auckland where there are no wine shops, pubs or restaurants.

The Dalmatian wine growers have remained a very important section of the industry. It was a close community. A morning spent listening to reminiscences produced some fascinating snippets of wine history. Joe and Peter Babich remember how their father made his wine. The work was all manual. He had a hand crusher with rollers. The vats were filled by buckets. The press was a basket press that was turned by hand; you walked round it in a circle just like a donkey. It took an hour to press a quarter of a tonne of grapes and the juice was transferred by bucket or by a hand pump. Things began to be mechanized towards the end of the 1940s, as tractors started to replace horses in the vineyards and the first electric crusher appeared.

The Babiches also remembered the advent of the hybrid varieties. Hitherto, European *vitis vinifera* varieties such as Pineau and Hermitage had been grown, as well as the *labrusca* varieties like Isabella, which had originally been introduced as rootstock to combat phylloxera. Bragato had condemned them for their 'foxy flavour, lack of sugar and excess of acidity'. The industry had lacked the means to combat rot, downy mildew and oidium efficiently and this had led the Ministry of Agriculture to introduce hybrids towards the end of the 1930s. Vines like Seibel 5455 and 5437 were hailed as being marvellous for they were easy to grow and produced grapes in abundance – as much as 10 tonnes per acre (25 tonnes per hectare). If you had clean, healthy grapes, you could not fail to make palatable wine. It was all dessert wine, for the Anglo-Saxon section of the population was the biggest influence in the market and wanted 'port' and 'sherry' styles, whereas the Dalmatians themselves preferred table wines.

The hybrids had body and guts, and also very marked acidity. Although the flesh was coloured, everything was fermented on the skins. The use of water in winemaking became an essential part of the process, for if you did not water the hybrid juice the acid levels would be too high and the wine would taste like lemon juice. The formula was very simple. If the acidity was 25 per cent too high, you simply increased the volume by 25 per cent with water. The addition of sugar provided the necessary sweetness to reach an alcohol level of at least 15° and yet more sugar and alcohol could be added if necessary. If it was made properly, the wine apparently tasted quite respectable, but the problem was that the method laid the way open for all manner of abuse. However, at the time the hybrids were seen as the great white hope as they were neither prone to disease nor virused like some of the *vitis vinifera* varieties.

Peter Fredatovich remembered his father planting Albany Surprise, which he sold as a table grape. It had the advantage of ripening early, so it helped the cash flow and enabled you to pay for your winemaking materials. It was all done with ready cash; they did not know what a bank manager was. Albany Surprise was not bad for 'sherry'. They also had some Pinot Meunier, but his father got rid of it as its extremely tight bunches made it highly prone to rot.

'Port' was more popular before the war and afterwards there was a boom for 'sherry', mainly sweet and medium sweet – in fact, the sweeter the better. It was sold by the half-gallon, with customers supplying their own flagon which was filled from the barrel. The base wine was always the same and blended according to the desired level of sweetness. Spirit was bought from other winemakers, until they acquired their own still. Enormous quantities of sugar, water and grape skins were mixed together, and this mixture was distilled. It was all strictly controlled by customs.

Fredatovich also remembered making his own barrels from totara, which was the only suitable New Zealand wood. One year, there was a strike at the sugar works at vintage time. However, the sugar company's drivers obtained a dispensation to deliver to the wineries. 'We were in the cactus, worried sick that we would not get the sugar we needed.' His father was against anything mechanized and their first tractor was bought in the early 1950s, quite against his father's wishes. Before that, they had used a wheelbarrow to bring in the grapes, four boxes per load. Barrels were used for fermentation, then concrete vats, then, very soon, stainless-steel ones, as the wine industry benefited from the influence of the hygiene requirements of the dairy industry.

Rose and Jim Delegat's grandfather arrived in New Zealand in 1924. He was already married, but left his wife and four children behind while he went to make his fortune. 'New Zealand was America; we didn't know anything about it.' He was a contract farmer rather than a gumdigger, but did not have any money to go home; then in 1939 he decided that his family should join him. One of his daughters, Vida Delegat, remembers how she spoke no

English and that it was very hard to find a job. Even now, she has a strong Croatian accent. Her sister Matja Selak remembers the journey out, how it took two months, going through the Suez Canal in an Italian cargo ship. She was fourteen when she arrived in New Zealand and had to learn English with nursery school children.

Winemaking methods were initially fairly primitive, but gradually evolved. Melba Brajkovich remembers how everything was done by hand, how the flagons for bottling were washed and labelled, and the wine siphoned from the barrel. She also remembers holding the hoops as her husband Mate made totara barrels. Talking to these people, you feel that there is a real camaraderie of heritage and of shared experiences. Henderson, where most of them settled, remains the heart of the Dalmatian winemaking community.

The first signs of the shift away from 'port' and 'sherry' came in the 1950s. Mate Selak made a 'claret', a dry red wine and also a dry white, all from the same grape varieties, Seibels, but vinified in a different way. He was one of the very first to make a sparkling wine, a carbonated wine called Champelle. His wife remembers how he loved doing the riddling. 'It was his pride and joy. He was like a baby with a new toy,' seeing the grapes being picked, with people singing. Yet it was hard trying to sell the wine, travelling from hotel to hotel with samples. But if you didn't sell, you had no money to buy bread. At that time, Kumeu River, or San Marino as the winery was called then, produced some 120,000 gallons a year of 'port' and 'sherry'.

Corbans began making their first table wines prompted by Alex Corban, who in 1948 was the first New Zealander to graduate from Roseworthy College in Australia. It remains the first choice for many aspiring New Zealand winemakers. Corban developed Riesling Sylvaner, as Müller-Thurgau was then called, and also Pinotage. The Babich brothers remembered the meetings of a group called the Young Winemakers' Club which began in about 1960. They tasted each other's wines, which helped to develop their judging skills, and Joe Babich admitted ruefully that there were a few headaches the next morning. What struck them was how much better the *vitis vinifera* wines were than the hybrids. That is when the balance started to shift, moving back to the classic grape varieties of Europe once again. Unfortunately there was initially some-

THE WINES OF NEW ZEALAND

thing of a false start, influenced by Helmut Becker, the eminent Geisenheim professor. When he came out to New Zealand in the 1960s, he enthused about the similarity of conditions with the Rhineland of Germany and encouraged the planting of Müller-Thurgau. In fact, New Zealand is generally much warmer, but none the less his advice was followed and it is only now that Müller-Thurgau is finally beginning to fall from favour, lying behind Chardonnay but not yet Sauvignon in the grape popularity stakes.

As recently as in 1965, the two most widely planted varieties were still Baco 22A, which was allowed only in Armagnac at the time, and Albany Surprise, which does not feature in that form in any other vineyard in the world, or, to quote a succinct comment in a report issued by Cooks, 'The first is prohibited in most European winemaking districts and the second would be if anyone proposed to plant it.' Frank Berrysmith, the government viticulturist, conducted a survey of grape plantings. If you compare the 1960 survey with that of 1965, Cabernet Sauvignon has moved into ninth place with 14.5 hectares (36 acres), and Riesling Sylvaner was fifth with 30 hectares (74 acres) in 1965 and seventh with 18 hectares (45 acres) five years earlier. In the 1960 survey, the only other *vitis vinifera* varieties were Chasselas (which is of doubtful value as a wine grape), Pinot Meunier, Palomino, Pedro Ximenez and something called Gamay Gloriod, among twelve named varieties. By 1965, Gamay Gloriod had slipped out of the top twelve; Chasselas, Pedro Ximenez and Pinot Meunier were still there and, apart from the newcomer Cabernet Sauvignon, all the rest were hybrids.

Although *vitis vinifera* had not completely disappeared from New Zealand, it was certainly in danger of sinking into a mire of fortified wines and hybrids. André Simon's 'New Zealand Holiday', an article published in the journal of the International Wine and Food Society in the winter of 1964, makes fascinating reading, giving some idea of the state of the wine industry at the time. He visited vineyards and wineries around Auckland; met Alister McKissock, now at Aspen Ridge, at the Te Kauwhata Research Station; described a dinner with the Marist brothers; and visited Tom McDonald at McWilliam's in Hawke's Bay, as well as a 'shakes' factory in Masterton which provided powder which was dropped into milk or water to flavour it. The laboratory there was apparently more fascinating than any in the wineries.

Simon particularly praised the Tom McDonald Cabernet of 1949, but he was also complimentary about some other wines. The McWilliam's Private Bins of Pinot Chardonnay, which were not for sale, of the 1958, 1960, 1962 and 1963 vintages 'all possessed a distinctly Pinot character and a higher appeal than any other New Zealand wine known to me'. McWilliam's Cresta Doré, a Müller-Thurgau, was described as a fresh and pleasant wine, and a 1960 Bakano, their brand of dry red, was found to be a good dry wine. His very first taste of New Zealand wine was a Corbans Palomino 'flor sherry' – Corbans were in fact the first to make a commercial 'flor sherry' in 1962, using the Australian process of flor induction – and he tasted other Corbans wines of which the 1963 Riesling and 1961 Cabernet were the best. At the Te Kauwhata Research Station, a medium sweet 'sherry', a blend of Palomino and Dr Hogg Muscat, was found to be 'a curious wine, but with a distinctly vinous character'. The next wine, labelled 'Sauterne', was 'curiouser' and without vinous character, and was in fact made of apples. A so-called 'Madeira', made from various Seibels with a caramel addition, was thought the best. The Marist brothers insisted on him tasting liqueurs 'of which they are surprisingly proud', but he tactfully refrains from saying what he thought of them. One cannot help suspecting that the 1955 Moët and Ayla, and 1950 and 1948 Lafite provided by the Auckland Wine & Food Society came as very welcome relief!

There was no doubt that interest in table wine was growing, along with the realization of the inadequacies of the hybrid varieties. One of the factors that prompted the gradual and then quickening move away from hybrids was the interest taken by foreign companies in the industry. McWilliam's had led the way, establishing a vineyard and winery in Hawke's Bay in 1947, subsequently merging with McDonald's in 1961. Penfolds of Australia also wanted their share of the New Zealand market and decided to establish a vineyard with the creation of Penfolds Wines (NZ) Ltd. Gilbey's had a brief flirtation with Nobilo in Huapai and Seppelts likewise with Vidal in Hawke's Bay. In most instances, this foreign involvement was fairly short-lived and the companies in question soon reverted to New Zealand ownership. Today, the main foreign investment lies with Montana and Corbans, but at a distance, as well as the involvement of Yalumba, Rothbury and Domaine Chandon in Marlborough, and the Japanese ownership of De Redcliffe. Kemblefield is American owned and there are other foreign individuals participating in the industry.

The industry had also begun to be more self-critical. A wine exhibition that was to become the Air New Zealand Wine Awards was started in 1957. The list of results for 1967 makes interesting reading. There were eleven classes: unfermented grape juice, four table-wine categories not exceeding 25 per cent proof spirit (dry white, sweet white and dry red table wine, and sparkling and carbonated wine); the over 25 per cent proof spirit covered various categories of 'sherry' (dry, medium and sweet), Muscat and 'port'. The conditions of entry stated very firmly that all entries must be the product of bona fide established winemakers, made from pure grape juice from grapes grown in New Zealand, and the wine processed and matured in New Zealand by the entrant.

Among the winners were many names that are familiar today. The table wines showed a tendency to borrow European names. Pleasant Valley's 'Hock' won a bronze medal and so did Vidal's 'Chablis'. There were no gold medals in the dry white category, nor in the dry red, which included entrants like Pleasant Valley 'Burgundy', Lombardi Red Seibel 'Chianti' style and McWilliam's Bakano, as well as Western Vineyard Cabernet Sauvignon 'Claret' 1965, with a bronze and a silver for their 'Gamay de Beaujolais' 1966. 'Sauterne' or 'Sauternes' featured heavily in the sweet white category and a wine called Totara Gold won the only gold medal among the table wines. In the sparkling wine category Eastern Vineyards submitted Château de Thierry 'Champagne' Demi Sec, alongside Nobilo's Golden Drop Wines, as it was then called, with a sparkling Ruby dry, which won a silver.

Among the winners in the fortified wine category there were several familiar winery names, such as Pleasant Valley's 'Frontignac' in the 'port' section. The medium sweet 'sherry' class included Vidal's Sweet Luscious 'Sherry' Special Reserve, and Villa Maria's Golden 'Sherry', while Delegat's 'Madeira' featured under the full sweet 'sherry' class. The 'port' descriptions included harmony 'port', cellarman's special 'port', ruby 'port' rich red Italian styled, mild 'port' and unfortified 'port', as well as simple tawny, reserve and old ruby. How very different from the 1992 competition in which I participated as a judge, just twenty-five years later, when we tasted, by varietal, rows of Sauvignon and Chardonnay, Pinot Noir and Cabernet Sauvignon, and the 'port' and 'sherry' classes had shrunk to virtual insignificance.

The industry began to expand significantly towards the end of the 1960s. Licensing laws were gradually becoming more relaxed, which helped sales. Island isolation had been a factor in wine appreciation, or lack of it. Many New Zealanders encountered wine for the first time when they were stationed in European wine regions during the Second World War, and only then when the supply of beer ran dry, and wine was always quickly abandoned in favour of beer whenever possible. But some did become more appreciative. The arrival of countless Europeans brought their wine traditions and cultures to the country, and the numerous New Zealanders who have travelled to Europe since the war have absorbed some enthusiasm for wine. That influence continues. Wine has become fashionable.

The story of Montana's development of Marlborough and their imaginative step to plant Sauvignon as well as Müller-Thurgau is told in the Marlborough chapter. However, in charting the course of the history of the industry, it undoubtedly marks a milestone: New Zealand's entry into modern wine production. It came at a time when others were examining the boundaries of viticulture and looking at the feasibility of growing grapes in areas which had never previously been considered, or had been neglected since the first tentative plantings in the last century. There has been the most amazing flowering of New Zealand viticulture in the last twenty years or so. Inevitably, there were casualties. Some wineries found it difficult to adjust to the production of table wines with a growing international flavour and were simply unable to improve their winemaking standards.

The emergence of the contract grape grower also encouraged the development of more vineyards. Hitherto, it had been customary for a winery to produce all its own grapes, but some began to encourage farmers looking for a new crop on their land to consider viticulture. The wineries provided the vines and advice for the novice grape growers in return for a contract for their fruit. This phenomenon particularly gathered momentum as Montana began to plant in Marlborough, and encouraged others to follow their example. Plantings increased in Poverty Bay and Hawke's Bay; in contrast, the Auckland area declined in importance.

A key development of the 1970s was the creation of the Wine Institute, which continues to control the industry today. It consists of an executive committee which represents the three categories of wineries: small, medium and large, according to their annual production. There are just four companies in the large category, with annual sales exceeding 2 million litres: Montana, Corbans, the Villa Maria group and recent newcomers Nobilo's. Twelve companies fall into the middle category, while the small category – where annual sales do not exceed 200,000 litres – contains the largest number of members: 188 in 1995.

One of the prime movers was the indefatigable Terry Dunleavy, who then became the Institute's first executive officer. Dunleavy would describe himself as a political animal and a frustrated politician. He enjoys the political machinations of negotiations, and did indeed unsuccessfully stand for parliament in Napier in 1969. Then he joined the wine industry, working for Montana, and organized the planting ceremony in Marlborough in 1973, with a barbecue of twenty-four lambs, masterminded by Ivan Selak. Dunleavy was successful in bringing about a meeting of the ways between the Viticultural Association (mainly consisting of small Dalmatian growers), the regional body of Hawke's Bay Association and the New Zealand Wine Council. It was no mean achievement, given the diverse points of view of these three groups. Dunleavy then went on to enjoy a successful career as the representative of the New Zealand wine industry from 1976 until his retirement in 1990.

I asked Dunleavy to highlight his career and to name his three finest moments. They are worth recording for their significance in the development of the industry. First was his pride at seeing New Zealand as the featured nation at the London Wine Trade Fair in 1988; second, his thrill at shaking the Queen's hand at the Wine Institute's Field Day in Marlborough in 1990; and finally, the excitement of sitting on the visitors' bench in the New Zealand Parliament when the Sale of Liquor Act was amended in 1990 to allow the sale of table wine in supermarkets, which now accounts for about one-third of all domestic sales.

Meanwhile, despite the growth of the industry, there were still mutterings that the illegal practice of adding water to wine was continued by many wineries in order to stretch their production. Denis Irwin at Matawhero went as far as to say that in 1975 he was the only one not putting water into his wine. The issue came to a head in 1981 when several wineries produced large volumes of 'flavoured wines', mainly as cask wines. This resulted in an outcry of adverse publicity and an amendment to the Food and Drug Regulations which dropped the 'flavoured wine' category. From 1983, water was allowed in wine only as part of the process of including a legal additive. Production figures dropped dramatically the following year, from 57.7 million litres in 1983 to 41.7 million litres in 1984. New Zealand wines were finally on track for quality production.

No industry ever develops at a constant pace. There are leaps forward and steps backward. The 1980s saw a dip in growth. There were wineries with financial problems that came near to disappearing in the aftermath of a price war, company mergers and, more significantly, a conviction that too many vineyards were causing a grape glut. What followed in the mid-1980s was the vine pull. Growers who had planted vines at the behest of the larger companies found themselves asked to pull up their livelihood. Murray and Daphne Brown, who now run Cairnbrae Wines in Marlborough, vividly remember being summoned to a meeting of the Corbans growers three days before Christmas in 1985 and being asked to pull up a vineyard which had only just come into production. In fact, many of the vines that were pulled up were varieties that were no longer desirable – not just the hybrids, but vines like Chasselas, Palomino and Müller-Thurgau. The government offered to fund the vine pull up to $10 million, and the grape growers were paid $6,175 per hectare, thereby reducing the country's vineyard area by one-quarter. Some 1,517 hectares (3,748 acres) of vines were destroyed and apparently over sixty grape growers left the business. Ironically, the following vintages, 1987 and 1988, were both small harvests which exacerbated the effects of the vine pull. Ten years later, the vineyards are growing apace.

The first 150 years of the New Zealand wine industry has been a fascinating story of personalities, problems and performances; an amazing shift of flavours and grape varieties; of periods of despair and of optimism. Today, the industry is not without its problems, but it can take its place in the world market-place with its shoulders high. The preoccupations of the mid-1990s and what the future holds are the subject of the next chapter.

3

The New Zealand Wine Industry Today

The fortunes of the New Zealand wine industry have soared spectacularly over the last decade or so. The year 1980 could represent a watershed in the development of the industry – not for any one particular event, but for an overall gathering of momentum, marking the time when so many new areas and wineries were poised to blossom. So many of the new developments in the industry have taken place since 1980, with the ensuing decade seeing an amazing expansion and development that is set to continue up to the millennium and beyond.

After the vine pull of the mid-1980s and a shake-up in the ownership and profile of some of the big players, the industry now looks set on a steady course of growth and development, with the expansion of new areas, the introduction of other grape varieties and the instigation of a system of registered origin. Which is not to say that there are no problems lurking beneath the surface. There are. How easy is it to make a living from growing grapes and producing wine? Has the recent growth been too fast and uncoordinated? Who will buy this increased production? Can the growth be sustained? How many of the new entrants to the industry, particularly the so-called 'lifestylers', will survive? There are many unanswered questions and, in reply, only time will tell . .

New Zealand's dramatic success on the export market, and in particular on the British market, has enhanced the credibility of its wines. Avery's of Bristol, pioneer importers of other New World wines, had shipped Cresta Doré and Bakano from McWilliam's at the beginning of the 1970s, which they followed with a selection of wines from a handful of other wineries after John Avery had been the British judge at the New Zealand Wine Competition in 1978. But it was only in the next decade that the export trade became a viable option. Talk to Terry Dunleavy and he will tell you that as recently as 1980 there was but a handful of people in the industry who believed in the export trade: himself, Frank Yukich of Montana and John Buck of Te Mata. Dunleavy credits Ernie Hunter with the idea of the formation of the Wine Guild, a body designed to promote exports.

On the British market, one man has done more than anyone else single-handedly to promote the cause of New Zealand wine. When Richard Goodman arrived in Britain in 1980, he encountered complete ignorance as to the existence of New Zealand wine. Pigheaded tenacity and persistence are what kept him nibbling away at the market, gradually increasing Cooks's sales to 25,000 cases from his one-bedroom flat in Southfields that doubled as an office. A change in the ownership of Cooks led to a change of policy and a move by Goodman to Montana, where he saw sales rise from a meagre 4,000 cases in 1986 to 180,000 cases in 1992. Although Goodman has now moved on to pastures new, Montana's sales are still growing. His wisdom was to base the sales drive on three key varietals – Sauvignon, Chardonnay and Cabernet Sauvignon – all retailing at the same price, with the result that Montana is now one of the leading brands on the British market. Goodman considers that the big breakthrough for New Zealand and Montana came when they sold more Chardonnay than Sauvignon, thus demonstrating that the consumer was beginning to realize that New Zealand meant more than just one grape variety.

Dunleavy described Richard Goodman as one of the unsung heroes of the New Zealand wine industry. He also mentioned Margaret Harvey in the same breath. She is a New Zealander who was working as a pharmacist at the London Clinic when she took the imaginative step in 1985 of setting up a business, Fine Wines of New Zealand, to import a range of New Zealand wines. Her early shipments included wines from Matua Valley, Babich, Morton Estate, Delegat's and other wineries that could be described as the *crème de la crème* of the New Zealand industry. They were very familiar to Harvey, but completely unknown on the British market.

Back in 1985, the idea of wine from New Zealand was considered something of a joke – an attitude not so dissimilar to the reaction some people have to the idea of English wine today – and it took a lot of energy to convince people to take it seriously. Harvey considers that her big breakthrough was a listing by the

Miller Howe in the Lake District. Once a restaurant with an international reputation was prepared to accept New Zealand wine, others began to follow suit. Many of Harvey's initial agencies have moved on to larger companies as their production and sales have grown, but they should recognize the debt they owe Harvey for the tremendous groundwork she accomplished, paving the way for their present successes. Fine Wines of New Zealand celebrated its tenth anniversary in 1995 and continues to import from a small, highly select band of New Zealand wineries.

The next breakthrough came with the advent of Cloudy Bay on the market. For some reason, this was a wine that caught the collective imagination. The evocative image on the label of the Richmond Hills of Marlborough, and a highly successful marketing policy, turned Cloudy Bay Sauvignon into an overnight success story, making it the most desirable of wines, even to the extent that it was subject to sales quotas. New Zealand wine had arrived. Depending on the state of your wallet and your aspirations, you selected Montana or Cloudy Bay, and the choice has continued to grow. In 1994, sales to the United Kingdom accounted for just over 68 per cent of all exports, representing over fifty different wineries. There is no doubt that we have been captivated by the exciting new flavour of Sauvignon, for Sauvignon from New Zealand is quite unlike the same grape produced in any other part of the world, with its immediate appeal and distinctive taste.

However, the Wine Guild is all too aware of the fickleness of the consumer and the undesirability of relying on just the one export market, and is now turning its attention to other countries. New Zealand exhibited for the first time at the international wine fair Vinexpo in Bordeaux in 1995, and the Wine Guild is looking at the export potential in Germany, North America and Australia, while individual wineries are considering other countries. Nobilo's have achieved an enormous success with White Cloud in Sweden. However, there is no doubt that there is a certain empathy between New Zealand and Britain. New Zealand's place on the British market is now well established and although it may be competing with wines from all over the world on our wine shelves, its position among them is assured.

The vine pull of the mid-1980s can now be seen as a minor blip in the growth of the vineyard area, as Appendix 1 shows the area of vines planted and in production since 1985. New Zealand is now firmly set on a course of expansion, with the boundaries of land considered suitable for viticulture being stretched to the utmost. New areas are being planted, such as Mohaka, between Gisborne and Hawke's Bay, while Motueka, north of Nelson, is another possibility. Established areas are expanding. In Hawke's Bay, vineyards are moving away from the coastal area and being developed inland along the Ngaruroro and Tutaekuri River valleys. In Marlborough, there are the first plantings in the Waihopai Valley and a growing number of vineyards in the Awatere Valley. In fact, vines are appearing in the most unlikely places, as diverse as the far north, close to the Ninety Mile Beach, to Great Barrier Island, and in the centre of the North Island. Grapes grow well in much of New Zealand; the problem is to determine where they grow best. Someone has said that the best New Zealand vineyards have not yet been planted. That may no longer be so, but certainly no area will be ignored.

The expansion in the vineyards comes from three directions. The first is from established wineries seeking to expand their sources of grapes, with the aim to have those sources under their own control, rather than in the hands of contract growers. Then there are the people who are turning to wine as an alternative career. They have often worked successfully in some other field, have tired of their particular rat-race and fallen in love with wine to the extent that they want it to become a full-time occupation. Finally, there are farmers with land who would like to diversify their activity and move away from a dependence on pastoral farming, and maybe also earn more money growing grapes than grazing sheep.

The older established wineries are the most secure and well funded, with the resources to finance expansion and the knowledge that there is a market for their wines. A winery such as Villa Maria or Matua Valley is keen to explore the avenue of new grape varieties and expanding areas, and approaches the situation in a very reasoned and well-thought-out way.

There has been a phenomenal increase from 130 to 204 wineries between 1990 and 1995, and it is hard to imagine that all of these will survive. Some will realize they have no future and give up; others will grow and establish a balanced and an appropriate economy of scale. There is no doubt that the industry is growing fast, but that is in fact what was planned. A recent Wine Institute survey suggests that another 2,000 hectares would be needed by 1998, which was, in fact, already achieved by the end of 1995. There were 6,100 hectares planted at the end of 1993, 6,680 at the end of 1994 and a total of 8,000 expected by the end of 1995, representing a breath-taking increase of 30 per cent in the vineyard area in just three years. The industry really did need to grow, but some people are losing their nerve at such a rapid expansion.

Inevitably, there are those who mutter that this unbridled expansion cannot continue and foresee darkly that the bubble will burst. They may be the prophets of doom. The cracks appear in the instance of some of the lifestylers, who have launched into the venture without any serious realization of the capital requirements of the wine industry. A wine press is expensive, vats are expensive. Often they have had no wine training of any kind, although sometimes they have worked in a scientific environment which helps them make the transition. As Stan Chifney, an expert on vaccines, said of winemaking, 'I could do it with my eyes blindfolded.' Alternatively, they realize that they have no experience and have to hire the services of a qualified oenologist. John Loughlin at Waimarama employs Nick Sage, who also consults for some other wineries in Hawke's Bay. Mark Rattray in Canterbury makes wine not just for himself. The numerous grape growers who use the services of Vintech, now Rapaura Vintners (of which more on page 258), in Marlborough also have to engage a consultant winemaker.

Once your wine is made, you have to sell it, and in a country where each vintage brings a plethora of new labels on to the market, that is no mean feat. Those with more astute marketing ability may find a national distributor; some rely on the fact that there may be very little, if any, immediate competition in their area and sell from the winery gate, while others open a restaurant or café, which provides a ready outlet for their wine and forms part of their marketing strategy, but can also bring other problems in its wake. The examples of the winery restaurant are numerous; some are successful and other less so. French Farm in Canterbury is a sad example of an instance where accountants decided to concentrate on the restaurant and not the winery, having initially thought that there were larger profits to be had in the wine trade than there in fact are.

You cannot help feeling that some of the people involved in the new small wineries have been seduced by the romantic appeal of wine and simply do not realize what excruciatingly hard work it is, a relentless full-time job, without any financial security. There is a definite suspicion that many of the small wineries are under-capitalized and dependent on the sympathy of their bank managers for survival. And to quote John Buck, he cannot believe that begging on your knees in front of your bank manager is any kind of lifestyle. The question is, how cost effective are these small wineries? The likelihood is that there will be a fall-out, and maybe mergers, enabling some of them to become more efficient. But there will always be new people eager to take the same career leap. In some ways, the lifestylers have a choice. If they have the resources, they can set up a boutique winery with a vineyard, or they can simply buy grapes from a contract grower and concentrate on a winery, or alternatively grow grapes and have their wine made for them.

Maybe the simplest way to join the wine industry would be to plant Sauvignon in Marlborough. Rather than buying land outright, you could find somebody with some spare land, persuade them to plant vines and, in return, make them a shareholder in the venture. The wine would be made for you by Rapaura Vintners so that the only capital expense would be the cost of your vines. Everything else could be bought as you need it, with annual bills for vineyard labour and treatment, and winemaking facilities.

The contract growers are in a different position. They have had it good and they have had it bad. Grapes are an agricultural crop and in years when the crop is small, prices go up, and in years when the harvest is large, prices fall, relentlessly following the laws of supply and demand. Contract growers are in the best position when they have a long-term partnership with a winery for which quality is key motivation. Then they will be well rewarded, receiving a good market price for their grapes and a bonus for special work in the vineyard, such as a particular canopy management, low yield and exceptional grapes. Ideally, the winery and grower work closely together, with the winery advising on its requirements which the grower fulfils. Contracts are usually based on acreage and paid according to the size of the crop, specifying a minimum sugar ripeness with a bonus for additional sugar. Thus in a large harvest, the winery receives more grapes and pays accordingly. Usually, the price of grapes is reflected in the wholesale price of the bottle of wine. This means that a grower who has produced exceptional quality grapes which go into a winery's special reserve will be suitably remunerated.

When they want to develop an area, some wineries will encourage the existing farmers to plant vines for them, which is what happened when Montana was starting up in Marlborough. At present, about 70 per cent of all the industry's grape requirements are grown under contract. However, if a winery does not control the source of its grapes it runs the risk of receiving bad grapes, and the wineries are planting more and more vineyards in order to have a more direct control over their grape supply. Probably by 2000 the contract growers will have shrunk in importance to producing just half the industry's needs. Some growers play the open market for grapes, but it can be difficult, with uncertain and irregular rewards. However, when there is a dearth of grapes, it means that prices can escalate, with Chardonnay reaching as much as NZ$2,500 per tonne. With the short vintages of 1992 and 1993, grape prices have been high, which has encouraged some planting. Sometimes it is the wineries who are blamed for high prices, and sometimes they are accused of forcing prices down. Ultimately, it is the grape growers who are at the end of the line.

It is possible to earn a fair living from growing grapes. Ideally you need about 16 hectares of vines, and no debts or mortgage on your land. But that is where the problem lies for some of the new plantings, for the price of land has risen dramatically in the last few years. Many of the established small wineries say that they would simply not be able to afford to start up now because land prices have soared, making it prohibitive to buy vineyard land. Examples of this include the auction of a plot of land in Martinborough in 1994 which fetched $8,000 per acre ($19,768 per hectare). In 1980, you could have bought land for $6,177 per hectare ($2,500 per acre), and not so long before that, land was going for a song at $1,235 per hectare ($500 an acre). By 1988, it had reached $17,297 ($7,000). In some areas, land costs as much as $34,594 ($14,000). However, land does continue to change hands. Alan Limmer reckons that 1,000 hectares were sold in Hawke's Bay in 1994 and that 1,200 hectares of new vineyards were planted in that one year alone. And once you have acquired your land, it costs between $10,000–11,500 per hectare to plant your vineyard, allowing for grafted vines, trellis and fencing, drainage, fertilizers and the preparation of the land as well as equipment, going up to as much as $30,000 per hectare to include irrigation.

Once they have become growers, many people then want to go on to make their own wine. Someone remarked rather cynically that as a grape grower in Marlborough you are nobody. To be somebody, you must have your own label, irrespective of the fact that the wine is made for you under contract. The growers see this as a way of improving the return on their land and then, of course, the next stage is the investment in a winery, but that is a step which leads to far greater overheads and capital commitment. There is a feeling that some of the newcomers are dreamers. The industry needs stability and how do you interest solid investors if the industry has no solid foundations? That is a singularly pessimistic outlook. However, a more realistic hard truth is the suggestion that 10 per cent of the wineries make 90 per cent of the profits – a fact that should provide food for thought for any potential newcomer.

However, the industry is attracting some solid investment, even from overseas. Kemblefield in Hawke's Bay represents a sound American interest and there are other projects funded by foreign money which have yet to come on-stream. An American has planted a significant-sized vineyard in Waipara, apparently with sparkling wine production in mind. Spencer Hill in Nelson has been set up by yet another American, Philip Jones, who sold a successful business in California. There is also some Italian interest in Hawke's Bay, and Japanese too, as well as at De Redcliffe, and Australian involvement in Marlborough.

Although New Zealand is not hampered by the kind of restrictions that the old world imposes on viticultural expansion, the development of new vineyards can bring problems with existing agriculture. Planning requirements, and what they call resource management consents, demand an application for a change in the use of the site, and the requirements of a vineyard or winery may not always meet with a sympathetic reception. If a winery is close to a residential area, there may be complaints about noise. The winery may have problems with the disposal of dirty water and winery effluent. If the vineyards are close to other farming land, problems may arise over sprays. Most of New Zealand's farmers have been accustomed to spraying as and when they liked, without any consideration for other crops, but the proximity of vineyards has affected that freedom. John Kemble at Kemblefield suffered when a sheep farmer treated his pasture with a hormone spray that combats thistles. It is also lethal to vines after budbreak and can travel as far as 20 kilometres if the wind is blowing in the wrong direction, as it was in this instance. Traditional farmers and the grape growers, who may well be newcomers to the land, often have different needs and attitudes. The pastoral farmer cannot understand how you can make money out of one or two 12-hectare (4- or 5-acre) plots and sees viticulture as toy farming. The two do not always coexist happily.

Meanwhile, pastoral farming makes a very significant contribution to the New Zealand economy, while wine is more of a flagship, representing the icing on the cake. However, there is no doubt that viticulture has brought affluence to areas which were far from thriving. The town of Martinborough is an obvious example. When once it was a rundown sheep town, it is now prosperous, welcoming the tourists who come to visit the wineries, spending money as they do so, and, equally important, it is a place with a real identity.

In Hawke's Bay, the wine industry makes about $60 million a year, as opposed to the apple industry which grosses $120 million. Kiwi fruit, sheep farming and forestry are also more important than wine in the region's economy, but while they are all fairly static in their performance, there is no doubt that wine is a expanding industry. Not only is production itself growing, but wine brings the tourists who are eager to explore the winery trails, trying the wines for themselves and sampling the winery restaurants. It all adds a buoyancy to the local economy.

No other industry is so site selective, and that will be reinforced by the new system of registered origin, which should come into operation for the wines of the 1996 vintage. The government has been working on this scheme since 1990 and in 1994 passed the Geographic Indications Act. Alongside this stands the GATT agreement to protect the intellectual property of associations with a geographic indication. This means that New Zealand can no longer use terms like 'sherry', 'Chablis' or 'Sauternes' for the domestic market. Administrative boundaries have been established in New Zealand, in conjunction with the New Zealand Geographic Board and based on the river control authorities. Broadly, these areas are Northland, Auckland including Waiheke Island, the Waikato, the

Bay of Plenty, Gisborne, Hawke's Bay, Wellington which extends north of Masterton, Nelson, Marlborough, Canterbury and Central Otago. Within these large areas there will be smaller subdivisions. For example, Wellington will probably be divided into Gladstone, Martinborough, Masterton and, on the west coast, Otaki. Then within those divisions, there will be yet smaller areas, and even vineyards named after specific geographic features, such as Gimblett Road and Swamp Road in Hawke's Bay. As in most European wine regions, the key percentage is 85 per cent, so that 15 per cent from another vintage, area or grape variety is acceptable. Unfortunately a complete list of registered origins is not available at the time of writing.

Allowance is also made for synonyms, historical factors and the two languages. This means that Gisborne, for instance, can be called not only Poverty Bay but also its Maori name Turanganui a Kiwa. The geographical name must be accompanied by the words 'registered origin' in order to avoid any confusion with names that may appear to be geographical but are not, such as Cloudy Bay or Shingle Peak. Above all, a label must not be confusing, for the aim is to guarantee to the consumer that the origin of the wine is that which is stated on the label. There is no other guarantee of quality, as is sometimes implied in the appellation systems of Europe. In order not to impose restrictions as regards the blending of wines from different areas, it is possible to mention more than one region on a label.

The Wine Institute felt very strongly that the boundaries should be based purely on a geographical location and not on any climatic or soil criteria. Although wine was the first product to establish these regional delimitations, the same boundaries will also apply to other crops such as apples or kiwi fruit. Essentially little will change on the labels, apart from a guarantee of origin. The wineries have to keep adequate records, showing how much they produce, along with the quantity of any grapes they have purchased, so that they can satisfy the authorities in the event of an inspection.

The small vintages of the early 1990s have caused a shortage of wine for the domestic market, as well as restrictions on the export market. Fifty per cent of New Zealand's domestic consumption is bulk bag-in-the box wine and much of that demand has been satisfied by Australian wine making up New Zealand–Australian blends, while some have even included some European wine. However, this is a temporary situation which has been alleviated by a large vintage in 1995 and pressure on supply will also be reduced as so many new vineyards come into production. Normally, only about 15 to 20 per cent of domestic consumption does not come from New Zealand, but recently that figure has been far higher, as much as 50 per cent, but it will drop significantly. Incidentally, for the sake of comparison, only 2 per cent of Australia's consumption comes from outside the continent.

On the domestic market, the biggest growth area is Chardonnay. Sauvignon does well too, as do blends of Cabernet and Merlot rather than pure Cabernet Sauvignon. There is also great excitement about Riesling. Rather like the British, the average New Zealander goes for cheap and cheerful wines. The average spend is $10 a bottle, which gives you a bottle of Montana Sauvignon on special offer or a more commonplace Müller-Thurgau. The action is in the $12–15 price bracket, with a good choice of Chardonnay, Sauvignon and Cabernet. The government takes its cut in the form of $1.50 excise duty as well as 12.5 per cent VAT. In some ways, New Zealand still has a very undeveloped wine culture. It is growing, but the average New Zealander is at heart a beer drinker and, as in Britain, most wine is drunk within hours of its purchase. The concept of buying wine to lay it down for consumption in a few years' time is still in its infancy.

The two main annual competitions, the Air New Zealand Wine Awards and the Easter Show, excite a lot of interest among wineries and consumers. As part of a young industry, the New Zealand wine producers do not have the confidence of their counterparts in Europe. The show system is very symptomatic of that hesitancy. They need the reassurance that comes from winning an award, and they are very keen to pit their wines against each other and to learn from the comparisons. Foreign judges, one Australian and one British, are invited to participate in the Air New Zealand Wine Awards so that New Zealand's wines can be placed in an international context. Naturally, the results excite much interest and reputations can certainly be started, if not created, on the strength of one win.

Philip Gregan, the astute young executive director of the Wine Institute, currently sees two clouds on the horizon of the industry: the high grape prices and the high dollar, both of which affect New Zealand's position on the international market, but may be only temporary. Grape prices determine the ultimate price of every bottle of wine and affect New Zealand's competitiveness. This is compounded by the strong dollar (the exchange rate was at the time of writing about $2.30 to the pound) which makes New Zealand wines expensive in the foreign market-place and also affects their position on the domestic market by making imported wines cheaper. This, of course, may change, but it may well lead wineries to re-evaluate their involvement in the export market.

The thinkers in the industry are aware of the harsh realities. They see the transition from a highly protected local industry into a competitive international industry. The future will be one of extreme competition which you have to be very fit to withstand, for New Zealand is now competing with the rest of the world, not with other New Zealand products. New Zealand will only ever be a small wine-producing country. It will never be able to produce large volumes of cheap wine for export and so it must concentrate on high quality and good value, and leave the bulk-wine market to Australia, South America and South Africa. The key is to be competitive and to produce wine at a price that people will pay.

As can be seen in the chapter on grape varieties, there is a keen interest in new varieties for New Zealand. The choice of varietals will therefore expand significantly and New Zealand will move away from its strong alignment with Sauvignon in the mind of the consumer. There is an undeniable long-term faith in viticulture and a conviction that the only way forward is to plant more and increase the vineyard area, with both established varieties and new varieties. Essentially, New Zealand must continue doing what it does best: making wines with a wonderful intensity of fruit, the product of long cool ripening seasons. New Zealand has a more temperate climate than any other New World wine-producing country. Therein lies its originality which, above all, it must maintain. If it does, the future looks good.

4

Viticulture: How to Control the Vines

Geologically New Zealand is a very new country, as the world's youngest land mass and only 50 million years old. In European terms, that makes it a mere adolescent. The Alps are 60 million years old and the Jurassic limestone of Chablis even older at 180 million years. Lake Taupo, one of the scenic spots of the North Island, was created only 20,000 years ago and parts of Hawke's Bay are very much more recent. The two main islands are a splendid confusion of geology, the result of countless earthquakes and volcanic eruptions. You can fly over extinct volcanic craters in Auckland harbour, and New Zealand is known as the shaky isles for a reason: its eastern seaboard from Gisborne, through Napier, then Wellington, and on down the west coast of the South Island, lies on the edge of a great fault line, the same two plates that make California so vulnerable to earthquakes.

For viticulture, this means that the soils are very young, very confused, and also very fertile. An area like Hawke's Bay forms a geological jigsaw of different soil types which are only just being plotted. The one soil type in which New Zealand is poor, which can be found in Europe, is weathered limestone. Only Waipara, to the north of Christchurch, claims to have the fragmented limestone similar to that of the hills of Burgundy.

Consequently, New Zealand viticulture is in a state of flux. While the technical expertise in most wineries reaches a very high level of competence, prompted partly by the stringent standards and technical expertise of the dairy industry, the overriding feeling is that there is still much to be done in the vineyard. They are still learning which grape varieties grow best on which soils, which rootstocks suit which varieties, and what are the most appropriate systems of training, trellising and pruning. Three main preoccupations concern them: site selection, the need to control the vigour of the vines, and the essential requirement to bring sunlight into the vines in order to ripen the grapes fully in the cooler climate of the world's southernmost vineyards. Then within these parameters, there are other concerns. Phylloxera is spreading and birds constitute one of the main vineyard pests.

Vines throughout New Zealand seem to have a tendency to excessive vigour. The key factors relating to vigour are climatic and environmental. Vigour reflects the health of the vine, and both phylloxera and viral infections can slow it down considerably. However, in most areas the vines tend to produce lavish canopies of green leaves which, of course, deter the ripening process as the leaves shade the grapes and the vine's energy is misdirected towards leaf production rather than grape ripening. There are all kinds of explanations offered as to why vigour is such an overriding problem in New Zealand, whereas in European vineyards it is rarely discussed. New Zealand soils have high natural fertility, which inevitably results in high vigour. Excessive rainfall, which can and does occur, encourages the vines to grow prolifically. Another theory is that the explanation lies in the moisture-holding capacity of the soils. New Zealand has high water tables, so vines, even in free-draining soils, are able to tap water without too much difficulty. This means that the difference between vigorous and non-vigorous soil is its water-holding capacity, and this is one of the criteria which needs to be applied in site selection. If there is an ample water supply, there is nothing to check the growth of a healthy vine.

Given that vigour is a fact of life of New Zealand viticulture, the main problem is to control the vine, and the need to prune and train it in order to obtain the ripest possible fruit. In this field, Dr Richard Smart, a talented and outspoken Australian who was government viticulturist between 1982 and 1988, has played a vital advisory role, doing much to determine the future face of New Zealand vineyards and, since then, many others in different parts of the world, from England to South America. His book *Sunlight into Wine* elaborates on his thoughts and theories, expounding the need to bring light into the canopy. He emphasizes the effect of sun exposure of grape clusters and leaves on wine quality, reiterating that they need to be well exposed to the sun.

Shade in the canopy reduces wine quality, especially in a cool climate like New Zealand. Above all, the vine should be in balance. He explains the high vigour by the new viticultural technology. Improvements in pest, disease and weed control with the use of agricultural chemicals have enhanced the health of the vines, along with the availability of virus-free material for new vineyards and the improved application of fertilizers. There has also been a tendency to select sites where the soil is deep and fertile, and that factor, combined with high summer rainfall or generous irrigation, has inevitably resulted in vigorous vines. Allan Clarke from the Vine Improvement Group explains how there was a high residue of fertility from the previous farming activity, such as dairy farming, and often the vineyard sites that were chosen in the 1970s were those with high natural fertility. The main aim was a high yield and so the obvious choice was a flat fertile site. Now that the industry is coming of age, there is a distinct move towards infertile sites, such as Gimblett Road in Hawke's Bay and the 'tough, mean clay soils' of Waiheke, with a choice of sites that do not retain water, allowing for better vigour control. There is also growing interest in hillside sites, of which the Terraces at Esk Valley is an early example, and which may well prove a future source of fine wines.

In each region, site selection is receiving greater consideration. For example, in Hawke's Bay there is a distinct move away from the Heretaunga Plains, which have reserves of moisture under the soil, towards more arid, stony country further away from the coast. The deep fertile sites would be far better for apple orchards and other market gardening. Urban pressure also makes an impact on site selection. Vineyards in the suburbs of Auckland are decreasing, not only because the humid climatic conditions can make grape growing difficult, but also because the urban sprawl renders the land more profitable for housing. Urban proximity can create disputes over noise and spray drift.

Problems in the vineyard can arise from canopy shade, as well as from overcropping and excessive vigour. An inadequate trellis system results in too much shade in the canopy, which in turn adversely affects the yield and quality of the grapes. The vine has a vegetative growth cycle which favours shoot growth over fruit production, so it is necessary to break the cycle using root-zone management to devigorate the vines. Grass cover crops compete with the vines for water and nutrients, and also limit erosion.

In the search for the best possible fruit, various different training systems are practised. Some are well established and others are more experimental. One of the most articulate supporters of Smart's principles is David Hoskins at Heron's Flight. He was greatly influenced by the Cool Climate Symposium held in Auckland in 1988 at which the buzz words were 'canopy management'. He found Smart's attitude refreshingly unhampered by any traditions, as it would have been in Europe. At Heron's Flight, where the soil is a mixture of water-retaining clay and loam, Hoskins has espoused the big-vine theory in an open lyre system. The principle behind it is that the big vine is devigorated by being allowed to grow and the result is 6 metres of cordon in two branches per vine. Two vines are planted side by side, 1 metre apart, with the canopy widening out so that the gap between the two at the top is 1.5 metres. This means that you are able to work within the canopy. The angle is the key, allowing the sunlight to enter the canopy and ripen the fruit, and excessive vegetation is removed regularly, leaving enough for the grapes to ripen.

Michael Brajkovich at Kumeu River is very enthusiastic about the lyre system of trellising, which was developed in Bordeaux. The difference between the vineyards at Kumeu River and Heron's Fight is that Brajkovich's vines are trained into two curtains forming a lyre, rather than having two vines side by side. This allows for an open canopy with good light at the centre of the vine and good ripening of the fruit.

Scott Henry is another catchword trellising system in New Zealand, which was developed by the eponymous grape grower in Oregon in the 1970s and was found to be suitable for fertile soil. Again, it depends on a divided canopy, with some shoots going up and others down, working on the principle that the longer something is held erect, the longer it will carry on growing, so a collapsing canopy automatically devigorates and loses steam. The main advantage of Scott Henry in New Zealand is that it is very easy to modify from 'vertical shoot positioning' – the standard New Zealand training of an undivided canopy, with two parallel canes and all the shoots going up, which tended to produce too much shaded canopy, although it had the advantage of being easy to spray. if there was a risk of fungal disease. The Scott Henry system increases the surface area, but half the shoots are devigorated by being trained downwards, resulting in a significant increase in sugar and yields.

Sylvoz is another system that is currently being tried and tested. It consists of a permanent cordon along the wire, with the fruiting canes trained down at pruning so that the shoots grow vertically, supported by movable wires. This entails a redistribution of photosynthesis, but with the same amount of foliage as Scott Henry. It is well suited to mechanical harvesting and, again, has resulted in healthier fruit. More light coming into an increased canopy surface means that the vine is able to ripen a larger crop. Indeed, some would accuse it of overcropping. There are also the advantages of better spray penetration, with a more open canopy and greater air circulation, thereby reducing the risk of disease. The aim is to regulate the leaf area and crop to match, so that the vine is in balance. The textbooks state that you need fifteen leaves per bunch of grapes, but more work is needed on the relationship between the leaves and the grapes, and their respective positions.

Other systems include the Geneva Double Curtain and Te Kauwhata Two-Tier system, but they are tending to be supplanted by Scott Henry or Sylvoz.

Spacing is also a consideration. Most New World vineyards were established after the mechanization of agriculture. This means that the vines were automatically planted in rows wide enough to allow for the passage of a tractor. It is only now that the European idea of close-spaced vines is being considered; even then, the vines may be as close as 1 metre within the row, but will still be in rows 3 metres apart to accommodate the tractor and harvester. In the recently planted Te Motu vineyard on Waiheke, they have spacing of 1 metre by 2 metres, instead of the more usual 3 metres by 1.5 metres, and they are also looking at 4-metre-wide planting but admit that is probably too wide. The Villa Maria Group's new vineyard in Hawke's Bay is planted in narrower rows of 1.8 by 1.5 metres, which they find improves the quality of the fruit while maintaining a good yield.

High-density planting may be another option for combating vigour in that it results in competition among the vines for nutrients, but in fertile sites this can have the opposite effect and encourage growth as the vines compete with each other and overproduce foliage. The optimum vine spacing is dictated by the potential of the soil, so that a soil that encourages growth requires wider spaced rows, while closer spaced vines perform better in low-potential soils. It is all a question of balance. There is a trial in Hawke's Bay of a vineyard that is 1 metre by 1.5, a hillside site with 6,666 plants per hectare. Danny Schuster at Omihi Hills in Waipara has a vineyard of Pinot Noir on limestone, planted in what he called close spacing of 2 metres by 1 metre. Any closer and you need special machinery, but there is now more equipment available which is suitable for narrower rows. Essentially, however, most New Zealand planting is determined by the tractor width and everything is still very much in the trial-and-error phase.

What is being planted is the subject of enormous development, with a staggering increase in the variety of grapes, rootstock and clones. Initially, the introduction of new varieties depended very much on particular enthusiasms. In the 1970s, it was up to individuals to import anything that had caught their fancy. Denis Irwin's father at Matawhero was responsible for some of the more original imports of the 1970s, such as a Gewürztraminer from California. Helmut Becker from the Geisenheim Institute brought in a huge range of disease-resistant vines, such as Reichensteiner, Optima and Scheurebe. Few of them actually caught on, although they were evaluated. According to Joe Corban, Becker brought in a suitcase of vines and played havoc! The process was often thwarted by bureaucratic ineptitude, combined with New Zealand's understandably strict quarantine laws. However, the process of vine importation, run by the Department of Agriculture, was draconian and out of date. Tony Molloy of St Nesbit can entertain you at length with his attempts to import Petit Verdot. He finally acquired five vines after nine years, which culminated in threats of court injunctions. Happily, the process has now become much more streamlined and flexible with the backing of the Vine Improvement Group, which also involves local nurserymen in each area, encouraging growers to plant source blocks of new imports.

Joe Corban at Riverlea Nurseries is an important figure in the work of propagation and vine development. He is an immediately likeable man with a fervent enthusiasm for what he is doing. Viticulture is in his blood and he has worked as a viticulturist all his life, first for Corbans and now running his own nursery. He drove me around his vineyards. He has some 20 hectares (50 acres) of vines, with 100 kilometres of plastic tunnelling. There were rows of closely planted vines, all beautifully neat and tended with loving care, representing around 300 different combinations of grape varieties, clones and rootstock. The performance of the various combinations can then be appraised, with the most successful being supplied to the industry.

Usually, the imported material has to spend two years in quarantine, or only one if it comes from an accredited source such as UC Davis in California, or possibly ANTAV in France which may soon be accredited. Originally, any import had to be virus free, but this is no longer necessary if the potential import is suffering from a virus or disease that already exists in New Zealand. There are ten official imports allowed each year, with a five-year plan that pays more attention to better clones of proven varieties rather than new varieties. However, private individuals are also allowed to bring in vine material at a cost of $2,500 per item, a price which tends to discourage private enterprise. Once the vine is out of quarantine, then it can be propagated freely.

Clones of particular varieties are discussed in the following chapter. Suffice it to say here that the choice is growing by the year and will continue to do so. What also has to be determined is the suitability of different rootstock and how they relate to different soils, grape varieties and particular clones. Kim Goldwater talked of when he planted his first vines in 1978. The only rootstock available was a high-vigour one, 1202, with the advantage that it propagated well and was easy to graft, but of course resulted in vigorous vines. Now everyone is looking at low-vigour rootstocks. John Stichbury at Jackson Estate is currently trying out about twenty-seven different rootstocks, of which he anticipates ultimately using just five, including maybe 3306 and Riparia Gloire. At Cloudy Bay, they are experimenting with new clones and rootstocks in their own nurseries which supply their growers so as not to be dependent on the official research organizations. They are concentrating on six in particular, including 101-14 for Sauvignon and Schwarzman for Chardonnay. As yet, no one really knows which are the most suitable rootstocks.

Timing is another aspect in the use of rootstock. For example, the Mendoza clone of Chardonnay tends to burst bud earlier than others, but spring frost can be a problem in Marlborough, so the solution would be a rootstock which delays its budbreak. However, the rootstock must not change the character of the fruit and there must be an affinity between the rootstock and the vine. Another consideration is the factor that some rootstocks perform better in different soils. Joe Corban, in his work on rootstocks, considers that 420-A may be the only vigour-reducing rootstock which really does produce smaller vines. He disputes the commonly held view that 3309 reduces vigour. 101-14 may lead to earlier ripening, by one or two weeks. Basically he says that if the soil is rich, they all perform the same. There is still much to discover and, according to Allan Clarke of the Vine Improvement Group, 'an exciting new quality barrier to go through'.

Meanwhile, phylloxera has not yet affected all the vineyards of New Zealand, so that rootstocks are not essential for new plantings. Phylloxera first arrived in New Zealand in 1885 with some vine cuttings. Romeo Bragato offered advice about grafting vines as the remedy. However, not all the regions are affected to the same extent. Phylloxera was first detected in Hawke's Bay in 1900. Now three-quarters of all the vineyards there are planted on grafted vines and all should be grafted within a decade. In contrast, Martinborough, which is a much newer area, is still a phylloxera-free zone, but for how long remains to be seen. Marlborough survived about ten years before phylloxera first appeared in the mid-1980s and there is now a huge demand for rootstock, with extensive replanting.

However, some of the new vineyards are still planted with ungrafted vines. This may seem short-sighted in the extreme, but if you are lucky, you may last on ungrafted vines for as long as ten years. Then there are financial considerations. The price difference between a grafted and an ungrafted vine is significant: 30–40 cents for a vine on its own roots, as opposed to $2.50–3.30 for a grafted one. I was also told that it is possible to set the expense of replanting a vineyard, as opposed to planting a new one, against tax. Quite simply, there is not enough rootstock available to meet the demand. Replanting also allows for a change in the composition of the vineyards. To quote Ivan Sutherland, Cloudy Bay's viticulturist, the sooner Müller-Thurgau is out of Marlborough the better, and that will happen with the replanting.

Some of the replanting is being done block by block. Others, such as Hunter's, have preferred to interplant between the existing vines, which means that you lose only a year's fruit from the vineyard. You can easily spot the vines with phylloxera as they have lots of yellow leaves, and look thin and spindly. However, they still continue to produce fruit and if they have a good root system it does not really matter so much if the voracious louse has eaten half of it. It might be suggested that phylloxera could be useful as a devigorator, but it also affects the quality and flavour of the fruit. Initially it seems that vines only slightly infected by phylloxera produce superb grapes, as a result of the improved fruit exposure, with less canopy shading and lower yields, but after a couple of years the grapes start to suffer from weak, diluted flavours, with low acidity and low sugars.

Irrigation has a significant effect on the vigour of the vine. The Marlborough Research Centre has been conducting trials on irrigation in an attempt to change a prevailing attitude of using it as an insurance policy. If water is available, it is very easy simply to turn on the tap. However, some areas of potential vineyard, such as the Waihopai Valley in Marlborough, do not have water available. The short answer to the question, 'Do vines need irrigation?' is, 'No.' However, much depends on the soil and on its water-retaining capacity, in both topsoil and subsoil.

Irrigation is one way of manipulating the vigour of the vine and the quality of the fruit. It can delay maturity as the vine thinks that it should still be growing, rather than concentrating on ripening its grapes. This can make a difference to the timing of the vintage of one or two weeks, which in Marlborough, where they may have autumn frosts, could be crucial. Water stress, therefore, can be a positive factor. The shoots of the vine are very sensitive to water stress, whereas the fruit is not, so you can effect shoot stress without affecting the fruit. Essentially, if the plant is stressed, it starts to think about the future, so it concentrates on producing fruit rather than more shoots.

Currently the Marlborough council allows 12 litres per vine per day, a figure based on work at Lincoln College and the Marlborough Research Centre. As recently as 1994, the daily allowance was 24 litres, which the research centre considered excessive. At Kemblefield in Hawke's Bay John Kemble found no restriction on irrigation. He had to apply to use the water source and he is allowed 30 litres per second for twenty hours per day. He considered irrigation essential during the initial phase of the vineyard, to help the young vines establish themselves, but once they have reached the subsoil below the free-draining soil it is less critical. If the vines do not establish a good root system quickly, you run the risk of losing them in a drought.

A cover crop or no cover crop is a yet another factor in vineyard management and vigour control. A cover crop such as chicory or rye grass will take water out of the soil and help control the vigour of the vines by establishing water deficiency in the soil. However, if you have a cover crop, you also run a higher risk of damage from frost, although if the crop is merely short-cropped grass, there is little difference between that and bare soil. Bare soil has the advantage of heating up more quickly and storing more energy to release overnight. Grass transpires, losing more heat and taking up less heat, while a low-growing cover crop between the vines helps suppress weeds. At Martinborough Vineyard they put straw down around the vines to discourage the weeds, but one disadvantage becomes apparent in strong winds, such as those in Martin-borough, when the straw blows all over the vineyard.

At Waimarama, the north-facing vineyard slopes are grassed and, essentially, the grass controls the water supply. They pro-gramme the irrigation meticulously, with thirty-nine gauges in the soil and an electronic controller. At Cloudy Bay they are also working with neutron probes so that the vines will be irrigated only when necessary and the whole process is much more carefully controlled. This is essential for Sauvignon, which tends to excessive vigour if it is given too much water.

Leaf plucking and shoot trimming are other factors in the control of the vine, which allow more light into the canopy and form part of the seasonal work in the vineyard. Leaf plucking exposes the grapes to sunlight, making for a riper crop, but if it is done to excess, the grapes are left quite bare, with the vines almost obscenely naked. However, it can significantly alter the flavour of the grapes, making for a distinctly riper taste. This is particularly noticeable in Sauvignon Blanc in Marlborough, where vines that have not been leaf plucked produce much more herbaceous flavours than those that have.

Shoot removal, while taking away excessive vegetation and exposing the grapes, usually results in further shoot growth. The purists feel that leaf plucking is a symptom that the vine is out of balance, as is green harvesting which entails the removal of bunches of grapes after flowering if the crop threatens to be excessive. The vines should be managed in harmony with their surroundings and, of course, the more work that is necessary in the vineyard, the higher the ultimate cost of production.

Another way of affecting the crop, which is only at an experimental stage, is girdling. At St Helena they are trying it for their Mendoza clone of Chardonnay, cutting into the trunk of the vine a week before flowering. After about three or four weeks the wood calluses over. The idea is to prevent the carbohydrates from going back into the root system, which results in a better setting, as Mendoza is particularly prone to *millerandage*, or 'hen and chicken' as New Zealanders call it. Trials in Marlborough over the last seven years or so have resulted in a 50 per cent increase in the crop. However, there is a fear that ultimately it will weaken the vine and make it more susceptible to disease by creating what is initially an open wound.

The seasonal work of vineyard management is not dissimilar to other vineyards in other parts of the world. However, it is all quite highly mechanized, with line trimmers, leaf pluckers and sprayers, and increasingly sophisticated tractors with digital computer controls.

New Zealand vineyards suffer from many of the same diseases as European vineyards. Botrytis sprays are used to combat rot which is a problem in damp, humid conditions. Powdery mildew or oidium are also prevalent, for which there are conventional treatments. There is also a research project to establish a pattern between the weather and outbreaks of disease, with work on disease prediction to enable a more efficient use of fungicides, thereby entailing a reduction in spray programmes. This means that you treat your vines whenever an outbreak of disease is likely to be prompted by a climatic condition. One spraying costs $260 per hectare, which represents no mean saving. Wineries with very committed viticulturists carry out an immense amount of monitoring, accumulating detailed data which they can use to manage their vineyards more efficiently.

As for viruses, leaf-roll virus is the most common and is the subject of some research. The chief factor in its spread is the mealy bug, which enjoys the climate of the warmer vineyards such as Auckland, Hawke's Bay and Gisborne. It is found in Marlborough, too, but is not considered a problem there as the low humidity and cool nights keep it under control. Further south it is too cool. The mealy bug does not fly but crawls from one vine to the next and may also be spread by pruning. Insecticides are used to keep it at bay, but once a vineyard has leaf-roll virus, the only long-term solution is to replant.

The use of fertilizers is generally sensible as there is reasonable fertility in the soil and, of course, in some instances too much. Any deficiencies of potassium, phosphorus, magnesium, or nitrogen can easily be ascertained and corrected as part of good vineyard management. As for organic viticulture, the most committed exponents are the Milltons in Gisborne, who are accredited with Bio-Gro status from the New Zealand Biological Producers' Council, and who also follow Rudolf Steiner's principles of bio-dynamics. Rippon Vineyard has also just been accredited with Bio-Gro status, while Stephen White at Stonyridge is among others to follow organic viticulture.

One of the most common hazards for the grapes is birds, in particular the pretty green waxeyes, described by Alan Limmer as 'another bit of detritus from Australia'. They make a noise which sounds like a fingernail squeaking on a blackboard, setting your teeth on edge. The waxeyes do not actually eat the grapes, but a flock of them can cause devastation in a vineyard of nearly ripe grapes. They prick each one and take the merest sip of juice, and of course this makes the grapes immediately susceptible to infection and rot. Vineyard managers stretch their imagination in thinking up all manner of bird scarers. You can see some colourful scarecrows in the vineyards. Longview has large balloons floating over the vines. Others have mock hawks and kites. There are various noise devices, but these can eventually become habit forming and indeed alert the birds to the presence of something sweet and juicy to eat.

The most usual deterrent is to net the vines, which is expensive, costing about $5,000 per hectare, and the nets have only limited life as they can tear easily. Even then, the wily little waxeyes can wriggle under the nets and, once trapped, do untold damage. They are a protected species, so you are not allowed to shoot them as a deterrent, only when they are actually feasting on your grapes. A possible salvation might be the New Zealand hawk which is an endangered species. If more hawks could be established in the vineyard areas, they might act as effective predators and keep the smaller bird population at bay. Another option which could be developed is the fact that birds are scared of lights.

Waxeyes are not the only culprits. Starlings are also a problem. They were first introduced to New Zealand to eat the grass grubs which destroy grazing pasture. Glenn Thomas at Vavasour described them as very resourceful birds, citing the example of how, when their normal food sources were destroyed by floods in Gisborne in the aftermath of cyclone Bola, they turned their attention to the vineyards and simply stripped them of grapes.

Frost, both in spring and autumn, causes concern in the cooler vineyards from Martinborough southwards. Helicopters are one way of combating it. The Giesen brothers in Canterbury usually have a helicopter on standby during the crucial period of the spring. You pay a small fee for the standby facility, but once the helicopter takes to the air it costs you $1,000 per hour, which is not an insignificant sum. However, it may make all the difference between having wine to sell and having none at all. In Martinborough too, some of the wineries, such as Martinborough Vineyard, avail themselves of a helicopter if frost is predicted. The helicopter will take to the sky when the thermometer drops to 0°C and can raise the temperature to 5°C by churning up the air. It is effective, provided that there is no more than 100 feet of frosted air. Some of the new growers in Central Otago are planning to build large windmills which could have a similar effect to the helicopters, churning up the cold air and preventing the formation of frost. However, for this they need planning permission. No one mentioned any of the frost-prevention systems that you find in Chablis – spray systems or heaters – so it seems the choice is either a helicopter or a prayer.

Finally, the grapes are ready for picking. Harvest dates can vary considerably; the earliest might be February in Gisborne and the vintage can last until well into May or even June in Central Otago. Some grapes are hand picked, namely those intended for finer sparkling wines and for any table wines that require whole-bunch pressing, entailing the inclusion of some stalks. Normally, the majority of New Zealand vineyards are highly mechanized with mechanical harvesters to pick the grapes. These machines have become highly sophisticated and much more gentle in their technique than the early machines that violently shook the vines. They can now even pick whole bunches, and gather up much fewer leaves and mouldy grapes than earlier machines. According to Allan Scott in Marlborough, they could even be used for sparkling wine. If you wish to harvest in the cool of the early morning, it is much easier to use a machine. They do this at Jackson Estate, bringing in the grapes between five and ten o'clock in the morning, when the fruit will be only about 12°C in temperature.

The age of the vines has a significant effect on flavour. In European terms, a vine is considered to have reached its peak of production at about fifteen years old and will have at least another ten years of full productive life in front of it. In New Zealand, a fifteen-year-old vine is a rare thing, and there are numerous very young vineyards, a situation which is exaggerated even more by the considerable replanting programme necessitated by phylloxera. It has been observed that the first couple of crops off a vineyard often produce very good fruit, ripening beautifully, but then the flavour tails off for about ten years, stemming from a tendency of the vine to overproduce. Essentially the vine needs time to settle down and develop its full root structure. Once the majority of New Zealand vineyards have come of age, the flavour in the wines can only improve.

In so many wine-producing countries, in both the new and the old worlds, greater emphasis has been placed on work in the cellar, while the vineyards have been left to take care of themselves. It is only now that vineyards are being given the attention that they deserve and winemakers are realizing how essential it is to have vineyards that are in balance and which give them the grapes that they need for fine-flavoured wine. New Zealand is no exception in this. Its technology in the cellar is abreast of all the latest developments, but in the vineyard there is still much to be done, with so much to learn about clones and rootstocks, training systems and irrigation. The refreshing aspect of all this is that there are no hard-and-fast rules and no appellation regulations controlling production methods, so that everything is possible and New Zealand remains completely unbound by tradition. It is the responsibility of the individual winery to obtain the best quality grapes, which in turn will produce the finest possible wine, with minimal intervention in the cellar.

5

Grape Varieties: Life beyond Sauvignon

New Zealand is poised on the edge of a veritable explosion in the choice of grape varieties available to its winemakers. Sauvignon and Chardonnay are the two principal quality white varieties, while Müller-Thurgau currently supplies much of the bulk drinking. Cabernet Sauvignon, Merlot and Pinot Noir account for most of the better red wines, but the choice is growing year by year as new varieties emerge from quarantine. There is an innate curiosity about the potential of the vineyards which pushes back the frontiers each year. It is not just the grape variety that is considered, but the clone of that variety, while rootstocks represent yet another piece in the puzzle. Then there is the evolution in winemaking styles, which is more significant for some varieties than for others. Again, there is much to discover.

To quote Allan Clarke of the Vine Improvement Board, 'their shopping list is a bottomless pit', prompted by a continual reassessment of existing varieties, maintaining some and rejecting others, combined with an infinite curiosity about the unknown, which is fed by the need for greater diversification. New Zealand has achieved an enormous success with Sauvignon, closely followed by Chardonnay, and now it is time to offer a broader choice. That is not to say that they should stop doing what they do well, but on the contrary that they should also try other varieties so as not to be too single-minded in their pursuit of Sauvignon. This chapter looks at the various grape varieties and what is done to them in the cellar.

SAUVIGNON – AND SÉMILLON

Sauvignon is the grape variety that put New Zealand on the international wine map. In Marlborough in particular, it has produced a flavour quite unlike Sauvignon from anywhere else in the world: a uniquely juicy, sappy flavour; a powerful combination of pungent gooseberries, cats and asparagus. Methoxypyrazines have been identified as the compounds that give Sauvignon its distinctive flavour. They make the taste of New Zealand Sauvignon blatantly obvious, unashamedly pushy and completely different from any Sauvignon that has ever come from France. It is a wine that you either love or hate. Subtle it ain't, but delicious it is. There are methoxypyrazines in French Sauvignon too, but their impact is less marked. In distinct contrast, Sauvignon from the Loire Valley, particularly from Sancerre and Pouilly Fumé, is more delicate and distinctly understated, while Sauvignon from Bordeaux is a little more solid and flatter in flavour. Its success has been nothing short of astonishing, and what is even more surprising is that all the plantings of Sauvignon in New Zealand originate from just one single clone which would have been lost but for the efforts of Ross Spence.

There was some Sauvignon at the Te Kauwhata Research Station, but it was diseased and virused. However, Spence had a hunch that there was potential, then he found a healthy vine in a Corbans trial block – just one vine that had originated from Davis – which was healthy and virus free. It was UCD 1. He propagated it, grafted it and put it into production when he started Matua Valley in 1974. Meanwhile, he sold cuttings to Montana for their vineyards in Marlborough. Initially there was resistance to Sauvignon Blanc on the label, but when Robert Mondavi visited New Zealand he suggested that Matua Valley call their wine Fumé Blanc, which is what they did at first. However, for Montana, Sauvignon on the label was accepted – as it now is for everyone else – to describe an unoaked wine, while Fumé Blanc refers to a Sauvignon that has had some contact with wood.

Marlborough is virtually synonymous with Sauvignon, for that is where it is most widely planted and where it produces its most typical and characteristic flavours. Nelson, which is a little warmer, tends to make wines that have just a touch more weight than those of Marlborough, while Sauvignon from Hawke's Bay is less aggressively pungent, fuller and stonier, with more tropical flavour.

A wine like Te Mata's Castle Hill could even be said to have a little more subtlety. There is little Sauvignon grown around Auckland, with Kumeu River providing a successful exception, or in Gisborne, as the climate tends to be too warm. In Central Otago and Canterbury, it competes in popularity with other varieties and produces wines with quite firm acidity. Most of the Auckland wineries obtain their Sauvignon from Marlborough, either from their own vineyards or from contract growers. They used to truck their grapes north, but now they tend to use the facilities of Vintech, or Rapaura Vintners as it has been called since mid-1995.

Sauvignon is a simple wine to make. In contrast with Chardonnay, it provides little choice for the winemaker but 'sells like hot cakes' and generates lots of welcome cash flow. What more does a winery want, except that it does not provide the winemaking challenges of Chardonnay, Pinot Noir, or even Riesling. It is a very straightforward winemaking process. You crush the grapes, ferment the juice, carefully controlling the temperature, stabilize the wine and bottle it, then it is ready for sale. However, there are nuances of flavour which come not only from what is done in the cellar, but also reflect how the vines are treated in the vineyard.

Herbaceous overtones in Sauvignon are an indication that the grapes are not as ripe as they might be. Without sunshine, Sauvignon takes on a grassy character. Leaf plucking to expose the grapes properly to sunlight can remove some of the herbaceous flavours, and the timing of the leaf plucking also has an effect on flavour. According to Neil McCallum of Dry River, if you leaf pluck after *véraison*, you will obtain a capsicum, bell-pepper character, while leaf plucking before *véraison* gives a stone-fruit flavour. Ripe fruit adds an extra degree of alcohol which improves the flavour and balance, as does a blend of fruit picked at various levels of ripeness, between 21.5° and 25° Brix, which is possible in years where the grapes are ripening well and the harvest is not threatened by heavy rain. It adds an extra dimension.

The fermentation should be long and slow, taking about four and a half weeks in stainless-steel vats at about 9–10°C, but slightly higher at the beginning and end. Most of the grapes are machine picked and if they are then sent up to Auckland for vinification, some skin contact is inevitable. Deacidification and chaptalization are both possible. Alternatively, the level of acidity can be reduced by varying amounts of malolactic fermentation. However, Denis Dubordieu of Château Reynon in the Graves has proved by his experiments with lees stirring that Burgundian techniques do not work with Sauvignon, while a malolactic fermentation encourages the loss of freshness and fruit.

Then it is simply a question of blending, stabilizing, filtering and bottling. Sometimes the blends vary according to their destination. Canadians apparently have a sweeter tooth than the British for their Sauvignon, so a little more residual sugar is deliberately left in their wine. Usually Sauvignon has about 3 or 4 grams per litre, depending on the vintage, which still makes it a dry wine, but with enough sugar to take off harsh edges of acidity.

Another element of diversity is the use of Sémillon in the blend, in an amount which may vary from as little as 2 to as much as 15 per cent. Sémillon tastes similar but different, adding an extra element of complexity in what could easily be a one-dimensional wine. It can add backbone to compensate for overripe Sauvignon which has turned flabby, or have a slight softening effect if the Sauvignon is overtly acidic. Ross Spence worked on two Sémillon clones while he was developing the Sauvignon. One died, leaving UCD 2, which has provided all New Zealand's plantings of Sémillon.

You occasionally find a pure Sémillon varietal in New Zealand. Merlen is one exception, but most is destined for a blend, usually with Sauvignon. New Zealand Sémillon is said to be different from Australian because of the different ripening conditions. Maybe it would also have ageing potential if it were able to ripen properly, but the clone is virused and rarely does. Michael Brajkovich of Kumeu River also believes in the potential of Sémillon and manages to achieve ripe fruit, but with only a low yield. Maybe the introduction of better clones will remedy the situation.

Oak is another flavour factor for Sauvignon. Sometimes it is subtle and understated, as in Cloudy Bay where the wine spends about four months in wood, including just 4 or 5 per cent of new oak. They describe the oak as a palate filler and find that it enhances the longevity of the wine. The generally accepted view is that New Zealand Sauvignon does not age – neither, for that matter, does French Sauvignon. However, there are exceptions which certainly Cloudy Bay can prove. Even the more humble Montana Sauvignon held its own more than adequately at a vertical tasting of its first ten vintages.

Sometimes the oak can be more overtly obvious, removing the Sauvignon fruit and replacing it with something resembling an oak infusion which is not always successful. Oak can cover up any green flavours and mask an excess of acidity. At Gibbston Valley, oak is used to distinguish between the fruit they obtain from Marlborough, redolent of gooseberries, and their own Central Otago fruit, a third of which goes into wood with a malolactic fermentation, giving the wine a firm green-pea character. They are clearly not imitating Marlborough.

Morton Estate makes a Fumé Blanc that is all barrel fermented and spends three or four months in oak. For my tastebuds, it compares unfavourably with their Hawke's Bay Sauvignon, which has an appealing mineral quality about it. Hunter's oak-aged Sauvignon includes about 40 per cent oak-aged wine, while the rest is fermented in stainless steel, making a lean, oaky palate with underlying juicy fruit. They try not to have too much oak; just enough to add an extra dimension and allow for greater ageing potential.

The Antipodean makes what they describe as a Graves-style white: a blend of 80 per cent Sauvignon/20 per cent Sémillon. The two varieties are barrel fermented together and spend twelve months in oak. I would not disagree with the French comparison, for the flavour is full and grassy and slightly nutty, with good fruit and acidity, not unlike a finely oaked Graves.

Mark Mason at Sacred Hill has worked with Denis Dubordieu at Château Reynon and is very much influenced by his ideas. He is eager to develop the idea that New Zealand Sauvignon can indeed age and sees that varietal as the strength of Sacred Hill. His Noble Selection is a rare example of a sweet Sauvignon made from mainly botrytized grapes and barrel fermented to taste of honey and marmalade.

At Vavasour, Glenn Thomas is moving away from the grassy thin acidic style of Sauvignon to wines with more fruit ripeness. He wants good crisp fruit with some firm body; wines with the minimal amount of residual sugar that will go with food. Crisp acidity will always be a component of Sauvignon, but the flavour must be ripe as well. The Vavasour Reserve Sauvignon includes a proportion of barrel-fermented wine that is lees stirred, then blended with tank-fermented wine that has been left on the lees without stirring. Here, Thomas's aim is maturation without the wine absorbing obvious oak flavours – a fine line to tread. However, the

Awatere Valley gives Sauvignon with more of a flinty character that is quite different from the Wairau Valley and the rest of Marlborough.

What will be fascinating to observe in the coming years is the development of New Zealand Sauvignon as new clones come on-stream. Not unnaturally, there is the attitude 'if it ain't broke, don't fix it', and New Zealand Sauvignon is working brilliantly. On the other hand, to place all your eggs in one basket is perhaps risky, and they are haunted by the possibility of doing even better. So new clones have been brought into the country by the Vine Improvement Group and three clones from Bordeaux, as well as one from Italy, have just been released. The first fruit from them will be produced in 1996 and the results assessed. Curiously, perhaps, there are no clones available from the Loire Valley. Allan Clarke of the Vine Improvement Group ruefully admitted that 'the French are a bit prickly about the competition', as well they may be.

CHARDONNAY

Vineyards of Chardonnay now outnumber those of Sauvignon and also Müller-Thurgau. It is the most widely planted grape variety and continues to be so, with a plethora of new vineyards all over the country, from Northland down to Central Otago, as shown in Appendix 2. Although Marlborough is synonymous with Sauvignon in international eyes, it does in fact produce more than a third of the country's Chardonnay, with Gisborne and Hawke's Bay the other two main areas.

There are enormous climatic differences between the regions, but that is to Chardonnay's advantage. It is the most adaptable of vines, performing well in a variety of climatic conditions, and it is not fussy about soil type. It may suffer damage from spring frosts in cooler regions as it has an early budbreak, but it generally ripens well, without too many problems in the vineyard, and gives consistent yields. Gisborne, the self-proclaimed Chardonnay capital of New Zealand, is the warmest area, producing some soft ripe Chardonnay – wines that are mass produced and above all fruit driven, uncomplicated and easy to drink, along with others from individual vineyards which have more stature and structure, but always with the characteristic ripeness of Gisborne.

Hawke's Bay also produces ripe fruit with a rich flavour, but the acidity is more apparent; in the cooler areas of Marlborough and nearby Nelson, a lemony quality appears in the fruit. Canterbury and Central Otago are cooler still. Critics of Marlborough Chardonnay claim that it does not have the potential for long-term development of Hawke's Bay and Gisborne, and that the acidity levels are too high to make a balanced wine when the grapes are fully ripe. That said, there are numerous producers of Chardonnay in Marlborough who would dispute it. However, many of the new plantings of Chardonnay in Marlborough are destined for sparkling wine. It is Hawke's Bay that is widely considered to produce the best Chardonnay, although Gisborne may usurp that position about one year in five. Gisborne Chardonnay develops quickly and appeals early, but also has some staying power, as illustrated by Millton's 1986. The high clay content in the soil of Gisborne partly accounts for the riper, richer flavours which make Gisborne Chardonnay more accessible and explain why Montana's Gisborne Chardonnay is their biggest selling wine.

However, there is no doubt that winemaking techniques mask many of the regional variations. Chardonnay is a winemaker's delight. Since it is not an aromatic variety, winemakers do not have to concentrate on extracting the true fruit and flavour of the grapes, as they do with Sauvignon or Riesling. Instead, they can have a wonderful time playing with all manner of vinification techniques. And, of course, Chardonnay is a vital ingredient of sparkling wine, of which there are a growing number in Marlborough in particular (see pages 93–8).

A winery with vineyards in more than one area may well try different techniques in order to encapsulate the individual flavour of each. Brent Marris at Delegat's explained how he develops the tropical character of Hawke's Bay Chardonnay, fermenting it in tank, then ageing it in wood, with at least six months on the lees. Here the emphasis is on fruit, with oak as a support. In contrast, Oyster Bay Marlborough Chardonnay is fermented in wood, three-quarters new, and the barrels are lees stirred. Marris finds the Marlborough fruit very powerful, so it needs oak to tone it down and give it some definition.

There has been a breath-taking evolution in New Zealand Chardonnay over the past decade. The first wines were simple and unoaked. Then Chardonnay was matured in old oak, quickly followed by new wood. It was realized that the fruit and oak would marry better if their wines were actually fermented in oak, preferably new French *barriques*. John Hancock was the very first winemaker in New Zealand to ferment Chardonnay in oak, as recently as 1983, when he was at Delegat's. In the early 1980s, people were happy with fruit-driven wines, with a layer of oak added. Now barrel fermentation gives a better balance to the wine.

New Zealand winemakers are very conscious of the different French coopers and pay great attention to the provenance of their barrels. They are more likely to tell you the name of their cooper – be it Demptos, François Frères, or whoever – than the precise provenance of the oak – Tronçais, Nevers, or even American – although they might mention that the wood is tight grained and indicate the degree of toasting in the barrels. Some use American oak for cheaper wines, or better still American oak seasoned by French coopers such as Demptos, the *bordelais* company who now have associates in Napa. Delegat's buy from them with a guarantee of two years' air-drying of the wood, and they also have the length of charring stamped on the barrel rim. Twenty minutes is too short; longer is better, with quite a high initial temperature which gradually cools, giving more depth and a more attractive smoky character to the wine. A different cooper can make a significant impact on wine quality, as Delegat's found when they changed coopers recently.

Often Chardonnay is often kept on the fine lees for several months, with regular lees stirring, which tones down some of the fruit and adds an element of yeastiness. It is necessary to achieve the balance between maturing the wine in wood sufficiently without allowing it to become overoaked. The length of barrel maturation can therefore vary from just two or three months to a year or more.

Barrels are expensive. A good quality French *barrique* of 225 litres from a cooper such as Dagaud & Jaegle currently costs NZ$1,000, while Ricard can produce a cheaper barrel for about $800. They charge $1,110 for a 350-litre hogshead and $1,325 for a 500-litre puncheon, which represents a considerable saving per litre. The 500-litre puncheon gives a deeper layer of lees at the bottom, resulting in a more reductive character, with more yeast autolysis, but with less impact from the wood and oxidation. In comparison, an American oak barrel of 225 litres made by a French cooper will cost $540. Generally, American oak gives sweeter vanilla and banana flavours, with a more aggressive character than the subtle French oak. However, the French coopers seem to be able to tone down some of the overt flavours of the American oak.

For serious economy on wood, the option is oak chips which make for a fatter, buttery, more 'Australian' style of Chardonnay. The size of the chips varies considerably from virtually sawdust granules to matchsticks and bigger shards. You calculate how much you need by weight according to the volume of wine, usually 3 to 5 grams per litre, and they are tied up in a muslin bag. The oak must be properly seasoned and toasted or else you will obtain only harsh, aggressive flavours. Usually they are made from American oak; it is also possible to obtain French oak chips, but they are at least twice as expensive. The smaller the chips, the more extraction of oak flavours, so generally small chips are used for Chardonnay and bigger chips for red wine.

The two extremes of style which illustrate the range of flavour of New Zealand Chardonnay are the unoaked Nobilo's Poverty Bay Chardonnay and Kumeu River Chardonnay. The first is simple, possibly one dimensional; it does not even see an oak chip and tastes not unlike a fairly full Mâcon Blanc. The second aspires to emulate something rather fine from the Côte de Beaune – a Meursault or a Puligny-Montrachet and is given the full Burgundian treatment, including whole-bunch pressing, fermentation by natural yeast, a serious amount of new oak, a full malolactic fermentation and regular lees stirring which helps to break down the yeast. The result is one of the most distinctive of New Zealand Chardonnays.

Another master of Chardonnay is Tim Finn at Neudorf, who explained how his style has evolved over the years. First of all, better vineyard management has given him riper fruit. In 1991 he began to experiment with new oak, also the first year in which he tried whole-bunch pressing to move away from an extracted character. Hand-picked fruit makes for a slower pressing and much better juice. There is no skin contact, which avoids phenolics and the resulting bitterness, and consequently any need for fining. Before, when he had the inevitable skin contact from mechanically harvested fruit, his Chardonnay would fall to pieces after not too many years; now, it is much more elegant with good staying power and length.

Between the two extremes is a veritable medley of different flavours and techniques. Both chaptalization and deacidification are possible, and practised when the inadequacies of the vintage make it necessary. A malolactic fermentation may also improve a wine's balance, for it is better to convert the malic acid than to remove acidity artificially. The proportion of malolactic fermentation in Chardonnay may range from all to nothing, depending on the vintage. The argument against malolactic fermentation is that it can make the wine too soft and result in a loss of fruit.

Alan Johnson at Palliser explained his vinification process for Chardonnay in precise detail. All the fruit is mechanically harvested so that there are no whole bunches. The grapes are crushed and pressed, the juice is settled for forty-eight hours then racked, and the fermentation started with cultured yeast. About a third of the way through, the juice is put into wood, of which about one-quarter is new, mainly from Taransaud and Dagaud & Jaegle. Johnson attaches great importance to the cooper and the oak is usually Vosges or a tight-grained oak from the Massif Central. The wine spends nine months in wood, but without any lees stirring as that would add too much of a yeasty character. He puts fairly clean juice into the barrels. However, some juice solids are important because they add structure, while lees stirring makes for faster development. Oak has a different effect on bright wine and on wine containing solids. If bright wine goes into wood, the oak becomes more dominant than in a wine with solids. Johnson determines the percentage of malolactic fermentation by the characteristics of the vintage. In 1994 it was about 60 per cent and a little more in the cooler vintage of 1993, and only 30 per cent in 1991. If the malolactic fermentation does not start of its own accord, you can inoculate for it. At the end of the ageing period, the wine is cold stabilized and bottled.

I wondered whether it would be possible for New Zealand, with its cool climate, to produce an unoaked Chardonnay that resembled an unoaked Chablis and developed in the same way. For the moment it seems unlikely. The first hurdle to overcome is the psychological barrier. New Zealanders expect Chardonnay to taste of oak; if it doesn't, they expect to pay considerably less for it. On the domestic market, oak chips are preferable to no oak. Another suggested reason is that there is a simple difference between the composition of the grapes in Chablis and in, say,

Marlborough. In Chablis, the grapes have a high acid level and a low pH, whereas in Marlborough, both the acidity level and the pH are high. Apparently a high pH in the grapes can be rectified in the vineyard by canopy management and the control of vigour. A high pH can make for more a unstable wine, which may require more sulphur, whereas a low pH gives an attractive leanness to a young Chardonnay. However, in some instances there is a move away from the obviously oak-driven styles of Chardonnay. Coopers Creek are even considering a unoaked Chardonnay from Marlborough, but for the moment their Reserve Chardonnay is fermented one-third in new oak, one-third in one-year-old oak and one-third in tank, then blended together in order to tone down the effect of the oak.

The other style variation for Chardonnay is the occasional example of sweet wine, when the quirks of nature have allowed for a botrytized wine, such as Seibel's 1991 Noble Late Harvest Chardonnay from Hawke's Bay, which was described as a complete fluke with 100 per cent botrytis. Morton Estate produced one in 1994 which has fermented slowly in oak for several months, from April until the end of October, and will spend a further three or four months in wood. Millton Vineyard have another example.

Many of the Chardonnay vineyards are still very young. Vines are in their prime when they are about twenty years old and there are very few, if indeed any, Chardonnay vineyards that are as mature in New Zealand. Pinot Chardonnay was mentioned in a viticultural report of 1917, but not by Bragato, and more was brought into the country in the 1920s. However, most of the vines were infected by leaf-roll virus and did not thrive. It was not until the mid-1980s that there was a concerted effort to improve the quality of Chardonnay with the introduction of six new clones between 1982 and 1985. This has helped to encourage the development of Chardonnay with a dramatic increase in acreage from 394 hectares in 1986 to about 1,200 in 1992. In 1995 it reached 1,917 hectares, to account for 23 per cent of the vineyard total. At the same time, vineyard sites are being considered more carefully, with selections of better fruit being used for reserve wines or sold under a specific vineyard name, such as Babich's Irongate or Matua Valley's Judd Estate.

There are now several different clones of Chardonnay in New Zealand, not all of which have been fully assessed through vineyard and cellar. The most popular is the Mendoza or McCrae clone which originated from Davis and was introduced from Australia by McWilliam's in the 1970s. McCrae was the Hawke's Bay grower who first planted it in New Zealand. It often suffers from a poor set, resulting in very irregular yields – anything between 1 and 4 tonnes per acre. If the flowering takes place in inclement weather, it causes what is called hen and chicken, with both large and small berries. The small berries give a higher skin-to-juice ratio, making for a richer, sweeter flavoured juice with a good balance, high alcohol and high acid. However, the high alcohol can have the disadvantage of inhibiting the malolactic fermentation. This is the clone that a winery chooses to plant in its own vineyards, or else growers are paid a premium for it to compensate for the lower yields.

Clone 6 came from Davis, again via Australia, and is not dissimilar to Mendoza but is more consistent, with a better set and medium-sized bunches. It complements Mendoza well, giving softness and fruitiness to balance Mendoza's acidity. There is clone 15 too, also from Davis, which is as yet unproven, as is clone 7. Clones 4 and 5 produce big juicy bunches of grapes, usually with thin acidic juice, which makes them perfect for sparkling wine. Then there are Burgundian clones coming into the picture as plantings mature, such as clone 96, which gives a consistent but medium-to-low yield, and 2/23, which is similar to clone 6 but with a higher yield.

However, there is no doubt that the progress of the last few years will be more than matched in the next decade. Basic cellar techniques have been mastered. It now depends upon the work in the vineyard and as new clones are developed, they will open up new possibilities in the winery. Meanwhile, there are some very exciting Chardonnays waiting for our enjoyment.

RIESLING

Maybe Riesling is the unsung hero of New Zealand white wines. Although this is the grape variety of all great white wines of the Rhine and Mosel, it has sadly fallen from favour with the decline in popularity of German wine, the image of which has been spoilt by cheap and nasty Liebfraumilch tarring the fine estate wines with the same brush. This is grossly unfair to what some people would claim to be the world's greatest white grape variety. Riesling offers an intriguing diversity of taste, responding to variations of site and *terroir*, and producing different flavours depending on the ripeness of the grapes. In Germany it can make half a dozen different wines from the same vineyard, depending on how and when the grapes are picked. With Chardonnay, everything depends upon the wine-maker; for Riesling, significant differences also come from the soil and climate too.

Riesling performs at its best in a cool climate with a long ripening season and warm autumns. That is just what the vineyards of New Zealand, from Martinborough southwards, are able to provide. Marlborough and Canterbury, especially Waipara and also Central Otago, may prove to be particularly successful. The flavour range in New Zealand Riesling is almost as diverse as that of Germany, with the main difference that New Zealand Riesling tends to be fuller, with a higher alcohol level. Often the wines are left with a little residual sugar so that they are medium dry. Botrytized Riesling is not uncommon, either.

Although Riesling has been around in New Zealand since the early days of viticulture, it is only in the last few years that it has made any kind of impression. Romeo Bragato mentioned it as suitable variety, but without much enthusiasm, and it virtually disappeared from view. In 1975, there were just 8 hectares planted in Hawke's Bay and half a hectare in Auckland, but since then the momentum has gathered.

My introduction to the charms of New Zealand Riesling came with my first visit to the Giesen brothers in the summer of 1991. A 1989 Canterbury Dry Riesling was delicately honeyed, with lemony acidity. A Late Harvest Riesling had a hint of botrytis, while the 1990 Botrytis Riesling was redolent of ripe honey, apricots and peaches. The grapes had been left on the vines until early May and the fermentation stopped to retain the sweetness. The remaining yeast had been removed by centrifuge and the resulting wine was luscious and balanced, not at all cloying. Also in 1989 they picked some Riesling with a record 54° Brix, which they had blended with some botrytized Müller-Thurgau to make a Trocken-beerenauslese style, with a taste of dried raisins and apricots. In this instance the fermentation stopped naturally and the total production was just 600 half-bottles.

For the Giesens, the intrinsic character of New Zealand Riesling is very dominant fruit, combined with a very good acidity balance. The wine should be crisp, refreshing and peachy. They consider that it is usually too fruity to achieve the kerosene character that can be obtained on the Mosel.

Four years on, they were concentrating on dry Riesling, aiming to make a wine to age, which would not be sold for at least two and half years after bottling. This is quite contrary to the usual New Zealand practice of drinking most Riesling within six months of the vintage. The 1994s that I tasted were lean and lemony, while the 1991 had developed a slightly slatey nose, with good mineral notes and a hint of honey on the palate. It would improve still more.

The vinification process for Riesling is quite straightforward, usually consisting of a cool fermentation in stainless-steel tanks, or maybe occasionally in wood. Matthew Donaldson at Pegasus Bay ferments half his juice with solids, and cold settles the other half before fermentation, which gives some extra complexity. The wine then spends eight months on the fine lees, which gives it a lemony, limey finish. Broadly speaking, the vinification process is not so different from Sauvignon. Other Canterbury wineries have produced some good Rieslings too, and John McCaskey at Glenmark laughingly described it as the Waipara weed because it grows so well in that area.

In Central Otago, the long autumns favour Riesling. Black Ridge made a good 1994, without needing to chaptalize or deacidify, as did Gibbston Valley and Chard Farm, producing wines with fresh stony acidity.

In contrast, Marlborough Riesling tends to be fuller and slightly sweeter, but with a considerable capacity to age, as Alan McCorkindale demonstrated with a vertical tasting of Stoneleigh Riesling from 1994 back to 1986. As five times winner of the Air New Zealand Riesling trophy, he is the undisputed master of the variety in New Zealand. It is also a variety he particularly enjoys making. Quizzed about the differences in longevity between New Zealand and Germany, he suggested that the stony soil of his vineyards in Marlborough gave more fruit and made for quicker development. He thought that the climate bore some similarity to the Palatinate region of Germany, although in fact it is generally warmer, with Marlborough averaging 2,395 sunshine hours, as opposed to 1,712 in the Palatinate and 1,574 in the Mosel.

Almuth Lorenz at Merlen makes her Riesling as light in alcohol as possible and with minimum skin contact to avoid any bitterness. Late harvest and botrytis Riesling present another challenge. Her 1991 Magic Merlen was left on vines until June and fermented in small barrels until January, when the fermentation stopped of its own accord. It then spent a further six months on its lees.

The Stichbury brothers at Jackson Estate are also Riesling supporters. They are convinced that the varietal is set for a comeback, but meanwhile discreetly label their wine Marlborough Riesling Dry, placing emphasis on provenance rather than variety. They too made a successful botrytis wine in 1991 which is ageing beautifully.

Grove Mill prefer Riesling with some residual sugar, 20–30 grams per litre, as opposed to about 12 grams for a dry style. That way you can make a better wine, retaining more acidity, with a lower pH and higher extract. In fact, Dave Pearce's aim is a Mosel Auslese, but with a little more body and alcohol, which is what he achieved with his 1991.

At Dry River, Neil McCallum is an ardent Riesling enthusiast. He finds that in New Zealand the botrytis can be too obvious and phenolic, overwhelming the flavour of the grape variety. His 1991 Riesling, which approximates to a Spätlese, was harmonious peaches, apricots and honey, and some slatey kerosene notes, all in perfect balance. McCallum has also produced some botrytized wine which can only be described as simply delicious. Other wineries produce Riesling. Martinborough Vineyard produces both a dry and a late harvest, and the new winery Nga Waka shows potential. Chris Lintz remains true to his German ancestry and makes New Zealand's only sparkling Riesling.

Allen Hogan at Te Whare Ra in Marlborough is convinced of the suitability of Marlborough for botrytis. He was the first Marlborough winemaker to produce a botrytis wine and explained that it is not his vineyard that is particularly prone to botrytis, but the combination of heavy dews and warm days which create a humid microclimate in the canopy. He encourages the noble rot still more by refraining from using botrytis sprays. He also explained that the standard New Zealand Riesling clone has very open bunches, which makes it less prone to botrytis; a new clone with tighter bunches from South Australia, which he is currently planting, should prove more satisfactory. Riesling is also one of the varieties used by Rongopai for their late harvest wines.

The full potential of Riesling is still to be realized, with an infinite variety of wines – from the austerely dry, through degrees of delicate honey, to some richly luscious sweet wines.

PINOT GRIS

The grape variety of which we are going to see an enormous increase in the coming years is Pinot Gris. Dry River, with Neil McCallum's enthusiasm for the flavours of Alsace, has already established a reputation for the variety, and several others are interested in its possibilities, maybe as a alternative challenge to Chardonnay.

Pinot Gris was an early arrival in New Zealand and was praised by Bragato in that 'it bears heavily and produces an excellent white wine'. Along with other varieties, it fell out of favour and only now is beginning to enjoy something of a revival in fashion. The early import was Tokay *à petits grains* which was a low cropper and has indeed been pulled up in Alsace. Tokay *à grands grains* gives larger crops, but the quality of flavour is not so good. None the less, it rarely produces more than 1.5 to 2 tonnes per acre, with small berries. New clones are now being brought in by the Vine Improvement Group from Alsace and from Geisenheim.

McCallum's vinification is perfectly straightforward. The grapes are pressed without any skin contact, as that is unnecessary for enhancing flavour if the grapes are fully ripe. It gives concentrated fruit with good body and extract, and a certain creamy texture.

There are now at least five vineyards of Pinot Gris in Martinborough, inspired by McCallum's fine example. Martinborough Vineyard had its first crop in 1995 and a new enterprise, Margrain, has planted some. Dennis Roberts formerly at Gladstone described it as the 'next unknown white'.

McCallum's cuttings came from the Mission Vineyard. The continuity of Pinot Gris had been maintained, but in a rather unsatisfactory, over-fertile vineyard at Meeanee in Hawke's Bay, where it was used for bulk wine. Now they have replanted on a more suitable site with the aim of making a more serious wine, maybe as part of their Jewelstone range.

In Hawke's Bay, for the moment, Brookfield remain the principal exponent of the varietal. Robertson's planting is of the original clone, with small berries and small bunches. He does not find it an easy variety to handle and says he took a few years to learn how to balance a tiny bit of oak with the tannins in the skins. Minimum skin contact is necessary to prevent colour from the pink skins of the ripe grapes tainting the juice. He has now established a new Pinot Gris vineyard. The last crop off his original vineyard was in 1992, but the site was too fertile and the vines were affected by phylloxera, so he decided to replant in stonier soil and is very excited about the potential as the bunches seem to set better.

Ross Spence, one of New Zealand's most innovative viticulturists, is very enthusiastic about the potential of Pinot Gris. Matua Valley had their first crop from a vineyard in Marlborough in 1995.

There is a little Pinot Gris in Canterbury, at Larcomb and at St Helena, while Waipara Springs are interested in planting some. Central Otago is a potential source of gentle aromatic Pinot Gris at Gibbston Valley, where it is lightly spicy with a little residual sugar to balance the acidity. They first made it in 1987 and found that it ages beautifully, with good extract. Rob Hay at Chard Farm suggested that Hawke's Bay was too hot for Pinot Gris, as it likes to ripen fully but slowly, like Pinot Noir. He would like to try fermenting it in older oak, as the body and extract lend themselves to oak in the same way as Chardonnay. Sadly, their last crop was eaten by the birds.

PINOT BLANC

Pinot Blanc, again, was an early arrival in New Zealand and was recommended by Bragato for doing well in all districts and making good wine, but then disappeared from view. Pinot Blanc lies somewhat in the shadow of Pinot Gris, as its flavour is not so distinctive. For the moment, I know of only St Helena and Omihi Hills that produce it as a varietal wine. In fact, Danny Schuster buys his fruit from St Helena, who have 2 hectares (5 acres) in production. At St Helena there has been some experimentation with methods. 1989 was soft and grassy, and 1990 did not see any wood either, but it was a very ripe year with some botrytis, making a rich, leafy-textured wine. The 1991, which was given just a little wood, has matured into something not too dissimilar to Chablis, with some elegance and fruit, while the 1994 was partially barrel fermented and aged in old wood for six months. With the 1995, they intend to revert to no oak ageing.

Danny Schuster described Pinot Blanc as 'poor man's Chardonnay', and makes it in a very similar way. He obtains fruit from Hawke's Bay as well as St Helena and claims to use three-quarters of the total production of New Zealand Pinot Blanc. The grapes are pressed in Hawke's Bay, then fermented in Waipara in old French wood which is at least three years old. The wine spends eight months in wood. Schuster avoids a malolactic fermentation and gives the wine some lees contact, making a wine that is rich, long and refined, with good acidity.

Matua Valley have also planted Pinot Blanc in Marlborough and feel that, like Pinot Gris, it has much to offer. As yet, the full potential of Pinot Blanc and Pinot Gris has to be realized. It will be exciting to observe their evolution in the coming vintages.

MÜLLER-THURGAU

Müller Thurgau was introduced to New Zealand by the government viticulturist Charles Woodfin in the 1930s, along with various other even less attractive varieties – hybrids such as Baco 22A and some numbered Seibels. It was merely one of the crowd until Alex and Joe Corban, as winemaker and viticulturist respectively, began to pay it a little more attention in the 1960s, producing what they called Riverlea Riesling. Müller-Thurgau was at that time more commonly called Riesling Sylvaner. This was the first white varietal table wine to be made from *vitis vinifera* grapes for many years, marking a watershed in New Zealand viticulture. The Babich brothers remembered it well when it was tasted at the Young Winemakers' Club, along with the first Pinotage produced by Corbans at the same time. 'We were so impressed how much better than hybrids they were and this marked the start of the return to the classic varieties.' George Fistonich was equally enthusiastic, remembering that when Müller-Thurgau came along in the late 1960s, it was 'like discovering a new clone of Chardonnay today.

We did not have to drink Blue Nun or Deinhard Green Label any more; we could make our own.' And he did in 1970.

Helmut Becker of the Geisenheim Institute also encouraged the spread of Müller-Thurgau. He drew comparisons between Germany and New Zealand which, on reflection, are now considered ill-founded. In some ways he takes responsibility for sending New Zealand down the dead-end corridor of Müller-Thurgau, whereas her viticulture might now be much further advanced if she had moved on swiftly from the first Riesling Sylvaner to Sauvignon or Chardonnay. In 1960, Riesling Sylvaner accounted for just 45 (18.2 hectares) acres of vineyard; by 1965, it had increased to 74 acres (30 hectares) and continued to grow steadily until the vine pull of 1986 saw the uprooting of vast acres of Müller-Thurgau. Chardonnay now outranks it, but not yet Sauvignon.

The appeal of Müller-Thurgau is that it is an easy variety to cultivate and is liked by contract growers for its regular yields. It is an early ripener, but can be susceptible to wet weather at the harvest and succumbs easily to rot. It has played a significant role as a blending variety, mixed with a bit of Dr Hogg Muscat or Palomino or whatever is to hand, and rendered lightly sweet by a little residual sugar or the addition of some sweet reserve. Cresta Doré from McWilliam's became a household name, as did Montana's Wohnsiedler. Today, Müller-Thurgau is a vital constituent of Nobilo's White Cloud and Montana's Misty Peak.

The one person to give me a Müller-Thurgau of which they were genuinely proud as a serious wine, rather than a marketing exercise, was Denis Irwin at Matawhero. His 1989 Riesling Sylvaner Dry Reserve, tasted in 1994, threw a completely new light on my usual preconceived ideas about Müller-Thurgau. Instead, this was a wine with an amazingly intense flavour, with some apricot fruit and good mouthfeel. The 1993 tasted at the same time was still very young, pithy and undeveloped, with fresh acidity. But that was very much the exception to the rule, illustrating Irwin's originality and desire to go against the flow.

More characteristic is Nobilo's White Cloud, which is mainly Müller-Thurgau with 15 per cent Sauvignon and just a smidgen of Muscat to give the wine a lift. It has a flowery taste characteristic of well-vinified Müller-Thurgau, with a little sweetness on the finish. In other words, it is totally inoffensive and completely unmemorable. Wohnsiedler Müller-Thurgau is quite sweet and flowery, while Montana's recent introduction, Misty Peak, made from Müller-Thurgau with a hint of Muscat and Gewürztraminer, is quite soft and innocuous, with a hint of spice. It was prompted by the visible success of White Cloud which they saw was uncontested.

DR HOGG MUSCAT

Dr Hogg Muscat is another variety that has been grown in New Zealand for a number of years. In reality it is an old English table grape and is not used for wine production anywhere else in the world. In the past it has been a constituent of fortified dessert wines and nowadays it features in blends with Müller-Thurgau, such as White Cloud. It is also used for some of the sweet sparkling wines on the domestic market, such as Montana's Bernardino Asti Spumante look-alike and also Fricante. It grows well in Gisborne, where it is the most popular variety after Müller-Thurgau and Chardonnay.

Another manifestation of it is in Matua Valley's Late Harvest Muscat, which is full and grapey, with good acidity, not unlike a *vin doux naturel* from Beaumes de Venise or Frontignan, but with only 10.5° alcohol, which makes it altogether more refreshing.

OTHER GERMANIC VARIETIES

There are other Germanic grape varieties, vestiges of the influence of Helmut Becker in New Zealand's viticultural development. Almuth Lorenz at Merlen produces a Morio-Muscat, in deference to her origins in the Rheinhessen, which she describes as Morio-Muscat country. It is her Müller-Thurgau replacement and she has just over 1 hectare (3 acres) which has been in production since 1991. It tastes much less overpowering than German Morio-Muscat, with some sweet pineappley fruit. The fermentation is stopped, leaving 25 grams per litre residual sugar.

At Lintz you will find an example of Optima. Montana brought it into New Zealand in the early 1970s with a view to blending it with Müller-Thurgau. Chris Lintz has planted just six rows to see how it goes and in 1993 produced an Optima Noble Selection from fully botrytized grapes, which is almost a Trockenbeerenauslese in its sweetness. In Germany, Optima reaches very high *oechsle* levels much more easily than Riesling.

There is Reichensteiner, used mainly for blending. Osteiner, which is produced at Rippon Vineyard, tends to be rather acidic. Norbert Seibel has made the only example of New Zealand Scheurebe, which was grown originally for Corban's bulk white. There are the occasional sightings of Bacchus, Ehrenfelser and also Sylvaner.

BREIDECKER

Breidecker is peculiar to New Zealand. It was developed at Geisenheim specifically for New Zealand and is a cross of Müller-Thurgau and Seibel 7053. It is named after Heinrich Breidecker, a German immigrant who made wine at Kohukohu in the Hokianga on the North Island, and was first planted in New Zealand in 1962.

Breidecker was valued for its resistance to rot, which is typical of its hybrid parentage, as well as its generous yields and early ripening. On the other hand, its flavour is singularly unremarkable. I have only once tasted a pure Breidecker, at Larcomb, when it was soft and grassy, with a little acidity and a faintly appley nose, providing easy but unexciting drinking. It is usually blended with Riesling and Sauvignon, as in St Jerome's Estate Dry White, and its main virtue is doubtless cash flow.

CHASSELAS

Chasselas, which offers much more enjoyment as a table grape, has been grown in New Zealand since the last century, for it was among the grapes shown to Bragato by the French settlers at Akaroa. Today, there are just 92 hectares of Chasselas. It is used as a blending variety, for it lacks flavour, as it usually does when it is used as a wine grape in Europe, notably in Savoie, Baden and Switzerland.

PALOMINO

Palomino is diminishing in importance as the domestic market for 'sherry' declines, for which it has been a mainstay. In 1992 there were just 72 hectares, as opposed to 347 hectares in 1960, when it was the most important *vitis vinifera* variety, and third in the ratings after Baco 22A and Albany Surprise.

CHENIN BLANC

Two other white varieties feature in the top ten chart: Gewürztram iner and Chenin Blanc. Chenin Blanc has also been used primarily as a blending grape, adding flavour and body to Müller-Thurgau, but the few examples of the varietal demonstrate that it does deserve to be taken more seriously. It enjoys the cool climate of New Zealand, where it seems to ripen more efficiently than in the coolest years of the Loire Valley, where the acidity can be searingly eye-watering. It was Collards 1990 Chenin Blanc which made me look at the variety in a new light. A small amount of the wine was given just a few weeks' wood maturation which added a hint of extra complexity, with some good rounded fruit, honey, peaches and balancing acidity. According to Lionel Collard, the problem with Chenin is that it is badly cultivated mainly for bag-in-box wines, especially in Gisborne, and that has given it a bad name. What it needs is good canopy management and modest yields, 3 to 5 tonnes to the acre (7 to 12 tonnes per hectare), rather than double, which will bring out its flavour. Collards were the first to make it as a dry rather than a medium sweet wine. Theirs is a blend of Te Kauwhata and Hawke's Bay fruit. The Te Kauwhata fruit is grown on clay and is fleshier, whereas the Hawke's Bay fruit is more minerally. Their 1994 was given a little more oak and has a delicate grassy character, with a hint of honey on the finish.

Lincoln produce a varietal Chenin for the export market, and James Millton in Gisborne considers it to be one of their strengths, along with Riesling and Chardonnay. Stan Chifney grows it successfully in Martinborough, and Esk Valley in Hawke's Bay also take their Chenin seriously, giving it four months of oak ageing for an extra dimension. They also made a botrytis Chenin for the first time in 1992. In fact, this Reserve Botrytis Bunch Selection was three parts Chenin to one part Chardonnay. The Chardonnay ripened a month earlier and was kept in new French oak for a month while the Chenin was fermented before blending the two. The Chenin was bunch thinned, to the extent that 40 per cent of the grapes were removed; in addition, it was leaf, plucked on the west side of the rows to expose the grapes to the afternoon sun. The humidity necessary for botrytis came from the morning dew and the vines were netted to keep the birds at bay. Whereas Esk Valley's dry wine was kept in wood, the sweet wine relies on fruit for its flavour, with ripe pineapple and peaches, proving the point that Chenin Blanc had been planted in New Zealand for all the wrong reasons.

GEWÜRZTRAMINER

As for Gewürztraminer, there are some very successful examples, both sweet and dry. It was first introduced as Roter Traminer by the Department of Agriculture in 1953, but performed badly, probably as a result of the defects in the original plant material. Consequently, it was ignored. But since then things have improved, although it can still be a temperamental variety to grow, producing fairly low yields especially if the weather is bad at flowering. For wine growers, the basic problem with Gewürztraminer is quite simply that it doesn't make money. It is a low cropper at 2.5 to 3 tonnes per acre and growers are lucky if they can find someone to pay more than $700 to $800 per tonne. Chardonnay is a much more remunerative proposition.

The largest concentration of plantings is in Gisborne, but there is also a significant amount in Hawke's Bay and Marlborough, as well as some in Central Otago. Verdun Burgess and Mike Wolter at Black Ridge have made a very convincing Gewürztraminer in both 1993 and 1994, a delightfully understated wine with some delicate spice and good mouthfeel. At Rippon Vineyard they have two different clones of Gewürztraminer, one that is very floral and the other rather plain in comparison, but when Clothilde Chauvet experimented with skin contact, the dull one took on body and roundness while the floral clone curiously lost its flavour. The two were blended and the end result was delicately spicy, neither overpowering nor too sweet, with Central Otago's grip and elegance.

In Marlborough I have enjoyed Gewürztraminer from Te Whare Ra: a youthful 1994 with subtle orange spice and a delicious maturing 1986 when it was nine years old. Allen Hogan finds it a challenging variety to vinify, as it must be absolutely ripe and is very phenolic, which can lead to bitterness on the finish. Grove Mill has also produced good Gewürztraminer with ripe mouth-filling flavours when the fruit is available.

In Nelson, Hermann Seifried has made ice wine from Gewürztraminer by selecting the ripest bunches and freezing them to concentrate the juice. The resulting wine is very intense and concentrated. The Mission in Hawke's Bay has also made an ice wine from artificially frozen grapes. It has a slightly roasted character, but is not especially spicy, just full and sweet.

Alan Limmer at Stonecroft explained that with too much botrytis Gewürztraminer loses its varietal character. He made a late harvest in 1994 with 30° Brix and only a little botrytis, as he wanted to retain the characteristic spiciness. It was sweet and smooth, with spicy orange-peel fruit and acidity. He also makes a dry version with some restrained spice, but finds that it can be difficult to keep the right balance with Gewürztraminer.

From Gisborne, Matawhero Gewürztraminer has been one of the star wines of the region. Denis Irwin encouraged his father to plant Gewürztraminer when he was studying in Germany. A clone was imported from Davis and the vines are now twenty years old. Irwin is particularly excited by his 1994, which is everything that Gewürztraminer should be, with a distinctive toasted spicy nose, with good structure, acidity, body and fruit, and a certain indefinable something. Irwin thinks it the best Gewürztraminer he has produced since 1974.

Montana are also looking at Gewürztraminer in Gisborne, considering Geisenheim clones 11, 12, and 13. They are developing a vineyard at Patutahi which has light, dry free-draining soil which is suitable for Gewürztraminer. The vineyard is protected from the cold southerlies and rainfall is low. The 1993 is spicy, without being blowsy; ripe and harmonious. It was hand picked, given quite long skin contact, then gently pressed. The juice was cleaned, fermented and vinified in the standard way, and the 1994 promises equally well.

Villa Maria's Reserve Gewürztraminer is solidly spicy. They aim for a dry, oily Alsace style and, with that in mind, keep it on the large lees for a while. The fruit comes from their vineyard near Auckland airport.

Neil McCallum at Dry River loves Alsace and for that reason has Gewürztraminer, as well as Riesling and Pinot Gris. He feels that there may be something of a resurgence in the popularity of Gewürztraminer and revels in its lovely hedonistic flavour. The wine is fermented as dry as possible. The 1992 had an orange-peel nose, with delicate spicy flavours, while the 1994 was still quite closed when it was six months old. It will develop some exotic fruit flavours. New Zealand Gewürztraminer never seems to have the rich, oily opulence of some Alsace Gewürztraminer, but is none the worse for that. Instead, it is elegantly spicy and under-stated, compared to some of the opulently blowsy flavours of Alsace.

Dry River has also produced a Botrytis Bunch Selection which equates to Beerenauslese or the lower end of the scale of Sélection de Grains Nobles. It is a difficult wine to make because you must have structure in a sweet wine. In Riesling that can be provided by acidity, but Gewürztraminer is low in acidity so the other option is alcohol, or else the wine is too flabby. Oak could be another possibility, in the way that it adds structure to Sauternes. This example certainly packed a punch of alcohol on the finish, with some concentrated ripe spicy flavours.

CABERNET SAUVIGNON AND OTHER BORDEAUX GRAPE VARIETIES

Cabernet Sauvignon arrived fairly early on in New Zealand's wine history. It may have been among the vines introduced by James Busby and, along with Cabernet Franc, was mentioned by Romeo Bragato as being suitable for the climate. Bragato particularly recommended it in Auckland, the Waikato and Hawke's Bay, as 'it withstands the extremes of climate well . . . and the wine produced is of an excellent quality'. However, apart from the occasional example of McDonald's Cabernet Sauvignon, it was, like most of the better varietals, lost in a mire of hybrids until the beginnings of a revival in interest in the 1970s, with a considerable increase in plantings later in the decade. This has continued so that it is now New Zealand's fourth most widely planted variety and most popular red grape.

While it is Bordeaux that represents the epitome of fine Cabernet Sauvignon, blended with Merlot, Cabernet Franc and maybe other varieties, Cabernet Sauvignon has travelled readily not only to the New World, but also to other vineyards of Europe, such as Tuscany and the South of France, where it was not a traditional variety. It adapts easily to different conditions, settling well into California, Australia, Chile and South Africa. It is to red wine what Chardonnay is to white: a feasible challenge. While it is at its best in Bordeaux as one of the constituents of a blend, in the New World it is often produced as a pure varietal.

In New Zealand, despite Bragato's encouragement, Cabernet Sauvignon has not always been a success. The flavour has suffered from the effects of unripe grapes, characterized by a green herbaceousness, which may be acceptable on the home market but compares unfavourably with examples from France or Australia. However, with the revival of interest in the variety there has been a steady improvement in flavour, which is partly the result of much better vineyard management. With the increase of sunlight into the vines and more effective systems of training, producing riper grapes with a greater emphasis on tannin structure, the taste of New Zealand Cabernet Sauvignon has become much more satisfying.

In general geographic terms, Cabernet Sauvignon thrives where Pinot Noir sulks, and where Pinot Noir flourishes, Cabernet Sauvignon fails to ripen. Needless to say, there are exceptions to this generalization. The two varieties meet in Martinborough, but I have yet to find really satisfactory ripe Cabernet Sauvignon there. There is also Cabernet Sauvignon on the South Island, but again, with rare exceptions such as Fromm in Marlborough, most Cabernet Sauvignon is rather thin and weedy. That said, Ivan Donaldson of Pegasus Bay pleads the cause of Cabernet in Waipara very fluently, pointing out that much of the early plantings of Cabernet came from virused vines. In his vineyard he has observed a significant difference in the ripening ability of the virused cuttings, compared with some healthy vines from Hawke's Bay. When the grapes from the Hawke's Bay vines had reached 20° Brix, the fruit from the virused vines was still at only 16° Brix. Donaldson would also argue that trellising systems are all important and the introduction of Scott Henry has made a significant impact on the ripening process. He also considers that Cabernet Franc and Merlot are essential to fill out the flavour of the Cabernet Sauvignon.

Hawke's Bay and Waiheke Island rival each other as to which area produces the best Cabernet Sauvignon. There are good examples from the Auckland area too, as well as from Matakana and even further north. These are areas where the climate is warm enough for the grapes to ripen fully. Hawke's Bay has the advantage of virtually limitless availability of land for vineyards, whereas Waiheke is seriously constrained. It is limited for sites, for some terrain is too steep and in some areas it has problems with wind. Hawke's Bay's potential for red wine, with such a wide variety of different sites, is enormous. There is shingle, which suits Cabernet and there is clay, which Merlot prefers, and some with underground supplies of water.

If a winery chooses to concentrate on just one style of wine, so far it has always been a wine inspired by fine claret. There are several examples, such as Stonyridge and Te Motu on Waiheke, St Nesbit in South Auckland, Waitakere on the outskirts of Kumeu and Waimarama in Hawke's Bay. For others, such as St Jerome, Te Mata and Kumeu River, it may not be their only wine, but is the one on which they place greatest emphasis and importance. Usually Cabernet Sauvignon is the main component, but often it is blended with other Bordeaux varieties: mainly Cabernet Franc and Merlot, occasionally Malbec and, more rarely, Petit Verdot.

Vinification methods very much follow those of Bordeaux, with a fairly lengthy period of maturation in new and older wood. Usually the barrels are French, the standard Bordeaux *barriques* of 225 litres, but sometimes they are made of American oak, partly because it is cheaper and also gives a softer flavour. The blending of the different varieties may take place soon before bottling or earlier on in the maturation process. There is the usual attention to racking and topping up of the barrels. The fermentation and maceration periods tend to be quite long, up to three weeks, which softens the tannins and adds depth of flavour, with regular plunging and/or pumping over. Davorin Ozich of St Jerome attributes a longer maceration period and longer ageing in wood to his sojourn in Bordeaux during a vintage.

The most sophisticated vinification equipment and facilities for red wine are to be seen at Te Mata, with its overhead plunging system designed to obtain a controlled tannin extraction without any tough tannins. The aim is to avoid moving the pips. The tanks are quite broad in diameter and the cap is totally soaked by a downward thrust of 1.3 tonnes. Insulation helps maintain a regular fermentation temperature of 30°C, while the elegant underground barrel cellar keeps the wine at a gentle 12°C during the ageing period.

A significant influence on the quality of basic New Zealand Cabernet has been the association between Cordier in Bordeaux and Montana, which was intended particularly to improve their Church Road Cabernet, but will also have an effect for other Cabernets in their repertoire. The most essential feature has been the emphasis on the importance of the grapes, combined with the gentle handling of the cap. Ivan Donaldson again argues that wine-making techniques can do much to remove the accusations of herbaceousness, for fermentation at a warmer temperature and a good regular aeration of the juice removes many of the grassy flavours that spoil New Zealand Cabernet Sauvignon.

New clones of Cabernet Sauvignon are becoming available as they are released from quarantine, namely three French clones and one Australian. This is seen as an exciting new development as it will be the first time that New Zealand has had Cabernet Sauvignon clones from France. Any others, after the very first original plantings, have come from Australia or California.

There are occasional pure Merlots, but usually Merlot needs Cabernet for some backbone or else it can be soft and flabby. Similarly, Merlot is useful in filling out the hollow in Cabernet Sauvignon, remedying what is sometimes described as a 'doughnut wine'. Generally, Cabernet Merlot has more appeal as a blend than Merlot Cabernet. However, Esk Valley in Hawke's Bay favour Merlot, basing their reputation for red wines on it, and their Terraces vineyard is half-planted with Merlot along with smaller amounts of other Bordeaux varieties. C. J. Pask have also produced a very competent ripe plummy Merlot. Some see Merlot as the easy choice when you cannot obtain ripe Cabernet Sauvignon, providing a useful substitute. However, in the vineyard Merlot is adversely affected by cool weather at flowering which reduces its crop. Ideally in a Cabernet Merlot blend, both varieties should be fully ripe.

Cabernet Franc makes a lighter, fruitier style of wine, but too much in a blend can cut the tannin, rather like a detergent cutting the grease in the washing-up water. Michael Brajkovich, who described Cabernet Franc as the unsung hero of New Zealand reds, produces a successful example of the varietal which is modelled on Chinon, with fresh, ripe fruit, making it easy to drink, with a little tannin and some acidity. He says it is a problem to convince New Zealanders that it is an appropriate wine as they expect their red wines to be heavy and Australian in style and do not understand something that is light and thirst-quenching. However, it fills a gap in the flavour range.

Brajkovich is more enthusiastic about Merlot than Cabernet Sauvignon, probably influenced by his friendship with the Moueix family of Château Petrus. He finds that Merlot is more tolerant of not being fully ripe, and that Cabernet Sauvignon is very difficult to obtain consistently ripe. Consequently, he does make a Merlot Cabernet blend which has a certain *bordelais* character about it. The precise percentages of the components vary with each vintage and are aged separately for one year, then blended together for a further year's ageing before bottling.

Malbec is another variety which has aroused interest but is proving problematic because its yields are tiny and in most years is not a viable financial proposition for growers who would like some return on their plantings. It is not a recent introduction but featured in the grape survey of 1965, with just 14.5 acres (5.9 hectares). At Stonyridge it produces half the average crop of Cabernet Sauvignon, but Stephen White loves it. However, he described it as an accountant's nightmare. Chris Pask is disillusioned by it, reckoning that he cannot afford to grow it if it only produces half a tonne of grapes off 5 acres (2 hectares), when he needs 1.5 to 2 tonnes of grapes per acre. However, the cask sample of the 1994 I was given to taste was deliciously perfumed, with silky fruit and some tannin.

For the moment, Stephen White at Stonyridge and Tony Molloy at St Nesbit are the sole supporters of Petit Verdot, which provides just a minute part of their wine. Molloy does not have any Malbec, so this makes White the only producer of all five Bordeaux grape varieties, and a suitably serious wine Larose is too.

PINOT NOIR

Pinot Noir is a temperamental grape variety. Even in its native Burgundy it can be reluctant to show its true quality; as for crossing oceans to the various ends of the New World, that is quite another matter. Of all the numerous varieties planted in the New World, Pinot Noir has adapted with the most difficulty, responding badly to warmer climates, not to mention ill-judged vinification techniques. It has sulked unrepentantly, producing bitter, clumsy wines and prompting the question, 'Why bother?' But we all know that when Pinot Noir is at its best, it is truly great, capable of producing some of the finest red wine in the world. That is the challenge that has been accepted, in Martinborough and the South Island, as well with some recent plantings in the cooler parts of Hawke's Bay.

Pinot Noir was first planted in New Zealand as early as 1897, at Masterton in the Wairarapa, not too far from Martinborough. Romeo Bragato wrote that Pinot Noir 'ordinarily bears well and yields a nice wine'. However, it was not until 1976 that the first commercial Pinot Noir was produced by Nobilo's. More impact was made by a 1982 Pinot Noir from St Helena in Canterbury, from vineyards just outside the city of Christchurch. Martinborough Vineyard followed with Larry McKenna's first vintage in 1986, with others in Martinborough close behind. In Canterbury the limestone hills of Waipara seem a natural home for Pinot Noir, with fine examples from Mark Rattray, Waipara Springs, Omihi Hills and Pegasus Bay.

New Zealand's advantage over the rest of the New World is that it has a longer growing season than anywhere else in the southern hemisphere, with a cooler climate combined with more daylight hours. That is not to say that Martinborough and Central Otago do not have summers. They do; but Martinborough in particular has cold winters, dry summers and long autumns with a low annual rainfall, all of which Pinot Noir vines relish. It ripens relatively early, but also budbreak comes early, making it vulnerable to spring frosts, and its tight, compact bunches can make it susceptible to rot.

Clones really matter. Many of the early plantings of Pinot Noir in New Zealand were of the Bachtobel clone which can be singularly uninspiring in flavour, producing rather stewed, insipid wine, not dissimilar to a tamarillo or tree tomato in taste. Bachtobel is now used more and more for sparkling wine, in which its defects are less apparent and its deficiencies can be camouflaged by bubbles.

Another widely planted clone is 10/5, which gives good colour and considerably better flavour than Bachtobel, but can lack intensity and is also used for sparkling wine. The introduction of the

Pommard clone, otherwise known as the Davis clone 5, which is widely planted in Oregon, has done much to improve the quality of Pinot Noir in New Zealand and really does produce some convincing flavours. So far it remains the most promising clone and has been responsible for the recent successes of New Zealand Pinot Noir.

Another clone, grown at Ata Rangi, is named after an Auckland customs officer. Apparently, someone surreptitiously purloined a vine cutting from Domaine de la Romanée Conti and attempted to take it through Auckland customs smuggled in a boot. Malcolm Abel was the customs officer who confiscated the offending vine, but instead of destroying it he followed its progress through quarantine, planted it and, for a short time before his premature death in 1982, ran his own small winery outside Auckland.

Various other clones are mentioned in the context of Pinot Noir. There is Mariafeld which comes from Switzerland. Other American clones include 2/10, and clone 13 from Davis, which does better in Martinborough than in Marlborough, but generally lacks weight and may prove more suitable for sparkling wine. The D5 clone is quite widely planted in Nelson. Originally it was thought to be Gamay and can give quite a stalky flavour to the wine. Finally, two new clones from Burgundy have just been planted, including 115 from Morey-Saint-Denis, as well as an Italian one. It is too early to rate their performance.

Vinification methods entail a considerable variety of different techniques, all of which are discussed and dissected at the annual Pinot Noir conference, modelled on the Oregon conference, with about sixty participants from wineries all over the country.

So many different factors come into play. Some favour Guy Accad's controversial methods of extended cool maceration before fermentation, but are horrified by his high sulphur levels. This may be a reflection of the fact that many New Zealand cellars are better equipped with refrigeration facilities, providing more efficient temperature controls. There are so many permutations and choices possible for Pinot Noir. The winemaker may consider extended cool maceration, longer or shorter times on the skins, and percentages of whole bunches, entailing the inclusion of stalks which must be absolutely ripe or else they will impart green flavours. They have to decide whether to plunge or pump over, with varying fermentation temperatures up to as much as 32°C to extract the utmost flavour, in open or closed fermenting tanks. Then the wine goes into wood, new or older oak, for varying lengths of time, entailing racking, with or without air. These are all possibilities with Pinot Noir.

Neil McCallum described Pinot Noir as a soft round ball. It should not be edgy. He prefers to hand plunge so that the skins are handled very gently. He wants good soft velvet tannins, combined with the lovely Martinborough fruit, and he avoids aeration as it can remove the character of the wine which once lost will not return. Another master of Pinot Noir, Clive Paton at Ata Rangi, favours a cold soak for two weeks, keeping it below 10°C, then gradually starting the fermentation, bringing the temperature up to 32°C, maintaining it at about 28–30°C, then running the juice off the skins. That makes about three weeks' total skin-contact time – for one lot of wine. For his old, fifteen-year-old vines he opts for less pre-fermentation maceration, observing that the French are not as controlled as we are and don't worry too much. They let nature take its course.

Paton considers that 20 to 25 per cent new oak is enough for Pinot Noir. He is very aware that the subtlety of the variety can easily be upset. The wonderful Pinot Noir fruit must be kept; at the same time, he is trying to evolve his style so as to have more muscle in his wine, but always retaining the fruit. You learn something every year.

For Alan McCorkindale at Stoneleigh it is essential to use a variety of techniques, with variations on Accad's methods as well as more traditional methods, all of which makes for interesting blending, which is part of the challenge. He also finds that a little chaptalization towards the end of the fermentation helps to use up the last remaining yeast.

Tim Finn at Neudorf considers the problem with New Zealand Pinot Noir is that it can be too big and jammy, without enough structure – a fault of the 10/5 clone, which tends to overripen. You need to ensure some tannin from the stalks and skins for balance, and aeration also helps reduce the jamminess. Finn also observes that Pinot Noir needs a warm temperature at the peak of the fermentation or else 'you just get lolly water'! He finds that addition of a little sugar towards the end of the fermentation gives the dying yeast something to feed on, so that it creates glycerol and therefore more richness in the mouth.

All will agree that diversity is the key with Pinot Noir. You cannot use just one technique. Several variations enhance the flavour. Accad's method can give increased concentration and it blends well with more traditional wines. Alan Brady at Gibbston Valley, when discussing his 1993 Pinot Noir, said that he constructed the wine by blending.

At Rippon Vineyard, Clothilde Chauvet said that she tried different techniques with different barrels, such as whole-bunch pressing with a particularly ripe block. The inclusion of stems has the advantage of slowing down the fermentation, which is beneficial when you want it to last for ten rather than two days. Also, if Pinot Noir is picked too ripe it does not age well as it loses its structure and the stems, in that instance, add some welcome tannin. At Rippon they have five different clones – 5, 6, 13, 2/10 and 10/5 – which are each fermented separately then blended together, selecting the best barrels which complement each other. Chauvet's 1993 Pinot Noir was one of the stars of the vintage. But to quote Rob Hay of Chard Farm, 'As for Central Otago, we have not seen the best yet, especially for Pinot Noir.'

GAMAY
One of the gaps in the New Zealand flavour spectrum is light, fruity, easy-to-drink wine, as New Zealanders tend to think that they should follow the Australian example and produce seriously oaked and firmly structured red wines. A variety called Gamay Gloriod features in the grape surveys of the 1960s, but that was a white variety which was very prone to rot and has now disappeared without trace. With the flavour gap in mind there is a growing interest in Gamay, and Matua Valley have planted small plots of it in Hawke's Bay, Gisborne and Marlborough in order to compare its characteristics in the three different areas. This will be a space to watch.

PINOT MEUNIER
Pinot Meunier has been in New Zealand for a long time. Bragato called it Mueller Burgundy and thought it one of the most suitable varieties for the climate. 'It is somewhat subject to attacks of mould in late wet seasons but generally speaking bears heavily here and in

normal seasons produces a good crop of high-class wine.' In 1960, it was the fifth most important variety in the country with 52 acres (21 hectares); by 1965, it had dropped to eleventh position with nearly 33 acres (13 hectares). Today, it is enjoying a little revival in interest as a constituent of sparkling wine.

Daniel Le Brun has one of the few vineyards of Pinot Meunier in New Zealand and has recently begun to include some in his non-vintage brut and also in his rosé sparkling wine. He find that it adds softness and rounds off any acidity. Alan McCorkindale has just planted an acre (40 ares) of it at Stoneleigh and thinks that it should prove an interesting component in their sparkling wine for its fruit flavours. It retains its fruit, making the wine more approachable when young, so that it needs less time on the lees. He took his cuttings from Hunter's block, which is grown for them by Phil Rose of Wairau River under a long-term agreement. It is more forward than Pinot Noir, filling out the middle palate, whereas Pinot Noir fills out the back palate. Also in Marlborough, Johanneshof Cellars are planning to include some in their blend and see it as a palate extender.

There is also a little Pinot Meunier in Martinborough. The story goes that Michael Eden, who was one-time vineyard manager at the Mission in Hawke's Bay, found some gnarled old Pinot Meunier vines from which he took cuttings that he planted in Martinborough in the early 1980s. Chris Lintz uses some of it for his rosé, which in 1994 was made entirely from Pinot Meunier.

SYRAH AND OTHER RHÔNE VARIETIES
In New Zealand this grape variety is called Syrah rather than Shiraz, following the nomenclature of the Rhône Valley, rather than that of New Zealand's nearest neighbours and closest vineyards across the Tasman Sea.

Syrah arrived in New Zealand early on in its viticultural history. Romeo Bragato described the Hermitage he was given by Mr Beetham in the Wairarapa: 'I was given a taste of Hermitage wine six years old, and it was certainly of prime quality.' In concluding his report he recommended Black Hermitage as one of the most suitable varieties for the climate. 'The Hermitage will, in your colony, give heavy yields, and wine of first quality; it is of a hardy nature and will resist disease better than most other varieties and should compose at last one-half of the vineyard.' Incidentally, he also recommended White Hermitage for white wine. His advice might have been taken, for in the Department of Agriculture Bulletin of 1914 Syrah was mentioned as one of the principal varieties in the main vineyards of Hawke's Bay. S. F. Anderson, Bragato's successor as government viticulturist, wrote in 1917 that Syrah was being grown 'in nearly all our vineyards, but the trouble with this variety has been an unevenness in ripening its fruit'. That is probably still true today, for Syrah ripens as late as Cabernet Sauvignon, but is not as hardy and can be badly affected by rain.

In the northern Rhône Valley, where Syrah produces its most stylish wines, it enjoys the heat of summer on well-exposed slopes such as the Côte-Rôtie, and the hills of Hermitage and Cornas. In Australia, too, the Barossa Valley produces some of the most successful examples of the variety outside France.

After its initial success in New Zealand, it disappeared from view, remaining in the country at the Te Kauwhata Research Station. Alan Limmer of Stonecroft, who is one of New Zealand's staunchest supporters of Syrah, remembered how he helped with the vintage at Te Kauwhata in 1984 and saw the wine that the research station made, which provided a very good reason for not planting Syrah. However, he was not to be so easily daunted. He planted his first Syrah in 1984, just one experimental row, and has produced a wine every year since 1987 with his first release coming in late 1990. Limmer is a passionate Rhône enthusiast. He loves the taste of Syrah and vinifies it in much the same way as Cabernet Sauvignon, with a long period of skin contact followed by barrel ageing. Such has been its success that Syrah now accounts for half his production.

Morton Estate planted Syrah in 1991 in their Hawke's Bay vineyard and produced their first crop in 1994, just 1 tonne off 1 hectare. A cask sample was appealingly peppery and, with such a tiny quantity, it will probably be blended with Cabernet Sauvignon.

Te Mata are also looking hard at Syrah and extending their acreage from an initial 2 acres (just under 1 hectare) planted in 1989, both for Te Mata and in their new Woodthorpe vineyard. They are considering a new French clone 470 which is still in quarantine but has been identified by the French as the best clone from a choice of nine from the Rhône Valley. Sadly, there will be no 1994 Bullnose Syrah as the vineyard was devastated by hail.

In Martinborough, Syrah has been one of the three components of Clive Paton's original blend, Célèbre. In 1994, Syrah provided 10 to 15 per cent of the blend, giving some very concentrated berry fruit, while in comparison his Cabernet was slightly herbaceous. The Syrah certainly tasted the riper of the two varieties and may prove more successful, for the difference between ripe and unripe Syrah is less marked than with Cabernet.

There is Syrah in Marlborough, too. Vavasour have planted some in the hotter, drier Awatere Valley and 1990 was their first vintage. However, none was bottled in either 1992 or 1993 as the vintages were so marginal, and only a very limited quantity was produced in 1994. However, the 1991 shows what happens in a good year, with a good varietal nose, a spicy, peppery character, and some elegant blackcurrant gum fruit on the palate. The wine spent twelve months in 500-litre Nevers puncheons.

Even in Central Otago you find Syrah. It is one of the varieties in Rippon Vineyard's house red as Rolfe Mills is especially enthusiastic about it. It is planted in a part of the vineyard that forms a particular heat trap, otherwise it would be difficult to ripen so far south.

Despite its early presence in the country, Syrah is a new variety for New Zealand to master, with a growing interest from an increasing number of wineries, particularly in Hawke's Bay. It may prove problematic as inconsistency is one of its characteristics in a marginal climate, ripening well one year but not the next.

OTHER RHÔNE VARIETIES

Other Rhône varieties are also attracting interest, such as Mourvèdre, Cinsaut and Grenache, as well as Viognier, and to a much lesser extent Marsanne and Roussanne.

Grenache is already in the country. It came from Davis and ripened well when Tom McDonald grew it, but then fell from favour. Now there may be a revival of interest along with other varieties from the Rhône. Cinsaut featured in the 1965 grape survey and there was some Mataro, which is the Australian synonym for Mourvèdre. Other imports of Cinsaut and Mourvèdre came out of quarantine in 1995, and Stephen White produced a small amount of Grenache and Mourvèdre in 1994, which he intends to blend with his Syrah.

Neil McCallum was the first to attempt to bring in Viognier, but his cuttings were snarled up in bureaucratic quarantine regulations. Te Mata were more successful and planted their first Viognier in November 1994. McCallum now has a few vines planted, but they were affected by frost. As Viognier is a late ripener, there are some doubts as to whether it will ripen. The same applies to Marsanne and Roussanne, and as yet no one is putting them to the test.

Petite Sirah, which the French call Durif, was brought from Davis in the 1970s. It is a very minor player indeed in the Rhône Valley and in New Zealand has proved unsuccessful for the simple reason that it does not ripen properly.

OTHER REDS

Pinotage

Pinotage features in the ratings as New Zealand's fifth most important red variety, with 73 hectares in production in 1995. This South African variety, developed by Professor Perold in the Cape in 1925, is a cross between Pinot Noir and Cinsaut, which the South Africans confusingly call Hermitage. Pinotage enjoyed a flush of popularity at the same time as Müller-Thurgau in the late 1960s, at the beginning of the move to replace the hybrid varieties with *vitis vinifera*. The Babich brothers remembered Corbans making the first Pinotage in 1964.

There are a handful of examples of Pinotage today. Nobilo's grow it at Huapai, where with its thick skins it is able to resist the prevailing humidity. They ferment it in open-top vats, taking it off the skins after about twelve days, putting it into tanks for the malolactic fermentation to take place, then keeping it in 500-litre puncheons of French oak for about eighteen months. The 1991 is quite ripe and alcoholic, almost raisiny, with some berry fruit, as well as that hint of earthiness which can be characteristic of Pinotage.

I preferred a lighter example from Pleasant Valley, made without any wood and intended for early drinking. It had a hint of astringency, balanced by some berry fruit.

Peter Hubscher of Montana is recorded as saying that Pinotage is the most underrated grape variety in New Zealand. Montana have a new planting of it in Hawke's Bay. The 1994 tank samples tasted ripe and fruity, deep-coloured frothing wine with tannin and acidity. Montana also feel that Pinotage could do well in Gisborne in the right free-draining soil. While some like Grove Mill have pulled it up, others are planting it and the figures show that the overall trend is an increase.

Zinfandel

For the moment, Zinfandel is totally unproven in New Zealand. The Californian John Kemble has nursed it through quarantine so that he can plant it at Kemblefield in Hawke's Bay. He is also giving some cuttings to Alan Limmer, so it will be a question of 'watch this space'. Kemble, who has had good experience of producing Zinfandel at Ravenswood in Sonoma Valley, sees the potential problem as summer rainfall. Zinfandel has large tight bunches of thin-skinned grapes and rain makes it all too easy for rot to develop. However, Hawke's Bay is probably the best choice of anywhere in New Zealand for this variety.

ITALIAN VARIETIES

As horizons broaden, so there is immense interest in moving away from the conventional choices of grape varieties. Sangiovese has inspired interest, although there are definite doubts as to whether it will ripen because it needs a much longer ripening season than Cabernet Sauvignon. In Tuscany, where the two varieties are grown side by side, Sangiovese is picked as much as three weeks later than Cabernet Sauvignon.

However, Italian varieties are enjoying a fashion trend and there are small plots of various varieties on an experimental basis, mainly on the North Island. Montana admit to dabbling in Italian varieties, looking at grapes which will produce flavour rather than yields. They have plantings in Hawke's Bay of Sangiovese, Nebbiolo, Dolcetto, Marzemino, Lagrein, Barbera and Teroldego. For the moment it is all very experimental, but a Montepulciano clone of Sangiovese is showing promise. Dolcetto featured also in Bragato's list of suitable grape varieties, but then disappeared from view.

David Hoskins at Heron's Flight in Matakana has an acre (40 ares) of Sangiovese with just two different clones, and dreams of making a so-called Super Tuscan blend with Cabernet Sauvignon. At the other end of the North Island, Clive Paton has planted some Sangiovese in the warmest part of his vineyard, along with some Nebbiolo, just to see how they go. Alan Laurenson of Limeburners Bay shares his enthusiasm for Italian varieties, with an experimental row of Sangiovese, and others coming through quarantine.

On the South Island, some introductory Sangiovese has been shared between Hunter's, Montana and Fromm. Allan Clarke of the Vine Improvement Group suggested Freisa as a red option and Cortese for white. Essentially, it is an open field to see what will grow where.

6

Sparkling Wine

While it is logical to look at winemaking methods for table wine under the respective grape varieties, sparkling wine encompass several varieties and so it seems simpler to give it a separate chapter.

The first sparkling wine, following the Champagne method, was produced at the Mission Vineyard by Brother John around 1960 using Pinot Meunier, Pinot Gris and Folle Blanche. It was called Fontanella and there was both white and pink, made in a brut style. Next came Selaks with a wine they called Champelle. San Marino was another early wine; then came Montana with Lindauer, and now the choice of sparkling wine is poised to expand enormously. As recently as 1991, there were just four sparkling wines included in the annual New Zealand tasting in London: two from Montana, Lindauer and Deutz Cuvée Marlborough, as well as one each from Morton Estate and Selaks. Four years later the range had widened to ten, with wines from Daniel Le Brun, Mills Reef, Pelorus from Cloudy Bay, and two examples from Nautilus, the New Zealand arm of the large Australian producer Yalumba.

However, there are numerous other sparkling wines standing in the wings in various stages of development. Some represent little more than a couple of years of base wines, while others are almost ready for release, and there are yet others which are destined for the domestic market and have not left New Zealand's shores. There is a strong feeling in Marlborough that sparkling wine could well be the next fashion trend. Sauvignon is now firmly established. Chardonnay now outnumbers Sauvignon and with the anticipated increase in production there will be more Chardonnay available. This could well find a useful outlet in sparkling wine, especially as there is a view in some quarters that Chardonnay does not always ripen sufficiently in Marlborough to make good table wine.

Although others had produced sparkling wine before, Montana really put New Zealand sparkling wine on the map. The company's association with Deutz Champagne has proved to be a successful partnership, resulting in the creation of Deutz Cuvée Marlborough. Meanwhile, Lindauer, which Montana was already making, has improved significantly in its wake. Deutz, like other Champagne houses, had realized that the possibilities of growth within the Champagne region were limited and that the alternative was to look at other parts of the world. Where most have turned to California, they saw the advantages of the cool climate vineyards of New Zealand. And in Montana they found a partner prepared to follow their winemaking instructions to the letter, investing in the necessary equipment and making the wine exactly to specification.

The first purchase was a new Coquard press which is very gentle and slowly squeezes the hand-picked grapes. The juice is classified in the same way as Champagne. Eight tonnes are pressed at one time: 1 tonne of grapes yields 510 litres which constitute the *cuvée*; the subsequent 100 litres make up the first *taille*; the second *taille* consists of whatever may be left over. The second *taille* is certainly never used for Cuvée Marlborough, or indeed for Lindauer. The juice then undergoes a carefully controlled fermentation and malolactic fermentation in the normal way.

The exact blend, carried out with the help of André Lallier from Champagne Deutz, is not divulged. In any case, the proportion of Pinot Noir and Chardonnay varies from year to year, for the aim is consistency of style. Montana wants the body and fullness which comes from Pinot Noir; it therefore tends to dominate the Chardonnay, but not overwhelm it. No Pinot Meunier is used, but the blend usually includes a small proportion of wine from the previous year. The wine spends about two years on its lees and is then sent to Auckland for riddling and disgorging. There, Montana has constructed the most extraordinary giant giropalettes, quite unlike anything I have ever seen anywhere else in the world. Four great blue-steel beasts each holding four pallets of 110-dozen bottles tower up above you, with a computer controlling their every movement.

The main differences between Deutz Cuvée Marlborough and Lindauer are that the grapes are mechanically harvested and come not just from Marlborough but also from the warmer regions of Gisborne and Hawke's Bay. The final blend happens in Auckland, with each area first putting its wines together, making a total of some thirty different components in all. Broadly speaking, the blend is fairly similar to Cuvée Marlborough in that there is a slight dominance of Pinot Noir and no Pinot Meunier.

The other significant difference is that Lindauer is made by the transfer method to avoid the time-consuming and costly processes of riddling and disgorging. And, of course, these differences show in the glass. Cuvée Marlborough has a delicate creaminess with some backbone, while Lindauer has less finesse and is more solid and overtly fruity, but is none the worse for that. Twin Rivers is Montana's sparkling wine that comes from Hawke's Bay alone and is so called as there is a river on either side of the vineyard. It follows the method of Cuvée Deutz: a blend of Pinot Noir and Chardonnay, with eighteen months on the lees, making quite a full, yeasty, rounded wine.

Most of the growing interest in sparkling-wine production has come in the wake of the table wines. Cloudy Bay made Sauvignon before Pelorus. Hunter's Brut forms part of the range in a winery that makes several different varietals. The same is true for Morton Estate, Matua Valley, Selaks and others. For the moment, there are just two sparkling-wine specialists in New Zealand for whom bubbles represent their main production. They are Cellier Le Brun in Marlborough and Parker MC in Gisborne, of which more in the relevant chapters. In virtually every instance, the blend of grape varieties follows that of Champagne: Chardonnay and Pinot Noir, with possibly a little Pinot Meunier as more comes into production. Chris Lintz in Martinborough is the only producer to have moved away from Champagne and produce a Riesling-based sparkling wine.

Deutz is not the only Champagne house to show an interest in New Zealand. Kevin Judd at Cloudy Bay had already begun to work on the development of a sparkling wine when Veuve Clicquot bought a majority interest in the winery. Needless to say they encouraged the project and the result is Pelorus, named after the dolphin that used to swim in the Marlborough Sound. The first vintage of Pelorus was 1987, and the style and method have not changed significantly since. In 1987, Cloudy Bay used grapes from just two vineyards; now the grapes come from six or seven, with a greater variety of clones of Chardonnay and Pinot Noir. As is mentioned in the sections on these grape varieties, there is much discussion about the suitability of various clones for table wine rather than sparkling wine, and vice versa. The most common Pinot Noir clone for sparkling wine is Bachtobel – the one that was first planted in New Zealand – as its lack of colour makes it appropriate for sparkling wine. As for Chardonnay, the recently introduced clone 6, with higher yields than Mendoza, is considered most suitable.

For Pelorus, the method of production is absolutely classic, using traditional *pupitres* for riddling after about three years on the lees. The grapes are picked fairly ripe, though still earlier than for table wine, with the aim of making a rich, full-bodied wine, as is the style of their 1990 vintage.

At Highfield, Michel Drappier of Champagne Drappier is the consultant for a sparkling-wine project that is still in its infancy. The first release will be in 1997. The association with Drappier came about through the Japanese partner of Highfield, Shin Yokoi, who is the agent for Drappier in Tokyo. Tony Hooper, the wine-maker at Highfield, has spent time in Champagne; Michel Drappier comments on samples and suggests picking dates. For the moment, the grapes, in equal proportions of Pinot Noir and Chardonnay, all come from one vineyard. Quizzed as to the differences between New Zealand sparkling wine and Champagne itself, Drappier thought it was the lack of finesse. In New Zealand there is an intensity of fruit, but it needs more depth. Also, pH levels tend to be higher in New Zealand and if you are to keep the wine on the lees for a long time, as they intend to, with at least three years' ageing, you do need a lower pH. This is something on which they are working.

Corbans already produce Amadeus, mainly from grapes grown on the South Island, but Alan McCorkindale admits that he is developing what he calls 'a super-premium *méthode champenoise*' which will not be ready until about 1998 or 1999. For the moment, Pinot Noir is the main component, but he has also planted an acre (40 ares) of Pinot Meunier which should add an interesting dimension of fruit. This will be something to watch. Jackson and Gillan are, as I write, only a few months away from releasing a sparkling wine, while Wairau River and Lawson's Dry Hills also have projects in the pipeline. Johanneshof have cellars tunnelled out of the hillside, designed especially to provide the ideal conditions of humidity and a constant temperature for the maturation of sparkling wine. A small amount of their base wine is aged in wood for an extra layer of flavour, and Pinot Meunier will be included in the blend along with Pinot Noir and Chardonnay. Again, base wines have been made since 1991, but as yet nothing has been released on to the market.

Australians recognize the quality of New Zealand fruit for sparkling wine. Nautilus, which is part of Yalumba, produce sparkling wine from Marlborough, while Domaine Chandon in Australia have an association with Hunter's for the production of Domaine Chandon in New Zealand. Tony Jordan, from Domaine Chandon, Australia, advises Hunter's on their own wine and masterminds Domaine Chandon's New Zealand wine, which is sold only on the domestic market. Hunter's produce a very much smaller amount and say that they are aiming for a more forward style, so that the wine spends longer on the lees before disgorging. They have also enjoyed some input from Richard Geoffroy, one of the oenologists at Moët & Chandon in Epernay, who has advised on picking times simply by tasting berries in the vineyard and has helped with fermentation rates, gradually encouraging them to fine-tune their process. It began in 1987 as a bit of a hobby, but is gradually becoming a more significant part of their production.

For Morton Estate, the production of sparkling wine is important enough to warrant a separate cellar for storage and giropalettes. Here, Pinot Noir accounts for 60 to 70 per cent of the blend as there is a heavy demand for Chardonnay for their table wine. The non-vintage wine spends twelve months on the lees, with fruit being the main objective, while the vintage stays for four years on the lees. Perversely, I preferred the fruitier non-vintage.

Matua Valley has developed its sparkling wine considerably since the first vintage in 1987. Their 1990 was made from Auckland fruit, three parts Pinot Noir to one part Chardonnay, and a fifth of the blend was aged in wood. It spent two years on its lees and was given a low dosage of 7–8 grams. It tasted full and toasted, with a lightly herbal tang. The 1991 was made in the same way from 60 per cent Pinot Noir and 40 per cent Chardonnay, all from Marlborough, but it had a more delicate palate, with more elegance too.

Although Selaks were one of the earlier producers of sparkling wine, it was only recently that it became a serious part of their production. They have hand-operated giropalettes and the wines spend at least two years on the lees. The Dry has a light dosage, while the Brut, with a slightly higher dosage, is made from the same base of two-thirds Pinot Noir to one-third Chardonnay, and is slightly fuller.

While the main interest is currently centred on Marlborough, there is a view that even more potential may exist further south in Canterbury, although for the moment only the Giesen brothers admit to considering sparkling wine, and even then fairly tentatively. Central Otago, too, may have something to offer, but as yet there is no evidence to support the case.

7
Northland

The frontiers of viticulture in New Zealand are expanding, both north and south. The recent plantings of vines of Central Otago have been criticized as mad and foolhardy, and even less likely is a successful vineyard at Kaitaia, overlooking the sand dunes of the Ninety Mile Beach in the far north of the North Island. There is also a flourishing winery at Whangarai and a growing number of vineyards outside Warkworth in the Matakana Valley. But, of course, it was in Northland that Samuel Marsden first planted vines at Kerikeri in the Bay of Islands in 1819.

Heron's Flight

We drove up from Auckland through sleepy Helensville to Warkworth, a pretty little town on the Matakana River, and found Heron's Flight off the Matakana road close by. If you carry on further, past Matakana itself, you will reach the sea, where there is the marine reserve of Goat Island and botanical gardens on Kawau Island which were created by an early Governor-General.

The countryside is gentle and rolling, enjoying the warm sunshine of late January. Scottish settlers first arrived here in the 1850s. Today, it is an area of dairy farming and there are orchards of apples and other fruit, making it the fruit bowl of Auckland. Originally the fruit was transported by barge down the Matakana River and then on by sea to Auckland. Now vines are beginning to appear amid the orchards and pastureland. David Hoskins and Mary Evans have been producing wine at Heron's Flight since the mid-1980s. Hoskins came from Philadelphia and has been in New Zealand since 1971. He spent two years looking for suitable vineyard land and kept returning to the Matakana Valley, despite its unproven track record for viticulture. However, the climate is good, generally hot and dry but with some tempering maritime influence, and he and Evans liked the area as a place to live and bring up a family.

Hoskins is tall and lanky, with thinning blond hair and a passionate enthusiasm about his wine. His education centred on an unusual combination of a chemistry degree followed by a second degree in philosophy, and all the while wine has been a consuming interest. Evans has a more down-to-earth approach about the difficulties and problems involved in running your own winery, and the essential commitment.

We walked round the vineyards while Hoskins elaborated on his enthusiasm for Richard Smart's big-vine theory. He had attended the Cool Climate Symposium in Auckland in 1988, at which the buzz words had been canopy management. Essentially, the big vine devigorates itself by simply being allowed to grow as it wishes. The soil at Heron's Flight is clay loam and its water-retaining properties make for quite vigorous vines. Humidity is their main climatic problem, causing fungal diseases against which it is necessary to spray. Consequently, Hoskins has planted his vines with the main objective of restricting their vigour and at the same time maintaining good aeration, with well-exposed fruit.

Heron's Flight is named after two families of herons that live in the pine trees on the boundary of the vineyard. They are quite tame and fortunately, unlike most New Zealand birds, show no desire to supplement their diet with grapes. The 4-hectare (10-acre) vineyard is planted mainly with Cabernet Sauvignon and Chardonnay, as well as a smaller amount of Cabernet Franc and Merlot, and an experimental block of Sangiovese, prompted by Hoskins's keen interest in the so-called Super Tuscans: the blends of Sangiovese and Cabernet Sauvignon which do not currently conform to any Italian wine law.

The first vintage of Heron's Flight was 1991, from which we tasted the Cabernet Sauvignon – a solid, smoky wine with good cedarwood notes, balancing tannin and an elegant finish. It spent ten days on the skins during fermentation and was aged in wood for twelve months. The wine met with instant acclaim and Hoskins admits that it has been a difficult act to follow. He was lucky to begin with such a good vintage, when the subsequent years have been more problematic. If they do not have sufficient heat, the grapes, though technically ripe, lack richness. 1992 was cold and wet and 1993, although dry, was equally cool. 1994 was dry and hot, and consequently has produced wine with the qualities of 1991, with good ripe fruit and soft tannins. Sadly, 1995 was spoilt by intermittent rain from mid-January, with the result that they picked no Cabernet Sauvignon at all and have made only simple early-drinking wines from the other varieties.

The first Chardonnay vintage, with two wines, was 1994. One was fermented in stainless steel and kept for just four weeks in old barrels to produce an uncomplicated fruit-driven wine, while the other was barrel fermented to give some appealing toasted notes and rounded fruit. A Cabernet blush is a pretty pink addition to his range.

Hoskins's mentor in the wine industry is Alex Corban, who guided him through his first vintage. Corban was one of the pioneers of the modern era of New Zealand winemaking, the first New Zealander to attend Roseworthy College in Australia and the first chairman of the Wine Institute. He was also responsible for introducing refrigeration to New Zealand winemaking in the 1960s. Hoskins has plans for a winery adjoining his vineyard, but for the moment rents a nearby winery that was once a cow shed and is now furnished with old dairy vats that are used for fermentations, as well as a bladder press and barrels.

Heron's Flight, Sharp Road, (RD 2) Matakana, Warkworth, telephone/fax: (09) 422 7915

The Antipodean

The Antipodean winery adjoins Hoskins's winery. It has had a chequered history since its grand opening by the Vuletic brothers in 1985, with a maiden vintage that was sold at an astronomical $95 per bottle – a price significantly higher than any other bottle of New Zealand wine at the time. The brothers' father, in good Dalmatian tradition, had always made wine, but his sons had determined upon a new start. They followed with the 1986 and 1987 vintages, but in 1988 cyclone Bola wreaked havoc and no wine was made. Then in 1989 a family dispute intervened. The two brothers, Jim and Peter, were unable to agree on how the winery should be run and a legal battle ensued, resulting in the division of the property. Today, the Antipodean is run by

Michelle Chignell who has bought her husband Peter's share in the estate. She is a lawyer by profession but is taking a sabbatical to run the winery, which she says she is enjoying much more than the stressful and negative aspects of the legal world.

A new small winery was built for the 1990 vintage to replace the cow shed now used by Heron's Flight. It is well equipped with open-top fermenters and a good number of barrels. Chignell now concentrates on four wines, expanding the Antipodean's initial range. There is an unusual white wine that is a blend of 20 per cent Sémillon and 80 per cent Sauvignon, fermented together in wood to produce, after twelve months of barrel ageing, a wine that is not unlike a good white Graves. It is full in the mouth, slightly nutty and lightly grassy, with good acidity and fruit.

There is a Syrah which is labelled the Iconoclast as it breaks away from the existing stereotype that Syrah will not ripen. The 1990 certainly did, beautifully, with medium-weight peppery fruit, and very convincing varietal characters and soft tannins. Whether the same success was repeated in subsequent more difficult vintages I am unable to say. Syrah was planted in the mid-1980s in a particularly warm, well-exposed part of the vineyard at the top of a north-facing slope. For the moment, the production is tiny – just two barrels a year.

The principal red wine, labelled The Antipodean, is a Bordeaux blend of approximately 60 per cent Cabernet, 30 per cent Merlot and 5 to 10 per cent Malbec. In some years they also make a second wine called Obiter (a legal term meaning an aside in a judicial judgment), which includes any wine that does not go into The Antipodean. Normally, the blending is done before the wine is aged in barrel for as long as two years. The label is a dramatic image of a Coptic cross with keys. The keys originate from the winery's legal associations. The cross relates to a family story of a Vuletic ancestor who prayed for a child; when it was born, a cross was made in gratitude from the family jewellery. The 1994, tasted from barrel, was closed and smoky, with firm fruit and tight tannin; the 1991 was still very closed, with good fruit and backbone, with soft tannins.

For the moment, these are the only two wineries in production in the Matakana area, but there are at least six other vineyards being planted, some with winery projects in the pipeline. Certainly it would seem that Matakana has the potential to produce ripe red wine in the best vintages.

The Antipodean, Tongue Farm Road, (PO Box 5) Matakana, telephone/fax: (09) 422 7957

Longview

From Warkworth we headed further north to Whangarei, where Mario and Barbara Vuletich run Longview Estate. They are distantly related to the Vuletic brothers of The Antipodean. Mario's father started the vineyard and winery selling 'port', 'sherry' and table wines under the Continental label. When he died, his son decided to uproot the old Seibels and Albany Surprise and replant them with *vitis vinifera* varieties – mainly Cabernet Sauvignon, Merlot and some Cabernet Franc, as well as little Pinot Noir and Syrah, and some Chardonnay. It is for his red wine that he really wants to be known. The change of name from Continental to Longview marks a change of image as well as a shift away from Dalmatian tradition. Longview reflects the view from the winery, of the wide open expanse of water of Bream Bay with the Whangarei Heights behind. In the foreground are the vineyards, with colourful flying scarecrows bearing clownlike faces to protect the vines from the ravages of the birds.

Vuletich talked about his family. His grandfather had been given some gumfields in Dargaville, closer to the west coast, and his father was just sixteen when he came to New Zealand. He ran a general store, but ultimately wanted to return to working on the land. Vuletich remembers, as a schoolkid in 1969, helping his father chop down bush to clear the land for planting vines. His mother is still alive and helps in the winery shop, for most of their wine is sold locally. They feel very isolated and left out of the mainstream of New Zealand viticulture as there are no other wineries or vineyards in the immediate vicinity.

None the less, Vuletich argues passionately for the suitability of this area for viticulture. He has the Irish gift of the gab and it would be difficult to get a word in edgeways to suggest an opposite point of view. But he is fervent in his conviction, and a self-confessed workaholic who is determined to succeed. Although Northland is considered too humid for viticulture, Vuletich argues that the humidity is not a problem for the thick-skinned grapes, only for the more fragile hybrids which split more easily.

The soil here is alluvial clay, with free-draining brown rock. The vines face south-west, which is the direction of the prevailing wind, and benefit from the sea breezes. They do need to spray regularly against disease, usually every couple of weeks depending on the weather, but generally about a dozen times a year, stopping two months before the harvest.

Certainly, recent vintages of Cabernet and Merlot show potential. A 1993 Cabernet had none of the herbaceousness so often associated with New Zealand, but instead some good ripe fruit and solid tannins. A 1993 Cabernet Merlot blend was tighter and firmer, while the 1994 Merlot, tasted from barrel, had an attractive smoky nose, with plenty of fruit, balancing tannin and a long finish.

Vuletich also continues to satisfy his father's old customers for Gumdigger's Port, which is sweet and spirity with notes of liquorice. It is made from Cabernet and Merlot. There is also a table wine made from White Diamond, a cross between Niagara and Albany Surprise, which has the sweet jelly-baby, foxy character that is typical of a hybrid.

You cannot fail to admire Vuletich's tenacity and enthusiasm. If determination and energy are anything to go by he certainly deserves to succeed, and maybe others will join him in Whangarei.

Longview Estate, SH 1, Otaika, (PO Box 6041) Whangarei, telephone: (09) 438 7227

Okahu Estate

Sadly, time did not permit us to continue north all the way up to Kaitaia and Okahu Estate at the southern end of the Ninety Mile Beach. Instead we had to turn south, returning to Auckland on the dusty dirt track, an apology for a road that runs past Kaipara Harbour with views of the water. My impressions of Okahu Estate are therefore based on a tasting in the Wine Institute's office.

Monty Knight is the driving force behind Okahu Estate. He has about 2 hectares (5 acres) of vines which were first planted in 1984 and supplements his needs by buying in grapes from further south. Ninety Mile Red is a blend of 70 per cent Cabernet Sauvignon topped up with equal parts of Syrah, Pinotage, Merlot and Cabernet Franc, and aged in barrel. Unfortunately, none was available for tasting. A pure Syrah is planned for release in late 1995. The Ninety Mile White is a blend of 70 per cent Chardonnay, 15 per cent of Sémillon and 15 per cent Arnsberger – a Riesling × Riesling cross developed at the Geisenheim Institute for its rot resistance. Part of the wine is fermented in oak, part of it undergoes a malolactic fermentation, and the wine is left on its lees for seven months with regular lees stirring to enhance its flavour. I found the 1994 quite rounded, with delicate oak and good fruit.

The fruit for the Clifton Chardonnay comes from further south, from a vineyard at Te Hana near the town of Wellsford, south of Whangarei. It is fermented in oak and aged in barrel for seven months, again with regular lees stirring. The result is a lean, oaky-flavoured wine, with good acidity, that was not overtly buttery. Knight is encouraging others to plant vines in the Northland area, at Kerikeri and Doubtless Bay, convinced as he is, like Mario Vuletich, of the viability of Northland as a wine region.

Finally, there was Old Brother John's Tawny Port which mainly comes from Cabernet with a small amount of some other varieties. It is aged for five years in oak puncheons and subjected to extremes of temperature, rather like an old Maury or Rivesaltes from the South of France, to achieve its fine tawny colour. Then it is blended in a solera system so that a little wine remains from the previous year. As for taste, it has soft liquorice on the palate, with some sweet nougat on the nose.

Okahu Estate, Cnr Okahu Road/Main Highway to Ahipara, (PO Box 388) Kaitaia, telephone: (09) 408 0888/2066, fax: (09) 408 1890.

8

Auckland

The history of the Auckland area is very much linked with the development of the New Zealand wine industry, described on pages 28–39. Many of the Dalmatian immigrants bought land in what were then the villages of Huapai, Kumeu and Henderson, in order to be close to a population centre which would provide a ready market for their produce. There was no consideration as to whether the area was in fact suitable for viticulture. What mattered was that the land was cheap and fertile.

This area is home to many of the large family wineries. Often, as other areas have developed, they have bought land in Marlborough, Gisborne and Hawke's Bay, or have established long-term agreements with grape growers in those regions. Their own original vineyards are tending to disappear as the land becomes more profitable for urban development.

The suitability of Auckland for grape growing is often criticized. However, there are those who do support it most ardently, such as Michael Brajkovich of Kumeu River and Tony Molloy of St Nesbit in South Auckland. The critics believe the climate to be too warm and wet. It is true that the sometimes excessive humidity demands particular attention in the vineyards, but Michael Brajkovich would argue that any good viticulturist can overcome this problem. There are years when Auckland enjoys an advantage over the rest of the country, such as 1993, which was warm and dry while the temperatures remained cool elsewhere. Sometimes, however, the vintage can be spoilt by heavy rain. There is also the contention that the clay soil is too heavy and fertile for vines. As will be seen, many of the Auckland wineries do source their fruit from elsewhere, with a range of wines from both the South and North Islands.

WEST AUCKLAND: HENDERSON, HUAPAI, KUMEU AND WAIMAUKU

Babich Wines

Although Babich are one of the early families of Dalmatian immigrants making their traditional wines, they have moved with the times under the direction of two brothers, Peter and Joe. Their father Josip, who was one of seven sons, arrived in New Zealand in 1910 at the age of fourteen to join other brothers who were mining in the gumfields near Kaitaia at the top of the North Island. Josip planted vines, following the Dalmatian farming traditions, then moved south in 1919 and bought land in Henderson. Today, Peter runs the business, helped by their marketing expert Neill Culley, while Joe is the winemaker and their sister Maureen deals with the paperwork.

Babich is an attractive winery to visit, with a welcoming tasting room, in the less developed part of Henderson, somewhat off the beaten track down Babich Road. Whereas once this fertile area was the fruit bowl of Auckland, it is now succumbing to the relentless encroachment of suburbia. However, they do still retain some vineyards around the winery, including Palomino for the small amount of fortified wine which they continue to make in deference to their early origins. They are a friendly family with views of the industry they are prepared to share.

Babich are known above all for their range of Chardonnays. This is the varietal on which they stake their reputation, most notably on the Irongate Chardonnay from a particularly fine site in Hawke's Bay on Gimblett Road. They do not own the vineyard, but have a long-term contract for its fruit. However, the brothers were so impressed by the consistent quality of the fruit from the Irongate Vineyard that they have established a new vineyard, in which they have the majority shareholding, on a site close by, just separated from the Irongate vineyard by the Ngaruroro River. This is called the Mara Estate, in memory of their mother who died in 1994. The soil there is river silt, whereas Irongate is shingle from an old river bed. Their third Chardonnay is a simple Hawke's Bay wine, a blend of wine from as many as three vineyards which is intended for relatively early drinking, with an appealing combination of fruit and oak.

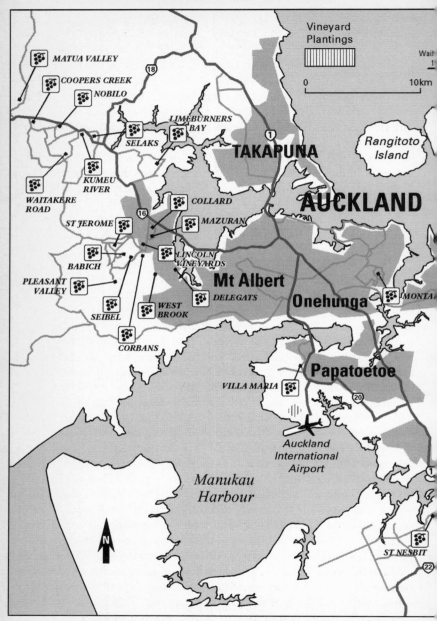

Auckland (North Island)

Sauvignon, Cabernet Sauvignon, Merlot and Syrah have all been planted on the Mara Estate, as well as Chardonnay. The 1992 Mara Chardonnay is solid and buttery with good fruit, while the 1992 Irongate Chardonnay is a much more complex wine and is intended to be so, with barrel fermentation, ageing on the lees and a high proportion of new oak, making a wine with a deliciously toasted character and numerous layers of flavour. The first vintage of Irongate Chardonnay was in 1985. There is also an Irongate Cabernet Merlot blend and, more adventurously, a Syrah from a 4.8-hectare (12-acre) block on the Mara Estate. I tasted a barrel sample of the 1994, which had the hallmark of Rowntree's black-currant fruit gums, and was young and peppery. Syrah presents a fresh challenge, with a new variety to master. The Babich brothers also feel that they need to diversify with white wine too. There is so much Chardonnay and Sauvignon, maybe they should consider Pinot Gris or Riesling. Whatever they choose, they are moving with the times.

Babich Wines, Babich Road, Henderson, telephone: (09) 833 7859, fax: (09) 833 9929

Collard Brothers

The Collards were Huguenot refugees who settled in Kent after the Revocation of the Edict of Nantes, and grew fruit and hops. Then John Collard came out to New Zealand as an orchard instructor for the Department of Agriculture in 1910. He bought land in Henderson, the existing winery site on Lincoln Road, when it was still a cart track linking fields and orchards, and not part of the busy urban sprawl of Auckland. He planted fruit trees and bushes, and married Dorothy Averill whose two brothers ran the Averill winery. It was at their suggestion that John Collard's sons, Lionel and Brian, began crushing their grapes and making wine.

Today, the winery is run by the next generation: Bruce, who is a talented winemaker, and his brother Geoffrey, who oversees the vineyards. However, Lionel remains firmly in charge, presenting the public face of Collards to visitors like me. Although he has visited England only once in his life, and as recently as the mid-1980s, he sees it as home and retains a very English stance about him, with something of the English gentleman. I am not sure if he plays golf, but he would not be out of place in a Kentish village golf club and he can recite extracts of Gilbert and Sullivan's *HMS Pinafore*. Bruce Collard is a gentle, rather shy man, who, to quote his father, 'plays the juice like a piano'. And it is true. Taste a range of Collard's wines and Bruce's talent shines out.

Most original of the Collard range is their Chenin Blanc, which made me see the varietal in a new light the first time I tasted it. Collards were the first to make a dry Chenin. So often in New Zealand it is destined for bag-in-the-box wines and little attention paid to it. Collards provide a rare exception, making a wine that is a blend of Hawke's Bay and Te Kauwhata fruit. The 1994 vintage has just a hint of oak and some attractive grassy fruit, with a touch of honey and good acidity. The minimum of oak maturation gives it an extra layer of complexity.

Collards are particularly known for their Rothesay vineyard in the Waikoukou Valley near Waimauku, from which they make Sauvignon and Chardonnay, and also a Cabernet Merlot blend. The 1994 Rothesay Sauvignon is firm and pithy, with some weight and body; the 1993 Rothesay Chardonnay has layers of flavour, with a buttery, toasted character. The 1989 Rothesay Chardonnay was one of my star wines on my very first visit to New Zealand in 1991. They also produce a Hawke's Bay, a Poverty Bay and a Marlborough Chardonnay, and aim to bring out the character of the different areas, avoiding over-oaking and over-vinification, and simply allowing the juice to dictate the style of the wine. Riesling is another white wine with which they achieve elegant results, based on Geoffrey Collard's experience in Germany.

As for red wine, they have planted Pinot Noir in Marlborough in a joint project whereby they provided the landowner with vine cuttings. The first vintages show promise.

Collard Brothers, 303 Lincoln Road, Henderson, telephone: (09) 838 8341, fax: (09) 837 5840

Coopers Creek

The genial Andrew Hendry is the man behind Coopers Creek. He and a partner Randy Weaver set up the winery at the beginning of the 1980s, buying land outside Huapai in 1980, planting a 4-hectare (10-acre) vineyard, and building a winery in 1982. Hendry is an accountant by training who worked for Penfolds, then wanted a more direct involvement with the industry. However, his professional expertise stands him in good stead for running an efficient winery. Weaver has since returned to the United States and the wine is made by Kim Crawford, a Roseworthy graduate whose career has included Arrowfield in the Hunter Valley, Stags Leap in Napa Valley and Backsberg in South Africa, before joining Coopers Creek in 1988. There is a flair about Crawford's winemaking, while Hendry is relaxed with a dry wit.

Coopers Creek takes its name from the nearby creek on the main road out of Huapai. The winery is a neat, functional warehouse with a small forest of stainless-steel vats outside that have a capacity of 550 tonnes. Their reputation rests upon Chardonnay and Riesling. They now have a vineyard in Hawke's Bay with the inappropriate but memorable name of Swamp Road. In addition, they buy grapes from Marlborough and Gisborne. The 1992 Swamp Road Chardonnay demonstrates a shift away from a very oak-driven style to a blend that is partly fermented in new oak, partly in one-year-old oak and partly in tank, in equal proportions. The result is some toasted notes on the nose and a certain firm, lean backbone on the palate. Crawford would even consider trying a non-oaked Chardonnay from Marlborough if the yield was as low as 2.5 tonnes per acre. He is also experimenting with a sweet Chardonnay, made for the first time in 1994 from grapes that reached 36° Brix which were fermented in oak.

Riesling comes, maybe unusually, from a vineyard in Hawke's Bay, close to the coast so that it is cooled by the sea breezes and enjoys a long ripening period. The vintage is usually about three weeks later than in vineyards further inland, at the end rather than the beginning of April. A Late Harvest Riesling comes off the same block. Here, they aim for ripeness rather than botrytis and it is made only in the best years, such as 1994, 1991 and 1990. The 1994 is delicately honeyed without being too heavy or cloying, while the dry Riesling is appealingly flowery.

As for red wine, they have planted a vineyard of Pinot Noir on a limestone hillside in Hawke's Bay and they also produce a Cabernet Merlot blend from the home vineyard. Sparkling wine is something they are playing with, and they are also considering Chenin Blanc, inspired by the examples of Collards and Esk Valley, recognizing that it is an underrated variety.

Coopers Creek Vineyard, 601 State Highway 16, Huapai, (PO Box 140) Kumeu, telephone: (09) 412 8560, fax: (09) 412 8375

Corbans

Corbans are New Zealand's second-largest wine producer and, as such, one of the three or four big players that dominate the industry. Yet despite their size, they maintain a strong profile of individuality and a firm insistence that big can be beautiful. Their winemakers are allowed, in some instances, as much personal expression as if they were making wine for a smaller family concern, rather than a larger corporation. More specific details of their activities in Marlborough, Hawke's Bay and Gisborne are given in those chapters. What follows here is a broad outline as, for the time being, the Corbans head office is in Henderson, at the old homestead of the Corban family.

The original company was founded by a Lebanese immigrant, Assid Abraham Corban, who arrived New Zealand in 1892. Ten years later he planted 1.6 hectares (4 acres) of vines at his Mount Lebanon vineyard in Henderson, which was then a village to the north of Auckland. The full story is told by Dick Scott in his book *A Stake in the Country*, which gives an inkling of just how hard life was for the early wine growers. The first vineyards included varieties such as Black Hamburgh, Golden Chasselas, Albany Surprise and Pinot Meunier, some for table grapes and some for wine. Romeo Bragato described the Mount Lebanon vineyard as 'the model vineyard of New Zealand and an object lesson to grape growers'. The Corban family survived the problems created by New Zealand's flirtation with prohibition, and in their heyday, still as a family concern, were the largest wine producers in the country, playing a vital part in the development of the industry.

Today, no member of the family remains with the company. In 1948, Alex Corban was the first New Zealander to graduate in oenology from Roseworthy College in Australia, which was a milestone at the time, and his son Alwyn runs the successful Ngatarawa winery in Hawke's Bay. Alex's cousin Joe is a leading viticulturist in the forefront of the introduction of new clones and rootstocks, while other members of the family have diversified into different walks of life. As for the company itself, it has undergone the vicissitudes and take-overs that beset so many large organizations.

Corbans is now an amalgamation of three companies: the original Corbans; Cooks, which was set up in the Te Kauwhata area in 1972 and named after the explorer who first charted the coastline of New Zealand; and the New Zealand arm of the Australian company McWilliam's, in which Cooks took a majority shareholding in 1984 before merging with Corbans in 1987. They in turn are owned by the DB Group, who in turn are part of Asia Pacific Breweries in Singapore, and the ultimate responsibility now lies with Heineken as the major shareholders. However, winemaking and marketing and all the decisions of running a wine company are centred on the old Corbans homestead in Henderson. Marketing guru Noel Scanlan is general manager and the winemaking is masterminded by the intensely blue-eyed Kerry Hitchcock.

Corbans wines are found under several different labels and qualities. Best of all is their recently introduced Cottage Block range, for which the winemakers in Gisborne, Hawke's Bay and Marlborough are allowed full rein to make exactly the wine they wish, handcrafted from hand-picked fruit, sparing no expense, or virtually none, and without any regard for the final quantity available for sale. Cottage Block Chardonnay from each area makes a fascinating comparison, demonstrating the quality and characteristics of each region. There is also a Cabernet Merlot blend from Hawke's Bay, as well as a Pinot Noir and a botrytized Riesling from Marlborough.

Next down the quality ladder come Corbans Private Bin and Cooks Winemaker's Reserve, as well as the regional labels: Stoneleigh in Marlborough and Longridge in Hawke's Bay. What they call their *négociant* label of Robard & Butler also includes some good wines, notably the Amberley Riesling from a vineyard north of Christchurch which is vinified in Marlborough. Then there is a range of basic varietals, either under the Cooks or Corbans label. Cooks tends to feature more widely on the export market, especially in Britain. Corbans prefer to ignore the smaller regions, leaving Nelson, Martinborough and Central Otago to the family wineries, for there is not the same scope for development as in Marlborough, Hawke's Bay or Gisborne.

For the year 2000 they are already planning the Millennium Reserve, a very limited release of 750 magnums of 1992 Hawke's Bay Cabernet Sauvignon, the best wine of the vintage, which they are planning to sell at $250 apiece. And who knows what they will plan for their centenary celebrations in the year 2002.

Corbans Wines, 426–448 Great North Road, (PO Box 21183)

Henderson, Auckland, telephone: (09) 837 3390, fax: (09) 836 0005

Delegat's Wine Estate

Delegat's is run by a formidable but friendly brother-and-sister team, Jim and Rose Delegat, with their young winemaker Brent Marris. This is very much a family company, especially after a brief flirtation with an outside shareholder following financial difficulties during the price war of the mid-1980s. However, it is now back firmly in Jim and Rose's control. Their father Nikola founded the winery, buying land in 1947, some years after his first arrival in New Zealand from Dalmatia, and building a winery three years later in 1950. He began with 2 hectares (5 acres) in Henderson, planted with olive trees as well as vines – Palomino, Baco 22A and Seibel – for 'port' and 'sherry'.

The attractive weatherboard building that now houses the winery office was once the family home where both Jim and Rose were born. What is now the winery shop was their father's original winery. The change of direction from fortified wines happened in 1979 with the arrival of John Hancock, a young Australian who went on to create the reputation of Morton Estate and is now involved with a new venture in Hawke's Bay. Brent Marris has been the winemaker at Delegat's since 1985. In that time, their range has been streamlined into just nine wines that come from Hawke's Bay, under the Delegat's label, and Proprietors Reserve for the best wines, or from Marlborough under the Oyster Bay label. Riesling and Gewürztraminer have been dropped, and they are concentrating on Chardonnay, Sauvignon Blanc, Cabernet and Merlot. They also admit to considering Syrah for Hawke's Bay and produced a Pinot Noir from the Wairarapa in 1994, after encouraging a sheep farmer to change direction and plant 12 hectares (30 acres) of Pinot Noir as well as some Chardonnay. They had to hold his hand as he had never grown grapes before.

I wandered round the winery with Jim and Brent, tasting from barrels, followed by Brent's friendly hound, Bacchus. A barrel sample of Hawke's Bay Chardonnay from their own vineyards will form the backbone of their Proprietors Reserve range. It is barrel fermented and lees stirred regularly every two weeks, and was showing good acidity and elegant fruit. Delegat's have three different vineyards in Hawke's Bay, one on the free-draining shingle of Gimblett Road, and one very close by so that it is similar in soil composition, while the Vicarage Vineyard on Swamp Road has much heavier soil with more clay. A sample of Oyster Bay Chardonnay was more lemony with firm acidity, in keeping with the characteristics of Marlborough. Oyster Bay Sauvignon – named after a whaling village in the Marlborough Sound – is fresh and pithy, while a Hawke's Bay Sauvignon Fumé is for my tastebuds too overtly oaky, with little varietal character.

With red wines they are aiming for a concentration of fruit, but with elegance rather than power. The 1994 Cabernet Sauvignon from Gimblett Road had some appealing smoky fruit and the Merlot had the ripe flavours of the vintage.

Delegat's pay great attention to work in the vineyard as the prime means of obtaining good fruit, with strict controls and attention to detail, and with an increasing number of vineyards in the hands of the winery rather than contract growers. In the winery, a change of cooper a couple of years ago has enhanced the quality of the wine. I have certainly found that I appreciate Delegat's wines more and more after each visit.

Delegat's Wine Estate, Hepburn Road, Henderson, telephone: (09) 836 0129, fax: (09) 836 3282

Kumeu River

Kumeu River stands for Chardonnay and Merlot, and above all for West Auckland. Contrary to the current trend among Auckland wineries, who prefer to source their grapes from other areas, the Brajkovich family insist on the importance of having ultimate control over their vineyards which are all in the Kumeu area.

This is a friendly family company. Mate Brajkovich bought land in Kumeu in 1944. There was already an acre of Albany Surprise, but he planted more vines – Seibel, Palomino and Baco 22A – and built a winery in 1950 which is today incorporated into the enlarged winery building. His widow Melba laughingly said that every time they had a baby, they built another extension to the winery. Mate Brajkovich died in 1991, but Melba continues her involvement in the business along with their three sons: Michael who is the winemaker; Milan, whose main interest is viticulture; and Paul, who is responsible for sales and marketing. And if you should see a little old lady with a wizened, wrinkled face, dressed all in black, sitting in the sun outside the winery, that is Kate, Melba's mother-in-law, who, when I met her, had just celebrated her 92nd birthday. The winery was originally called the San Marino Winery, with a reputation for 'port' and 'sherry', and also some dry white and red table wine, but the name was officially changed to Kumeu River in 1989. Brajkovich is used as a second label, usually for wines for earlier drinking.

Michael Brajkovich would feature in everyone's short list of New Zealand's most talented winemakers. He was the star pupil of his year at Roseworthy and talks about his wines with quiet modesty, combined with complete confidence in his philosophy and methods. There is an understated flair in his techniques. His Chardonnays stand out from the normal run of New Zealand Chardonnays, with their very European, or more precisely, Burgundian style. For a start they undergo a full malolactic fermentation, which is extremely unusual for New Zealand. They have layers of flavour. Initially they may seem quite mature, with a much less obviously fruit-driven style, but with considerable subtlety and concentration of flavour. They do not always show well in blind tastings as they stand out as being awkwardly different, but sip them with a meal and you have a treat.

There is also a simple Brajkovich Chardonnay which is made without any contact with oak to produce a light, uncomplicated wine, and more specifically a Brajkovich Auckland Chardonnay which includes fruit from Mangere in the south, as well as Kumeu, and is vinified in the same way as the Kumeu River Chardonnay but given less contact with new oak. In 1993 came the first vintage from a recently purchased plot adjoining the winery which they have planted with Chardonnay to produce a wine they call Mate's Chardonnay.

They used Sémillon for the first time in 1992, adding a small amount to their Sauvignon. Very ripe Sauvignon, as it was in 1992, runs the risk of turning flabby and Sémillon adds some backbone. Fermented in mostly old wood, the 1993 Sauvignon Sémillon blend, with the proportion increased from 15 to 30 per cent, had some firm nutty fruit, with good backbone and structure.

Merlot is Michael's other enthusiasm, in preference to Cabernet which ripens less consistently, whereas Merlot is more tolerant of not always being fully ripe. Michael is possibly influenced by his friendly relationship with the Moueix family of Château Pétrus. He spent the 1983 vintage with them at Château Magdeleine in Saint-Emilion, working with Merlot. So it is that Merlot dominates the Kumeu River Red, with some Cabernet Sauvignon and less Cabernet Franc to make a wine with some European elegance, good fruit and soft tannins. The method is very much that of Bordeaux, with two and a half weeks on the skins, slow pumping over, and taking great care to produce only soft tannins, nothing harsh or aggressive. Another original wine is the Brajkovich Cabernet Franc, which could be described as a Chinon look-alike as it has some ripe berry fruit with a bit of acidity and tannin, and is perfect for early drinking. It is quite unlike most other New Zealand red wine.

Michael Brajkovich is adamant about the importance of running your own vineyards. The microclimate of Kumeu is quite warm and wet, making botrytis a potential hazard, but this can be averted by exposing the trellis and leaf plucking. The soil is clay loam, with sandstone underneath. They grow grass between the rows, enabling the water to run off or evaporate. If the soil was cultivated it would absorb water much more easily. All their new vineyards are on the lyre system, making for good ventilation and fruit exposure. They are gradually increasing their vineyard holdings, either buying land themselves or working very closely with growers who have planted vines for them. And although they are firmly committed to Kumeu, they are also looking at Masterton and considering the potential of the Wairarapa, maybe for Pinot Gris and Pinot Blanc, as well as Chardonnay and Sémillon; but that is a project for the future.

Kumeu River Wines, 550 Highway 16, (PO Box 24) Kumeu, 1454 Auckland, telephone: (09) 412 8415, fax: (09) 412 7627

Limeburners Bay

Limeburners Bay, although part of Huapai, is closer to Hobsonville in West Auckland. It seems a curious name for a winery. The explanation is that it is situated close to the upper reaches of the Waitemata Harbour, where early settler Rice Owen Clark burnt shells for lime to improve the quality of his too-sour soil. The winery was created by Alan Laurenson with his Danish wife Jetta. They first planted vines in 1978 and, until they built their own winery in 1987, made their wines in other people's cellars. Laurenson comes from a farming family, but has worked in industry in Europe. He took oenology courses and his wife is a horticulturist by training. On their 6.5-hectare (16-acre) vineyard they have Cabernet Sauvignon, Cabernet Franc, Merlot, Sémillon, Chardonnay and Sauvignon. All their fruit comes from West Auckland. Laurenson is also greatly interested in Italian varieties and has planted a row of Sangiovese. When we met, he had other varieties in quarantine: Teroldego, Marzemino, Dolcetto, Barbera and Prosecco.

There is a certain originality about the wines of Limeburners Bay. A Sémillon Chardonnay blend is made by adding fermented Chardonnay to Sémillon must, which sounds rather like New Zealand's answer to the *governo* process of Chianti, making for a second fermentation. This was first done by accident in 1989, but has been repeated in subsequent years, perhaps with uncertain results. With Chardonnay, Laurenson tries to avoid an excess of oak. He gave me his first Chardonnay, the 1987 vintage, which certainly had some appealing leafy fruit when it was five years old, while the 1990 had a more mature nuttiness.

A Pinotage had the earthiness you sometimes find with that variety, while a range of different vintages of Cabernet showed some attractive cedarwood notes, sometimes with hints of herbaceousness. Most original of all is a Dessert Cabernet, made rather like a *vin doux naturel* from the South of France. The grapes must be very ripe and the fermentation is stopped by the addition of brandy to achieve an alcoholic degree of 17. The wine is kept in oak for two years, and the taste is sweet and inky, with some tannin and herbal notes. I was not sure how much I really liked it, but it could certainly be New Zealand's equivalent of Rivesaltes.

Limeburners Bay Vineyards, 112 Hobsonville Road, Hobsonville, telephone/fax: (09) 416 8844

Lincoln Vineyards

Lincoln is a family winery that was known above all for its 'ports' and 'sherries'. The first Peter Fredatovich arrived in New Zealand in 1923 but did not acquire any land until 1937. He kept cows, planted an apple orchard and grew vegetables as well as vines on a plot of land that is now on the busy Lincoln Road in Henderson.

That is where the winery still stands, with an inviting-looking shop. Apart from a 2.5-hectare (6-acre) block in Henderson, most of their grapes come from contract growers in Gisborne, Hawke's Bay and Marlborough. Their other Auckland vineyard at Brigham's Creek has recently been uprooted in order to concentrate instead on Hawke's Bay. The first Peter's son, another Peter, developed the winery until his retirement, and now it is a third Peter and his brother John who run the company. Until recently their winemaker was Nick Chan, whose stepfather is Gilbert Chan from Totara, but he has now gone on to pastures new in California and has been replaced by Iain Trembath.

However, Nick Chan played a significant part in the transformation of Lincoln from an old-fashioned producer of 'ports' and 'sherries' into a mainstream table-wine producer. Peter Fredatovich saw Chan's arrival in 1985 as a turning point. They planted Chardonnay and Cabernet Sauvignon, and the shift towards table wine has continued. However, on my first visit to the winery they still had the old totara barrels used for maturing 'port' and 'sherry'. An Old Tawny Port tasted of walnuts and nougat, with chocolatey overtones, but they are slowly phasing out that side of their production.

Today, they concentrate on different styles of Chardonnay from various vineyards in Gisborne with a top-label Vintage Selection and the Parkland Vineyard, which also provides the base for the Vintage Selection but undergoes different treatment, including some ageing in American oak, making for a fatter, fuller wine than the more elegant Vintage Selection. A basic Gisborne Chardonnay from a blend of vineyards is ripe and buttery, although it includes a proportion of wine fermented in tank, as well as in some older barrels. French oak is used only for the best Chardonnay.

There are similar variations for the red wines based on Cabernet and Merlot, with a cheaper red made from Merlot blended with some Cabernet Franc. The 1991 Vintage Selection from the home vineyard contains 20 per cent Merlot, making a solid, rounded wine, while a 1993 with equal amounts of Merlot and Cabernet, including some Merlot from Hawke's Bay, has some attractive blackcurrant fruit. It will be interesting to see how this winery develops, with a new winemaker and a more energetic approach to the export market.

Lincoln Vineyards, 130 Lincoln Road, Henderson, telephone: (09) 838 6944, fax: (09) 838 6984

Matua Valley

I always enjoy my visits to Matua Valley. The two brothers Ross and Bill Spence perform an entertaining double act with wit and humour sparking off each other, stemming maybe from the combination of an Irish father and a Dalmatian mother. The young winemaker at Matua Valley, Mark Robertson, is more quietly spoken but, given the brothers' ebullience, perhaps that is no bad thing. The younger brother Bill is lanky and gregarious, but his sociable, relaxed manner belies a shrewd, observant brain. However, Ross, with equal wit, is the thinker of the pair and always has good thoughts on the current state of the industry and its development. He has also played a significant role in the industry, for it was he who isolated and propagated the single clone of Sauvignon that has been planted throughout New Zealand in the last twenty years.

The brothers' father Rod set up Spence Wines in Henderson in the 1940s, producing 'port' and 'Sauternes' and such like. Ross studied viticulture and winemaking at Fresno in California and, after a brief spell working with his father, decided to grow his own grapes. He remains a viticulturist at heart. He bought 4 hectares (10 acres) of land in Huapai and began Matua Valley in 1974. Two years later, Bill joined him. Their first winery was an old tin shed, but the arrival of another shareholder and partner enabled them to build the winery in Waikoukou Valley outside Waimauku. From there, Matua Valley has gone from strength to strength, establishing vineyards and fine-tuning its winemaking processes.

Recent developments at Matua have concentrated on the vineyards with the ultimate aim of controlling as much of their own fruit as possible, with a replanting programme that includes their contract growers' vineyards. They have bought three new vineyards in Marlborough, Gisborne and Hawke's Bay. In Marlborough they have planted Pinot Gris, which was produced for the first time in 1995, and Pinot Blanc, of which the first crop will be 1996. They already own vineyards in Waimauku and Hawke's Bay. The Smith-Dartmoor Estate in the Dartmoor Valley of Hawke's Bay, in which they have a shareholding, is the source of good Chardonnay and a Cabernet Merlot blend. They also take Chardonnay from the Judd Estate, a hillside vineyard in Gisborne.

Chardonnay follows the characteristics of the different regions, with Smith-Dartmoor Estate producing a tighter wine, while Judd Estate has some concentrated fruit and a toasted character after some bottle ageing. Their most stylish Chardonnay is sold under the Ararimu label, a name which recalls that of the old Maori block, going back to when the government parcelled out the land in 7,000-acre lots. Matua Valley was on the edge on it. The wine is rich and toasted, with layers of flavour. The oak is well integrated, making a powerful wine but with immense style. The source of the fruit for Ararimu Chardonnay is Gisborne, while Ararimu Cabernet Sauvignon represents the best fruit from the Smith-Dartmoor estate. With Chardonnay they particularly concentrate on the style of the estate, for that is what they want in the bottle and then in the glass, so that Judd Estate is fruit driven, while Ararimu, with a high proportion of malolactic fermentation, has power but without coarseness.

Shingle Peak is the name used for their Marlborough wines, after a mountain in the Kaikoura Range, and the soil of the vineyard is appropriately shingle. The range consists of Cabernet Sauvignon, Rhine Riesling, Chardonnay and Sauvignon Blanc, using the facilities that were Vintech but are now called Rapaura Vintners, in which they have a share. They have built a new warehouse for the development of sparkling wine, also a significant part of the activity at Matua Valley. They began making sparkling wine in 1987 with a high proportion of Pinot Noir from a vineyard in Waimauku. The wine spends a couple of years on the lees and develops a biscuity character, with its corners rounded by a light dosage.

Ask Ross about the future and as a viticulturist he talks about vineyards, clonal selection, canopy management and new varieties. Matua Valley is moving towards a more ecologically friendly management of their vineyards and they are also experimenting with new varieties and clones, employing a student to carry out microvinifications for them. Pinot Gris is a particularly exciting prospect.

Matua Valley Wines, Waikoukou Valley Road, Waimauku, (PO Box 100) Kumeu, telephone: (09) 411 8301, fax: (09) 411 7982

Mazuran's

George Mazuran was one of the great personalities of the New Zealand wine industry. He has been described as 'a real gentleman' and attributed with saying, 'Wine is my life, not my business.' He came to New Zealand in 1926, gumdigging like so many Dalmatians, saved money and eventually bought land some twelve years later. Like most of Henderson at the time, it was dairy pasture and orchard land. Now it is on a busy main road out of Auckland. The fruit trees have disappeared and the bullock track has been tarmacked. Mazuran's first vines were planted in 1939 and his first wines made three years later. He became President of the Viticultural Association and immersed himself in the political machinations of the wine industry, proving an effective lobbyist who argued the viewpoint of the winemakers and achieved changes to the restrictive legislation. He was awarded the OBE for his services to the industry and died in 1982. His winery is now run by his son-in-law, Rado Hladilo.

There is still a small vineyard at the back of the winery planted with Palomino, Muscatel and several different hybrids. Hladilo admitted that things had slowed down since his wife died seven years ago, even though his son Anthony is involved with business, but somehow he has lost his zest for making wine. However, they still produce 'port' and 'sherry', as well as a small amount of table wine from Chardonnay, Cabernet and Merlot grown in their 3.5-hectare (9-acre) vineyard.

The winery has a licence to make its own brandy which is used for fortifying the 'port' and 'sherry', in preference to the whey spirit used by most of the other producers. It is the lees and grape skins that have been distilled in a stainless-steel still with a copper cooling coil that has two pipes, one for the spirit and the other for the faints, which run out into a separate bonded room that is strictly controlled by customs officials. There are totara barrels and old cognac barrels for storage, as well as a large kauri vat.

We tasted Mazuran Dry Sherry made from Palomino, which was quite nutty, followed by a 1960 Old Tawny from various hybrids, which was quite sweet and chocolatey. Next came a 1954, then a 1952 Old Tawny, which was sweet and rich with a slightly burnt finish. The 1970 is the youngest vintage they have for sale and they also make 'Madeira', a cross between 'port' and 'sherry', as well as young ruby from Cabernet Sauvignon. We finished with an Old Liqueur Muscat, which has been left in a barrel for forty-five years and simply bottled as it is needed. It was sweet and nutty, very concentrated, and remarkably moreish.

However, I left with the feeling that I had been in a time warp. Hladilo was sad in his widowhood, but with a wistful smile, and the events of the modern industry were passing him by, yet it did not worry him.

Mazuran's Vineyards, 225 Lincoln Road, Henderson, telephone/fax: (09) 838 6945

The House of Nobilo

After a choppy period during the mid-1980s when several wine companies suffered severe financial losses, the House of Nobilo is now very much a family company run by three brothers: Nick, Steve and Mark. Their father Nikola Nobilo came from the island of Korčula, where he had been a stonemason, just as the Second World War broke out and settled in Huapai in 1943. The family had made wine in the village of Lumbarda and a recent television programme, in a series called *Country Calendar*, recorded their return to their roots. Zuva, Nikola's wife, married him by proxy in 1939, with Nikola's brother standing in for him, before travelling out to join her husband in New Zealand. Now in her eighties, she is still a delightfully lively woman with a fountain of stories, not to mention a delicious line in whitebait fritters.

Nobilo's is now the largest family winery in New Zealand and has recently joined the small group of category three membership in the Wine Institute for those whose sales exceed 2 million litres per year. Their success with White Cloud is responsible, a brand that was launched in 1990. The name recalls the old Maori name for New Zealand, Aotea Roa, which translates as 'the land of the long white cloud'. It is mainly Müller-Thurgau, but with 15 per cent Sauvignon and just a hint of Muscat to give the wine a lift. Above all it is soft, with some flowery fruit and easy to drink. They were the first in the mid-1970s to use the name Müller-Thurgau, rather than that mouthful of a name Riesling Sylvaner. By 1982, there were forty-nine different Müller-Thurgaus on the domestic market, but Montana's recently introduced Misty Peak is now their main competitor. However, with their strong sales to

Sweden they are aiming for 1 million cases of White Cloud by the year 2000. New vineyards in Mohaka, an untapped area between Hawke's Bay and Gisborne, are being developed with White Cloud in mind. The first vintage was 1995 and 200 hectares (500 acres) will be in full production by 1997. Mohaka is a new area which is very similar to Gisborne as regards climate and soil. It is on the coast, sheltered by the mountains to the west and no grapes have been grown there before.

At the quality end of the market, Nobilo's are known above all for their range of Chardonnay. The Poverty Bay label unusually has no contact with oak and tastes rather like a full-bodied Mâcon. A Gisborne Chardonnay spends six months in oak to give it a richer flavour and then there are two specific vineyards from Gisborne: Tietjen and Dixon. Tietjen Chardonnay is partially barrel fermented, with some ripe tropical flavours, while Dixon Chardonnay is all fermented in oak and kept in wood for six months, allowing for some good oak integration and firm, buttery flavours. There is also a stylish Marlborough Chardonnay and inevitably a Sauvignon, from the Matador vineyard in Marlborough which is shared with Selaks.

As for red wines, they produce Cabernet Sauvignon from Marlborough and from their remaining vineyards in Huapai, and, more originally, Pinotage. The 1991 Pinotage has some berry fruit and was almost raisiny, with that slight earthiness which can be characteristic of the varietal. The wine spends eighteen months in 500-litre French barrels and provides an original flavour, demonstrating the suitability of Huapai – which means 'good fruit' in Maori – for red wine.

Nobilo Vintners, Station Road, Huapai, telephone: (09) 412 9148, fax: (09) 412 7124

Pleasant Valley

Pleasant Valley is the oldest family winery in New Zealand and has not changed hands since it was founded in 1902. Stephan Yelas's grandfather Stipan Jelich planted vines in the Henderson Valley in 1896 intending to produce table grapes, but when he found that there was no money to be made he turned to winemaking instead.

This is another winery that has undergone a change of direction in recent years. Stephan's father Moscow died in 1984, which is when Stephan took over. Moscow had enjoyed the boom of the 1960s and 1970s, but had been reluctant to countenance the move to table-wine production. Stephan is a viticulturist by training who says that he learnt winemaking in his own winery, usually with a qualified winemaker on hand for the vintage.

We wandered round the winery. It is old and atmospheric. There are stocks of old 'port', barrels of twenty- and twenty-five year-old wines made from Seibel hybrids which now sell extremely cheaply. A twenty-one-year-old 'port' retailed at $29 in 1995 and a ten-year-old at only $9.80. 'Sherry' is made from Dr Hogg Muscat, as well as pressings of Chenin and Müller-Thurgau that are not used for table wine. There is more of a demand for 'port', which therefore warrants more care, so better grapes are used for it, such as Pinotage and also Cabernet pressings.

We tasted in the winery café which attracts a lively passing tourist trade. Of the table wines, the Pinotage is the most original. There are very few producers of this South African variety in New Zealand and the 1994, which is intended for early drinking, had some fresh berry fruit and lively astringency. Chardonnay and Sauvignon grapes come from Hawke's Bay, and Gewürztraminer from Gisborne. There were flagons of 'sherry' – Amontillado dry, Amoroso medium and Oloroso sweet – as well as some two-year-old Rich Port. Best of all was the Founders Port with an average age of fifteen years, and the twenty-year-old Anniversary Port produced for their ninetieth-anniversary celebration, which was rich and spirity, but with a good concentration of fruit.

Pleasant Valley Wines, 322 Henderson Valley Road, Henderson, telephone: (09) 838 8857, fax: (09) 838 8456

St Jerome

Unlike most of the wineries of Dalmatian origin, St Jerome is a relatively new creation. Two brothers are behind it: Davorin and Miro Ozich. Their family had produced wine in Dalmatia for generations and their father continued to make a little 'port' after he arrived in New Zealand in 1954. Davorin, with a master's degree in biochemistry, worked in the pharmaceutical industry but had always wanted to make wine. His brother was a farmer and in 1981 they took the decision to enter the wine industry, bought land in Henderson, and in 1986 produced their first wine. St Jerome was the first Dalmatian saint, dating from the fourth century, and his feast day would be cause for family celebrations on 30 September.

There is a division of labour in that Miro concentrates on the vineyards while Davorin is responsible for the winemaking and sales. Their father is now retired, but continues to play with his 'port' which is sold under the Nova label. In 1987, Davorin worked a vintage at Château Cos d'Estournel, a classed-growth estate in Saint-Estèphe. This experience has made a significant impact on his winemaking methods, leading him to appreciate the benefits of a long maceration period at fermentation, which in turn allows for a longer maturation in wood. A fine red wine is their objective. There was a quantum leap in quality with the 1988 vintage when Davorin put into practice what he had learnt in the Médoc and produced a wonderfully concentrated blend of Cabernet Merlot. The 1991, when it was four years old, had immense style and certainly would not be out of place in a line-up of good claret, with some ripe cassis fruit and oak on the nose, and elegance combined with tannin and fruit on the palate. They consider that Auckland has had a more consistent climate than Hawke's Bay over the previous ten years, with good long summers to ripen the grapes. Humidity may be a problem, but can be overcome with good vineyard management and regular spraying. Their vineyard is a 7-hectare (18-acre) block on clay soil, a north-facing suntrap, with the average age of the vines now over ten years old.

The Ozich brothers also produce a lighter Cabernet for earlier drinking which spends about three months in old barrels, as opposed to three years in new barrels for their best wine. White wines include Sauvignon and Chardonnay from Hawke's Bay, Gewürztraminer and Riesling from a neighbour's vineyard, as well as St Jerome Vintage 'Port', made from Cabernet Sauvignon and aged in old totara barrels, making for some rounded liquorice fruit.

St Jerome Wines, 219 Metcalf Road, Henderson, telephone/fax: (09) 833 6205

Seibel

Norbert Seibel had a varied career in the wine industry before coming to New Zealand in 1979. He comes from Mainz, worked

in Alsace and then in the Rheinhessen at Oppenheim, before studying at the Geisenheim Institute. From there he went to South Africa,
joined the Distillers Company and ran the Bergkelder before Julius
Lazlo. Then he came to New Zealand for what was meant to be
a two-month visit in 1979, but stayed on to work for Corbans as
their chief winemaker until he grew tired of large-company politics
and wanted to fulfil his dream of having his own boutique winery.
He began making wine under his own name in 1987, first using
the facilities at Pleasant Valley, then at West Brook. Finally, in
1992 he bought the bankrupt winery of the Balic family's Golden
Sunset Vineyard. It had once enjoyed a good reputation, but had
ceased production in 1988.

Seibel has insignificant vineyards of his own, but prefers the
flexibility of buying in grapes. He wants to try varieties that are new
to New Zealand, such as Nobling, Morio-Muscat and Bacchus. He
is the only producer of Scheurebe, having identified a block of it
which originally went into Corbans bulk white. He also admits to
being 'a bit of Riesling fan, but not because I come from Germany'.
He likes its versatility, the fact that it can be sweet or dry, or any
flavour in between. We tasted a barrel-fermented dry Riesling
which I found quite oaky, but which undoubtedly needed time to
develop. A medium dry Riesling from Hawke's Bay had some
delicate honey and good acidity; a Late Harvest White Riesling,
with a good proportion of botrytized grapes, was full, ripe and
honeyed. When he was with Corbans, Seibel had predicted that
Marlborough could be a second Rheingau.

There is also a ripe Chenin Blanc, an oaked and an unoaked
Sauvignon (I preferred the oak-free version), and a barrel-
fermented Chardonnay. As for red wines, he is excited by Pinot
Noir but has not yet made any. He has produced, however, a
Cabernet Merlot blend with some rugged fruit. The winemaking
is carried out with meticulous attention to detail and Seibel is
fulfilling his dream, with the support of his wife, Silvia, who runs
the Kellercafé where you can taste his wines.

Seibel Wines, 113–117 Sturges Road, (PO Box 21660) Henderson, telephone/fax: (09) 836 6113

Selaks

Mate Selak was one of the great personalities of the industry. I was lucky enough to meet him, albeit briefly, on my first visit to Selaks in 1991 and remember a man of great charm. Subsequently I have spent time with his widow Matja, who reminisced about the old days. She explained how Mate had joined his uncle Marino, who had begun making wine in 1934. She talked of helping Mate to make barrels out of totara and of the shift from 'port' and 'sherry' to table wines, with claret, dry red and white wines, all coming from the same varieties but vinified in different ways. Today, Selaks is run by Mate's two sons: the amiable Ivan and rather more serious Michael who seems to feel the weight of responsibility. Darryl Woolley is their winemaker. However, it was Kevin Judd who first put Selaks in the limelight with his 1984 Sauvignon Blanc before moving on to Cloudy Bay.

Today, there is a strong emphasis on Marlborough in Selaks's profile, accounting for 80, if not 85 per cent of their production. Unlike most of the Auckland wineries, they have tended not to use the facilities of Vintech but, from the 1995 vintage, have their own facilities in Marlborough in partnership with Nobilo's, with whom they also share the fruit of the 121-hectare (300-acre) Matador Estate owned by John Webber. It represents a colossal $1.5 million investment. However, they are confident that quality will take a quantum leap, removing the need to truck fruit up to Auckland, which is a sixteen-hour journey at its quickest. Memories of the effects of a ferry strike in 1991 still linger. They will save transport costs, too, and above all have a real identity in Blenheim. From Marlborough they produce Sauvignon, Chardonnay, Riesling and a little Cabernet, Merlot and Sémillon, while the rest of their wines come from Gisborne, as well as a little Cabernet from Hawke's Bay. A token vineyard adjoins the winery.

Their range is still very much oriented towards white wine, with Chardonnay, Sauvignon from the Drylands vineyard in Marlborough, as well as a Sauvignon Sémillon blend which is fermented in new wood, and a growing interest in Riesling, both dry and sweet. They first made Marlborough Riesling in 1991. The 1993 dry Riesling is delightfully floral; a medium dry, slightly honeyed; and a 1994 Ice Wine made by freezing the grapes has some peachy honey and firm acidity. The best wines are sold under the Founders Selection label, provided the quality is up to scratch.

Mate Selak was one of the first to make sparkling wine and his wife Matje remembers how excited he was disgorging the first bottles. His sons took up the practice again in 1983. There is an Extra Dry wine, with very little dosage, that has an appealing nutty nose, and a Brut with 12 grams sugar of dosage that is fuller and richer. A little Pinot Meunier was planted in 1992 which will add an extra dimension to the wines, currently 70 per cent Pinot Noir and 30 per cent Chardonnay.

I left with the impression of a serious family winery that is quietly and determinedly going places.

Selaks Wines, Cnr Highway 16 and Old North Road, (PO Box 34) Kumeu, telephone: (09) 412 8609, fax: (09) 412 7524

Waitakere Road

Tim Harris is a tall, bespectacled lawyer who has turned wine writer and now winemaker. He first became interested in wine when he lived and worked in London. In 1986, he bought land in a syndicate of seven partners, all lawyers, from Mate Brajkovich of Kumeu River. Harris manages the vineyard and makes their wine, and since 1988 has also had his own adjoining vineyard of Cabernet. He admits to having had no professional winemaking training, but has learnt by experience from his mistakes – the 1990 was vinegar – and Michael Brajkovich has offered advice and help. Harris's first wines were made in the back of the garage which has now been extended into a neat shed, equipped with stainless-steel fermentation tanks and tight rows of barrels.

For the moment, Harris concentrates on red wine from Cabernet Sauvignon, Cabernet Franc and Merlot. However, he has another 4 hectares (10 acres) that he could plant, and wonders about Chardonnay and Pinot Gris. He reckons that Pinot Gris could cope with the Auckland humidity and would not give that taint of botrytis which sometimes spoils Auckland whites.

Harris is currently producing three red wines. Upper Case Red, with a legal ring, comes from the syndicate vineyard and has good fruit for relatively youthful drinking. The blend is predominantly Merlot, which suits the clay soil along the Waitakere Road, south-west of Kumeu. There is also Cabernet Sauvignon and Cabernet

Franc in Upper Case Red; and while Harris particularly likes the impact of the Merlot, he does not want too much Cabernet Franc as it can cut the tannin, rather in the same way that detergent cuts the grease in the washing-up water. Upper Case Red is mainly matured in old French barrels.

Harrier Rise, made from his vineyard of Cabernet Sauvignon and Merlot, is named after the hovering hawks that obligingly keep other smaller birds away from the grapes. The wine is structured and solid, with tight fruit. Selected Blend Vintage, or SBV for short, is a more rustic wine, a Bordeaux blend but for earlier drinking. In contrast, the 1991 Harrier Rise had developed some attractive cedarwood flavours on the palate, fulfilling Harris's aim of a wine with depth that will develop with ageing. It promises well for the future.

Waitakere Road Vineyard, 748 Waitakere Road, (PO Box 489) Kumeu, telephone/fax: (09) 412 7256

West Brook

West Brook is one of the many wineries set up by Dalmatian immigrants earlier in the century. However, in 1986 a change of name from Panorama to West Brook symbolized a change of direction. Anthony Ivicevich is the third generation. His grandfather and great-uncle bought land in Henderson in 1935 and a winery was built a couple of years later. The first wines, following the traditional 'port' and 'sherry' styles of the Dalmatians, were sold in old beer bottles for 1/6d. a bottle. Anthony Ivicevich's father had continued the tradition of fortified wine, with considerable reluctance to contemplate any change, and it was only when Anthony himself took over from his father in 1985 that they began producing table wine.

It entailed a considerable transformation. Ninety per cent of their production was fortified at the time, with thirty-six different labels for fortified wines and also liqueurs. Not only were there 'sherries', made from Baco 22A, Palomino and various Seibel varieties, but also fruit liqueurs, and cherry and apricot brandy. While the name of Panorama has been retained as the label for the remaining fortified wines, namely a little 'sherry' and old tawny 'port', the winery name was changed in 1986 and it remains very much a family affair. Anthony's son Michael is training at Wagga Wagga, and his wife Sue helps with paperwork and visitors.

West Brook is named after the nearby rail stop, and their better range of wine introduced in 1992 is labelled Blue Ridge, for the Waitakere Ranges seem blue in the distance. They have a small vineyard of Chardonnay, Cabernet and Merlot in Henderson, and buy in grapes from Hawke's Bay and Gisborne. Their most unusual wine is a Wood-Aged Sémillon which spends nine months in French *barriques* and American puncheons. The 1990 had a honeyed, leafy flavour with firm acidity. They also produce Chenin Blanc, in preference to Müller-Thurgau, for fruity easy drinking, as well as some lightly honeyed Riesling. The Blue Ridge range comprises Chardonnay, Sauvignon and a Cabernet Merlot.

The transformation in the winery has been effective. In 1995, 90 per cent of their production was table wine, while fortified wines remained as a very small part of the business. Anthony Ivicevich has great hopes for the future, especially with his son's professional training.

West Brook Winery, 34 Awaroa Road, (PO Box 21-443) Henderson, telephone/fax: (09) 838 8746

SOUTH AUCKLAND

Montana

Montana is the giant in the New Zealand wine industry, accounting for 40 per cent of the country's wine production and a comparable share in the vineyards. However, like all things it had small beginnings. Ivan Yukich came from Dalmatia, first as a lad of fifteen, then went back to Dalmatia to return again to New Zealand with a wife and two sons. He earned his living as a market gardener, then planted a small vineyard in the Waitakere Ranges west of Auckland calling it Montana, which is the Croatian word for 'mountain'. The first release of a Montana wine came in 1944.

The company grew under the impetus of his two sons: Mate, the viticulturist, and above all Frank, the winemaker and salesman. Frank Yukich had an unparalleled vision of expansion with the energy to match. He was responsible for the innovative planting in Marlborough and he had already expanded into Gisborne and the Waikato. It seemed that there were no limits to his vision. However, in 1973, the same year that the first vines were planted in Marlborough, Seagrams gained a significant shareholding in Montana with the result that Frank Yukich departed. There simply was not room for such a large personality in the Seagrams scheme of things.

Montana is now owned by Corporate Investments and today the head office and bottling facilities are in Glen Innes, a suburb of Auckland. They also have wineries in Hawke's Bay, Marlborough and Gisborne, descriptions of which are in the relevant chapters. Montana in Auckland is very much a central warehouse and bottling plant, a vast complex of vats for storage and blending.

To have an idea of the philosophy of Montana you need to talk to Peter Hubscher, an energetic stocky man with a sharp commercial brain who has been general manager of the company since 1991. I found it interesting to compare Montana with the other giant of the industry, Corbans. There are two main differences. Whereas Corbans allow their individual winemakers great freedom, Montana expect theirs to conform to company philosophy and pay attention to the collective corporate goal which is, above all, 'value for money'. People are allowed to be creative within their different areas, but they must produce good-quality wine on a large scale, and that they do. Montana's Marlborough Sauvignon has proved the point, in many cases providing wine drinkers who are newcomers to New Zealand with an easy introduction to a flavour that is inexpensive but packed with value. Montana put more money into that than into small specialized projects but, that said, Hubscher still maintains that they are 'dedicated to excellence in a commercial way'. The past few years have seen a dramatic improvement in some of their wines, particularly in their red wines from Hawke's Bay in conjunction with Cordier, and the development of their sparkling wines in association with Champagne Deutz.

Also significant, and quite different from Corbans, is the importance which they attach to their own vineyards. Instead of relying on contract growers for the bulk of their needs, they have over 1,000 hectares (2,500 acres) of vineyards in Marlborough, Hawke's Bay and Gisborne, and are continually working to improve those vineyards, replanting them or changing them by grafting to move away from Chasselas or Müller-Thurgau towards better varieties, with more suitable training and pruning methods. Where once the majority of their vineyards were used for bulk wine, the reverse is now true, with most intended for quality varietals. This allows them to realize greater returns off their own land. They are prepared to bid on the open market for bulk grapes if necessary, but they want to control their own destiny where quality varietals are concerned. They are continually evaluating different sites with this in mind.

There is no doubt that Montana has fulfilled Frank Yukich's vision for export horizons and will continue to do so, with a series of wines that demonstrate sound quality in quantity.

Montana Wines, 171 Pilkington Road, (PO Box 18 293) Glen Innes, telephone: (09) 570 8400, fax: (09) 570 8440

St Nesbit

Tony Molloy is a charming and articulate tax lawyer who planted a vineyard in the early 1980s on a southern arm of the Manukau Harbour at Karaka, south of Auckland. The land had originally been a dairy farm and the winery is an old cow shed fitted with stainless-steel milk tanks which transform easily into wine vats, except that they are much shallower than usual, but no matter.

St Nesbit is named after Molloy's grandfather Nesbit Sneddon, a former New Zealand cricket captain whom Molloy chose to canonize in respect of his uncle, a priest in Rome who first introduced him to wine. What is unusual about St Nesbit is that Molloy produces just one wine, unlike virtually any other New Zealand winery, and it is red wine in a country that is deemed to do best with whites. Cabernet Sauvignon, Cabernet Franc and Merlot are the main grape varieties, and soon there will be Petit Verdot and Malbec in the blend too. Exact proportions depend on the vintage. The 1989 was mainly Cabernet as the waxeyes feasted greedily on the Merlot. Petit Verdot has been much longer coming into production than Molloy would have wished, as his attempt to import the vines were foiled by bureaucratic import and quarantine regulations. Happily, the situation has been resolved.

Molloy's first vintage was 1984 and for his first few vintages he bought in grapes until his own vineyards came into production. I always admire Molloy's energy, for not only is he working full time as a Queen's Counsel, but he is also devoting almost equal attention to his wines and to his large family. St Nesbit is very much more than a hobby. It represents a challenge to prove that New Zealand is able to produce world-class red wines.

Molloy loves an opportunity to compare his various vintages. The first time I met him, I was treated to vertical tasting from 1984 to 1989 – in other words, every vintage he had made that was in bottle. There is a definite thread of similarity of flavour running through the wines, with characteristics that are not dissimilar to Bordeaux, but yet not quite claret. There is an underlying elegance, with soft tannins, some berry fruit, notes of cedarwood and a smoky quality. The wines do not have the weight or power that you can find on Waiheke or in Hawke's Bay, but above all they have elegance, in a certain indefinable European way.

Unusually for New Zealand, Molloy uses natural yeast and the wine spends about eighteen months in mostly new oak barrels. Molloy also gives his wine considerable bottle age before selling it. As I write in 1995, the current release is the 1989. The 1990 and 1991 are both still firm and tannic.

St Nesbit has been a lone vineyard in Karaka, but with the widespread explosion of grape growing others have followed Molloy's example. In the course of 1994, at least eight people have planted vines in the area.

St Nesbit, Hingaia Road, Papakura, (PO Box 2647) Auckland, telephone: (09) 379 0808, fax: (09) 377 6956

Villa Maria

If you should find yourself driving near Auckland airport behind a grey Mercedes with the number plate VILLA, you are tailing George Fistonich, the founder, general manager and principal shareholder of Villa Maria. While the Villa Maria group includes Vidal and Esk Valley in Hawke's Bay, it is Villa Maria itself that concerns us here. Fistonich's father Andrew arrived from Croatia in 1930. He worked in the gumfields and, in good Dalmatian tradition, made a bit of wine for his family and friends before finally becoming a licensed winemaker in 1949 with a tiny winery called Mountain Vineyards. Fistonich was destined for the building trade, but gave up his apprenticeship to found a new company, Villa Maria, in 1961. The name was chosen because it had an international ring to it.

The last time I met Fistonich, I encouraged him to reminisce. He was a one-man band for most of the 1960s, seeing the tail end of the old winemaking styles dominated by 'port' and 'sherry', and the start of the new. At the beginning, his winery was full of large old totara barrels without a single stainless-steel tank in sight. He was a member of the Young Winemakers' Club which included Ivan Selak, Joe Babich, Nick Nobilo and others who were curious about the potential for table wines. When Müller-Thurgau was first introduced in the late 1960s, it was like discovering a new clone of Chardonnay today. He remembered Bryce Rankin judging Müller-Thurgau and talking about the need to use refrigeration as recently as the beginning of the 1970s. The influence of Australian wine-makers has opened up the industry, increasing its acceptance of new ideas. It has been a veritable snowball.

However, Villa Maria still remains true to its early origins, continuing to produce the 'sherries' and 'ports' that its more elderly customers enjoy. As we tasted a range of varietals, with fine examples of Cabernet and Chardonnay, in an area adjoining Villa's shop, I watched the older generation arriving to fill up bottles of 'Golden Sherry' and 'Madeira Port'. Fistonich admitted that the 'sherries' all come from the same base wine, with more sweetening and caramel added according to the desired flavour. He remembered trying to improve the quality a few years ago, but the die-hard customers protested. This was the traditional taste of the immediate post-war wine drinker of New Zealand and that was what they wanted.

Yet I must emphasize that Villa Maria keeps well abreast of the winemaking developments of recent years with an excellent range of varietals. Kym Milne, the talented Australian winemaker, was at Villa Maria when I first visited the winery in 1991; since then, Grant Edmonds has continued Kym's good work. He has now moved on to make his own wine in Hawke's Bay and his place has been taken by Michelle Richardson, while overall winemaking responsibilities for the Villa Maria Group have been given to Andrew Phillips, an Australian who has been working with Brown Brothers in Victoria.

Essentially, Villa Maria's wines come in three categories. Best of all are the Reserve wines, followed by Cellar Selection, then Private Bin. Fistonich and Edmonds treated me to a comprehensive tasting of the range on my last visit in October 1994.

Highlights included the 1994 Private Bin Sauvignon from Marlborough, with some fresh, pithy gooseberries. This contrasted with the Reserve Sauvignon, also from Marlborough, which included a small amount of contact with oak. Just 10 per cent of the juice is put into wood, half new and half one-year-old barrels, half-way through the fermentation. The juice was very ripe in the first place. Edmonds likened it to Wattie's canned peaches and syrup which are familiar to all New Zealand children. Happily, the wine bore no relation to tinned peaches, but was ripe and mouth-filling, with some pungent Sauvignon fruit.

As for Chardonnay, they make two Private Bin wines: one from Gisborne, with the full, rich flavours of the region and one from Marlborough, which is tighter with firmer acidity. Reserve Chardonnay from Marlborough is more toasted in character, but always with good acid structure, while the barrel-fermented Chardonnay has a fine balance of oak and fruit. Villa Maria take credit for coining the phrase 'barrel fermented' and were one of the first to do so in the mid-1980s, along with John Hancock at Delegat's, then Morton Estate.

Private Bin Riesling comes from Marlborough, with some slatey, stony fruit and a hint of honey, confirming Edmonds's belief in the potential for Riesling in New Zealand. Villa Maria have also had great success with their Hawke's Bay Noble Riesling. It was first made in 1991. They actively encourage the botrytis by not spraying, which of course incurs the risk of grey rot instead. The 1993 is deliciously concentrated, with sweet peachy fruit and good acidity. A Reserve Gewürztraminer is produced from a vineyard near the airport. It has the dry, oily style of Alsace and a restrained nose.

Villa Maria already have a sound reputation for their red wines with Reserve Cabernet Sauvignon from Hawke's Bay. However, they anticipate great things for New Zealand in the next few years as they obtain better fruit from better vineyards, planted in the right areas on the right rootstock and with virus-free clones. Steve Smith, who is based in Hawke's Bay at Vidal's, is one of the country's most talented viticulturists and has been involved in the development of their new vineyards. They have just planted 40 hectares (100 acres) with Riesling, Chardonnay, Sauvignon and Sémillon in Marlborough in the Awatere Valley, further inland from Vavasour on a terrace about sixty feet above the river. They have also a new vineyard on Gimblett Road in Hawke's Bay, as well as another land purchase to plant. Gisborne, Hawke's Bay and Marlborough are the chief sources of their grapes as well as the odd local vineyard and some contract growers at Te Kauwhata. They believe in a certain flexibility regarding the different regions and also that regions can be blended to give you a consistency of style. In that instance, there are two names rather than one regional name on the label.

Villa Maria successfully weathered the turmoil in the industry during the mid-1980s and survived financial difficulties. Combined with Esk Valley and Vidal's, the Villa Maria Group is one of the big four players in the Wine Institute and is set to continue its progress into the next century.

Villa Maria Estate, 5 Kirkbride Road, (PO Box 43-046) Mangere, Auckland, telephone: (09) 275 6119, fax: (09) 275 6618

9

Waiheke Island

Waiheke is rather like the Isle of Wight. It is close enough to the mainland not to feel isolated, yet far enough away for the pace of life to change the moment you embark on the ferry that transports you across the Hauraki Gulf away from the bustle of Auckland and its lively harbour. There is something about the island atmosphere that makes me relax the moment I reach the landing stage at Matiatia Wharf. I always feel as though I am there on holiday, even if I have a day of wine tasting ahead of me.

Goldwater Estate

On my first visit, Kim and Jeanette Goldwater were there to greet me with a warm, friendly welcome. They were in effect the first to plant vines on the island back in 1978. There had been a small amount of 'port' and 'sherry' and a trickle of table wines produced by the Gradiska family at Ostend in the 1950s, but while some of the old hybrid vines remain, production had stopped some time ago. It was the Goldwaters' love affair with sailing that brought them to Waiheke in the first place, buying what New Zealanders call a holiday bach, a simple bungalow. From 1983 they have lived on the island permanently, devoting themselves to Goldwater Estate. Theirs is a delightful spot in Putiki Bay, with a weatherboard house and a small winery adjoining, surrounded by vines and with views over the bay.

The Goldwaters have 3.25 hectares (8 acres) of vines in production and were planning to plant another 2.43 hectares (6 acres) during the winter of 1995, taking cuttings from their own vines. In their own vineyards they concentrate on Cabernet Sauvignon and Merlot, while Chardonnay comes from the nearby Delamore vineyard and also from Marlborough, as does a Sauvignon. For the Goldwaters, Cabernet and Merlot are what Waiheke does best. 'It is our summer in a bottle,' said Jeanette, as we tasted their 1993 Cabernet Merlot. Although this was a cool year throughout most of the country, on Waiheke it was a wonderful summer, making for some lovely ripe fruit and wines with good extract, body and length – in other words, a reflection of the quality of Waiheke.

Waiheke Island does indeed have considerable advantages over the mainland for grape growing, for it is significantly drier than Auckland. The rain that comes across the Tasman Sea falls on Auckland, and on a fifty-year cycle statistics demonstrate that on average it has 30 per cent less rainfall than Auckland, though more than both Marlborough and Hawke's Bay. Most of the wineries and vineyards are on the north side of the island, as the prevailing winds tend to come from the south. The gentle sea breezes help dispose of any humidity, while the maritime influence tempers night-time temperatures. The greatest climatic hazards are cyclones, but happily these are a rare event. The island also has more hours of sunshine than Auckland, for there is less cloud cover and no mountains or forests to affect the cloud formation. You can often look out towards the mainland and see a bank of cloud that seems to stop a couple of miles short of the island. Consequently, the grapes often ripen as much as ten days earlier than in the vineyards around Auckland.

The soil is also quite different from the mainland. It is mainly volcanic, very poor and stony, free-draining, with seams of rock, some clay and a high magnesium content. Little grows in it. Before the development of the vineyards, any farmland was used for sheep and cattle, but the last two or three years have seen a veritable explosion in vineyard acreage, but as yet no significant increase in the number of wineries. For the moment, the production is vinified at existing wineries.

Goldwater Estate, 18 Causeway Road, Putiki Bay, Waiheke Island, telephone: (09) 372 7493, fax: (09) 372 6827

Stonyridge Vineyard

Stephen White at Stonyridge Vineyard was next to follow the Goldwaters' example. This is another enchanting spot, a pretty pink-façaded house with the winery underneath and a veranda that turns into a café at weekends, offering views of the vineyards on north-facing slopes. These are hillside vineyards, with good slopes providing the necessary exposure of sunlight to the vines, in contrast to the vineyards of the plains on the mainland. Rose bushes were in flower at the end of each row. With White's enthusiasm for all things Mediterranean, he has also planted olive trees which produce some tasty black olives, as well as fig trees and little cork oaks, laurel and oleander, and various southern herbs, rosemary and lavender, all of which enjoy the climate of Waiheke. White practises organic viticulture and his vines are planted 1 metre apart, which for New Zealand is very close indeed.

White studied horticulture at Lincoln College, then went to California and on to Bordeaux where he worked at Château d'Angludet. He sees Peter Sichel as his mentor and inspiration for the wines he is making at Stonyridge. His is the first New Zealand vineyard to have all five Bordeaux varieties: Cabernet Sauvignon, Cabernet Franc, Merlot and, more unusually, Malbec and Petit Verdot. The last is most unusual of all. Tony Molloy of St Nesbit was the first to bring it into the country at a time when the importation of vine cuttings was beset by bureaucratic as well as quarantine restrictions. White has just 1 per cent of Petit Verdot which has now produced three vintages. He is very enthusiastic about it, considering it ripens more easily on Waiheke than in the Gironde, and finds that it provides both colour and acidity. He also loves Malbec for its fruit and colour. It is big and strong when it is young, but the tannins do not last and it gives only half the average crop of Cabernet, making it an accountant's nightmare. White also produced a little Syrah for the first time in 1994, but he is not yet convinced of its quality. The fruit is good, but there is no guts to the wine, which may be a reflection on the youth of the vines. There is also a tiny amount of Grenache and Mourvèdre, but for the moment they are grown very much on an experimental basis.

The reputation of Stonyridge is built on White's Bordeaux blend which he calls Larose. The very first vintage was in 1985; 1987 saw the first serious wine. He pays great attention to the details of winemaking. He has a tiny barrel room under the house, with a neat cellar of stainless-steel tanks. Natural yeasts are used and the wine undergoes a fairly lengthy maceration after the primary fermentation to extract colour and substance. The wine spends a year in wood, mainly medium-toasted Nevers from Seguin Moreau, some of which is new and some two or three wines old. The barrels are racked every three months, but there is no fining or filtering and gravity is used as much as possible.

We tasted the 1993 to the accompaniment of Puccini's *Madame Butterfly* playing from the cellar. The precise blend of this vintage is 57 per cent Cabernet Sauvignon, 27 per cent Merlot, 9.5 per cent Malbec, 6 per cent Cabernet Franc and a minute 0.5 per cent Petit Verdot, which were blended together before the wine goes into barrel. When it was just two years old, the young Larose was showing immense concentration, with good tannin, fruit and length, and several layers of complexity. White aims for ripeness with cool-climate complexity, while maintaining the varietal character of the wine, which he certainly does with recognizable and stylish Cabernet Sauvignon. The 1994, tasted as a barrel sample, had a spicy nose of new oak and again good concentration, coming as it does from a smaller vintage. The 1992 was technically ripe, but lacked body, so White declassified it into a second label Airfields, so called because his winery is right by Waiheke's tiny airstrip.

Stonyridge Vineyard, 80 Onetangi Road, (PO Box 265) Ostend, Waiheke Island, telephone: (09) 372 8822

Peninsula Estate

The third winery is Peninsula, which takes its name from its dramatic position on Hakaimango Point, with a 2.43-hectare (6-acre) vineyard exposed to the elements on every side. There is a tower in the vineyard from which there are magnificent views of the Coromandel Peninsula, Oneroa Bay and other nearby vineyards. Doug Hamilton was a car mechanic running the local garage before he turned to viticulture and planted his first vines in 1986. He made his first wine three years later. Hamilton's vineyard consists mainly of Cabernet Sauvignon, with some Merlot, and a little Cabernet Franc and Malbec. He is very much concentrating on red wine. His 1993 Peninsula Cabernet Merlot has some ripe berry fruit and some solid, chunky tannins. It is good, but it lacks the finesse of White's wine. However, the 1991 was more elegant, with some smoky cedarwood flavours, but a little lacking in substance. It spent about one year in wood, in a functional cellar that is run by Hamilton's winemaker Chris Lush.

Peninsula Estate Wines, 52a Korora Road, Oneroa, Waiheke Island, telephone/fax: (09) 372 7866

Te Motu

The most recent arrival on the Waiheke wine scene, but not in the New Zealand wine industry, is Terry Dunleavy with his wine Te Motu. The name comes from the full Maori name for the island, Waiheke Te Motu, meaning 'the island of long shelter'. It was one of Terry's sons, Paul, who first had the idea of buying land on Waiheke with his father's involvement, and it is another son, John, who with his wife Debbie lives on the island and is responsible for the day-to-day running of the vineyard. After Terry's long involvement with the New Zealand wine industry, it seems appropriate on retiring as the Wine Institute's Executive Officer that he should turn his attention to the practical side of the industry with the dedication that he has exercised in its other fields.

The Dunleavys have bought a 11.73-hectare (29-acre) property just across the hill from Stonyridge and an old Maori pa in the Onetangi area by the airfield. So far they have planted 4 hectares (10 acres). They have Cabernet Sauvignon, Cabernet Franc and Merlot and are considering Petit Verdot, but not Malbec. The vineyard is neat and well maintained, with rose bushes at the end of the rows of vines and a windbag flapping for the benefit for any pilot landing on the tiny airstrip. A small shed constitutes the winery so far, which is where the grapes are fermented, but the maturation in wood takes place at Matua Valley. They are mainly using Demptos American oak, as well as some one-year-old French oak.

With Dunleavy's sense of occasion, the very first vine they planted was christened with a bottle of 1982 San Marino (now Kumeu River) Trinity made from Müller-Thurgau, Gewürztraminer and Riesling. The first vine of the second block enjoyed a 1951 Tom McDonald Cabernet which is highly prized among New Zealand's older vintages; that vineyard is now called the Tom McDonald block. The first vintage of 1993 Te Motu Cabernet Merlot is wonderfully concentrated, with closed cassis fruit on the nose and palate, with great length, extract and tannin. As Dunleavy quipped, this is definitely not a doughnut wine with a hollow middle. Indeed, it is one of the growing number of wines which belie the observation that New Zealand cannot produce good red wine.

Waiheke Vineyards, 76 Onetangi Road, Onetangi, Waiheke Island (21 Ocean View Road, Milford 1309, Auckland), telephone: (09) 486 3859, fax: (09) 486 2341

The Newcomers

There has been a intense mushrooming of vineyards on Waiheke in the last few years, with people planting vines on land that was considered pretty useless for anything else. Lifestyle and the appeal of living on an island that is so close to a thriving city are the main motives of the newcomers. In most instances, wine does not provide their main source of income. As a consequence of this growth, land prices have risen dramatically. Stephen White paid $40,000 for his 10-hectare (25-acre) block in 1982; in contrast, the adjoining 4-hectare (10-acre) plot with an attractive house, gardens and orchard sold in 1995 for $365,000. At the last count there were twenty vineyards on Waiheke, totalling about 66.8 hectares (165 acres), of which more than one-third have been planted since 1993.

So who are the newcomers? Rainer Eschenbruch, who worked with Tom van Dam at Rongopai, has planted 2 hectares (5 acres) of Merlot, Syrah and Pinot Noir, together with a German partner. Stephen White made the first vintage from Barry Fenton's new vineyard in 1992. Although the grape varieties are similar, the wine is apparently quite different in taste as the vines are grown on cooler terrain. Gulf Crest is another new vineyard in the Onetangi area close to Stonyridge and Waiheke Vineyards which has been set up by Dr Barnett Bond with three partners. So far they have planted Merlot and Cabernet Sauvignon on a splendid site overlooking Onetangi beach.

Doug Hamilton is involved in a project with his neighbour Robert Gilmour, who has planted Cabernet Sauvignon, Cabernet Franc, Merlot, Syrah and Chardonnay. Altogether there are five vineyards in the Church Bay area, including the Delamore vineyard of Chardonnay which supplies Goldwater Estate. Also at Church Bay there is ferry operator George Hudson's vineyard of Cabernet Sauvignon. These are all people who have other careers, such as Nick Jones of Croll Ridge, named after an early pioneering family. Millionaire John Spencer owns a sizeable portion of the eastern end of the island and has planted a 1.6-hectare (4-acre) vineyard. Tony Forsyth of the Sheffield Consulting Group is developing the Te Whau vineyard on the Te Whau Peninsula. The growth seems never-ending, prompting Kim Goldwater to comment that 'we are becoming a winery society, rather than a café society'.

GREAT BARRIER ISLAND

John Mellars

A postscript to Waiheke Island is provided by yet another new island vineyard on Great Barrier Island which lies some sixty-five kilometres out from Auckland harbour. You can see it in the distance from Waiheke. It is wetter as it is more exposed to the rain clouds, with higher mountains that encourage rainfall. An enthusiast by the name of John Mellars has planted vines there. Apparently he tried Pinot Noir first which did not work and now has 1.2 hectares (3 acres) of Cabernet and Merlot. The island is covered with forestry and park land. There are sheep and cattle and holiday homes, and it sounds as unlikely a place for a vineyard as when the Goldwaters first planted their vines on Waiheke Island.

  John Mellars of Great Barrier Island, Okupu Beach, Great Barrier Island, telephone: (09) 429 0361

10

Waikato and the Bay of Plenty

WAIKATO

The Waikato is a area of fertile agricultural land south of Auckland. There is the occasional winery, but they are situated there more for historical reasons than for any firm belief in the suitability of the land for viticulture. Indeed, they often source grapes from other areas. However, Romeo Bragato set up the Te Kauwhata Research Station in the Waikato at the end of the last century, although no one quite knows why he chose this area rather than any other. Driving south from Auckland to De Redcliffe you pass lush green fields. The area enjoys a climate similar to that of Auckland, with warm average temperatures and high humidity.

De Redcliffe

De Redcliffe was set up in 1976 by Chris Canning, who planted vineyards and built a winery which he called De Redcliffe after a family name. His first vintage was 1980. Things were going well, but then in 1987 he decided to increase production and at the same time to build a hotel, financed by a flotation on the Auckland stock exchange. But by 1990 they had overspent and the business was bought by Japanese company Otaka Holdings, who have refurbished both the hotel and the winery. Canning is no longer involved with De Redcliffe and the wine is made by Mark Compton who trained at Wagga Wagga and worked in the Barossa Valley, then at Montana, before joining De Redcliffe.

It is an attractive setting in the Mangatawhiri Valley, with a stylish and comfortable hotel called appropriately and unoriginally the Hotel du Vin, with a restaurant and an adjoining winery surrounded by vines. They are planted in a very stony site on what

145

was an old river bed. Dams in the nearby rivers reduce the level of the water-table further, but nevertheless irrigation is unnecessary. Chardonnay, Sémillon, Pinot Noir and Cabernet Sauvignon are grown here and account for about a third of De Redcliffe's grape requirements. In addition, they have developed vineyards in both Marlborough and Hawke's Bay which undeniably have enhanced the quality of their wines. In future, Cabernet and Merlot will be sourced entirely from Hawke's Bay, while Riesling and Sauvignon come from Marlborough.

The winery is neat and streamlined, with a variety of different-sized tanks allowing for flexibility in handling the grapes. The purchase of a new airbag press in 1991 resulted in a quantum leap forward in quality. You can look down on the insulated barrel hall from above. Work with the barrels is controlled with meticulous attention to detail, with topping up regularly every two weeks. The lees are not stirred as Compton wishes to avoid introducing oxygen into the wine. Everything is very carefully orchestrated and the resulting range of wines is sound and reliable, but maybe slightly lacking in flair.

Mangatawhiri Chardonnay is their most individual wine. It is quite structured and not overly oaked. The 1991 Marlborough Riesling was particularly attractive, with good slatey, honeyed characters. Cabernet Merlot tended to lack depth and we finished with a curious Dessert Cabernet which tasted rather like ratafia and is made by adding alcohol to the juice to stop the fermentation once it has reached 5°.

De Redcliffe, RD 1, Lyons Road, Pokeno (PO Box 7063, Wellesley Street, Auckland), telephone: (09) 302 3325, fax: (09) 303 3726

Aspen Ridge

Aspen Ridge at Te Kauwhata, just down the road from the old research station, is quite different in style. Alister McKissock has had a varied career, working at Davis in California, then at Te Kauwhata in the mid-1960s, before setting up his own small winery. It is the sort of place where Heath Robinson would feel quite at home. Alister and Isabelle now produce Harvest Red and Harvest White from an eclectic collection of grapes – such as Blauburgunder, Macabeo and Grüner Veltliner – as well as a dry 'sherry' from Palomino and a 'ruby port' in which there was a little of everything. There was even a coffee liqueur. The wines have remained in something of a time warp. What was a surprise and much more appealing was their sparkling Sauvignon juice, which had excellent varietal character, with lovely juicy fruit. This is how a teetotaller could appreciate the pungency of the grape variety.

Aspen Ridge Estate Wines, Waerenga Road, (RD 1) Te Kauwhata, telephone: (07) 826 3595, fax: (07) 826 3143

Rongopai

From Aspen Ridge I went to Rongopai, started in 1982 by Tom van Dam with his wife Faith and Rainer Eschenbruch, who is now involved with a vineyard on Waiheke. Both van Dam and Eschenbruch were scientists at Te Kauwhata and went into partnership buying land and planting vines in 1984 to make their first wines in 1986. Eschenbruch has since moved on and the van Dams, together with a new partner from Perth in Scotland, have just purchased the old facilities of the Te Kauwhata Research Station. When I met them, they were in the process of moving out of their original winery, a neat shed which they had simply outgrown – a leap from 2,000 to 12,500 square feet.

In fact Rongopai, which means 'five good senses' in Maori, existed as a winery in the 1930s and 1940s. It was owned by the Gordon family who produced 'port' and 'sherry' and some rather dubious table wines. It was at its most successful when it supplied the American soldiers stationed in New Zealand during the Second World War and it ceased production in the late 1960s.

Now, with the acquisition of the Te Kauwhata cellars, it has taken on new dimensions. There is a planned increase in production from 100 to 200 tonnes. The old winery presents quite a challenge as a relic of the early New Zealand wine industry, equipped with large concrete vats and huge old barrels that came from Germany.

They make a varied range of table wines, with two tiers of quality. Winemaker's Selection is for the better wines, and none was produced in 1992 or 1993. Their Sauvignon is ripe and fruity. It presents little choice for the winemaker, but it 'sells like hot cakes' and generates lots of cash flow. A Barrel Selection Sauvignon satisfies consumer demand, but van Dam admits that it does not excite him. Part of the wine is fermented then matured in oak for ten months, making a tight, oaky wine with underlying fruit. However, I was inclined to agree with van Dam's opinion of it.

Their Riesling was delicious, with a youthful, fresh 1994 and a riper, more mature 1993 that had notes of kerosene and a concentration of honey. The Chardonnay is ripe and toasted, and there is also some Pinot Noir which shows potential. However, the originality of Rongopai is its late harvest botrytized wines. Van Dam explained how their vineyards are virtually surrounded by water. The nearby Waikari Lake, which represents some 4,047 hectares (10,000 acres) of water that is only 3 metres deep, has a considerable effect on temperature and microclimate. In addition, there is the Waikato River and the Whangamarino wet lands, a vast expanse of swampland which helps to encourage the development of botrytis. A south-east wind is necessary to provide the combination of morning mist and afternoon sunshine which helps botrytis develop.

In their 4-hectare (10-acre) Swan Road vineyard they have planted varieties that are particularly susceptible to botrytis, early ripening and thin skinned, such as Würzer (a cross between Müller-Thurgau and Gewürztraminer), Müller-Thurgau, Scheurebe and Bacchus. The 1993 Botrytis Reserve is a blend of all four varieties, with a Germanic nose, and peaches, apricots and honey on the palate. A 1993 Botrytized Chardonnay reached a record 44° Brix, which van Dam celebrated by opening a bottle of 1979 Pol Roger.

The first year they made botrytis wine was in 1987. The 1987 Riesling Auslese was deep golden in colour, with apricots and marmalade on the nose, and considerable concentration of fruit on the palate, with balancing acidity to prevent a cloying finish. The 1991 Botrytized Riesling had the characteristics of noble rot, but still needed time to develop in November 1994.

The botrytis wines are presented in thin Italian grappa bottles with a stylish label design portraying the clear blue skies of New Zealand. Inevitably, quantities have varied from year to year, with 1987 a record vintage producing 16,000 bottles. None was made from 1988 to 1990, nor in 1995; in 1991 and 1992, just 2,000 bottles; in 1993, 8,500 bottles; and in 1994, 4,000 bottles. They have a delightful individuality that takes advantage of the particular microclimate of the vineyards.

Rongopai Wines, 71 Waerenga Road, (PO Box 35) Te Kauwhata, telephone: (07) 826 3141, fax: (07) 826 3462

Totara

Totara is the oldest winery of the Waikato. It was set up in the 1920s by Chinese immigrant Joe Ah-Chan from Canton, who in 1924 planted a vineyard of Albany Surprise outside the town of Thames at the foot of the Coromandel Peninsula. He made his first wine in 1929. Thames was an old gold-mining town and at one time even larger than Auckland. Totara was originally known as Goldleaf Vineyards, but the name was changed after the nearby Totara Valley in 1950 when the winery was bought by Stanley Chan. He was no relation, but another Chinese man who had run a fruit shop in an Auckland suburb and made wine out the back of the shop as a sideline.

Goldleaf Vineyards had begun with just one corrugated shed in 1924 which still exists. Totara has simply grown up around it, with extensions added in a hotchpotch fashion. Today, next to the winery they have just one vineyard of Cabernet Sauvignon which is really only for show; they source most of their grapes from Marlborough and Hawke's Bay and now make some sound table wines, mainly Chardonnay and Sauvignon.

However, Totara has had a chequered history. Gilbert Chan, one of Stanley Chan's four sons and the only one to remain involved with the winery, explained how he learnt winemaking the hard way: as a schoolboy he helped in the cellar and vineyard after school. In the early 1950s they grew hybrid varieties, mainly Seibels, and later in the decade they established a reputation as grape-juice producers, as well as making 'Sauternes' from Seibel, Baco 22A and Muscat. In the 1960s they began making liqueurs and Totara is still known for its Totara Café, which is not unlike the Mexican coffee liqueur Kahlua and has a loyal following.

In the 1970s they planted *vitis vinifera* varieties. They produced 'ports' and 'sherries', then tried the bag-in-box market using Müller-Thurgau, Chenin Blanc and Muscat, but with unfortunate consequences. Gilbert's oldest brother made some bad mistakes as managing director and the quality of their wines dipped sharply. In 1989 Kevin Honiss, who sees himself as something of a market-ing whiz-kid, became the principal shareholder and is now turning the company around with some measure of success. In 1990 they sourced the best grapes possible with the help of Wayne Thomas, who had been involved with Montana's original planting in Marlborough, and this was reflected in their wines. I was one of the judges of the Air New Zealand show to award a trophy to their 1990 Chardonnay, which had some lovely toasted European notes. Both the 1993 and 1994 Chardonnay show promise.

I also tried their 'ports' and 'sherries': a Tawny 'Port' made from Albany Surprise and an old Palomino 'Sherry' which had been aged in old barrels had a pleasing nuttiness.

Totara Vineyards, Main Road, RD 1, Thames, telephone: (07) 868 6798, fax: (07) 868 8729

Ohinemuri

The winery takes its name from the river that runs through the dramatic Karangahake Gorge. Ohinemuri means in Maori 'the maiden that was left behind' and refers to a Maori story about the daughter of a chieftain falling in love with the guardian of the river. Ohinemuri is a delightful spot, even on a rather grey spring morning. It is just on the edge of the Waikato and quite far from any other winery. This was gold-mining country and the scenery is wild and rugged.

Ohinemuri was started by Horst and Wendy Hillerich. Horst comes from the Rheingau, where he concentrated on Riesling at Weingut Hulbert in Eltville. He arrived in New Zealand at the invitation of James Millton in 1987 and liked it so much that he tore up his return air ticket, then he met his wife Wendy. They have built a functional winery shed, but the showpiece of their property is a charming Latvian timber cottage built by a set designer from Covent Garden. This is now the winery café, through which they sell most of their wines.

The terrain is far from suitable for growing grapes. They have just one small vineyard close by which is really just for show, and they buy in grapes from Hawke's Bay and Gisborne, but mainly from the Waikato where they seek out the drier microclimates. They concentrate on Sauvignon, Chardonnay and Riesling, and also make some Gewürztraminer and Pinotage. Hillerich laughingly remembered how the first time he tasted Marlborough Sauvignon he had thought that some chemical had been added to it to produce such a pungent flavour! His own Sauvignon is now equally ripe and pungent, or else it is in a Fumé Blanc style, making quite a heavily oaked wine. The Riesling inevitably has Germanic nuances, and the Pinotage is light in colour and fruity on the palate, making a refreshing light red wine which may be New Zealand's answer to young Beaujolais.

Ohinemuri Estate Wines, Moresby Street, Karangahake, (PO Box 137) Paeroa, telephone/fax: (07) 862 8874

From Ohinemuri I went on to the Bay of Plenty, an hour's drive away though the Kaimai Range.

THE BAY OF PLENTY

The name Bay of Plenty was given to this region by Captain Cook, in contrast to Poverty Bay further down the coast. The region is rich and fertile, and not very suitable for viticulture because the soil is too rich and the climate too humid. There are just three wineries in the Bay of Plenty (of which the main town is Tauranga): Morton Estate, Mills Reef and Kanuka Forest.

Kanuka Forest

Kanuka Forest came on-stream after my visit to the area with its first release in December 1994. Tony and Julia Hassell have been planting Cabernet Sauvignon, Merlot, Chardonnay and Sauvignon since 1989, and now have just over 2.5 hectares of vines. Their winery is named after a picturesque belt of coastal kanuka – tall thin trees more commonly called ti trees – that adjoin the winery.

Kanuka Forest Wines, Moore Road, (RD 2) Thornton, Whakatane, telephone/fax: (07) 304 9963

Morton Estate

The public face of Morton Estate has for several years been the ebullient John Hancock. However, he is now in the process of transferring his energies into a new project in Hawke's Bay. Morton Estate was set up by Morton Brown in 1983. He has the reputation of being the only man to have made money from the wine industry in the 1980s when Morton Estate was floated as a public company and bought by the Australian wine company Mildara for a not inconsiderable sum. It then became part of a holding company, Appellation Vineyards, and changed hands again in mid-1995, so that it now belongs to John Coney, a successful land developer with business interests in Canada and Australia.

It is a charming place. The main winery building is fronted by an attractive Cape Dutch house inspired by Morton Brown's holiday in South Africa, with a restaurant next door. The quality of the wines of Morton Estate has been firmly established by its winemakers John Hancock and Steve Bird. They have a token 5 hectares of Pinot Noir next to the winery, but most of their fruit comes from their own vineyards in Marlborough and Hawke's Bay. Self-sufficiency has been their aim.

Morton Estate has a reputation for its sparkling wine, made predominantly from Pinot Noir with some Chardonnay. The non-vintage wine is very much fruit driven in style and spends twelve months on the lees, in contrast to four years for the vintage wine. Morton Estate Brut is quite full and solid in the mouth, with some good fruit, and the 1990, the current release on my visit in late 1994, was rich and yeasty.

Bird and I wandered round the barrel hall tasting from cask to cask. Both their White and Black Label Chardonnay spend time in wood. For Bird, there is no such thing as too much oak, but often there may not be enough fruit. Chardonnay is the star of their table wines, their central focus and the variety for which they have developed most of their vineyards. I like both the White and Black Label. The first is quite delicate and lightly nutty, while the second is a more solid, substantial, stylish wine, with riper fruit and a fuller, nuttier taste, its good acidity enabling it to develop with bottle age, such as the 1989 when it was six years old. Black Label is made only in the best years from the best vats. They also make an unoaked Chardonnay in their Mill Road Hawke's Bay range and Stonecreek is the name of their new vineyard in Marlborough.

As for red wines, they are working on Pinot Noir, experimenting with different techniques, and have also planted Syrah which is only just coming into production. They may try blending it with Cabernet Sauvignon and they are also waiting for some Sangiovese to come out of quarantine. There is Cabernet and Merlot too, as well as Sauvignon, but for the moment Morton Estate stands for excellence in Chardonnay.

Morton Estate Winery, SH 2, (RD 2) Katikati, telephone: (07) 552 0795, fax: (07) 552 0651

Mills Reef

When I met Paddy Preston in the spring of 1994 he was between wineries. His old winery he described as topsy-turvy and the new winery at Bethlehem, on the outskirts of Tauranga, was still a building site which would be ready for the 1995 vintage, so we tasted Mill Reef wines at his house and I enjoyed wonderful views over the water of Tauranga Harbour.

The first vintage of Mills Reef was 1989. Before that, the Prestons had made kiwi-fruit wine which remains a large part of their business, especially for the Japanese market. In some ways it is not dissimilar to making white wine and you can use some of the same equipment. Kiwis are harvested after the grapes. They are crushed so that they look rather like porridge and an enzyme is added to encourage the juice to fall out of the pulp. Then the fruit is slowly pressed. The juice is settled in the same way as grape juice, and sugar and yeast are added. The fermentation takes place in stainless-steel tanks and the wine is bottled about three months later. They make both dry and sweet kiwi-fruit wine. The dry version is delicate in flavour, lightly floral, not so unlike a Müller-Thurgau.

As for wine, they concentrate on Riesling, Sauvignon and Chardonnay, and also make some sparkling wine and a little Cabernet Sauvignon, all from Hawke's Bay fruit, under three different labels: Mere Road Selection, Mills Reef Hawke's Bay range and Elspeth, after Paddy Preston's mother. Mere Road Chardonnay is for early drinking and is only partially barrel fermented so that it tastes delicately buttery with soft, easy fruit. Both the Hawke's Bay and Elspeth Chardonnay are fully barrel fermented, but Elspeth is given more new oak, and they come from different vineyards. Elspeth tends to be fuller, riper and fatter, with more layers of flavour. The sparkling wine is ripe and fruity, quite toasted, with a full palate.

Mills Reef Winery, Moffat Road, Bethlehem, (PO Box 2247) Tauranga, telephone: (07) 576 8800, fax: (07) 576 8824

From Mills Reef I could have travelled further south past Rotorua to the new and untapped area of Galatea, where there is just one lone winery, Covell Estate. Bob and Desarei Covell have established a small vineyard following biodynamic standards and have planted Pinot Noir, Chardonnay, Cabernet Sauvignon, Merlot and Riesling. Their first vintage was 1991.

Instead, from Tauranga I had a bumpy journey in a cigar tube of an aeroplane, up to Auckland and back out again in the same Metroliner (as they are called) to Gisborne. It was a relief to arrive on terra firma, with James Millton there to welcome me.

11

Gisborne

The town of Gisborne is close to the most easterly point of New Zealand, proudly proclaiming that it sees the first light of the new day, and for this reason all hotel rooms in the town are already booked for the millennium festivities. The cliffs that dominate Poverty Bay bear the name of Young Nick's Head, in memory of the member of Captain Cook's crew who first sighted land after a long voyage across the southern Pacific from the Society Islands. Sydney Parkinson, who was on the expedition as the botanist Joseph Banks's natural history painter, writes on 5th October 1769:

> 'We had light breezes from the NE and pleasant weather: about two o'clock in the afternoon one of our people, Nicholas Young, Surgeon's boy, descried a point of land from the starboard bow at about nine leagues distance, bearing W and by N. We bore up to it and at sunset we had a good view of it. . . . .We regaled ourselves in the evening upon the occasion; the land was called Young Nick's Head and the boy received his reward".

It was a gallon of rum.

First impressions were favourable. The *Endeavour* took anchor in the large bay. Cook observed several canoes, people upon the shore and some houses in the country. He described the land 'on the sea coast as high with white steep cliffs and inland are very high mountains. The face of the country is of a hilly surface and appears to be clothed with wood and verdure'. Sadly initial contacts with the Maoris were not happy. Cook had intended to name the bay Endeavour Bay, after his ship, but instead he called it Poverty Bay, 'as it did not afford a single item we wanted, except a little firewood.' There is a large Maori population in Gisborne today, and they would like the name changed to Turanganui a

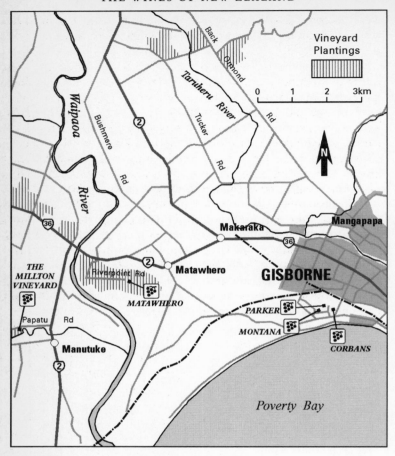

Gisborne (North Island)

Kiwi, to commemorate a Polynesian navigator, rather than have a constant reminder of the unfortunate incidents on Cook's arrival in New Zealand.

Today Gisborne is a lively little town, with a bustling centre and attractive weatherboard houses and pretty gardens in the residential area. The viewpoint from Kaiti hill offers a breathtaking vista over the bay and Young Nick's Head. As its foot is a maori marae, with some magnificent carvings. I stayed in the Whispering Sands Motel, which offered yet more wonderful views of the bay and the cliffs and the ocean beyond, and exhilarating walks along the beach after a day of intensive tasting. The beautiful coastline north of Gisborne towards Waikane beach is famous for surfing.

Vines were first planted in Gisborne in 1850, but this was something of a false start, as the Marist missionaries, Father Lampila and Brothers Basil and Florentin, sailing from Auckland, had mistaken Turanganui (as Gisborne was then called) for Hawke's Bay. Although they stayed long enough to plant vines they moved on the following year, further down the coast to their original destination. Father Lampila returned to Poverty Bay at the end of 1852 and recorded that he found the little vineyard that the brothers had planted bearing a small crop of well-ripened grapes, and, as wine for altar purposes was much needed, he spent some time in winemaking. But when he sent a small barrel of wine by sea to Hawke's Bay, the sailors broached the cask, drank the contents and refilled it with salt water. It was not an auspicious beginning to the Gisborne wine industry.

Romeo Bragato seems to have ignored Gisborne completely. From Napier he went on to Rotorua, and then to Te Puke and Tauranga. Next came an Austrian blacksmith, Peter Guschka, who planted about one hectare (a couple of acres) of Albany Surprise at the turn of the century, as a sideline. It was he, however, who helped and encouraged Friedrich Wohnsiedler to plant vines and set up Waihirere Wines. Wohnsiedler was born in Württemberg and brought up in a area where many of the population made their own wine for home consumption. He arrived in New Zealand at the turn of the century and first set up a small shop in Gisborne, but as a German national he was victim of anti-German sentiment after the First World War. His pork butchery and delicatessen was wrecked and in 1921 he turned to winemaking, planting vines at Ormond, to the north of the town, on a site that is today the source of one of Montana's single vineyard Chardonnays. First Wohnsiedler transported his wine by horse and cart, but by 1935 he had scraped together sufficient money to buy a motor car for his deliveries. Frank Thorpy in *Wine in New Zealand* describes how Wohnsiedler eventually established a winery that was noted for its double cellar of about 1200 feet, set, unusually for New Zealand at the time, four feet underground. At its peak Waihirere Wines was producing over 95,000 gallons a year, mainly of 'port', 'sherry' and 'madeira' and at his death in 1956 Wohnsiedler had a well established vineyard of about four hectares (ten acres).

The company continued to expand and by 1970 was responsible for over twenty hectares (fifty acres) of vines, as well as maintaining contracts with neighbouring farmers, growing such grapes as Baco 22A, Riesling Sylvaner, Palomino, Golden Chasselas, Pinot Meunier, Dr Hogg Muscat, Pinotage, Pinot Chardonnay and so on. As well as 'port' and 'sherry', they made Royal Muscat, 'Sauternes', 'moselle', dry white and red wines, Italian type vermouth and a formidable selection of cocktails and liqueurs.

Meanwhile Gisborne was attracting interest from other producers, notably Montana and Corbans, who had also developed contracts with local farmers, so that the vineyard area of Gisborne expanded dramatically from the mid-1960s. However the family-run Waihirere Wines encountered financial problems as it grew and finally in 1973 was bought by Montana. The name of Wohnsiedler lives on in one of their biggest selling lines for the domestic market, a light fruity Müller-Thurgau. Today the wine scene of Gisborne is dominated by Corbans and Montana, but there is more excitement and potential in the area than initially meets the eye.

Gisborne is cut off from the rest of the North Island by the Raukumara range, which isolates it climatically as well as geographically. The vineyards are mostly on the flats of Poverty Bay. Poverty Bay is in fact one large valley surrounded by hills on both sides and the flats are narrow valleys within it, separated by much smaller hills. There is a fine viewpoint where you can look down on what seems like a large plateau of vineyards. There is very little planting on the hillsides, as the ground is very unstable, with too much erosion to allow for steeply sloping vineyards. One of the main exceptions is a vineyard of Chardonnay and Pinot Noir planted by James Millton.

As well as vineyards, there are blocks of kiwi fruit, which are

protected by windbreaks, as well as orchards and acres of tomatoes, sweetcorn and squash. In fact tomatoes compete with grapes
in importance. There is competition for land for new plantings. In
1993 about 121 hectares (300 acres) of new vineyards were
planted, and in 1994 about another twenty (fifty), but the price of
land has risen, with 'the tomato guys paying ridiculous prices'. An
area of native bush, the kind of vegetation that Captain Cook
would have found, that once covered the area, is preserved at
Grays Bush. There are native trees such as kahikatea, which is a
white pine, and puriri. It is a small area of real forest, dense and
thick with just a little light filtering through the trees and birds
chattering noisily, making a dramatic contrast to the more peaceful
agricultural landscape.

There are considerable variations within the area, with nuances
of microclimate and soil. Specific areas are acquiring reputations,
such as Ormond, which is a narrow valley floor, which enjoys hot
dry summers with quite cold winters. Patutahi is a highly rated
area that is warm, with less rainfall than usual, as it is sheltered
from the cold southerlies. The soil is light and free draining and
suitable for Gewürztraminer and Chardonnay.

Climatically Gisborne has a higher heat summation with a long
growing season and warmer nights than Marlborough, which
boasts the highest sunshine hours, but has a shorter growing
season. Sea breezes temper the hotter years, with a prevailing north-
west wind. The main problem in Gisborne is humidity, and it tends
to have more autumn rainfall than other areas, 35 to 38 inches
per year, as opposed to Marlborough's 20 and Hawke's Bay's 30.
The depressions from the Tropics bring concentrated autumnal
rainfall, which can have a crucial effect on the vintage, resulting
in problems with rot. Normally they would try to control this with
preventive sprays and it can be overcome with good vineyard
management. The soil is very fertile, volcanic soil over sandstone.
The area is also prone to earthquakes as it lies on the main fault
line that runs along the ranges of the North Island. Apparently
this is easily visible from the air, but I have never seen it.

While Gisborne is known for Chardonnay and proclaims itself
to be The Chardonnay Capital of New Zealand, it is in fact Müller-
Thurgau that is still the most widely planted variety in the region,
used for wines like Montana's Wohnsiedler and their new Misty
Peak. Chardonnay comes next in order of importance, and then

Dr Hogg Muscat which features in Montana's Asti Spumante look-alike, Bernardino. It is New Zealand's biggest selling sparkling wine, but is not exported. However the great advantage of Chardonnay is that it is not too fussy about soil type and where it grows, so there is no doubt about its success in Gisborne.

Gisborne has been described as the breadbasket of the country, with the two key players, Montana and Corbans using the area to supply their needs for bulk wine. This image stems partly from the fact that there are few independent individual producers, to balance the profile of the area. However the reputation of Gisborne is growing as certain Auckland-based wineries have established vineyards in the area, including Nobilo's Dixon and Tietjen vineyards, Matua Valley's Judd Estate, as well as Montana's Ormond Estate and Corbans' Cottage Block Chardonnay.

Matawhero Wines

Even though the region is dominated by the two giants, the small producers have an individuality of their own, for some quite different reasons. Matawhereo was one of the original pacesetters, not just in Gisborne, but countrywide. Its wines were exported to Britain at the end of the 1970s, at a time when most of us were barely aware of the existence of New Zealand's wine industry. The first vines, Müller-Thurgau, were planted in 1968 by Bill Irwin, who not only was an enthusiastic and pioneering viticulturist, but also a bookseller. In the 1970s the importation of particular grape varieties and clones depended on individuals. This is what Irwin did, with great success. He brought in clones of Chardonnay, Gewürztraminer, Pinot Noir, Merlot and Cabernet.

His son Denis, who now runs Matawhero, is one of the more charismatic characters of the industry. His refreshing originality stems from a chequered and varied career, working for Nederburg in South Africa and spending time in Germany at the large cooperative at Breisach in Baden and at a small estate in the Rheingau. It was Denis who persuaded his father to plant Gewürztraminer, one of the varietals for which Matawhero is particularly known. Then during the 1980s be became obsessed by the Australian Gisborne, just outside Melbourne, and bought a vineyard there with the idea of taking Gisborne to Gisborne. He was also involved in the Bridge Hotel close to the winery, but both ventures brought financial complications in their wake. Irwin is now back at Matawhero, concentrating on rebuilding the reputation of the winery.

Tasting with Irwin is a fascinating experience, for wines are interspersed with Irwin's colourful views on life and wine. Subtlety and intellect are the things he most admires in a wine. He is anti wines that give everything at the first sip. It is the difference between a strip show at which the girl takes all her clothes off at once, or does it slowly. You have to introduce yourself to the wine and enjoy its ambience, the oak in the middle, the mystery at the bottom with a hook to make you want to sip it again. His wines are less obviously fruit driven than most other New Zealand wines and he makes wines that will develop and age more slowly than those of some of his colleagues. A 1989 Riesling Sylvaner threw a completely new light on Müller-Thurgau, with an unusually intense flavour for the variety, with weight and some wonderful apricot fruit. The 1993 version was still very young, with a fresh pithiness and some spritz.

Irwin is very reticent about detailing his winemaking methods. 'Late one night we think of something.' He sees oak as the vessel in which the wine is stored. 'I'm a wine merchant, not a timber merchant' and this sentiment was confirmed by a 1988 Chardonnay which had a lean mature style, with a European elegance. We wandered round his winery, which is a large shed full of stainless-steel tanks, tasting samples of Chardonnay and Sauvignon. His wines come solely from his own 24 hectare (60-acre) vineyard. The winery has taken the name of the particular area, with a separate block of vines called Bridge Estate after a dilapidated road bridge near by.

Irwin is particularly excited by his 1994 Gewürztraminer, which has characteristics that he has not seen since the 1974 vintage. It certainly had the most appealing, toasted spicy nose, with a very good fruit, acidity and body, making a distinctively stylish wine. A tank sample of 1993 Pinot Noir, which was about to go into barrel, showed considerable potential with some spicey fruit and vegetal undertones. A 1993 Syrah, also in vat, had some youthful peppery varietal character, with plenty of fruit, but not yet enough body, which may well be a reflection of the youth of the vines. 1990 was the first vintage of this variety at Matawhero. Although Gisborne is much more highly rated for its white wines, these reds certainly provided a convincing exception to the rule.

Matawhero Wines, Riverpoint Road, RD 1 Gisborne, telephone: (06) 8688366, fax: (06) 8679856

The Millton Vineyard

The Millton Vineyard is known as New Zealand's first registered organic vineyard, accredited by the Biological Producers' Council of New Zealand. Rippon have now followed suit, and others estates are working towards certification, and in some instances are very close to it, with transitional Bio-Gro status, such as Ata Rangi, Revington and Stonyridge, with others showing interest in organic viticulture. Not only are James and Annie Millton's methods organic, but they also follow the principles of Rudolf Steiner's bio-dynamics. They work by a predetermined calendar that establishes the best times for vineyard or cellar work by paying attention to the phases of the moon. For example, it is best to filter and rack when the moon is waning, while fermentations work better when the moon is rising. There is a lot of moisture in the vineyard when the moon is rising which subsides as the moon declines. This is the best time to spray with copper sulphate: it hardens the skins of the grapes and makes them more resistant to fungus.

James Millton arrived in Gisborne in 1980, 'looking for the ultimate vineyard' but, to quote Denis Irwin, you can spend your life looking for the ultimate vineyard, and he settled on Gisborne. His father-in-law was selling grapes to Montana, while James and Annie were becoming interested in organic viticulture. They questioned the enormous amounts of sprays used in the vineyard. A bill for chemicals in the mid-1970s came to between 35,000 and 40,000 dollars for just 4.45 hectares (11 acres) of vines. Their very first vintage was in 1984, but James spent the 1986 vintage at Château Soutard, an estate in St Emilion, then came back to New Zealand, leased vineyards, and bought them in 1989. They now have 3.44 hectares (8½ acres) of four different vineyards, mostly in the Manutuke district; the Opou Vineyard, which produces particularly good Riesling, as well as other varieties, the Riverpoint Vineyard at Matawhero for Chardonnay, the very steep Naboths Vineyard and a vineyard around the winery.

The Milltons believe that the strength of Gisborne lies in its soil, while the humidity results in wines, particularly Chardonnay, that have an early appeal which carries on as the wine develops. This was amply illustrated by a 1986 Chardonnay, which we enjoyed when it was eight years old. It had wonderful fruit, balanced with great elegance and structure. However they are still working out which varieties suit Gisborne best. They have decided on Riesling, Chenin blanc and Chardonnay, but are uncertain about Sauvignon. Gewürztraminer could also have a revival, but suffers from inconsistent yields, and resulting financial constraints. They also have one of the few steeply sloped vineyards of Gisborne, their Naboths Vineyard, which is planted with Chardonnay and Pinot Noir. They are very positive about the quality potential of Gisborne but recognized that it took a distinct dip at the end of the eighties when there was so much replanting of grafted vines to combat phylloxera. The only choice of rootstock at the time was SO4, which has proved neither suitable nor successful.

We tasted their current range of wines to the accompaniment of operatic arias over the loudspeaker in the cellar. First we looked at Chardonnay. Millton is adamant that contrary to popular perceptions, you can achieve delicacy from Gisborne Chardonnay. It is the percentage of new barrels that affects the final result, with a fine line between maturing the wine and overoaking it. He uses about ten per cent of new oak and would ideally like to keep his Chardonnay in barrel for a year or more. He is also obtaining some five hundred litre puncheons from the Tonnellerie de Bourgogne to see how they will perform. His 1993 Chardonnay comes from three different vineyards, with three different clones: clone 6 which gives softness and fruit; Mendoza which provides strength and acidity, and 2/23 which is very similar to clone 6, but with a more generous yield. The wine is blended in February and bottled in June or July and the resulting wine is one of great complexity and depth of flavour.

In contrast the 1992 Clos de Ste-Anne comes from their River point Vineyard with its low yielding vines, on which even more care has been lavished. The Milltons are convinced that a wine is conceived in the vineyard, and not in the cellar. They always use natural yeast and Clos de Ste-Anne Chardonnay undergoes a full malolactic fermentation, and tastes stylishly elegant, with good balance.

As for Riesling, Millton is inspired by Rainer Lingenfelder in the Palatinate. His 1994 Riesling from the Opou vineyard has a lovely honeyed character, with very good fruit and balancing acidity, possessing some of the elegant sweetness of the varietal. The fermentation is left to stop naturally, and in 1994 did so, leaving 27 grams per litre of residual sugar. The grapes were picked at the end of April, with some botrytis. A Spätlese was his aim, and he certainly succeeded.

The Milton Vineyard, Papatu Road, (PO Box 66) Manutuke, Gisborne, telephone: (06) 862 8680, fax: (06) 862 8869

Parker MC Ltd.

Phil Parker is another Gisborne original. His is the only winery in Gisborne, or come to that, in the North Island, that is dedicated to the production of sparkling wine. The winery name is Parker MC Ltd., with no prizes for guessing that MC stands for *méthode champenoise*. More zany is the elderly DC3, positioned as though it has crashed into the side of the winery building and adjoining wine bar which is appropriately named the Smash Palace. The concept is a great success. People arrive for a party, that may be in Madrid or Hawaii, board the plane and after a few drinks, return to the ground to find that the wine bar has been transformed, according to their destination, becoming alive with palm trees, or ladies with castanets dancing the flamenco. The bar provides an oasis of entertainment in the Gisborne industrial estate that adjoins the airport. View of Corbans immense tank farm from the windows of the DC3 may slightly detract from the charm. The bar is decorated with all manner of old signs, posters and bottles, and even a papier mâché budgie, for alternative bungee jumping, that is a leap over a budgie, rather than from a bridge. It is a winning formula, but Parker prefers to concentrate on his real enthusiasm: sparkling wine.

Parker is passionately committed to the region, lamenting that the large companies have promoted Marlborough and Hawke's Bay in favour of Gisborne. So many of their best grapes are taken to Auckland and lost in blends, thus confirming the image of Gisborne as a bulk wine area and a source of supply for cheap grapes. However a few key producers – such as Dennis Irwin, James Millton, the Spence brothers at Matua Valley and the Nobilos – have succeeded in extricating Gisborne from a descending spiral, by promoting some of the region's better fruit with their individual vineyard names. The larger companies have now become more enthusiastic about the quality of Gisborne with a positive recognition of the region's qualities.

Parker trained at Wagga Wagga, came to Gisborne, and decided to concentrate on sparkling wine 'because it is the toughest and more of a challenge'. He produces a range of sparkling wines out of a somewhat Heath Robinsonesque winery, using only Gisborne fruit, from his own vineyard, as well as some bought-in grapes. 1987 was his first vintage and he has kept base wines from every vintage, some of them in wood. Riddling is carried out by hand.

His 1990 Parker Classical Brut was my favourite in the range with some rounded yeasty fruit on the palate, quite a rich combination of Chardonnay and Pinot Noir, but then Krug is his inspiration. There is also Dry Flint, a blend of Chenin blanc and Sémillon, and a Rosé Brut made from Pinot Noir. A table wine, First Light Red, acknowledges Gisborne's position on the globe and a still Chardonnay is made for the wine bar.

Parker MC Ltd, 24 Banks Street, (PO Box 572) Gisborne, telephone/fax: (06) 867 6967

Revington Vineyard

Other members of the Gisborne wine scene include Ross Revington, who is behind the Revington label. He is a lawyer by profession who became interested in wine for the simplest reason of all: 'I enjoy drinking it'. In 1987 he seized an opportunity to buy a particularly reputed vineyard that had belonged to one of Gisborne's best grape growers, Peter Benson. The grapes were vinified at Grove Mill in Marlborough. Revington admitted to something of a mid-life crisis when he gave up law and became involved in setting up the Landfall winery with another partner. There has since been an amicable parting of the ways and the 1995 grapes were once again vinified at Grove Mill. Revington enjoys the work in the vineyard as relaxation from law, overseeing the vineyard management, and in 1994 attained transitional Bio-Gro status. However, if you have a winery the capital costs are enormous, in some instances disastrously so.

I tasted the Revington range at the Gisborne polytechnic. They concentrate on Gewürztraminer and Chardonnay, with good examples of both: an appealing dry spicy Gewürztraminer and a 1992 Chardonnay that showed good concentration and fruit, with underlying oak and a firm finish. The 1989 demonstrated its ageing potential as well as the intrinsic quality of the fruit.

The college has its own winemaking and viticultural department, with its own small vineyard and winemaking facilities, not only for teaching, but for research and experimental work. They are looking at yield estimation, working with grape growers to find an objective method of determining yields accurately prior to the harvest. They are also evaluating new clones of Chardonnay, as well as new grape varieties, including some curious German crosses such as Arnsberger, which is supposed to be resistant to rot and botrytis. A taste of Syrah from a glass demijohn had some fruity pepperiness.

Revington Vineyard, 110 Stout Street, Gisborne, telephone: (06) 867 3058

Shalimar

The newest entrant to the Gisborne winery scene is Shalimar. Alex Stuart had grown grapes for Montana for some twenty-five years, but had turned to peaches, nectarines and sweetcorn after the vine pull in 1986. However the family had always nurtured the ambition to produce their own wine. Shalimar is the name of the old farm, meaning the garden of peace, which is an appropriate image for a vineyard. Unusually they have a hillside vineyard which was planted in 1993, with Merlot, Cabernet Sauvignon, Sauvignon, as well as some Pinotage, and the following year, the first Pinot Gris in Gisborne. Their aim is show that Gisborne can make good red as well as white wine, which as yet remains unproven.

PO Box 1165, Gisborne. 09 862 7776

Montana

Despite the energy and commitment of the independent wineries and producers, Gisborne remains dominated by the two giants, Montana and Corbans. Montana is the biggest, with a breathtaking 21 million litres capacity, in three different wineries: the old Penfolds winery, for Montana now own Penfolds NZ; a winery at Ormond, on the site of the original Wohnsiedler winery and their main winery on the industrial estate. I wandered through the maze of tanks, glass in hand, with Roger McLernon, the area manager for Montana, and Steve Voysey, their Gisborne winemaker. McLernon is another very committed exponent of Gisborne, confidently predicting that it will be the 'next' area to hit the limelight. He is in a position to know for he has seen a considerable development in Gisborne over the last thirty-odd years. His father grew grapes and he first worked for Wohnsiedler, which is how he came to Montana.

This is the source of Montana's biggest selling single wine, Montana Gisborne Chardonnay, which was made for the first time in 1973. It paved the way for Chardonnay in bulk, with large blends of half a million litres or more of ripe, buttery, easy-to-drink fruity wine. Half comes from their own vineyards and half from contract growers. A small proportion is barrel fermented, using their enormous stacks of barrels, for Gisborne Chardonnay and for other wines, including their best Gisborne Chardonnay from the Ormond Estate. For this they use all French oak, three-quarters of which are new barrels. Whereas oak chips provide the conventional cheap way of obtaining an oaky effect in wine, Montana prefer to use barrels that have been shaved and remove just two millimetres off the inside surface in the fourth year of the barrel's life. They are following the example of Penfolds in Australia and proudly boast the only machine in New Zealand that can do this. They take the use of new barrels very seriously, particularly for Chardonnay. As well as French barrels they obtain American ones from a company in California, owned by Demptos Frères, which employs French cooperage techniques.

A single estate Gewürztraminer is a new venture, from the Patutahi Vineyard, with 'P' on the label. The grapes are hand picked and the vinification meticulous, with quite a long period of skin contact before a gentle pressing. The 1993 was attractively spicy, without being excessively blowsy.

Montana have begun to develop red wines in Gisborne only in the last two or three years. Their viticulturist, Warwick Bruce, is very keen, but it is a question of finding the right free-draining sites and ensuring the correct pruning and training to prevent excessive shading. Many of the original red varieties planted in Gisborne were riddled with virus. Now they have the advantage of healthy clones, which should make an enormous difference to quality.

There are large totara casks for 'sherry' and 'port'. They are able to grow a flor culture for fino, cultivating it first in the juice and then transferring it into tank when the alcohol is at an appropriate level. Montana Flor Fino made from Palomino has a dry nutty nose with a soft palate, and just the merest hint of a salty tang on the finish.

Montana Wines, Corner Lytton and Solander Street, (PO Box 1374) Gisborne, telephone: (06) 867 9819, fax: (06) 867 9817

Corbans

Corbans no longer own vineyards in Gisborne but rely on some fifty growers who cultivate about 404 hectares (1,000 acres) between them. Some are on long term and some on short term contracts, with three particularly important growers committed until 2002. Until the end of 1994 Simon Waghorn was responsible for the winemaking at Corbans in Gisborne but he has now left to run the new Whitehaven winery in Marlborough. His assistant, David Freschi, has taken over. Waghorn felt quite strongly that Corbans have suffered from not having their own vineyards. They have little control over yields, and if they want a low yield, they have to pay for a hypothetical larger yield.

Like Montana, Corbans are very committed to Chardonnay. They admit to the use of oak chippings in a Gisborne Chardonnay to an effect not dissimilar to cheap Australian Chardonnay, with some fat buttery fruit and hints of nougat. However they also recognize the intrinsic potential and quality in Gisborne Chardonnay and include it in their Cottage Block range. Partly in the interests of experimentation and partly as a public relations exercise, they have kept separate barrels of Chardonnay, one for each grower. The wines have been fermented in the same type of oak, with the same degree of toasting and the growers are all invited to a comparative tasting.

As well as classic *barriques* of 225 litres, they also have 350 litre barrels and 500 litre puncheons, which allow for less absorption of oak flavour and also less oxidation. They use both French and American oak. American oak gives more buttery, aggressive flavours, with notes of sweet vanilla and bananas, while French oak is much more subtle in its impact. For Cottage Block they use a variety of different coopers, aiming for a fairly Burgundian style of wine.

They said that in 1981 this was the most modern winery in the whole of the southern hemisphere, but it has suffered from the vagaries of ownership changes and company politics. Nowadays the bottom line on the cheque is signed by somebody at Heineken and there has been a considerable amount of new investment, with an expansion of the barrel cellar to allow for fermentation in barrel, as well as more sophisticated bag presses to replace the continuous process. It all augurs well.

Corbans Gisborne Winery, Solander Street, (PO Box 813) Gisborne, telephone: (06) 867 1269, fax: (06) 867 8467

Gisborne may have a reputation as the industry's breadbasket, but the wines that the region produces, including those individual vineyards marketed by some of the Auckland wineries, show an individuality of style and flavour in Chardonnay, as well as potential for Gewürztraminer and Riesling. The jury is still out on the reds.

12

Hawke's Bay

Hawke's Bay was named after Admiral Sir Edward Hawke. He was Captain Cook's hero and first Lord of the Admiralty until just before Cook left England on the voyage which led to the conclusive discovery and charting of New Zealand in 1779. Cook described the area as having 'the appearance of a very pleasant and fertile country'. Little did he know that two hundred-odd years later, Hawke's Bay would be considered one of New Zealand's best wine-growing areas, a source of increasingly fine red wine, as well as convincing whites, with a plethora of substantial wineries including the oldest in the country.

The principal town of Hawke's Bay is Napier. It is named after General Sir Charles Napier who played a part in the colonial history of India. In 1843 he defeated an Indian army at Meeanee and thereby suppressed the rulers of Sind, which prompted him to sent a telegram to the British government which read '*Peccavi*', Latin for 'I have sinned'. When Alfred Domett was appointed Commissioner of Crown Lands and Resident Magistrate, he extended the military associations with nomenclature to include Clive, Hastings and Havelock, after General Sir Henry Havelock who suppressed the Indian mutiny in 1857, then he went on to name streets after contemporary men of letters and science, such as Dickens, Thackeray, Faraday and Browning.

The centre of Napier was devastated by an earthquake in 1931. It was rebuilt with the result that the town now boasts the finest concentration of art deco buildings anywhere in the world. Many of the buildings have been preserved and restored to their former splendour, such as the Rothman's Building with its exuberant decoration. However, if you walk down Tennyson or Emerson Street ignore the garish shop windows and look at the façades above, which are a riot of colour and design. Some buildings did survive the earthquake, including the delightful weatherboard house with its delicate verandas and views of the Pacific Ocean which now houses a charming hotel, Mon Logis.

Mark Twain is supposed to have said of Napier, 'See Napier and spit!', but I am not sure quite why. There are also the remains of an old Maori fortress or pa. The old historical centre of Hawke's Bay is Taradale, with a parish church that was built in 1875, as well as the old McDonald winery building which is now part of the Montana complex. Hastings and Havelock North are the other towns of the area.

Hawke's Bay is one of the oldest wine regions of New Zealand. Marist brothers, missionaries from the Society of Mary, first planted vines here at Pakowhai in 1851. The Mission winery still exists, although not on the same site, which makes it the only New Zealand winery to have been founded in the last century and to have continued through the twentieth century under the same ownership.

In 1871 the Mission Vineyards benefited from the arrival of Brother Cyprien from France who, as Laurence Huchet, had learnt winemaking from his father in the Loire Valley. In 1879 a delegation from Lincolnshire, who were investigating emigration possibilities, wrote, 'Near Tutai Kuri we saw a garden in which a very large quantity of grapes were growing beautifully in the open air. The vines were arranged on trellis work and comprised a great many varieties, all apparently growing nearly equally well.' At the suggestion of the French consul in New Zealand, Count Alexandre d'Abbans, samples of the Mission wines from the 1885 to 1888 vintages were sent to the Paris exhibition of 1892 where one of them won a silver medal. Although the brothers were primarily making wine for the Eucharist, there are also records of them selling a little wine 'of a stomachic and tonic nature' in 1895. Romeo Bragato described the wine of which he was invited to partake at the Meeanee Mission Station as 'most exquisite and reminded me of the liqueur wine produced on the Greek Archipelago Islands'.

However, the Meeanee site was constantly threatened by floods from the Tutaekuri and Ngaruroro Rivers and in the winter of 1897 both broke their banks and flooded the plains of lower Meeanee. The vineyard was covered in silt and both cellar and

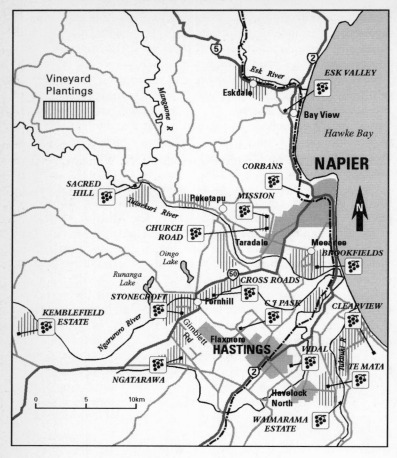

Hawke's Bay (North Island)

church flooded, so a decision was taken to move to higher ground. The brothers purchased 243 hectares (600 acres) of land at Green-meadows, from the estate of Henry Tiffen, who had also been another Hawke's Bay winemaker. The Mission is still there today.

Meanwhile, the interest of the rich landowners of Hawke's Bay had been sparked off by the activities of William Beetham in Masterton. As Dick Scott says in *Winemakers of New Zealand*, 'the novelty, if not the profitability of Beetham's hobby, attracted other East Coast landowners to grape growing', a sentiment which continues to provide a motivation today. J. N. Williams, Beetham's son-in-law, planted an acre of Pinot grapes in 1893, which he later expanded to 2.83 hectares (7 acres). Bernard Chambers planted vines at the Te Mata Station in Havelock North in 1892 after visiting vineyards in California, France and Australia; by 1897, he had 2 hectares (5 acres) of vines. His vineyard reached its peak in 1909 when there were 14 hectares (35 acres), producing 12,000 gallons of 'claret', 'hock' and 'Madeira'. The Australian manager J. O. Craike won gold medals for Te Mata at the Franco-British and Japanese-British Exhibitions. Te Mata today exhibit certificates from the International Exhibitions of Christchurch at which a gold medal was won for 'Madeira' in mid-1906 and for 'Hock' in 1907.

Most flamboyant of all was Henry Tiffen, originally a New Zealand company surveyor who had illegally occupied thousands of acres of Maori land in Hawke's Bay in the 1850s. His vineyard was not only his hobby but also the largest vineyard in New Zealand at the time. In 1890, at the age of 71, he had visited William Beetham in Masterton and tasted his wine. He was so inspired that he returned to Taradale and set up a vineyard and winery. He sent his manager to Australia to study the industry and so there were 8 miles of wire trellis supporting 10 acres of vines. Dick Scott described the vintage:

> A small army of fifty or more children, selected from a still greater number of applicants, was turned loose at 7 a.m. for a nine-hour day of picking. A mechanized press house carried the grapes by elevator to a second floor and fed them through stem-ming machines and crushers into a mobile wine press mounted on rails which emptied into a row of 1,162-gallon totara fer-menting vats – the only direct handling being that of a boy who shovelled the grapes on the elevator to begin the process.

No expense was spared and by 1896 the Australasian Fruit Growers' Conference of 1896 was given details of what was described as the premier vineyard of New Zealand, with 10 hectares (25 acres) of vines and 2.43 (6) more in preparation. The cost was estimated at £9,000.

Romeo Bragato visited all these vineyards and writes of them in his report. He described Mr Beetham and Mr Tiffen as 'of the class of men who cause important industries to flourish. They will ere long be in a position to place upon the New Zealand market wines in no respect inferior to those from the most celebrated vineyards of the Australian colonies.' Of Mr Tiffen's vineyard, he wrote:

It lies very low and in consequence it has become infected with oidium and black spot. This however can easily be remedied. The cellar is certainly a model of its kind . . . It is properly kept and fitted up with all modern appliances. In this cellar I saw some vats made of totara. This timber is destined to become largely used in connection with the winemaking industry. I am of the opinion that it is likely to be more durable than kauri, and will not communicate an unpleasant taste to the wine. In this vineyard the pinot, the proper grape for champagne, yielded a magnificent crop of the finest grapes seen by me. The soil and climate and quality of the grapes clearly prove the capabilities of this district for producing champagne and other wines.

After visiting the Mission Station he went to J. N. Williams, who had an acre vineyard planted with different varieties, the bulk being the two varieties of Pinots. The vines were doing exceedingly well in this vineyard and he intended to plant another 8 hectares (20 acres) with wine grapes. Mr Fitzroy of Hastings had half an acre of Black Hamburgh which, at the time of his visit on 20 March, were 'perfectly ripe, with exquisite bloom on them and the shape, size and colour of the berries was simply perfect. These grapes were superior in every respect to all the other grapes I had seen in other parts of New Zealand produced under glass.

'Mr. Chambers has a small vineyard of Pinots and a quarter-acre of Black Hamburghs which are doing well. Here I tasted a beautiful wine of similar type to that produced at the Meeanee Mission Station.' Then his final praise is his conclusion that the 'Hawke's Bay Province is, in my opinion, the most suitable for vineyard growing I have visited in New Zealand. It possesses thousands of acres which, by reason of the nature of the soil, natural drainage, and sufficiency of heat, will produce grapes of both table and winemaking varieties in rich abundance.'

In 1896, Henry Tiffen died and the Greenmeadows vineyard was taken over by his daughter Mrs A. M. Randall, who carried on making wine and expanded the vineyard to 14 hectares (35 acres) by 1905. She was then influenced by a manager who had turned prohibitionist and began to uproot the vines and turn the land into an orchard. The vineyard at Frimley Orchards was also ploughed up when new owners failed to make it pay. Only Bernard Chambers' Te Mata vineyard continued, but on a much smaller scale and under different ownership.

Meanwhile, Anthony Vidal had planted his first vines in Hawke's Bay in 1905, gradually extending his coastal vineyards at Te Awanga. His uncle was another early pioneer, but not in Hawke's Bay. José Sole, or Joseph Soler as his name became anglicized, had planted vines at Wanganui, but his nephew had moved to the more suitable area of Hawke's Bay and prospered. Vidal expanded the vineyard with the help of his three sons, buying land at Te Awanga, now the site of Clearview. Vidal's is now part of the Villa Maria group. Glenvale was founded by Englishman Robert Bird in 1933 and, as Esk Valley, has also become part of the Villa Maria group.

The Mission Brothers continued to make an impact in Hawke's Bay. A brother, Bartholomew Steinmetz of Luxemburg, left the Mission in 1897 to start his own vineyard. Rumours had it that he had also fallen in love and wanted to marry. In any case, he ran a successful vineyard and winery for some thirty years. In 1927 a young man called Tom McDonald, who was already working for him, took over the vineyard and winery and set up McDonald Wines.

Tom McDonald is one of the legendary figures of the Hawke's Bay wine industry. He is remembered for maintaining the reputation of the area for red wine, making it in the Bordeaux style at a time when most other producers favoured hybrids such as Baco Noir and Albany Surprise. André Simon was full of praise for McDonald's wines on a visit to New Zealand in 1964, comparing a 1949 McDonald Cabernet, 'a truly fine wine by any standards', with 1949 Château Margaux, which 'did not shame the New Zealand cousin of the same vintage'. In 1962 McWilliam's of Australia, who had already established vineyards in the area during the 1940s, amalgamated with McDonald's and Tom McDonald remained in charge of production. At that time McWilliam's Wines (NZ) Ltd. and Corbans of Henderson accounted for half the wine production of the country.

Today, the old McDonald winery building is part of Montana's Church Road complex, but Frank Thorpy describes the winery in its heyday, with the installation of modern machinery and equipment, and 526 acres (212 hectares) of vineyards in the Napier area. It was planted with a wide variety of different vines: Malbec, Pinot Meunier, Palomino, Pedro Ximenez, Baco 22A, various Seibels, Riesling Sylvaner, Pinot Chardonnay, Golden Chasselas, Gamay Gloriod, Grenache, Pinotage and Cabernet Sauvignon, from which they made most varieties of sweet and dry 'sherries', 'port' and muscatel, wine liqueurs and cocktails, and a sparkling, naturally fermented wine, both red and white. McWilliam's commercial table wines, white Cresta Doré and red Bakano, were household names throughout New Zealand, but Tom McDonald's real claim to fame was undoubtedly for his Cabernet Sauvignon and Pinot Chardonnay, and for continuing to make table wines when most of the industry was concentrating on 'port' and 'sherry' styles. The real shift once more towards *vitis vinifera* varieties did not really come, in effect, until the 1970s.

There is no doubt that Hawke's Bay is one of the most suitable areas in New Zealand for grape growing. The climate is drier than in Gisborne and around Auckland, although occasionally the area is subjected to heavy autumn rains. The most dramatic and devastating example of this was cyclone Bola in 1988. However, generally rainfall is low, which means that rot is not a problem, and the hours of sunshine are long. With an average heat summation of 1,460°, sunshine hours and temperatures are comparable to Bordeaux. The coastal area tends to be cooler, affected by sea breezes, and usually experiences more rain and humidity.

The area lies within the rainshadow of the Ruahine Range, part of the spinal cord of hills which run the length of the North Island from Hicks Bay to Wellington, protecting the eastern side of the island from prevailing westerlies. These are snow-capped for a large part of the year. The cold southerlies have usually finished by the end of November, although sometimes they can have an adverse effect on the flowering. Spring frost may also present

an occasional problem, but not to the same extent as in Martinborough or Marlborough.

The vineyard area lies mainly on the Heretaunga Plains. These
are crossed by three rivers which flow down from the Ruahine
Range: the Tutaekuri, Ngaruroro and Tukituki. The soil throughout the area is volcanic and, as such, is very varied. A guide to the
soils of the Heretaunga Plains gives over thirty different soil types,
with varying degrees of sand, loam and clay, shingle and gravel,
varying depths of topsoil, different fertility, irrigation needs and
natural drainage, all of which affect the vine, making a veritable
patchwork quilt of soils. Some are very good for viticulture and
others simply abysmal. On the plains the soil tends to be alluvial
and therefore more suitable for other crops. Elsewhere there are
areas of deep shingle, as well as layers of clay underneath a shallow
topsoil. Originally the vineyards tended to be located on the most
fertile sites, with more regard for convenience than precise site
selection. It is only in the last few years that a greater awareness
of the variations of soil and site has developed, resulting in a
definite move away from the coast to the drier shingly soil of the
river terraces.

The wine industry is now a vital part of the economy of Hawke's
Bay, but grapes are by no means the sole crop. This is very much
a region of market gardening and orchards, with apples and kiwi
fruit, especially on the heavier soils to the east of Hastings. Dairy
farming had been the predominant activity in the 1920s, then there
had been a perceptible shift to horticulture, including vines as
forming part of the agricultural mix. However, while viticulture
may rank fourth or fifth in the local economy it is set to grow in
importance, while other activities remain relatively static. The
interest in wine also brings the tourists, who in turn bring more
wealth to the area.

Today, one of the most prized sites in Hawke's Bay is Gimblett
Road, which ironically not so long ago was considered to be
wasteland. In 1982 Chris Pask of C. J. Pask was one of the first
to have the foresight to realize the suitability of this poor shingle
land. There was even a move to quarry shingle from the land rather
than from the river, which was ferociously resisted by the wine
industry. The decision in its favour was generally viewed as a
watershed and has prompted considerable interest from investors,
resulting in a rush of new plantings by wineries from Auckland as

well as those already in Hawke's Bay. The most isolated vineyards are among the most recent, such as those of the new winery of Kemblefield on river terraces along the Ngaruroro River.

With low rainfall, irrigation is generally deemed to be essential on the free-draining shingle soil, especially to help establish the young vines. However, once their root systems are developed it becomes less important. Phylloxera is rife in Hawke's Bay and consequently all new plantings are on grafted vines and have been for a number of years.

The reputation of Hawke's Bay rests firmly on Cabernet Sauvignon and Merlot for reds, and Chardonnay and Sauvignon for whites. However, several other grape varieties are being grown in the area and they are increasing in number and variety, with various experimental plantings. Montana admit to dabbling with numerous Italian varieties, not only the obvious Sangiovese and Nebbiolo. As will be seen, there is a growing amount of Syrah, not to mention Zinfandel.

Brookfields

Brookfields was first set up in 1937 by Robin Ellis whose family remained the owners for forty years. Then in 1977, when it was on the verge of closing down, the winery was bought by Peter Robertson. He has a biochemistry training and was working for McWilliam's as a chemist, but was tired of the big-company syndrome and very much wanted his own family business. Nearly twenty years on, Brookfields is running as he would like, retaining its manageable size producing between 7,000 and 9,000 cases per year, which ensures that Robertson remains very much in control as the winemaker.

His 1983 Cabernet Sauvignon was the wine that brought Brookfields to public attention. During the 1980s they have progressed by leaps and bounds, and now produce some serious white as well as red wines, with their own individual style. The winery itself is a charming, rustic fifty-year-old building, which is some age for New Zealand. The tasting and restaurant area is dominated by a wonderfully vivid mural by a local artist, Piera McCarthy. It is full of wit and colour, vivid pinks and reds, portraying two violins and a cello. The winery is at Meeanee, near the coast. As this is not such a suitable area for viticulture, most of Robertson's 18 hectares

(45 acres) of vines are further inland. The red wines come from Tukituki, Chardonnay from Fernhill and Sauvignon from Bridge Park.

Robinson is particularly enthusiastic about his reds. He makes wines that will develop with bottle age. They retain their youthful flavours for about five years, then go into a dumb tunnel from which they re-emerge, after a couple of years of dormancy, as something more complex and satisfying. With this in mind there is a heavy investment in new oak barrels each year and, above all, Robertson wants wines that will go with food.

Brookfields is one of the few to produce a Pinot Gris. It is not an easy grape to handle and Robertson admits that it took a few years to learn how to balance a tiny bit of oak with the tannins in the grape skins. He gives the wine minimal skin contact to prevent the pink-skinned grapes tainting the juice. The taste is satisfying, with some attractive dry spice.

Their Sauvignon is an oaked style. The wood provides a little body, which replaces the trace of residual sweetness often found in unoaked Sauvignon. As the wine ages, the oak marries with the fruit and broadens out. This was certainly true when comparing the 1994 and 1993 vintages. As for Chardonnay, he makes an Estate Chardonnay, and a Reserve Chardonnay which is fermented in oak, then spends a few months on the lees, making for a firm, lean-flavoured wine that is not too rich and blowsy. The Estate Chardonnay is more accessible in comparison.

However, it is to his red wines that Robertson devotes most of his attention and these are indeed serious wines. Depending on the vintage, but in a good year like 1991, he makes two wines: a pure Cabernet, and a blend of Cabernet Sauvignon with some Merlot and a little Cabernet Franc. It was interesting to compare the two. Mostly he uses new oak Nevers barrels. Each variety is aged separately for about six months, then he makes an initial blend followed by a final blend about a year later, towards the end of the maturation period. The pure Cabernet Sauvignon spends twenty months in wood, in older barrels initially, then in newer wood later. It is a sturdier, more structured wine, with firmer tannins and good fruit, while the Cabernet Merlot blend has more subtlety, softer tannins and ripe, rounded fruit. Both were very appealing in their different ways and characteristic of the Brookfields style.

Brookfields Vineyards, 376 Brookfield Road, Napier, (PO Box

7174, Taradale) Hawke's Bay, telephone (06) 834 4615, fax: (06) 834 4622

Clearview

Even on a grey spring morning, Clearview has a certain charm. It is a delightful spot, close to the sea at Te Awanga in the southern part of Hawke's Bay, with views of the coast and Cape Kidnappers which remembers an incident on Captain Cook's voyage. There is an old olive tree in front of the winery, as well as avocado trees, and I am reliably informed that the winery café provides one of the best lunches on the Hawke's Bay winery trail. Unfortunately I was there too early in the morning, with another three appointments before lunch, to verify this. However, I enjoyed the old photographs in the winery bar and there was a bottle of Vidal 1973 Te Awanga Claret, a wonderfully old-fashioned-looking label, more in keeping with the style of fifty years earlier.

Tim Turvey bought the property late in 1986 and began planting vines a couple of years later. This is where in 1916 Anthony Vidal first planted a vineyard of Palomino and other varieties. The site is protected by hills from prevailing southerlies. There are 5 hectares (12 acres) of Cabernet Sauvignon, Cabernet Franc, Merlot, Sauvignon and Chardonnay, all growing on stony, unirrigated land. Tim Turvey was away so I was shown round by his associate Kingsley, who was running the winery in Turvey's absence. He also has 6 hectares (15 acres) of vineyards on Gimblett Road comprising Cabernet Sauvignon, Cabernet Franc and Merlot, which are used for Clearview. They are very keen to control the source of their fruit.

It is a neat little winery, with fermentation tanks underground, a small basket press for the red wines, a small horizontal press for the whites and a compact barrel store room. Their key wines are an oaked Sauvignon, a Reserve Chardonnay and a Cabernet Merlot blend. The others, such as Te Awanga Sauvignon Blanc and Beachhead Chardonnay, are intended for sale in the restaurant. Production is just 20 tonnes per year, and that is how they intend to remain, one of the smallest boutique wineries in Hawke's Bay.

I tasted some impressive cask samples from the 1994 vintage: a concentrated Merlot, with good body and soft tannins; a smoky Cabernet Franc; and some tighter, leaner Cabernet Sauvignon. In

1993 they suffered the problems of a cool year and the Cabernet ripened late. Merlot was more successful, with some plummy fruit and firm tannins. As for whites, the 1994 Te Awanga Sauvignon was fresh and pithy with some tropical fruit flavours, while the Fumé, which is fermented in oak and given the full treatment of lees contact and some malolactic fermentation, was smoky with buttery new oak.

There was a feeling of quiet confidence, of a small compact winery run by people with precise objectives. It will be a name to watch for the future.

Clearview Estate Winery, Clifton Road, (RD 2) Te Awanga, Hastings, telephone: (06) 875 0150, fax: (06) 875 1258

Corbans

Corbans have a large winery on the industrial estate on the edge of Napier, dealing exclusively with Hawke's Bay fruit. Evan Ward is the winemaker. He has been in Hawke's Bay for some twenty years, adapting to big-company politics, as he has moved from McWilliam's, to Cooks, then on to Corbans. These are modern facilities, with a forest of tall stainless-steel vats some 12 metres high, and a large warehouse crammed with barrels.

Corbans have three main vineyards, each with a quite different soil type. There is the Omarunei vineyard. The name means 'great gathering' and in 1860 was the site of a Maori battle. Here 42 hectares (105 acres) are planted with Chardonnay, Gewürztraminer, Sauvignon and Cabernet Franc. Just across the river is the Ste-Neige vineyard, planted with Chardonnay, which represents a joint venture with a Japanese company. Corbans manage the vineyard and make the wine for them. Then there is the Tukituki vineyard in the valley behind Te Mata, where the soil is a hard clay pan and very stony, providing the source of their best Cabernet. Finally there is the Longridge vineyard, close to the sea at Haumoana, where they grow Chardonnay and Merlot.

Longridge gives its name to Corbans Hawke's Bay range, which includes an oak-aged Sauvignon Blanc, Chardonnay, Gewürztraminer, and a Cabernet Sauvignon blended with Merlot and Cabernet Franc. Like the winemakers in Marlborough and Gisborne, Ward is allowed a certain flexibility for the expression of his personal style, epitomized in the new Cottage Block range, to which he contributes a Chardonnay and a Cabernet Merlot. For Chardonnay, for example, Ward favours a small amount of malolactic fermentation and American in preference to French oak. This you can taste on the palate, with some vanilla flavours and more weight than other Hawke's Bay Chardonnays. In contrast, Longridge Chardonnay is less oaky and intended for relatively early drinking.

The first vintage of Cottage Block Cabernet Merlot was in 1992, with a blend of 60 per cent Cabernet Sauvignon, 25 per cent Merlot and 15 per cent Cabernet Franc. It suffers somewhat from the cool conditions of the year. There is some cassis fruit, but also an underlying herbaceous note. The 1991 Winemaker's Reserve Label, from a much better vintage, was more satisfying, with some ripe, plummy fruit.

Ward made Pinot Noir for the first time in 1994. Normally it forms part of the base wine for Amadeus, their traditional-method sparkling wine, but the fruit was simply too good in 1994 to lose it in bubbles. We tasted various barrel samples, with different vinification techniques, some with more skin contact, others with standard methods. There were hints of liquorice, but the wine was packed with tannin which overwhelmed the fruit, yet should soften after a year or so in wood.

This is just one part of the jigsaw that is Corbans.

Corbans Winery, Thames Street, (PO Box 25) Napier, telephone: (06) 835 4333, fax: (06) 835 9791

Crossroads

Crossroads is one of the new names in Hawke's Bay, producing its first wines in 1990 from purchased grapes in somebody else's winery. A winery was subsequently built for the 1994 vintage. It represents a joint venture between Malcolm Reeves and Lester O'Brien, who showed me round. He is a chemistry graduate and has had a varied career in computers, spending the previous ten years in Belgium. Then it was time to come back to New Zealand and, at Reeves' suggestion, start up this joint venture. Reeves was already a consultant to several wineries and wanted to make his own wine. They decided on the name of Crossroads, for that is just what the venture represents for both of them. They looked at Marlborough, but decided on Hawke's Bay for its more consistent climate and bought land in 1992, part of which was planted with

Müller-Thurgau. There are now 4 hectares (10 acres) of Cabernet Sauvignon, Cabernet Franc, Malbec and Merlot, and the Müller-Thurgau will disappear.

Riesling, Sauvignon and Chardonnay are bought in and, together with a Cabernet Merlot blend, are seen as the mainstay of the production. I tasted a range of wines with O'Brien. There was a 1991 Riesling, with some slatey notes and a hint of maturity, a lightly spicy 1994 Gewürztraminer, their first vintage of Pinot Noir from 1993, and some slightly herbaceous 1993 Cabernet Sauvignon.

Maybe for Chardonnay they will have three quality tiers: a reserve, a black label and what O'Brien called an entry level with minimum oaking, and fruit from Hawke's Bay and maybe also from Gisborne. The 1992 Chardonnay Reserve was ripe and buttery and mouth-filling, with an obvious toasted character, while the 1994 had good structure and more elegance.

This is very much a winery in the making, working out its projects for the future. It is a space to watch and is already finding its feet with the establishment of a good sales outlet.

Crossroads Wine Company, Korokipo Road, SH 50, Fernhill, (PO Box 1184) Napier, telephone: (06) 879 9737, fax: (06) 879 6068

Esk Valley

The Esk Valley winery is in a delightful spot on the coast at Bay View to the north of Napier. This winery began life as Glenvale in 1933. Robert Bird originally bought the land for a market garden and orchard, but found that there was little demand for table grapes during the Depression so he turned to winemaking. By the time of his death in 1961 he owned a 4-hectare (10-acre) vineyard and what was then a modern winery that had a reputation for 'sherry'. His son, and then his grandsons, took over, but Glenvale suffered in the price wars of the mid-1980s. It was bought by Villa Maria in 1987 and the name was changed to Esk Valley.

Winemaker Grant Edmonds was given the task of re-establishing the faded reputation of the winery. He remembers that Glenvale used to make some fifty different products – about ten wines and all kinds of curious liqueurs. Clearing out the cellars they found two pallets of various colouring and flavour additives. It was a prime example of a winery that had simply failed to move with the times. The core of the original winery, a solid white walled building, has been retained, with its old open-top concrete tanks which are virtually indestructible. They are the sort that you are more likely to find today in old-fashioned cellars in the South of France than in New Zealand. However, in deference to modernity, some have been lined with stainless steel.

Esk Valley has one of the more unusual vineyards of Hawke's Bay: a terraced vineyard from which they produce a wine called simply The Terraces. The site was first planted in the 1940s when the Bird family had built the terraces, but without any irrigation the vines had suffered, so they gave up the struggle and planted pine trees instead. It is a wonderful vineyard of just 1 hectare, which produces about 200 cases a year, facing due north, with no shade but with the temperatures tempered by the sea breezes. The soil is limestone with a little clay. In 1988 the pines were felled and the terraces planted with 50 per cent Merlot, 20 per cent Malbec, 20 per cent Cabernet Franc and 10 per cent Cabernet Sauvignon – but the components in the wine depend, of course, upon the vintage. 1991 was the first vintage of The Terraces, with a smoky nose and some cassis and tannin. The 1992 did not include any Cabernet Sauvignon as it was too herbaceous; none was made in 1993, and the 1994 was back on form with some concentration of fruit on the palate, and good structure and tannin. In 1995, although the later ripening Cabernet Sauvignon suffered from rain during the vintage, the other varieties were fully ripe and picked before the deluge so that the potential quality promises well.

Esk Valley is known for its Merlot and all its reserve red wines are based on that variety. As for white wines, they place particular emphasis on Chenin Blanc and are one of the few wineries to take that variety seriously. The 1993 is soft and honeyed, with the merest hint of oak. A botrytis Chenin was made for the first time in 1992, with some peachy fruit, and pineapple and apricot too. There was no oak ageing, with a reliance on the quality of the fruit for flavour. In 1994 they made two large glass jars of it, a wine with 145 grams of residual sugar, which equates to a Trockenbeerenauslese. This time it had been barrel fermented and would have been delicious, but disaster struck when the transporter dropped them!

Gordon Russell, who took over as winemaker from Grant

Edmonds in 1993, also makes Liqueur Muscat which he calls his toy. This is New Zealand's equivalent to ratafia, as the juice is not fermented at all because spirit is added, then it is kept in wood. The flavour is rich and sweet, with a dry finish, rather like Madeira cake.

Finally, mention must be made of the winery's pest-control officer, a sleek ginger cat called Muscat who looked extremely well fed.

Esk Valley Estate, 735 Main Road North, (PO Box 111, Bay View) Napier, telephone: (06) 836 6411, fax: (06) 836 6413

Kemblefield

Kemblefield is one of the newcomers to the Hawke's Bay winery scene. The name comes from the two partners, John Kemble and Kaar Fields. Both are Californians. Kemble trained at UC Davis and has been involved with Ravenswood in the Sonoma Valley since 1978, of which he is still a director and shareholder. Then he and Fields began looking at the possibility of doing something in northern California, but could not find anything suitable. A chance meeting with a New Zealander brought Kemble across the Pacific to see what New Zealand had to offer. He liked what he saw. He was equally impressed by Martinborough and Marlborough, but opted for Hawke's Bay and found his site in April 1992.

Kemblefield represents a considerable investment and a serious commitment to the area and the industry. Kemble and Fields have bought a total of almost 145 hectares (360 acres) of river terraces at Mangatahi on the Ngaruroro River, near Morton Estate's Riverview vineyard. However, for the moment it is the only winery in this particular isolated area. They looked specifically for a location with moderate to low vigour and with good free-draining soil. The winery, designed by a Napier architect, was ready for the 1993 vintage. At the moment it comprises 500 square feet, but is cleverly designed so that the building can easily double in size simply by unbolting and moving the front to allow the side walls to be extended. It is well conceived and streamlined.

They are planning to concentrate on the Bordeaux varieties: Cabernet Sauvignon and Cabernet Franc, Merlot, and a little Malbec and Petit Verdot. Eventually, they are also planning on Zinfandel. The cuttings were imported in November 1993 and needed to spend two growing seasons in quarantine. This means that they were able to start propagating them in January 1995, so it will be some time before we see the first New Zealand Zinfandel. Kemble does see a potential problem. Zinfandel produces large but tight bunches of thin-skinned grapes and with the potential summer rainfall in Hawke's Bay, this may result in rot. As for white varieties, they have planted Chardonnay and Sauvignon, with some Pinot Gris and a little Gewürztraminer.

For the moment, everything is still very much in its initial stages. Kemble is enjoying the challenge of changing continents and indeed hemispheres. He jokes about the problems he had with the New Zealand immigration authorities who suggested that he needed to go on a diet before they would consider granting him residency! He is a stocky, curly-haired, relaxed Californian who would fit very well into New Zealand, and he finds the New Zealanders friendly, helpful, and ready to exchange ideas and information. He is adapting his winemaking style to suit New Zealand grapes. It was a difficult vintage in 1993, and the acidity level in the Chardonnay grapes allowed for a full malolactic fermentation and some chaptalization, which is not allowed in California.

His first wines, from the 1993 vintage, include some buttery Chardonnay, two different Sauvignons: a standard unoaked wine, and a reserve which is barrel fermented, left on the lees for five months and given a full malolactic fermentation, which is unusual for New Zealand Sauvignon. As for reds, there are two: one based on Merlot and the other on Cabernet Sauvignon. The 1993s did not avoid the herbaceousness of the cool year, but barrel samples of the 1994s promise well. There is no doubt that this is a space to watch.

Kemblefield Estate Winery, Aorangi Road, RD 1, Hastings, telephone: (06) 874 9649, fax: (06) 874 9457

Montana at Church Road

Montana's Church Road winery is on the site of Tom McDonald's old winery in Taradale. McWilliam's amalgamated with McDonald's in 1962, then a series of take-overs and company turnabouts led to McWilliam's being bought out by Cooks and retreating to Australia. Then, in turn, Cooks were taken over by Corbans and the Church Road winery was allowed to run down. The last grapes were crushed there by Cooks in 1981. Montana bought the site in 1989 and renovated and extended the facilities so that the winery is now a modern complex of vats and barrels.

The most significant aspect of Montana's activities in Hawke's Bay is their joint venture with Cordier. There is no doubt that the *bordelais* influence has radically improved the quality of their red wines. A before-and-after tasting illustrated it vividly. The 1990 Church Road Cabernet, with 15 per cent Merlot, spent twelve months in wood, both French and American, and although the fruit was ripe, the wine still had a slightly earthy nose and hints of greenness on the palate. The 1991, from another good vintage, was aged only in French oak and had a smoky nose, with more finesse and good structure and fruit. The quality has continued to benefit from the continued association.

It was Peter Hubscher's idea. He realized that there was a need for improvement, especially in view of Montana's investment in new vineyards. Someone from Cordier worked the vintage at Church Road in 1991, introducing standard *bordelais* techniques, including a more gentle handling of the grapes. Tony Pritchard, the winemaker at Church Road since 1991 when he moved down from Gisborne, admits that it has been a humbling but hugely informative experience which has enhanced quality. They have now installed six large wooden fermentation vessels with closed tops for the 1995 vintage that came from the cognac coopers Radoux and will be assembled *in situ* by the French coopers.

The Church Road label is also used for some good Chardonnay. The aim with this varietal is for quite a heavy fruit-based wine, with some developed spicy wood for the Church Road Reserve. It does not come from a specific vineyard, but represents the best vineyards and the best barrels. Church Road Chardonnay has good fruit too, but less depth. They use both American and French oak, with varying proportions of malolactic fermentation. The first vintage was 1991 and was well received, so they are anxious to maintain a consistency of style within the vintage variations. Then they are working on a more complex Chardonnay made from hand-harvested fruit, which will give a leaner structure with extended lees contact, but with less new oak. However, with a couple of vintages of trial wines they need to convince the marketing people that there is a demand for yet another variation on Chardonnay.

Montana have extensive vineyards in Hawke's Bay, but so far none is sold under their individual names, although they are working on Phoenix Estate near Te Mata for Chardonnay. Twin Rivers is an established vineyard and also the name of their Hawke's Bay sparkling wine. This has benefited from the expertise of Champagne Deutz, in the wake of their work in Marlborough. The first release of Twin Rivers was 1992 and the blend was equal parts Chardonnay and Pinot Noir, but now they are increasing the proportion of Pinot Noir to two-thirds in an attempt to provide more complexity. The vineyard site is cooler than most in Hawke's Bay with a good airflow.

Montana's first vintage of Gewürztraminer from Hawke's Bay in 1994 had some appealing spice and a sweet finish. You feel with Montana that they are in a constant state of evaluation and that nothing stands still. Now they are looking at Italian grape varieties – Sangiovese, Nebbiolo and several others – and at new clones, which should also enhance quality. In fact, it is an unceasing quest for quality within the constraints of the marketing demands of a big company.

McDonald Winery (Montana Wines Ltd.), 150 Church Road, (PO Box 7095) Taradale, telephone: (06) 844 2053, fax: (06) 844 3378

The Mission Winery

The oldest winery of all is the Mission Winery. On my first visit there I was taken on a guided tour of the Mission itself by Brother Martin, who talked enthusiastically, hardly stopping to draw breath as he explained how the chapel had been rebuilt after the 1931 earthquake and boasted of the contents of the library with every edition of *The Imitation of Christ* and a first edition of Captain Cook's memoirs. It is housed in a lovely old weatherboard house on a hill above the winery, while the seminary is now in Auckland.

The winery is surrounded by vines, which in turn are protected by a semicircle of hills. This is one of their three vineyards. They have also established a new vineyard at Gimblett Road and have vineyards by the sea at Meeanee, which is not such a good site because of its proximity to the coast.

You enter the winery through the sales area where people still come to fill their own containers from large casks of 'fine old port' and 'maranella sherry'. They still have the original old casks in which they keep their fortified wines, as well as an old still for making brandy to fortify the 'port' and 'sherry'. A fortified altar wine, remembering the original reason for planting vines, is produced from Müller-Thurgau.

The Mission wines have improved significantly in recent years, partly because the brothers have allowed some investment in the winemaking facilities. They are in the middle of a five-year programme, buying new tanks and new refrigeration equipment. While the basic aim of the winery remains very much value for money, with a range of undemanding and affordable wines, they have extended their range of better wines. The Jewelstone label was launched as a reserve label for Chardonnay and Cabernet Sauvignon in 1991.

I wandered round the cellar with the winemaker Paul Mooney. He is a relaxed, amiable character who has been at the Mission for fifteen years and was originally trained by one of the brothers. We tasted the components of Jewelstone 1994 Cabernet from barrel, including the best Cabernet Franc which accounts for 15 per cent of the blend. Some 1994 Gewürztraminer, which was about to be bottled, was dry and spicy, and there were different barrels of Chardonnay for the Jewelstone reserve, which is finely tuned, with percentages of American and French oak, old and new wood, hand-picked fruit, whole-bunch pressed, and a proportion of malolactic fermentation. The 1991 is rich and toasted on the nose, with a lean structure and an underlying richness. None was made in 1993, which was a reflection on the vintage, and similarly no Jewelstone Cabernet, and none in 1992 either.

Their biggest seller, Sauvignon, has just a whisper of sweetness for commercial appeal, with a soft, grassy flavour. The 1994 Noble Nectar Botrytis Riesling represents their first sweet wine, with five pickings from two different vineyards looking for shrivelled berries. It was rich and concentrated, with the roasted notes of botrytis, and demonstrates how the Mission has moved with the times.

Mission Vineyards, Cnr Church and Avenue Roads, Greenmeadows, (PO Box 7043) Taradale, telephone: (06) 844 2259, fax: (06) 844 6023

Ngatarawa

Ngatarawa, meaning 'between the ridges' in Maori, is based on a partnership of two families, Glazebrook and Corban, which began in 1981. The Glazebrooks are big pastoral farmers with racing stables and the Ngatarawa's 18 hectares (44 acres) of vines are planted on their land. Alwyn Corban's great-grandfather founded Corbans in 1902, his father Alex has played an important role in the industry and Alwyn is now the only member of the family still involved with winemaking. He was working for McWilliam's but was keen to do something smaller at a time when Gary Glazebrook was looking for other investment opportunities. The result was Ngatarawa, where Corban is very much responsible for the day-to-day running, while Glazebrook is chairman of the board of directors. The first release from their own vines was in 1984.

Two-thirds of their fruit comes from their own vineyards which are in a particularly dry part of Hawke's Bay. The soil is free draining, with about eighteen inches of fine loam over shingle. They have Sauvignon, Chardonnay, Riesling, Cabernet Sauvignon, Cabernet Franc and Merlot, from which they produce two ranges of wine: the top Glazebrook range, which consists of a Cabernet Merlot blend, Chardonnay and a botrytis Riesling; and the Stables range for more accessible wines, with a Cabernet Merlot, Chardonnay, Sauvignon, a late harvest Riesling and maybe a dry Riesling.

The name Stables picks up the horse racing of the Glazebrook family. A horse appears in the logo on the label and the winery is built around old racing stables. It is an attractive spot. On my last visit we sat outside in the spring sunshine, tasting through Corban's wines. The old stable doors are painted dark green, on white walls, with a pond full of water lilies. In fact, the stable doors camouflage the storage and bottling facilities, and a more functional winery is hidden away at the back.

Corban's wines have a distinctive originality and individuality which sometimes go against the mainstream of New Zealand flavours. The Stables Sauvignon has firm stony fruit and good weight, and is appealingly discreet, compared to some. A 1993 Dry Riesling, the first made since 1989, was fresh and lemony with a hint of honey. This is a wine that could certainly develop with bottle age. I have always enjoyed the Glazebrook Chardonnay, which in the past has been called Alwyn Chardonnay. It is fermented in new

French oak from the Vosges and Massif Central and the result is a lean, structured wine, with tightly knit fruit and layers of complexity. Glazebrook Chardonnay is a wine to age for the toasted characters develop, but always with a certain restraint, as in both the 1991 and 1989 which had developed some lovely mature notes when it was six years old.

Glazebrook Cabernet, which includes some Merlot and maybe a little Cabernet Franc and Malbec, depending on the vintage, has a European elegance with some smoky cedarwood fruit and good, firm tannin. Each variety is put into oak separately, with the final blending after nine months, followed by a further three months in wood.

Late Harvest Riesling is just that, made from late-picked grapes with some botrytis, and has a honeyed sweetness and firm acidity. The Botrytis Riesling, originally named after Glazebrook's younger daughter Penny, is the most individual wine made from only botrytized grapes, resulting in a lovely roasted quality, with a barley-sugar nose and a brilliant concentration of honey and acidity, marmalade and dried apricots. The 1987 was fermented in stainless steel, while the 1992 was barrel fermented and was still quite undeveloped when it was three years old. Corban actively encourages the development of botrytis by not spraying against rot, but then, of course, he runs the risk of grey rot. The Noble Selection was made in 1987 and 1988, but not in 1989 or 1990.

Corban has a committed sense of purpose. He wants to concentrate on what he is already doing. He is not interested in new grape varieties as he thinks that you can become distracted and lose focus. He still feels that he has lots to learn about clones, rootstocks and training systems. The emphasis is very much on 'estate-grown' wines, from a small winery of just under 200 tonnes per year, with a strong individuality.

Ngatarawa Wines, Ngatarawa Road, (RD 5) Hastings, telephone: (06) 879 7603, fax: (06) 879 6675

C. J. Pask

Chris Pask is a relaxed character with a friendly welcome who came out to New Zealand from Bury St Edmunds in 1960 and stayed. He has worked as a pilot for some twenty years, planting vines in the meanwhile, including the first vineyard on the now highly prized Gimblett Road. Nowadays he has given up flying and devotes his attention to his winery. His winemaker is Kate Radburnd, a talented Roseworthy graduate who in her previous post was responsible for many of Vidal's medal-winning wines.

The first time I visited C. J. Pask, in 1991, Radburnd had just arrived and I had a feeling that it was very much a winery in a transitional phase that needed time for Radburnd to make her mark. At the time, Pask described his winery building as 'home-made' and it has certainly become more streamlined in the last four or five years, with new equipment and a smarter tasting area.

Pask first planted in the Gimblett Road area in 1982. The land had been for sale for ages because everyone said it was too dry. Someone had tried growing tomatoes and even with irrigation they had not been successful. The soil is silt over the shingle of an old river bed which soaks up any water so that the moisture remains under the surface. Pask began with 40 hectares (100 acres) next to what is now the Irongate vineyard, which are gradually being extended and are planted mainly with Chardonnay, Cabernet Sauvignon, Cabernet Franc and Merlot. Some Malbec was also planted for a first crop in 1992, but is producing such tiny crops that it is not proving financially viable, even though a cask sample of the 1994 tasted quite delicious, with some rich plummy fruit. However, a crop of half a tonne off 2 hectares (5 acres) does make Pask wonder if he can afford to grow it.

Pask is especially enthusiastic about Pinot Noir, but it is a difficult grape variety to produce, both in the vineyard and in the cellar. I particularly liked a 1993 Reserve Chardonnay made from a selection of the best grapes which are all barrel fermented to give a wonderfully full, rich nose with a concentrated flavour of fruit and acidity. Radburnd's philosophy is to do as little as possible in the winemaking while working on the quality of the fruit. She is aiming to achieve more finesse in the wines, a greater consistency in style and quality, with a potential that is yet to be fulfilled.

C. J. Pask Winery, 1133 Omahu Road, (PO Box 849) Hastings, telephone: (06) 879 7906, fax: (06) 879 6428

Stonecroft

Dr Alan Limmer is articulate and highly motivated, with very clear aims and well-informed views on the industry. He has the objectivity of someone who has come to it fresh from another field, with a doctorate in chemistry. As a soil scientist he was running a laboratory, testing soil for residues and nutritional value for the horticultural industry. He had always been interested in wine and had always wanted to own some land. It was in his blood in that his grandfather was a farmer. However, he needed a purpose to the land and decided upon vines. He spent about six months looking at sites all over Hawke's Bay, from Esk Valley to Te Awanga, and decided on a sheltered stony site, a valley that had been pasture land on the Mere Road outside Hastings. He has planted 4 hectares (10 acres), with another 2 (5) to come into production.

Stonecroft is known above all for its Syrah, for it was Limmer who made the very first commercial example of the variety in New Zealand. He planted just one experimental row in 1984 and has made it since 1987, with the first release late in 1990. It now accounts for half of his production. He had seen the Syrah produced by the Te Kauwhata Research Station, which he says 'was a very good reason for not planting Syrah'. However, he likes a challenge and had a hunch that it might work. And it does. A cask sample of the 1994 was deep purple, with a lovely peppery nose typical of the variety, with some solid fruit. The 1993 was lighter, from the hardest of vintages, again with some peppery fruit. Limmer is also very enthusiastic about other varieties from the Rhône Valley. He is planting Cinsaut and Mourvèdre with a view to evaluating them. Grenache has been tried in New Zealand before but did not work, but then neither did Syrah. He would also like to try some Zinfandel when it is released from quarantine.

He also produces a Cabernet Merlot blend which is the subject of some experimentation each year, playing around with maceration times and the tannin structure. 'We don't do anything the same twice; it's now a very complicated plot.' His aim is complexity and length, and generally he feels that New Zealand reds are not tannic enough. He said that at the beginning his 1994 Cabernet Merlot was like a mouthful of sandpaper and he thought, 'No one will drink this, not even me!' But a few months on, although it was still tough and tannic, there was fruit there too. The problem is that it is quite different from the average New Zealand red wine which tends to be softer, sweeter and lightly herbaceous. The 1991 vintage had good solid fruit and tannin, with a structured back-bone, and certainly should continue to develop for a few years.

Limmer has also considered Sangiovese and Nebbiolo, but needs a very warm site and, even then, it can still be marginal. With his enthusiasm for the Rhône, he would like to try Marsanne. He is also interested in Viognier, and would even like to try some port varieties. But you can't do everything. As it was, he managed to obtain three out of the ten import slots for vines allowed for 1994.

As for established white varieties, he has Chardonnay, Sauvignon and Gewürztraminer. The Chardonnay is given the full works, with barrel fermentation, some malolactic fermentation and ageing on the lees for about six months until bottling. The amount of oak ageing has been reduced from twelve months. Limmer criticized the 1992 vintage, which did spend twelve months in oak, for its lack of elegance. The 1993 was quite delicate, long and balanced, with oak that was not too intense, while he was aiming for some-thing between the two when he gave the 1994 just ten months' ageing. Judging from the barrel sample, that is what he achieved, for it has richness combined with elegance and good fruit.

The Gewürztraminer is a particular favourite of his wife's and the 1994 is delicately understated and restrained, but with good fruit. He also tried a late harvest Gewürztraminer in 1994 which had a little botrytis, but not too much, as otherwise you lose the varietal character. It was sweet and spicy, with some orange-peel flavours and a distinctive note on which to finish our tasting.

Stonecroft, Mere Road, (RD 5) Hastings, telephone/fax: (06) 879 9610

Te Mata

Te Mata is one of the key players in the Hawke's Bay wine scene. As described on page 173, the winery was set up in the 1880s. I was told a rather charming story by John Buck, the present owner. Bernard Chambers was a Yorkshireman from Huddersfield who made a fortune in the Australian gold fields in the 1840s. He arrived in New Zealand in about 1851 with £150,000 of gold in his pocket and bought 35,000 acres of land in Hawke's Bay with the idea of creating a replica of old England through pastoral farming. He was a committed Quaker, with no interest at all in wine. However, his oldest son married a French girl who, so the story goes, said that the Havelock hills reminded her of Burgundy, but where was the red wine? And so the first vines were planted in the 1880s and the winery licence granted in 1896. Te Mata was exported to England in the early 1900s and won a gold medal at the White City Exhibition of 1909. Then in 1919 the landholding was divided. The winery was sold and suffered during the Depression. After a series of proprietors, it was finally bought by John Buck in 1978.

Just as Te Mata is a key winery, Buck is one of the key players to the extent that in 1995 he was awarded the OBE in the Queen's birthday honours list for his service to the industry. He studied economics and commerce; came to England and worked for Stowells of Chelsea, returned to New Zealand and ran wine retail businesses in Wellington. They were eventually sold to fund the purchase of Te Mata, which has gradually been transformed into one of the most spectacular wineries in the area. Buck is a man of immense energy, purpose and determination. You know that if he has set his mind on something he will achieve it, and he has taken on the bureaucrats in Brussels on New Zealand's behalf. He is full of ideas, with a quick wit and, with his wife Wendy, is a very genial host. He also has a keen sense of the financial realities of the wine industry but has invested seriously in it, and his sons look set to follow in his footsteps. Peter Cowley has been his winemaker since 1984.

The winery of Te Mata is one of the most striking architectural pieces of the area, designed by the New Zealand architect Ian Athfield, who also created a striking design for the Bucks's own house across the valley. The winery buildings, all in tranquil white, sit around an attractive landscaped courtyard with a fishpond. Most peaceful of all is the newest addition, the barrel cellar. Transported there blindfolded, you could be forgiven for thinking you were in a *chai* somewhere in the Médoc, not on the other side of the world, for the atmosphere and design is very much that of an ageing cellar in a Bordeaux château.

Te Mata is known above all for its Cabernet and Chardonnay. Chardonnay comes from the Elston vineyard, which is on a northeast-facing slope close to the winery. The winemaking includes fermentation in barrel, ageing in French oak for about nine months, with lees contact and a certain amount of malolactic fermentation. Ever since its first vintage in 1984, the resulting wine has been seriously good, with structure and balance and superb ageing potential. The 1989 was a particular success that has taken on several layers of complexity.

Coleraine is their best red wine, a blend of Cabernet Sauvignon and Merlot with some Cabernet Franc. Inevitably the proportions vary from vintage to vintage, but broadly are 75 per cent Cabernet Sauvignon, 20 per cent Merlot and 5 per cent Cabernet Franc. It originally came from just one small vineyard, but now the source has been extended to others. The vinification cellar has open-top tanks for standard red winemaking, but with a sophisticated system to allow for regular plunging of the cap, initially twice a day, reducing to once a day. They use a mechanical plunger that has a 1.3-tonne thrust downwards, is operated from the ceiling and can be easily moved from one vat to the next. Buck has seen this system in California, but no one else has it in either New Zealand or Australia. He is against *remontage* and pumping over, as he wants to control the tannin extraction and does not want to risk moving the pips and obtaining any harsh tannins. A substantial proportion of new oak is used for maturing the wine, and the barrels are topped up every week and racked every three months. There is no filtration and at the end of the second winter the wine is fined using real egg whites.

A vertical tasting of Coleraine is a fascinating experience, demonstrating the underlying characteristics of the wine since the first vintage in 1982. Some years have immense staying power, making wines to age, and the best vintages include 1985, 1989 and 1991. The wines have great style, with structure, fruit and tannin. They are not claret, yet they have the underlying elegance that is the hallmark of fine Bordeaux. Buck is sceptical about wines with a high proportion of Merlot, or even pure Merlot, seeing it as an easy choice and a substitute for when Cabernet Sauvignon fails to ripen properly.

Two Sauvignon wines, Castle Hill and Cape Crest, also comprise a significant part of Te Mata's output. The Castle Hill label recalls the origins of the Chambers family in a line drawing of the eponymous Huddersfield landmark. The flavour is characteristic of Hawke's Bay Sauvignon, with more body and weight than a Marlborough wine, while Cape Crest is more powerful still, even with ageing potential. Unlike Castle Hill, it has a touch of oak, with a third of it fermented in barrel. They have also planted some Viognier which was imported in 1994.

Bullnose Syrah is a new addition to their range. Syrah was first planted in 1989 at Te Mata and the first crop in 1992 showed some good varietal character. Sadly, there was none in 1994 as the vineyard was hit by hail, but the 1995 vintage promises well.

Nothing stands still at Te Mata from one visit to the next. Buck's restless energy always ensures that he has a new project. The current one is the new Woodthorpe vineyard at Okawa where about 142 hectares (350 acres) in a 210-hectare (520-acre) block of terraces above the Tutaekuri River are being planted with Chardonnay, Cabernet Sauvignon, Merlot, Cabernet Franc, a new clone of Syrah and some Viognier. Richard Smart is acting as consultant and they are looking at a computerized irrigation system which uses probes in the ground to activate the computer, ensuring that the water goes where it is needed. A new winery will eventually be built to service the vineyard and the wines will be kept quite separate from those of Te Mata. Woodthorpe is intended to be cost effective on a large scale, while Te Mata will always be small and beautifully handcrafted.

Te Mata Estate Winery, Te Mata Road, (PO Box 8335) Havelock North, telephone: (06) 877 4399, fax: (06) 877 4397

Vidal

Vidal is one of old established wineries in Hawke's Bay that has enjoyed a revival in its fortunes as part of the Villa Maria group. Anthony Vidal came out to New Zealand in 1888 at the age of twenty-two to join his uncle Joseph Soler who was making wine in Wanganui in the north. However, he realized the limitations of that area for viticulture, moved to Palmerston North, then on to Hawke's Bay, where he bought a property in Hastings. A few years later he established a vineyard at Te Awanga where Clearview is now situated. The winery passed to his sons who continued to make some respectable claret and Burgundy styles from Cabernet Sauvignon, Pinot Meunier and various hybrids. Then in 1972, Seppelts of Australia acquired a majority shareholding. A period of decline followed until George Fistonich bought the company in 1976.

I always enjoy visiting Vidal's. The winemaker is now Elise

Montgomery. She is a young, talented Roseworthy graduate who has worked in France, California and Australia before joining Villa Maria, then moving to Vidal in 1990. Her relaxed demeanour belies a keen attention to detail and she is a very committed wine-maker. It has been fascinating to see how her wines have evolved over the last five years. Vidal's are also lucky in having Steve Smith as their viticulturist, who is indisputably at the top of his profession in New Zealand with an unerring talent for choosing vineyard sites and sourcing fruit. Together they make a powerful combination.

The top label at Vidal's, as with all the Villa Maria group, is the Reserve range, while the Private Bin wines provide examples of good, sound varietals. The 1994 Sauvignon is fresh, with firm green-pea characters. The Fumé Blanc includes a little Sémillon and a touch of oak. Just 10 per cent is barrel fermented to provide some backbone. A Merlot Rosé is fresh and vibrant with ripe raspberry fruit. Montgomery's first attempt at Pinot Noir from a first crop off four-year-old vines on Gimblett Road came in 1993. It had some convincing fruit, with a good, silky finish. In 1994 she made her first botrytized wine, a Botrytis Selection Sémillon, with some honeyed apricot flavours, which I tried as a barrel sample.

Vidal's have above all a reputation for their red wines, with some serious Reserve wines: a Cabernet and Cabernet Merlot. The pure Cabernet Sauvignon comes from a vineyard at Clive with heavy soil and spends up to eighteen months in wood. One of the most convincing wines of recent vintages was the Reserve Cabernet Sauvignon Merlot, which has some very stylish fruit and balancing tannin. The first year in which Vidal's made really good reds was 1987 and the success has been repeated in the ensuing good vintages of Hawke's Bay.

Vidal Estate, 913 St Aubyns St East, (PO Box 48) Hastings, telephone: (06) 876 8105, fax: (06) 876 5312

Waimarama Estate

Waimarama is a beautiful spot, slightly apart from the mainstream of Hawke's Bay wineries down the road past Te Mata. The name in Maori means 'moonlight on the water'. From John Loughlin's house you have a view of the Tukituki River valley and apparently in the moonlight the river looks like a river of silver.

Dr Loughlin bought this land some twenty years ago, built a

house and planted a citrus orchard. He had first trained as a pharmacist, then studied medicine and became an eye surgeon. He describes winemaking as his third apprenticeship. His enthusiasm for wine began during a spell in England in the 1960s. At that stage, the wine culture of New Zealand was still extremely backward and the idea of a having a bottle of wine with your meal in a restaurant relatively unknown. Loughlin's consultant winemaker Nick Sage worked for Montana for several years but tired of the big company. He returned to Hawke's Bay to run the wine course at the polytechnic, and to act as a consultant to Waimarama and a handful of other wineries. Loughlin generously attributes Sage with much of the credit for the success of his wines, saying that he 'could not have got anywhere without Nick's help'.

For the moment, Waimarama focuses on just red wine. The citrus orchard was pulled up in 1987 and vines planted the following year, from which they obtained their first crop in 1991. The 3.6-hectare (9-acre) vineyard is planted mainly with Cabernet Sauvignon and Merlot, and a little Cabernet Franc, with the very specific intention of producing Bordeaux-style red wines. A friendly banter between Sage and Loughlin ensues with Sage accusing Loughlin of planting too much Cabernet Franc. He feels that although it is an interesting varietal, if you have too much – say, more than 8 per cent – in the blend, it can dominate the wine.

They have adopted a very traditional form of winemaking using a basket press and avoiding pumping the grapes or any excessive handling. Fermentation temperatures are carefully controlled with a three- to four-week maceration period. Each grape variety is kept separately in wood until the final blending just before bottling. The winery itself is neat and pristine, equipped with stainless-steel tanks for the fermentation, and well insulated for regulating the temperature. Loughlin pays meticulous attention to every detail, with his medical training coming into play.

We tasted cask samples of the 1994 vintage, some perfumed Cabernet Franc, a concentrated plummy Merlot, and a very smoky Cabernet Sauvignon. The 1993 vintage proved a difficult year in that the Merlot did not set properly and produced a very low crop, so they made a separate wine with the best of the Cabernet which is very elegant. The 1992 Cabernet Merlot is elegant and understated, with some smoky cedarwood notes, while the 1991 has developed more cedarwood characters, showing a similarity of style. New Zealand has a very undeveloped culture as far as keeping wine is concerned. In fact, most wine in New Zealand is consumed within hours of purchase and so although Loughlin would like his wine to age, he would also like it to be an agreeable drink when it is young, without any harsh tannins. That he is certainly achieving.

The last wine in their repertoire was rather unexpected: a Dessert Cabernet which is fortified with whey spirit and has a sweet, raisiny character.

Although Loughlin describes Waimarama as a retirement project, his son has bought an 11-hectare (27-acre) block of land and planted white varieties Sauvignon, Sémillon, Riesling and Chardonnay, with an ambition to make sweet wine. Somehow, I suspect that Waimarama will become Loughlin's third profession.

Waimarama Estate, 31 Waimarama Road, (PO Box 8213) Havelock North, telephone: (06) 877 6794, fax: (06) 877 6789

Sacred Hill

Sacred Hill takes its name from Puketapu, the site of a Maori battle between three tribes after which many were left for dead. The winery is thirty kilometres inland, hidden in the hills, away from most of the other vineyards of Hawke's Bay.

It is run by two brothers, David and Mark Mason. I met Mark who has the marketing diploma from Roseworthy College and is now involved with winemaking, along with Tony Bish who used to be at French Farm. Mark is a fast talker, bubbling with enthusiasm and full of ideas. You can sense his marketing background, but his winemaking experience also comes into play. He has worked with Denis Dubourdieu at Château Reynon in the Graves and, contrary to usual perceptions, is convinced that New Zealand Sauvignon can age. It is for its Sauvignon that Sacred Hill is known.

Their vineyards have considerable potential in terms of site selection. Two principal vineyards comprise 20 hectares (50 acres) on the valley floor and some 100 metres higher. There is Whitecliff, a 6-hectare (15-acre) plot planted in close rows, with 5,000 vines per hectare instead of the usual 2,000 or so. It stands on old volcanic soil, with red metal limestone, close to some dramatic limestone cliffs formed by the Tutaekuri River. Then there is the Dartmoor vineyard close to the winery. Dartmoor was the name given to the area by a bride who came out from England in the 1870s. She found the area so desolate that it reminded her of the bleak Devon moorlands. I found this hard to believe on a fine spring afternoon, but perhaps in deepest winter things are different.

Dartmoor and Whitecliff provide the names for the red and white wines respectively at the basic level, while there is a Reserve range for the better wines that includes three variations of Sauvignon and some Cabernet. Their first Chardonnay crop was not until 1995 and they are planting more red varieties, including Syrah and Merlot. However, for the moment their range is dominated by Sauvignon. There is Sauvignon Sauvage, made in 1994 without oak, to give some fresh lime flavours, and in 1992 with barrel fermentation and modelled on a young Graves. The 1993 Reserve Sauvignon is ripe and oaky and just a touch clumsy, while the Noble Selection, with 70 per cent botrytized grapes and barrel fermentation, is redolent of honey and marmalade, and with body and weight. It was a good note on which to leave Hawke's Bay.

Sacred Hill Winery, Dartmoor Road, Puketapu, (RD 6) Napier, telephone: (06) 844 2576, fax: (06) 844 3268

Eskdale and Others

This survey of Hawke's Bay wineries is by no means complete. Each year will see new labels and others will disappear. Constraints of time made it impossible to visit every single winery. Among the omissions the most serious is Eskdale Winegrowers which is run by Kim Salonius. He has a reputation for being something of a loner, a maverick winemaker who does not seek the limelight. His wines come from a 4-hectare vineyard first planted in 1973, from which he produces some individual Cabernet Sauvignon and Chardonnay. Sadly, I have never had an opportunity to taste them, but they have a reputation for flavoursome individuality.

Moteo is a label that made a brief appearance in 1991 and 1992. Peter Gough has a share in a Hawke's Bay vineyard and wanted to make wine from his grapes, which he did, borrowing the facilities at Ngatarawa to produce a Sauvignon and a Cabernet Merlot. The next stage, a winery of his own, would have required capital which he did not have. Now he is working at Ngatarawa and enjoying that challenge instead.

Tui Vale is a peripatetic label produced by Keith Crone from an isolated vineyard in traditional rough grazing country at Crown-thorpe, past Kemblefield on the opposite side of the valley. The vineyard actually belongs the Hyslop family, who otherwise are sheep farmers, but Crone, who is a qualified viticulturist, advises them on vineyard management. Some of his ideas about the industry go against the general current. He considers climate to be more important than soil: 'So much nonsense is written about soil.' It is a question of management. You need medium soil so that the vines are not overstressed, together with moderate drainage. His wines – Sauvignon, Chardonnay and Cabernet – have been made in various wineries, but eventually he is planning a winery in Hawke's Bay. The tui is a native New Zealand bird which features on the label.

John Hancock will be leaving Morton Estate in the Bay of Plenty at the end of 1997 to assume full-time responsibility for a project currently known as the Gimblett Road Estate Co. It involves a partnership of Hancock himself, a London restaurateur and an Auckland financier. An 18-hectare (45-acre) block was planted in 1994, with Chardonnay, Cabernet Sauvignon, Merlot and Syrah. They are also arranging for contract growers to produce Viognier, a complete unknown, as well as Chenin Blanc and Pinot Gris. However, the emphasis will be on red wines. Given Hancock's proven track record at Morton Estate, this will be another reputation to follow.

Grant Edmonds, who was the winemaker at Esk Valley and then at Villa Maria, left Auckland in 1995 to return to Hawke's Bay, where he and his wife Sue have planted 3 hectares of Merlot, Cabernet Sauvignon and Cabernet Franc. The first vintage of Redmetal Vineyards will be in 1996 and, again, this will be another name to watch. Meanwhile, Edmonds is acting as consultant to another new project, Alpha Domus, which produced its first red wines in 1995: a Bordeaux blend and a Pinot Noir. The whites – Chardonnay, Sauvignon and Sémillon – will come into production in 1996.

Mark Robertson, the winemaker at Matua Valley, together with his wife Jane Osborne, has bought 16 hectares (40 acres) of land in the Ngatarawa area of Hawke's Bay with the precise objective of filling what they perceive to be a gap in the market: the production of 'consistently ripe reds in commercial quantities'. So far they have planted 7 hectares (17 acres) with Cabernet Sauvignon,

Merlot and Grenache, and are considering Malbec, Cabernet Franc, Pinot Noir and Syrah for future plantings. Grenache is an unusual choice, but Robertson is particularly enthusiastic about this variety after his experience of working with it as a 'flying winemaker' in the South of France. They expect 1998 to be their first crop of any significance.

In 1993, Bruce Helliwell, together with his German wife, Anna-Barbara, began planting an 8-hectare (20-acre) stony site outside Hastings exclusively with red varieties, mainly Merlot, Cabernet Sauvignon and Syrah. They favour high density planting with 5,000 vines per hectare. Their first harvest will be in 1996 and they hope to release their first wine in 1998 under the name of Unison Vineyard. They explained how the name embodies their winemaking philisophies, combining their German and New Zealand heritages. There is no doubt that they will bring a European dimension to Hawke's bay, because Anna-Barbara trained as a viticulturist in Germany and studied oenology in Switzerland. As well as New Zealand, Bruce has also worked in California, Germany and most recently in the Chianti Classico estate of Castello di Cacchiano. The couple have also imported 250 olive trees from Tuscany, with a plan to make Hawke's Bay extra virgin olive oil, and also intend to continue their production of traditional balsamic vinegar.

Hawke's Bay has firmly established its reputation as one of the key vineyard areas of New Zealand, producing some of the country's most satisfying reds, as well as some enjoyable whites. There is a cohesion in the Hawke's Bay Vintners' Association, which now includes twenty-three members. They all have a long-term commitment to the wine industry, with common interests and goals that enable the Association to address the various problems its members encounter. They also organize an annual wine auction for the local Cranford Hospice as a modern version of the Hospices de Beaune sale. It began as a barrel auction and now includes outsize bottles as well.

One thing is certain: Hawke's Bay has changed dramatically in the last decade and is set to do so again in the next.

13

Martinborough

The night before my last visit to Martinborough, I stayed with friends in Wellington. A southerly was blowing hard, straight from Antarctica, buffeting the house with rain. It illustrated perfectly why Wellington merits the epithet 'windy'. Yet miraculously the next morning, the skies had cleared and we drove over the Rimu-taku Ranges in brilliant spring sunshine. In mid-October the gorse bushes were covered in bright yellow flowers. They are a British import and generally deemed a nuisance for they have overrun the native New Zealand bush, but on this particular morning they were resplendent in their glorious colour.

The road from Wellington to Martinborough twists and turns over the hills, offering some breath-taking views. However, wind can be a problem and the pass at the top is closed because of high winds more often than snow. Then at Featherston the road flattens out to reach the small town of Martinborough. It is an inconspicu-ous little place, offering not much of interest to the passing visitor. Ten years ago even Wellingtonians were uncertain of its where-abouts, but since vines have been planted there, and vineyards and wineries established in the mid-1980s, its fortunes have changed dramatically for the better. The name Martinborough has become synonymous with some of New Zealand's finest red wine. For many, Martinborough means Pinot Noir. From a sleepy town whose inhabitants scratched an uncertain living from farming pas-ture land for sheep and cattle, Martinborough has turned to wine. The living may still be difficult, but the success is more assured.

Martinborough was named after John Martin, a local landowner in the 1880s. Curiously, the central streets are in the configuration of the outline of the Union Jack, and many are named after the towns and cities that impressed John Martin on his grand tour, including Oxford Street, Ohio Street and Strasbourg Street.

Although Martinborough's viticultural success is recent, vines were grown in the Wairarapa, the area to the north of Wellington which has Masterton as its principal town, in the last century. The name Wairarapa means 'glistening waters'. In 1890 William Beetham, a gentleman farmer from Masterton with some 56,000 acres of land in the area, testified before the Flax and Other Industries Committee that he had been growing vines for seven years. As a young man he had spent several years in France and had returned to New Zealand not only with a French wife from Picardy, but with vines and a keen desire to produce his own wine. Beetham stated to the Commission that he was convinced of the suitability of large parts of New Zealand for viticulture, but considered that the country did not have sufficient heat to produce the dessert wine of Spain and Portugal. Therefore the production of table wine should be encouraged, and from the classic grape varieties of Europe. If the wine industry were to be established in New Zealand, it would give value to the poorer land that was not suited for pasture or growing grain.

Beetham began by planting just one-eighth of an acre in vines at his town house in Masterton in 1883, and continued to experiment with Pinot Noir, Pinot Meunier, Hermitage, Black Hamburgh, Black Muscat, Gold Chasselas and the white Spanish grape Doradillo. Over 3,000 cuttings, mostly Pinots and some Hermitage, were transplanted to a 1.2-hectare (3-acre) vineyard called Lansdowne in 1892. A reporter described the vintage in 1897, writing of how 'a team of children working for 2/- a day had picked 13½ tons of grapes from which Beetham's labourers had trodden 1,850 gallons of wine'. He then went to say that

> no objection can sensibly be taken to the method of crushing by the feet. These are cleanly washed in warm water, and one might as well object to bread that is kneaded by the hands as to grapes trodden out for wine making. The best wines are made in this way, for the seeds of the grapes are not crushed and their acrid soil pressed out into the must, to its detriment for wine making, under the soft feet and limited widths of the treaders, whereas in crushing machines, should the seed be nipped and smashed between the rollers, the wine is impaired.

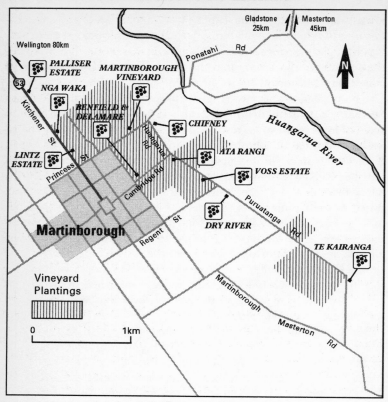

Martinborough (North Island)

Others were influenced or inspired by Beetham's example, notably Henry Tiffen at Taradale in Hawke's Bay. Apparently when Tiffen lunched with Beetham and tasted his wine he was so impressed that he said, 'This is enough for me,' returned to Hawke's Bay and planted his own vineyard.

The government viticulturist Romeo Bragato visited Beetham's vineyard at Lansdowne in 1895. He described four acres, chiefly planted with wine grapes, with vines that were well attended to, with the proper methods of cultivation and pruning. The vines were in a perfect condition of health, the grapes almost ripe, the berries well formed and rich in promise of bloom, and the crop a very heavy one. They were also free of any disease. Bragato was given a taste of six-year-old Hermitage wine, presumably Syrah, and found it to be of prime quality. He also mentioned a second vineyard at Masterton, owned by a Mr Bunny, that was planted with the same varieties as Beetham's and predicted that 'the excellent example set by these gentlemen will doubtless be shortly followed by numerous other settlers'.

Unfortunately, what Bragato could not foresee was New Zealand's inclination towards prohibition. The prohibitionists won their first victory in wine districts in 1908 in Masterton and also Eden, the area which includes Henderson outside Auckland, and voted no licence. W. G. Lamb, who ran the Taratua vineyards near Masterton, was prosecuted for selling from the vineyard and although the magistrate dismissed the charge, the Chief Justice Sir Robert Stout, an ardent prohibitionist, upheld the police appeal with the words, 'I will have no parley or rue with the sale of poison.' The 7,000 Pinot Noir vines were destroyed in 1909. Presumably Beetham's vineyard suffered a similar fate and viticulture disappeared from the Wairarapa for almost sixty years.

The real impetus to the current revival in Martinborough's viticultural fortunes came at the end of the 1970s. Dr Derek Milne, who was at one time head of the New Zealand Soil Bureau, and a specialist in soil physics and geology, wrote a report that examined the various parameters determining the successful cultivation of Pinot Noir, Cabernet Sauvignon and Riesling, looking specifically at rainfall and accumulated heat, as well as soil moisture. He considered the various vintage conditions of Bordeaux, Burgundy and Germany in the preceding twenty years and came to the clear conclusion that soil and climate control everything. A hot, dry area with drought-prone soil was essential, but it was impossible to assume that pastureland would be suitable; usually it was not.

Reasons of convenience and lifestyle led Milne to settle on Martinborough, rather than other equally feasible places such as Hawke's Bay or Marlborough. Quite simply, here was an area of gravelly free-draining soil in a region of low rainfall, within easy reach of Wellington. Milne therefore took a share in a venture that was to be called Martinborough Vineyard. In the way that things rarely happen in isolation, others were also considering Martinborough as a vineyard site. In fact, there were four pioneers: the partners of Martinborough Vineyard, Stan Chifney of Chifney Wines, Dr Neil McCallum at Dry River, and Clive Paton at Ata Rangi. The maiden vintage for all four was 1984, while a vineyard that was planted in 1978 by the then publisher Alister Taylor failed to survive. Taylor ran into debt, and rabbits and possums disposed of the vines. The land now belongs to another winery, Te Kairanga.

Since 1984 the sceptics who doubted the suitability of Martinborough have been proved wrong. Even with the experiences of viticulture at the end of the nineteenth century, there were still many who believed that grapes simply would not grow here and that the land was more suited to pasture for sheep and cattle. The town of Martinborough and much of the immediate surrounding land to the north-east lies on a terrace of free-draining gravel, bounded by the Ruamahunga and Huangarua Rivers. This is called the Martinborough Terrace and mention of it on the label causes some local dissension among those whose vineyards are not so favoured. Elsewhere in Martinborough there are more fertile silt loams as well as poorly drained clay loam overlaying silt pans.

The initial research demonstrated climatic similarities with the Côte d'Or, with average heat summation figures of 1,150 degree days for both regions. This makes Martinborough the coolest of the North Island wine regions, but it is also the driest. Rainfall in Martinborough is on average slightly higher than Burgundy, with 750mm per year, as opposed to 650–700mm in Burgundy. However, in comparison to other New Zealand regions it escapes some of the late summer and autumn rains that cause problems in Gisborne and Hawke's Bay. The cool, dry autumns provide the long ripening season that is particularly appreciated by Pinot Noir. Indeed in summer, drought can be a problem, resulting in some stressed vines. However, spring can be cool and damp, which in some years can make for an uneven flowering. Spring frosts can also cause unease and some wineries group together to employ a helicopter which remains on stand-by during the night. Martinborough's main climatic problem is wind. The first research showed that the area was not particularly windy, but it transpired that although conditions at the local weather centre in a sheltered spot some thirty miles north of Martinborough were relatively calm, in Martinborough itself the prevailing north-westerlies can blow fiercely. Indeed, one morning the car I was travelling in, which was no mean weight, was momentarily buffeted almost off the road. The strong wind necessitates windbreaks to protect the vineyards, as well as particular care in trellising the vines, as it has been known for an entire row to topple over, weighed down by unstable posts.

Martinborough Vineyard

The first ten years represent an important milestone in the life of any winery and provide a good moment for a retrospective review. This is what happened at Martinborough Vineyard in October 1994. The wines we tasted here in some ways provided an overview of how the whole area had developed in the previous decade. The evolution of style in the two varietals in question, Pinot Noir and Chardonnay, was fascinating to observe and taste. The tasting was hosted by Larry McKenna, the winemaker and also principal shareholder at Martinborough Vineyard. He is a Roseworthy-trained Australian who was working at Delegat's in 1986 when a phone call from John Hancock suggested that he might be interested in an opportunity at Martinborough Vineyard. Russell Schultz, the amateur winemaker who was a chemist by training, and the other partners had decided that if they were going to succeed, they needed to employ a professional. Larry McKenna simply rode down from Henderson on his motorbike. He liked what he saw and they liked him, so he stayed. Now, with his gruff charm he presents the public face of Martinborough Vineyard as well as making its highly distinctive wines.

In fact, the first two vintages of Martinborough Vineyard were not at all bad, considering that they were made by an amateur, but, with the arrival of McKenna, quality took a quantum leap forward. However, McKenna would be the first to admit that a considerable learning process has taken place over the first decade. With Chardonnay, this had included the use of barrels for fermentation, a practice that was only just beginning to appear in New Zealand in the mid-1980s. At Martinborough Vineyard the 1985 Chardonnay was fermented entirely in new oak, and over successive years a mixture of old and new barrels has been used.

All the time the aim has been for greater levels of complexity, moving away from the purely fruit-driven flavours of so many New Zealand Chardonnays. This is gradually being achieved by a continual process of experimentation that includes skin contact and different levels of charring in the barrels. The early wines did not undergo a malolactic fermentation at all, whereas later vintages may have a full malolactic, as in the cool years of 1992 and 1993, and just one-third in the warmer 1994. A proportion of whole-bunch pressing adds more structure to the wine. Then, of course, the first vines which were planted in 1980 are now that much older, which in turn enhances the depth of flavour.

McKenna sees 1991 as the watershed in his Chardonnay learning process. However, his favourite vintage is the 1988. It was a year that produced ripe fruit which has been delicately handled, achieving some appealing toasted notes on the nose and palate, and, nearly seven years on, some lovely mature flavours. The 1989 was also showing considerable depth, but with a fuller, more fleshy style. The influence of the malolactic fermentation, which provides some of the mealy, nutty flavours of fine Meursault, was apparent.

However, while the Chardonnay is good, it is the Pinot Noir that really excites and provides the challenge for several, but by no means all, the winemakers of Martinborough. Again, the ten vintages showed the results of a learning curve in the achievement of greater complexity and depth of flavour. Over the decade there has been a shift towards longer fermentation and maceration times, with longer periods in oak. Since 1990, a percentage of whole bunches has been included in the fermentation to make a wine with more tannin. Not only does this give a better structure, but it also fixes the colour. Different yeasts have been tried and now they are looking at different clones in the vineyard.

The star of the line-up of Pinot Noir was indisputably the 1991 Reserve, a special wine that was produced in that particularly fine vintage. It illustrates a first experiment with longer barrel ageing, for eighteen as opposed to twelve months, and comes from a selection of the very best fruit. The result is simply delicious and everything that a great Pinot Noir should be: a wine with a wonderful chocolately richness and immense subtlety and depth of flavour. The ordinary 1991 had also begun to develop some appealing farmyardy notes, while the younger vintages were still very undeveloped with youthful raspberry fruit, tannin and acidity. The 1989 had some ripe fruit and the 1988 some lovely vegetal flavours with an elegant finish.

As well as Chardonnay and Pinot Noir, Martinborough Vineyard also produces good Sauvignon with full, pungent fruit, some perfumed rich, spicy Gewürztraminer, and two styles of Riesling: a slatey dry wine and a honeyed sweet late harvest. The first 6 hectares (15 acres) of vines were planted in 1979 and 1980; now there is a total of 10 hectares (25 acres), as well as other vineyards which they tend but do not own. Pinot Noir and Chardonnay form the greater part of the vineyards, with several different clones of each. The winery itself is a large functional shed.

Martinborough Vineyard, Princess Street, (PO Box 85) Martinborough, telephone: (06) 306 9955, fax: (06) 306 9217

Dry River

Dr Neil McCallum at Dry River was also, like Derek Milne, a Department of Scientific and Industrial Research (DSIR) scientist with a passion for wine. He has a committed desire to produce fine wine, quite simply nothing but the best, and in his own thoughtful way that is what he is quietly achieving at Dry River. Although McCallum has no formal training in winemaking, he is a research chemist with a doctorate from Oxford University. He has the aptitude to read the theory and then translate it into a practical application, with a sound knowledge and appreciation of the controls and checks that are necessary. The winery name refers to a nearby river that regularly runs dry. In fact, in most years such is the demand for McCallum's wines that his cellar runs dry. By October there is usually a sign outside the winery gate explaining that there will no more wine until the next vintage.

The first vines at Dry River were planted in 1979 when McCallum bought a 9-hectare (22-acre) paddock, of which he planted 4.85 hectares (12 acres) with Sauvignon, Pinot Gris and Gewürztraminer. He obtains Riesling from the Craighall Estate, where the vineyard is owned by someone else, and, as he put it, McCallum 'calls the shots'. Chardonnay was not planted until 1985, as in 1979 there were simply no good Chardonnay clones available; in any case, McCallum's particular enthusiasm is for Alsace. Sauvignon was also considered pretty exciting then, but now he is considering pulling it up as everyone else is producing it. Pinot Noir was grafted later and he has Viognier in the pipeline. An initial importation was snarled up in the bureaucratic red tape of quarantine laws, then first planting was affected by frost, so we are unlikely to see Dry River Viognier until the end of the century.

The first time I visited Dry River, in February 1991, McCallum considered that he was very much at the experimental stage with his Pinot Noir. He showed me his second vintage, the 1990, in which he had successfully obtained some appealing berry fruit. Four vintages later, levels of complexity had evolved dramatically. This time we tasted no fewer than seventeen different cask samples of the 1994 vintage. The wines came from two different vineyards, Dry River itself and Craighall, with variations of techniques. Some included a high proportion of whole-bunch pressing and some no stalks at all; some a period of cold maceration à la Guy Accad, but without the high sulphur levels he normally uses, and some shorter periods of skin maceration. Different coopers are used, such as François Frères, Seguin Moreau, Radoux, Dagaud & Jaegle, and as for age, the barrels may be anything from brand new to three years old. The variations were fascinating to compare, with subtle nuances of fruit and tannin. Ultimately, all the barrels will be blended together to make one potentially delicious whole. Meanwhile, the 1993 vintage demonstrated a change of direction, away from immediate fruit flavours of the first vintages towards a wine with more structure, but without too many muscles. It was elegant and appealing, with some raspberry fruit and sufficient tannin to provide some backbone.

For McCallum, the major hurdle in making Pinot Noir in Martinborough is the achievement of ripe tannins while preserving the lovely Martinborough fruit characters. Therefore he avoids some traditional practices – for instance, the aeration of Pinot Noir – pointing out that once you remove the character, you cannot get it back. Any oxidation is therefore carefully controlled, with him tending to favour more reductive techniques. He allows the fermentation temperatures to take their course, letting them rise to about 32°C, and twelve months is the usual period of oak ageing. In fact, more than for Pinot Noir, Dry River has a reputation for Pinot Gris. This is a varietal that really excites McCallum, with his enthusiasm for the flavours of Alsace. He aims for an understated style, with the flavours of ripe fruit, without the manipulations of input from the winemaker. This is certainly what he achieved with the 1992 vintage, which was delightfully fragrant with a good concentration of fruit, high extract and a delicately creamy flavour. The vinification is straightforward, without any skin contact. Dry River's example has attracted further interest in Pinot Gris with a suggestion that it may be the next unknown white to hit the limelight. There are certainly at least five other vineyards of Pinot Gris, planted if not yet in production, in Martinborough.

The Riesling excites too. There is a dry style, with a delicate spicy character. This is the kind of Riesling that demands bottle age, which is McCallum's aim. He wants his wines to have a long life in the cellar first. A 1991 Riesling was more like a Spätlese, with elegantly honeyed notes, peaches and apricots, and balancing acidity, all in harmony. He has also made some very successful Late Harvest Riesling, as well as some deliciously concentrated Botrytis Bunch Selection Gewürztraminer. While acidity provides the structure in sweet Riesling, in Gewürztraminer it is more problematic: the variety is low in acid and therefore needs alcohol or else it would be flabby. Consequently, it is quite alcoholic on the finish.

McCallum comes across as a thoughtful winemaker. He has an intellectual approach to his wines and is ready to share his enthusiasm and ideas. An hour spent tasting with him is a thought-provoking and inspiring experience.

Dry River Wines, Puruatanga Road, (PO Box 72) Martinborough, telephone/fax: (06) 306 9388

Ata Rangi

Ata Rangi means 'new beginning', which is what it was for Clive Paton. He used to be a dairy farmer but wanted a more rewarding challenge, so he settled in Martinborough in 1980, following the general hunch that there was viticultural potential there. He made a little wine in 1984, but his first commercial vintage was 1985. In the winery he works with his wife Phyll Pattie, while his sister Alison is responsible for the vineyards. Her new husband Oliver also helps with the winemaking. They now source grapes from some 12 hectares (30 acres), from which they make just three wines: Chardonnay, Pinot Noir and Célèbre.

Célèbre is their most original wine, for it is a blend of Cabernet Sauvignon, Merlot and Syrah. However, some Nebbiolo and Sangiovese have also been planted in the warmest part of their vineyard just to see how they perform. Paton is optimistic that the warm Martinborough autumns will help to ripen them. If they prove successful he will reduce the proportion of Cabernet in Célèbre as he finds that five years out of ten, it is impossible to avoid the herbaceous notes of unripe Cabernet. He finds that even Syrah tends to taste riper than the Cabernet. In any case, as Célèbre is very much his own creation, he can make it how he will. He is aiming for an intriguing mixture of Bordeaux, the Rhône Valley and Italy. The 1990 Célèbre, drunk in October 1994, had several layers of flavour with good fruit, structured tannin and balance.

In 1990, Paton worked in Mercurey, then with Patrice Rion in Nuits-St-Georges the vintage, an experience which has greatly influenced his ideas, giving him the confidence to go to the limits and concentrate on the structure of Pinot Noir. As he says, so much New Zealand Pinot Noir is purely fruit driven and needs better structure. This is what he is now achieving with his wines, while still retaining the essential fruit of the variety. It is not an easy path to tread as the subtlety of Pinot Noir can be easily upset. We tasted three different cask samples of 1994. One came from fifteen-year-old vines, which is old for New Zealand, and had some good sweet fruit. With it, Paton had tried a modified version of the Accad method, while for a second cask he had extended the cold soak for two weeks, then allowed the juice to ferment. The third cask contained 25 per cent whole bunches. It was definitely an example, as it should be, of the three parts making an even greater whole.

Paton and Pattie are also working hard on improving their Chardonnay. An investment in a new airbag press has made a considerable difference to the quality of the juice. They are also working on longer lees contact and giving their wines less time in oak. About one-third of the barrels are new, from the Tonnellerie de

Mercurey, Seguin Moreau and François Frères. They like tight-grained barrels, with light toast, that give a good concentration of fruit with firm structure.

Ata Rangi Vineyard, Puruatanga Road, (PO Box 43) Martinborough, telephone/fax: (06) 306 9570

Chifney Wines

The fourth pioneer in Martinborough was Stan Chifney, a mildly eccentric and enthusiastic character who is an expert on vaccines. He is also a talented violinist, with his cellar doubling up as a practice room, and plays with the Greytown orchestra. He is almost a father figure to the Martinborough wine industry, for it was in his winery that the first vintages of Martinborough Vineyard, Ata Rangi and Dry River were made in 1984, and subsequently it has been used by others without their own winery. He was born in Britain, but lived in various parts of the world before coming to live and work in the Hutt Valley between Martinborough and Wellington in 1972. He explained how he had always produced home-made wines and had bought grapes with Russell Schultz, the first winemaker at Martinborough Vineyard. In Chifney's words, they made lousy wine from lousy grapes from Gisborne, but the excitement was there. When he was contemplating retirement, he heard talk of the feasibility of Martinborough as a vineyard area. He came to look for himself and bought 4 hectares (10 acres) and a house for what 10 ares (a quarter of an acre) would have cost him in Hawke's Bay. As he had worked in laboratories all his life, he said, 'I could do this blindfolded.' Unlike the other pioneers, he is an enthusiastic exponent of Cabernet Sauvignon and feels very strongly that there is a case for arguing the suitability of Martinborough for that variety. In any case, at the beginning nobody really knew what would do well. The research figures may have resembled Burgundy, but others considered that they would also be suitable for Cabernet and Merlot. As well as Cabernet, Chifney also planted Chenin Blanc.

A visit provides an excuse for Chifney to open bottles galore with unfailing generosity, offering a taste of just about every wine he has made in the previous ten years. Cabernet Sauvignon can suffer from the cooler climate of Martinborough and in some years, notably 1993 and 1992, none was made as it failed to ripen fully, producing green-pepper flavours. However, there is an overall consistency of style, with the best vintages, namely 1988 and 1990, producing some attractive cedarwood flavours. Chifney is adamant that he is making a Martinborough wine, not an imitation of Bordeaux. These earlier wines were pure Cabernet Sauvignon, but his 1994 included some Cabernet Franc and Merlot. The Chenin Blanc has some delicately honeyed fruit, with a dry finish. His address is Huangarua Road, which appropriately means in Maori 'a place of two fruits' – in other words, both red and white grapes.

Chifney Wines, Huangarua Road, Martinborough, telephone/fax: (06) 306 9495

Benfield & Delamare

There are others who share Stan Chifney's enthusiasm for the grape varieties of Bordeaux, but it does seem that, more often than not, the dice have been heavily loaded against them. Bill Benfield of Benfield & Delamare is a Wellington-based architect who was looking to establish a vineyard. Back in 1987 he saw a shed bearing a for-sale notice in Cambridge Road and a block of land in Oxford Street, on which he has planted Cabernet Sauvignon, Merlot, Cabernet Franc and Malbec. At the time, Martinborough had as yet to establish a reputation for Pinot Noir and 'Bordeaux reds seemed a good punt'. Benfield had access to climatic and soil data, which led him to believe that Cabernet Sauvignon would be a feasible option. His first vintage in 1990 had some good fruit and elegant flavours, and the 1991 also shows some potential, but subsequent years have been less successful. A hard spring frost on 28 November killed some mature vines, leaving him with just one barrel of wine in 1992. The 1993 was also adversely affected by the weather and in 1994 bad weather at the flowering reduced his yield to just half a tonne per acre, while rain spoilt the vintage in 1995.

Benfield & Delamare, Cambridge Road, (35 New York Street) Martinborough, telephone/fax: (06) 306 9926

Alexander Vineyard

Benfield introduced me to another newcomer to Martinborough, Kingsley Alexander, who has launched his label Alexander Vineyard. His first vintage, the 1994, was made at Benfield's winery from Cabernet Sauvignon with some Cabernet Franc. A tasting of a cask sample in October 1994 promised well, with some blackcurrant fruit and a touch of sweet oak. However, I could not help feeling that such determination, even obstinacy, might be going against the mainstream, contrary to the true potential of Martinborough.

Alexander Vineyard, Dublin Street Extension, (PO Box 87) Martinborough, telephone: (06) 306 9389

Te Kairanga

Chris Buring, the genial winemaker at Te Kairanga, was more blunt. He gave me a cask sample of his 1994 Cabernet Sauvignon and said, 'Now you know why I want to pull it up.' Quite simply, even though 1994 was a warmer year than either 1993 or 1992, the tannins were still green. Buring is convinced that Martinborough is too cold for Cabernet Sauvignon. His winemaking background is firmly Australian. He comes from the Barossa Valley, where his great-uncle was Leo Buring. However, the family company was bought by Lindemans and the name no longer has any particular identity but is one of the many brand names of Southcorp. There are no more members of the family left in the Australian wine industry. Buring trained at Davis and worked for Lindemans for twenty-three years, finally as the senior winemaker at Caradoc, where, he said ruefully, 'They make nearly as much wine as the whole of New Zealand.' Then it was time for a change and he came to Te Kairanga in 1990.

Te Kairanga was started originally by Tom and Robin Draper. They bought land in Martinborough in 1983, including Alister Taylor's old vineyard site, and planted vines as a semi-retirement activity. Their first vintage was 1988, which was when the winery came into operation. Since then, the Drapers have fully retired and Te Kairanga is now run by Andrew Shackleton. In Maori, Te Kairanga means 'the place where the soil is rich and food plentiful'. In some ways this is something of a misnomer as the vineyard sites are not fertile, but the river terraces are eminently suitable for growing vines, forming a dramatic vineyard site at the foot of hills. They now have 26 hectares (65 acres) planted with Chardonnay, Pinot Noir, Sauvignon Blanc, Cabernet Sauvignon, Cabernet Franc and Merlot. They would like to try Riesling. Here, Buring is influenced by his Barossa Valley origins and he foresees the winery concentrating on Chardonnay, Pinot Noir and Riesling in the future. They also make some easier, more commercial wines: Castlepoint Dry White and Red, named after a beach resort on the Wairarapa coast, and also a Rosé Dry, which is fruity without being sweet, avoiding the trap, unlike many New Zealand rosés, of being what Buring calls a lollipop wine.

Te Kairanga Wines, Martins Road, (PO Box 52) Martinborough, telephone: (06) 306 9122, fax: (06) 306 9322

Palliser Estate

The other estate which has made a significant contribution to Martinborough's growing international reputation is Palliser. It is named after Cape Palliser, the southernmost point of the North Island. Sir Hugh Palliser was a British admiral who had a significant effect on the career of Captain Cook. Palliser Estate Wines was originally started by Wyatt Creech, who is currently MP for the Wairarapa and Minister for Revenue. He planted his 10-hectare (24-acre) Om Santi vineyard in 1982 and formed a company to raise the money for a winery. Although Creech is still a shareholder, today the public face of Palliser is presented by Richard Riddiford, who is a member of an old Martinborough family and heads the board of directors. He has had a varied career in other fields and consequently has a broad international view of things. Since 1991, Allan Johnson has been the winemaker. He is a New Zealander who graduated from Roseworthy, then worked at Capel Vale in Western Australia until the time was right to come home. Palliser's first vintage, the 1989, was made at Martinborough Vineyard, and the winery was ready in time for the 1990 vintage.

At Palliser they concentrate on four main varietals: Riesling, Sauvignon, Chardonnay and Pinot Noir. The winemaking style is thoughtful, with careful attention to detail. With Pinot Noir, Johnson is still working out what suits his fruit best, trying out a long pre-fermentation maceration of five or six days, at 5–10°C, and allowing the fermentation temperature to rise to 32°C. He does some plunging and some pumping, uses some whole bunches, and combines some pressed juice with the free-run juice. He uses closed rotary fermenters, as well as open-top vats. Aeration is very carefully controlled and the wine spends twelve months in French oak barrels, a quarter of which are new. Then it needs at least two years in bottle. As described on p. 63, equal care is given in Chardonnay.

Compared with winemaking in Australia, Johnson finds the climate in New Zealand so much more variable, leading to a much wider range of possibilities. Your technique has to be changed to accommodate the grapes. The most significant difference is that summer is over before the harvest starts in New Zealand, whereas in Western Australia he had to cope with high temperatures outside as well as inside the cellar. Whereas in Australia you have to add acidity, in New Zealand if you add anything it is sugar, and you may have to reduce acidity. Usually, the harvest in Martinborough is spread out over four or five weeks, although in 1994 it was much more compact, between 11 and 28 April.

Palliser Sauvignon is a good yardstick for the variety, with a ripe, juicy, green-pea nose and mouth-filling fruit. It is very much a fruit-driven style and comes half-way between the fuller bodied flavours of Hawke's Bay and the leaner, pithy acidity of Marlborough. Occasionally it may have just a touch of oak, 2 to 5 per cent, and just a hint of residual sugar, as little as 4 grams per litre, which makes it firmly dry, as the limit is 5 grams per litre. The Riesling also confirms the potential for that variety in New Zealand, with delicate honeyed notes and balancing acidity.

Palliser Estate, Kitchener Street, (PO Box 110) Martinborough, telephone: (06) 306 9019, fax: (06) 306 9946

It seems that new wineries are opening all the time, and not just within the immediate confines of Martinborough. Some are looking further north towards Masterton, where Bloomfield Vineyards are already established. Stan Chifney's young partner, a Dutchman called Michael Nebus whose family already have vineyards at Borba in the Alentejo region of southern Portugal, has bought 20 hectares (50 acres) of land near Gladstone, between Masterton and Martinborough. He is proposing to plant Cabernet Sauvignon and Merlot, as well as Chardonnay and Sauvignon, as he considers the climate there to be warmer than on the Martinborough Terrace.

Gladstone Vineyard and Winery

Gladstone Winery – the nearby village was named after the British prime minister – lies in the Poatuhi Valley and is owned by Dennis

Roberts and his partner Richard Stone. Roberts was working as a vet in Wellington, but jokingly admits that a mid-life crisis prompted him to buy some former pastureland. He sold his veterinary practice and began growing vines and making wine. Nearly 3 hectares (7 acres) were planted in 1986 and 1987: Sauvignon and Riesling for white wine; Cabernet Sauvignon, Cabernet Franc and Merlot for reds. Roberts is not convinced that his particular area is suitable for Pinot Noir as it is warmer with less wind than Martinborough itself, but even so the warmish vintage of 1994 still proved marginal for Cabernet Sauvignon. However, much depends on canopy management and also the age of the vines which, for the moment, are still very young.

Roberts is quite philosophical about the change in lifestyle, but also sees some similarities. 'Animals cannot talk to you, neither can vines; you have to sense how an animal is feeling, in the same way that you discern how a wine is feeling.' The neat little winery was built for the 1991 vintage and it needs to acquire its own flora, for it should not be too squeaky clean. His Riesling promises well. The 1991 had a hint of maturity on the nose, with some honey and a firm backbone of acidity. A tiny amount of time in barrel opens up the fruit and rounds out the wine, with a touch of a gentle oxidation. This was inspired by correspondence with the winemaker at Léon Beyer in Alsace. Sauvignon also includes a very small proportion of barrel-fermented wine, with some well-integrated fruit and good mouthfeel.

Roberts's enthusiasm is infectious and his wines show enormous potential. His 1993 Sauvignon won the Air New Zealand trophy for that variety, which was a satisfying confirmation of his talent. And not only that, he makes the most wonderful bread, which we enjoyed for lunch with various New Zealand cheeses in the company of two sleeping Abyssinian cats, Ethie and Opie.

Sadly, since my visit Gladstone winery has been sold for personal reasons and the new owner is Christine Kernohan. Dennis Roberts will make the 1996 vintage.

Gladstone Vineyard and Winery, Gladstone Road, (PO Box 2) Gladstone, Wairarapa, telephone/fax: (06) 379 8563

Voss Estate

A change in lifestyle was also a key factor in the creation of Voss Estate. Gary and Annette Voss were marine biologists, but long weeks spent on boats in uncomfortable conditions began to pall. They bought their land in Martinborough in 1986 and planted 3 hectares (7.5 acres) of vines in 1988 with Chardonnay, Pinot Noir, Cabernet Sauvignon, Cabernet Franc and Merlot. Meanwhile, Voss spent a year at Wagga Wagga in New South Wales to fill the gaps in his scientific knowledge, while he learnt viticulture among the vines at De Redcliffe and Ata Rangi. However, as they have no irrigation their vines took time to become established and produce fruit, so that 1993 was their first vintage from their own vines.

We sat in the sitting room and tasted, looking out on the vineyard. The 1994 Sauvignon was delicate and grassy, and the 1994 Chardonnay made from Hawke's Bay fruit was fruit driven, full and buttery. The 1993 Pinot Noir was still very young and closed, with cherry and peppery fruit, after fourteen months in oak, while a barrel sample of the 1994 showed more promise with perfumed, ripe fruit. The 1993 Bordeaux blend demonstrated the problems of a cool vintage, with herbaceous sweet-and-sour fruit. They are considering grafting the Cabernet Sauvignon and just keeping the Merlot and Cabernet Franc.

Voss Estate, Puruatanga Road, (PO Box 78) Martinborough, telephone/fax: (06) 306 9668

Lintz Estate

Chris Lintz, although a New Zealander, has strong ties with Germany. His family had vineyards at Wawern on the Saar and he studied at the Geisenheim Institute. He worked for several German estates before returning to New Zealand to create his own. He planted a 9-hectare (20-acre) block of land in 1990 and his winery was built in time for the 1991 vintage. It now produces a considerable variety of different wines, including sparkling wine. In his vineyard he has Pinot Noir, Pinot Meunier, Merlot, Cabernet Franc and Cabernet Sauvignon, and for white wine he has Optima, Chardonnay, Gewürztraminer, Sauvignon and Riesling.

The sparkling wine is a Riesling Brut, which confirms his Germanic background and retains some individuality. Lintz uses the traditional method and the wine spends twenty-two months on the lees of the second fermentation. He uses his Pinot Meunier to make a vibrantly coloured rosé, rather than for sparkling wine. The Sauvignon he describes as '*barrique* matured', rather than oak aged, for six months, which gives quite a full, ripe flavour. Most individual is the 1993 Optima Noble Selection, which is almost as rich as Trockenbeerenauslese in concentration and sweetness, with 170 grams per litre of residual sugar. Montana first brought Optima into New Zealand in the early 1970s and used it to blend with Müller-Thurgau. Lintz has just six rows, to see how it goes. In 1994 he made just 40 litres, which he fermented in a glass jar in his sitting room to keep it sufficiently warm, thereby prolonging the fermentation and boosting the alcohol level. The 1993 was redolent of barley sugar, with lemony sweetness.

Lintz Estate, Kitchener Street, (PO Box 177) Martinborough, telephone: (06) 306 9174, fax: c/o (06) 306 9237

Nga Waka

Redundancy brought Roger Parkinson of Nga Waka to wine when it offered an opportunity to reassess his lifestyle. His enthusiasm for wine had initially been fired in Paris, where his father was a diplomat. Back in New Zealand, with a desk job in Wellington, he continued to be an avid consumer. When the opportunity came he decided to train at Roseworthy. His father had already bought a 25-hectare (10-acre) plot which they planted with Riesling, Sauvignon and Chardonnay. The early harvests were sold off and the first wine was made at Nga Waka in 1993, when Parkinson finally returned from Australia.

Parkinson aptly describes his winery as an elegant shed, inspired by a book by the New Zealand architect McGill called *The Elegant Shed*. It is neat and functional and unusually flooded with daylight, with a striking sloping roof, and is surrounded by vines. It was built in time for the 1994 vintage, with the last tanks arriving from Blenheim literally as the harvest started. Parkinson is particularly enthusiastic about his Riesling, which he models on the old Leo Buring wines of the 1970s, with the definite aim of a Riesling to keep and age. With only two vintages to taste, the potential was difficult to predict, but the young wines have delicate honeyed fruit, with good acidity and an elegant balance of flavour. The

Sauvignon is pungent and appealingly pithy, with a touch of what Parkinson called 'sweaty armpit character' which is typical of Martinborough Sauvignon. Then we tasted the three different components of the 1994 Chardonnay, one fermented in tank with no malolactic fermentation; the second fermented in lightly toasted oak again without a malolactic fermentation, and the third fermented in heavy toasted oak with a malolactic fermentation. A trial blend of the three seemed light and buttery, with good fruit.

Nga Waka means 'three canoes' and recalls the old Maori legends of Martinborough. The original name before John Martin arrived there was Waihenga, henga being a place where the Maoris dragged up their canoes and found sustenance. And with some imagination it is possible to discern in the hills forming a backdrop to the town the shape of three upturned canoes. Legend has it that this was where the Polynesian explorer Kupe brought his canoes to rest. In any case, the design of the three canoes on both the label and capsule makes a distinctive, eye-catching logo for Nga Waka.

Nga Waka Vineyard, Kitchener Street, (PO Box 128) Martinborough, telephone/fax: (06) 306 9832

There are other small wineries in and around Martinborough which time did not allow me to visit, such as Muirlea Rise, Winslow and Blue Rock, with other projects in the pipeline as pastureland is converted to vineyards. Even in the four years between my first and last visit to Martinborough, you can really sense the change in the atmosphere. Martinborough has acquired an identity and a prosperity that was not apparent before. The success of its wines brings visitors to the town, in particular for the annual wine festival, Toast Martinborough, which provides a golden opportunity to sample the flavours of the area.

14
Nelson

There is something very appealing about Nelson. It lies slightly apart from the mainstream of New Zealand viticulture, separated as it is from Marlborough by ranges of hills. It is a slow, winding road from Blenheim, with stunning scenery to match. These are the northernmost vineyards of the South Island, lying on almost the same latitude as those of Martinborough, as the two islands are separated by the stormy waters of the Cook Strait. The town itself, named after the admiral as a twin to Wellington across the waters, is still an important port, with car parts arriving regularly from Honda in Japan to supply the local factory. You can watch the tugs manoeuvring large cargo ships past the sand banks and islands into the port. The area is also known for its arts and crafts, with some superb potters attracted by the local clays, and the beaches on the Tasman Bay are popular during the Christmas holidays.

Leave Nelson behind you, drive through the suburb of Richmond, then further west, and you will find yourself in gentle rolling countryside, with a backdrop of the Richmond Ranges and the highest peak, Mount Richmond, snow-capped for much of the year. The vineyards of Nelson divide into three areas: the Waimea Plains that border the Tasman and include the large Rabbit Island in the bay; Upper Moutere, with its quietly undulating hillsides; and finally Mapua, which is furthest from the town and closer to the coast, with just one winery.

For several years, winemaking in Nelson was dominated by just two wineries: Weingut Seifried, as it was first called, and Neudorf. However, in the last four or five years, a couple of the small original wineries have changed hands, giving them new impetus, newcomers have built new wineries and yet more vineyards are being planted. Nelson will never attain the scale of Marlborough or Hawke's Bay, but that is part of its charm. As Tim Finn of Neudorf put it, 'The frustration of making wine in an unfashionable area adds an extra dimension of enjoyment, not to mention challenge.'

The first settlers to land in the area were Germans from Silesia, with two boats arriving in 1843 and 1844. They were peasant farmers who were accustomed to small plots of land on which they would cultivate a variety of different crops, including vines. Their approach was quite different from the sheep-farming immigrants in other parts of the country who carved up the land into vast tracts of several thousand acres. These Germans were smallholders whose division of the land suited the landscape. They had been attracted by the glowing prospects for viticulture that the New Zealand Company had promised them. There were 140 on the St Pauli and 200 on the Skiold, and the *Nelson Examiner* welcomed them warmly: 'No emigrants are more valuable than the Germans and we hail the intended cultivation of the vines by them with unfeigned pleasure.' However, the new arrivals found the hillsides that were thick with New Zealand bush hard to clear. Many departed, disillusioned, for the infant vineyards of the Barossa Valley of South Australia.

After this initial faltering beginning, the early history of Nelson's viticulture was somewhat chequered. Mention is made of substantial winemakers F. H. M. Ellis & Sons at Motupipi near Takaka, further round the coast past Motueka, who from 1868 produced wine from grapes and other fruit, and apparently remained in production until 1939, when the winery was converted into a woolshed.

There were Christopher and Peter Frank, who had been winemakers in Nelson since the 1870s with 1 acre of Golden Chasselas. Romeo Bragato describes his visit to Nelson, and in particular to Mr Frank's vineyard, in some detail.

On the 12th March, the grapes, chiefly of the Golden Chasselas variety were quite ripe and the berry was of such an unusually large size for this variety that I was somewhat puzzled at first to give the precise name. After an examination of the vines I had no hesitation in pronouncing them to be Golden Chasselas. These were of excellent flavour, full of saccharine matter and a really first-class table grape.

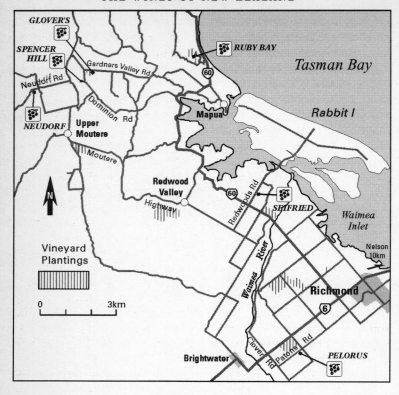

Nelson (South Island)

He then mentions a visit to a Mr Bradley who had a small vineyard and states that from what he saw of Nelson, he would have no hesitation in advising the residents to plant vines on a large scale for winemaking purposes, and also a few of suitable table varieties.

From Nelson itself he went to Richmond and visited a Mr King. 'Although the grapes grown in this vineyard were chiefly table varieties, Mr King has succeeded in making after a primitive manner a wine that would compare favourably with the best wine of its class produced in Europe.' Again, he finds the district 'decidedly suited to the cultivation of vines and fruit trees'. He also visited Motueka, to the north of Nelson on the west side of the Tasman Bay, which again is admirably suited to vine and fruit culture. He inspected Mr Ellis's winery, which he had been told was infected with phylloxera, but after careful examination found it entirely free from 'that dread pest, the vines being in a fine healthy and luxuriant condition'. Bragato went on to state that he considered it a criminal act for people who are not possessed of the necessary knowledge to enable them to judge, to assert that a vineyard is phylloxera affected. 'They have not the slightest conception of the injury they are inflicting upon the industry. Such rumours unconsciously check the enthusiasm of those who are experimenting for the benefit of the whole colony, and curb the energies of all engaged in the industry.'

In addition, he was impressed by the suitability of Lower and Upper Moutere for the cultivation of the oak tree, *Quercus pedunculata*. 'Since leaving Europe I have never seen a district where this invaluable tree would be likely to succeed better.' He thought the New Zealand government would be taking a decidedly wise step were it to determine in the near future to convert portions of the districts into oak forests, in view of the possibility of New Zealand becoming a large wine-producing colony. 'It would be readily conceded that it would be a great national advantage to be able to draw upon your own forests for the oak timber required for making staves for casks and other winemaking utensils.' It seems that Bragato's advice fell on deaf ears.

It does not seem also that Bragato's enthusiasm for the suitability of Nelson for viticulture was acted upon to the extent that he might have hoped, although winemaking continued in a spasmodic way. A vineyard originally planted with Black Hamburgh table grapes in 1918 was taken over by Viggo du Fresne after the Second

World War. He planted Chardonnay, Sémillon and Pinot Meunier, which all succumbed to virus infections, and from about 1967 to 1976 he made red wines from hybrid Seibel varieties.

The next newcomer was Rod Neill who in 1972 set up Victory Grape Wines, named after Lord Nelson's ship, after initial trial plantings in 1967. He has Breidecker, Seibel 5455, Pinot Noir and Cabernet Sauvignon, and is still making wine today, but very much on a hobby scale, so that his wines are rarely seen and do not receive the same exposure as the other Nelson wineries. I have never tasted any. It is in effect Hermann and Agnes Seifried at Seifried Estate, and Tim and Judy Finn at Neudorf who have created for Nelson the reputation that it enjoys today, and only within the last ten years. Other wineries have followed in their wake.

Seifried Estate

Hermann Seifried is an Austrian from the Steiermark who studied viticulture in Germany. He arrived in New Zealand on 1 January 1971 without being able to speak a word of English. He remembers his first few weeks as a linguistic fog. Twenty-five years on, he is forthright and articulate about the wine industry in general, and his own estate in particular. It was, in fact, the Apple and Pear Board that initially brought him to New Zealand, but in 1973 he bought 12.14 hectares (30 acres) of land, intending to plant strawberries, but plumped for vines instead.

Seifried's choice of Nelson was determined by the fact that he was already there, and he had met his wife Agnes who, although a Southlander, was settled in Nelson as a teacher. There was the potential market of holidaymakers and the conditions for growing grapes were good. Nelson has a long growing season with long sunshine hours, less extremes of temperature than Marlborough and no serious spring frosts.

On their first 2 hectares (5 acres), the Seifrieds planted thirteen different grape varieties, a choice determined simply by what was available. There were no significant vineyards of *vitis vinifera* varieties for table wine in Nelson at the time, just Albany Surprise for red wine and Palomino for 'sherry', so there was no previous experience on which to draw. Their first vines included Müller-Thurgau, Chardonnay, Gewürztraminer, Pinot Noir, Silvaner (in order to make a 'Chablis'), Golden Chasselas, Grey Riesling, Pinot Blanc and Gamay, and they were one of the first to plant Riesling in New Zealand. It was a real fruit salad of a vineyard, to enable them to find out what was particularly suitable for the area. Although there was no phylloxera in Nelson, all the vines were grafted as an insurance policy.

The development of the winery over the last twenty years, or indeed over the last five since my first visit, has been dramatic. In the spring of 1995 they had 52 hectares (130 acres) of vines in production, a further 12 (30) or so coming into production within the next year or two, and yet another 12 hectares (30 acres) of land which they intend to plant, in three distinct areas. One is close to their existing winery in Upper Moutere, on a north-facing slope, where the soil is quite heavy clay and quite fertile. The second is in Redwood Valley, near Upper Moutere, where the soil is a combination of sandstone and rocks embedded in clay. The topsoil is shallow and infertile, and the vines struggle to survive here. Finally, their third vineyard is planted on a sandy and stony river flat, where the vines can tap the underground river at 12 to 14 feet, while the soil itself is very free draining. This vineyard is planted around their new restaurant and conference centre on the road to Rabbit Island, which is where they are also planning a new winery. They have quite outgrown their present winery, crammed as it is with various sizes of tanks and barrels, providing their winemaker Jane Cooper with untold logistical problems.

Seifried is very much a viticulturist at heart. He grafts all his own vines and has his own nursery for rootstock. He admitted to a twenty-year learning curve, making every possible mistake, but now he has a very high success rate. The main problem for young vines is frost. Jane Cooper trained at Lincoln College in Christchurch and, until 1992, was the assistant winemaker under Saralinda MacMillan, who has moved on to other things, of which more later. Agnes Seifried copes with all the administrative day-to-day details.

From the thirteen original varieties, they have concentrated on just a handful. Chardonnay, Sauvignon, Riesling and Pinot Noir are the four that they consider perform particularly well in Nelson, and certainly that is proved on taste. Their 1994 Sauvignon has some firm acidity, with good fruit and a hint of residual sugar to soften the finish. The 1994 Riesling is delicately lemony and honeyed, while the 1993 had started to mature, with a hint of petrol, and filled out with some richer peachy notes. They find that the clay of Upper Moutere provides fruit with a lot of flavour.

Seifrieds' Chardonnay has developed some stature over the years. Old Coach Road Chardonnay, after the old highway from Nelson to Motueka, is their basic wine, with less and older oak, while the Redwood Valley Chardonnay is a fuller, more complex wine, with half the juice barrel fermented and half the wine aged in oak. Finally, there is a wine that is entirely barrel fermented, which is also given six months of extended lees contact to make a rich, mouth-filling Chardonnay. Although 1976 was their first Chardonnay vintage, they consider that it took them ten years to produce a really good wine, and recent vintages have shown a fine development, with wines that will age and develop further with maturity.

I have found their Pinot Noir less satisfying, which I think is the fault of the Bachtobel clone rather than any winemaking defects. They are now increasing the plantings of other clones, gradually introducing some 10/5 as well as D5. Cabernet Sauvignon also suffers from climatic deficiencies and tends to have some of the herbaceousness characteristic of cool-climate Cabernet. Really, Nelson is marginal for Cabernet.

In keeping with Seifried's Austrian origins, dessert wines are a speciality of the estate. Gewürztraminer can be difficult as it tends to set badly, resulting in low yields. A Gewürztraminer Ice Wine is produced by artificial rather than natural means, in that the grapes are hand selected then frozen before pressing, which gives a rich, intense, but not overtly spicy flavour. Late Harvest Riesling is produced in the best years by leaving the grapes on the vines for another six weeks so that they are dried and raisiny, rather than affected by botrytis. The flavour is richly redolent of apricots.

I also have to thank Agnes Seifried, if indeed thank is the appropriate word, for my first and last taste of Albany Surprise. It was a blush wine made from the grapes grown in neighbours' gardens and sold as a fund-raising exercise for the local hospital. It had the distinctive foxy hybrid taste of grape jelly which can only make one thankful that New Zealand viticulture has moved on to much better things.

Seifried Estate, Redwood Road, Appleby, RD Richmond, (PO Box 18, Upper Moutere) Nelson, telephone: (03) 543 2795, fax: (03) 543 2809

Neudorf Vineyards

Tim and Judy Finn planted their first vines in 1976 and made their first wine in 1982. They came to Nelson from Wellington, and to grape growing and winemaking as a second career choice. Tim was an agricultural scientist and Judy a journalist when they decided that it was time for a change. Tim, with his scientific background, was already interested in viticulture and winemaking, and now they are both firmly committed to Neudorf and to Nelson. They looked at other more fashionable areas, but dismissed Martinborough because of the wind. Nelson appealed as they liked the climate, with its early spring. There is slightly higher rainfall than Marlborough, although Upper Moutere is distinctly drier than the town of Nelson itself, with the rain falling mainly in the winter. In fact, the vineyards of Upper Moutere lie in the rainshadow of the Moutere Hills and the weather is very predictable. You can see it coming across the Tasman Sea, and the long days and cool nights ripen the fruit well.

I asked about vintage differences, to which Judy jokingly replied, 'It depends what mood Tim is in,' but this relaxed attitude belies a very serious and committed approach to winemaking, not to mention an innate talent, especially for Chardonnay. A comprehensive tasting of recent vintages demonstrated an evolution in style. There has been a change in vineyard management. Earlier vintages were not as ripe, for the canopy was less open, resulting in more herbaceous flavours. Now with smaller crops and more leaf plucking, they are developing a riper style. They aim for a maximum of 3.5 tonnes per acre of Chardonnay, when it would be perfectly easy to obtain 4 or 5 tonnes. There was a change of method in the cellar in 1991: they experimented with new oak, and tried some whole-bunch pressing of Chardonnay that removed some of the extractive character. Tim liked it so much that now all their Chardonnay is whole-bunch pressed, which makes for a slow pressing resulting in much better juice. This way there is no skin contact, which means no phenolics in the wine and no bitterness. It also means that you do not need to fine your wine. Usually the wine has about eight months on the lees. Tim had tried skin contact for Chardonnay but found that, in time, the wine just fell to pieces.

In 1994, for the first time he produced two Chardonnays: Moutere Chardonnay and one which he calls a village wine that is an easier, earlier style of wine, with fewer dimensions than the more complex Moutere. The 1991 Moutere Chardonnay has been the star of the vintages since 1990, with some fine development, an elegant nose, not dissimilar to the mineral character of good Chablis, but with more weight in the mouth and good integration of oak to balance the fruit. The acidity in Nelson Chardonnay makes for long-lasting wines and Tim finds that his vineyards are particularly suitable in that the clay, which is broken up with bands of gravel, gives more depth to the fruit and retains some moisture.

Neudorf also produce some very satisfying Rhine Riesling. Their first attempt at a dry Riesling came in 1993 and very successful it was too, with a slatey note of maturity, balanced with honey and acidity. The 1994 was still very youthful, but riper. The Sauvignon is good too, while Pinot Noir continues to provide a challenge. Tim sees the problem of New Zealand Pinot Noir as that they can become too big and jammy, without enough structure. The 10/5 clone can easily overripen, so you need some tannin from the skins and stalks for balance. Some whole-bunch pressing works well, provided that the stalks themselves are ripe. Tim also has D5 and Pommard clones in his vineyard. Pinot Noir also needs a warm fermentation, peaking at about 32°C or else 'you get lolly water'. He had the help of Bruno Lorenzon, a winemaker from Mercurey, for the 1991 vintage, and found it a great learning experience. His Pinot Noir shows potential, but has not yet attained the heights of his Chardonnay.

The winery itself is an attractive hundred-year-old clapboard building, where we sat outside and tasted in the evening light. The cat Milligan, whose markings make him look as though he is wearing the long-nosed visor of a medieval knight, purred loudly as corks were pulled. You are always sure of a warm welcome at Neudorf. The first time I visited the Finns, I caught my plane to Rotorua with seconds to spare. Subsequent visits have usually made me late for the next appointment, such is their enthusiasm.

Neudorf Vineyards, Neudorf Road, (RD 2) Upper Moutere, telephone: (03) 543 2643, fax: (03) 543 2955

Pelorus Vineyard

Jenny and Andrew Greenhough bought the old Ranzau winery and renamed it Pelorus. Their first vintage was in 1991 and, like the

Finns, winemaking was a second career choice for them. They came down from Auckland, where Andrew had studied art history and gained some experience as a cellar hand at Villa Maria. Jenny's father is in the book trade, so they also provide a warehouse for his South Island sales. They realize the desirability of a second income to help the cash flow when faced with heavy investment in the winery. Their beginnings were small, with 2 hectares (5 acres) of vines, some in grape varieties such as Müller-Thurgau and Gewürztraminer that they did not want.

On my second visit in February 1995 considerable progress had been made, with 3 hectares (7 acres) in production, and another 3 hectares planted, as well as a new winery planned in an old kiwi-fruit packing shed. They have narrowed down their range from their own vineyards to Pinot Noir, Chardonnay and Riesling, and also buy in a little Sauvignon Blanc from contract growers in Nelson. Sauvignon is very much a cash crop and the growers like it as it does not depend on a low yield for quality, unlike Chardonnay or Pinot Noir. Their vineyards are on the Waimea Plains south of Richmond, where the soil is rocky, based on old river beds and the climate warmer than Upper Moutere. This is very much a region of market gardening, with apple orchards on the plains. There used to be tobacco and kiwi fruit too, but they are now disappearing. Instead, there are a growing number of grape growers looking for contracts with the existing wineries and demonstrating the same potential for expansion as in the other regions of New Zealand.

Greenhough recognizes a four-year learning process, admitting ruefully that it takes two or three years to get to the stage where you can own up to your own wines! Apart from his experience at Villa Maria, he has learnt from books and from talking to people. The winemakers in Nelson are a small band who are always ready to help each other out.

Now Greenhough can unashamedly admit to his wines. His Sauvignon is fresh and pithy, with a firm finish coming from a touch of oak. His Chardonnay has good solid oaky flavours and a tight-knit character that will open up with time. The Riesling is medium dry, with 25 grams of residual sugar, and some honeyed fruit and balancing acidity. Pinot Noir is still very much a challenge. After spending the 1994 vintage in Mercurey, he was full of new ideas to try for the next vintage. He and Jenny deserve to do well.

Pelorus Vineyard, Patons Road, RD 1, Richmond, telephone: (03) 542 3868, fax: (03) 542 3462

Glover's Vineyard

David Glover is a friendly, cheerful man who enjoys his own product and the food that goes with it. In New Zealand you can choose any six letters and numbers for your car number plate and, if I tell you that Glover's car registration is TANNIN, you can quickly ascertain the main characteristic of his red wines. As he says, he likes red wines that you can get your teeth into and will age for a few years. Most New Zealand Pinot Noir is too feeble for his taste.

We sat and tasted outside the compact and rather chaotic winery, looking at his vineyards and listening to Mozart while Max, the elderly black cat, basked in the sun on the table next to our bottles. Glover planted his first vines in 1984 with his first harvest in 1989. He is somebody else who caught the winemaking bug later in life, doing a viticulture course in Australia, where he worked for a while before returning to New Zealand. His son Michael is following in his father's footsteps, training at Wagga Wagga.

First we tasted the whites. There was some understated Sauvignon, with a good, firm finish. Nelson generally obtains more weight in Sauvignon than Marlborough. Then there was a slatey dry Riesling, with a hint of honey, as well as an off-dry one with more apricots, and a late harvest wine. However, for Glover white wine provides the cash flow. Serious wine is red and he certainly achieves tannins that would indicate a long life for his wines. His 1993 Pinot Noir has a solid chocolately character, with tannin that might initially seem excessive but, with development, should soften satisfactorily.

With both his Pinot Noir and Cabernet Sauvignon he achieves very small yields of only about 2 tonnes per acre, and if the berries are very small, the skin-to-juice ratio is high, giving lots of concentration of flavour. In 1995 his 1991 Cabernet Sauvignon, which spent seven months in new wood, had a firm cedarwood and pencil-shaving flavour, with a tight structure. The wine had spent less than three days on the skins but was plunged at regular intervals and the fermentation reached 35°C at its peak. Glover's vineyards are in a suntrap on the hill which helps the ripening process and the results are highly individual.

Glover's Vineyard, Gardner Valley Road, (RD 1) Upper Moutere, telephone: (03) 543 2698

Ruby Bay

The fifth winery of any size in Nelson is Ruby Bay, which was originally set up as Korepo by Craig Gass of Conders Bend in Marlborough, of whom more later. Sadly, family problems forced him to sell it to David Moore in 1990. Moore is British born but has lived in New Zealand for over twenty years. From lecturing on biochemistry at Christchurch he went to Roseworthy College and admits to becoming hooked on wine. It was the turning point for him and the evidence of his commitment is there at Ruby Bay.

Moore has 3 hectares (7 acres) in production at Mapua, as well as a grower establishing a 4-hectare (10-acre) vineyard for him as a retirement project. He also has plans for a terraced vineyard between the winery and the sea, as Ruby Bay takes its name from its position on the coast. There is a delightful view of the bay from the winery veranda where you can sit and taste, with a small restaurant and an attractive garden. The winery itself is small and compact, well equipped with presses, barrels and tanks. Chardonnay, Sauvignon, Riesling and Pinot Noir are the principal varieties, and he also dabbles in Cabernet but not very successfully. In 1993, the yield from his own Cabernet vineyard was so tiny that he supplemented it with some fruit from Hawke's Bay, but nevertheless the wine did not lose the characteristic herbaceousness.

Chardonnay is rich and mouth-filling, made with some American as well as French oak; and Riesling makes some fresh, lightly sweet, easy-to-drink wine which provides some welcome cash flow. The Pinot Noir is fresh and peppery, but Moore has yet to achieve the silkiness which characterizes the variety. Unfortunately, time spent helping with a vintage in Mercurey was not as rewarding as he had hoped.

Ruby Bay Wines, Korepo Road, (RD 1) Upper Moutere, telephone: (03) 540 2825, fax: (03) 540 2105

There are other developments to watch out for in the future. On a small scale, Saralinda MacMillan, the former winemaker at Seifried Estate who left when motherhood curtailed her winemaking activities, has made her own MacMillan Chardonnay since 1993. She has just four rows in a vineyard on the Waimea Plain that give her about 200 cases a year. With such a small quantity, she admits that she is able to lavish lots of tender loving care on the vines, almost as much as on her babies, and certainly the results were there to taste in the 1993. Her first vintage under her own name was not an easy one, but she has achieved a wine with good acidity and structure, and some attractive fruit. Her husband Hugh is a talented potter. When I visited them, he was just opening the kiln after firing some wonderful Mediterranean blue glazed goblets.

The other name to watch for in Nelson is Spencer Hill, a new winery that has been set up by an American, Philip Jones. His winery was built for the 1994 vintage and he has 75 hectares (30 acres) of vines – mainly Chardonnay and Sauvignon, with a little Merlot, Cabernet and Malbec – in the Moutere Hills, across the valley from Dave Glover. There is also a group of tobacco growers from Motueka, further round the coast, who are considering converting their land to vineyards, and other growers planting vineyards and maybe aspiring to make their own wine, or, if not, hoping to contract their grapes to an existing winery. Maybe in time there will be a demand for an operation similar to Rapaura Vintners in Marlborough. However, for the moment it all illustrates the buoyancy of even a small area like Nelson that is slightly off the beaten track.

15
Marlborough

Marlborough Sauvignon Blanc epitomizes the success of New Zealand wine. Indeed, in some quarters it is almost synonymous with New Zealand wine and yet the first vineyards of any significance were planted as recently as 1973 in an act of amazing vision and faith. Who could have predicted that what was rough sheep-grazing country would be turned into prime vineyard sites in the short span of twenty years?

The heart of Marlborough is the town of Blenheim: a cheerful, bustling place, with large signs on the outskirts that proudly boast 'New Zealand's sunniest city'. Cloudy Bay was the name given by Captain Cook to the large bay into which the Wairau River flows and the broad river valley is contained on both sides by hills. The Kaikoura Range dominates the skyline to the south. On my first visit to Blenheim, we drove up the scenic coastal road with views of the Pacific Ocean. On another occasion, I flew over the Cook Strait from Wellington. On a calm, clear day the views of the Picton Sound are breath-taking, but on a windy day the short hop in the Metroliner becomes a battle of nerves and stomach. A slower, but not necessarily smoother, approach would be to take the ferry from Wellington to Picton, but the Cook Strait is not known for its calm waters.

The early history of winemaking in Marlborough is patchy indeed. Romeo Bragato ignored the region completely, going straight to Nelson from Christchurch. Presumably there was nothing to warrant a visit. Cynthia Brook traces the early history of the region in *Marlborough Wines and Vines*. Once again, Captain Cook was the first European to land here in 1770, finding a safe haven in Queen Charlotte Sound in a bay he named Ship Cove, where he refurbished his ship in preparation for further

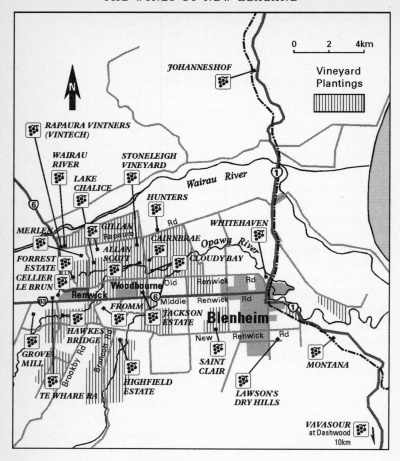

Marlborough (South Island)

exploration. In the 1820s, a whaling station was established; in the 1840s, the first colonists arrived looking for land to settle and farm. Most of the Wairau Valley was occupied during that decade, mainly for sheep farming, but crops were grown as well: oats, wheat and barley, hops, peas and potatoes.

The very first vintage of Marlborough wine was produced in 1875 by David Herd from the Auntsfield vineyard. Herd had first managed a large sheep farm for absentee landowners, but then acquired a 121-hectare (300-acre) block at the end of what is now called Paynter's Road, in the Fairhall area of Marlborough. The grapes were red Muscatel. The addition of brown sugar apparently helped the fermentation process and the wine was aged in old oak brandy casks. About 800 litres were made each year. The vineyard continued in production until 1931, for on Herd's death in 1905 his son-in-law Bill Paynter took over. Finally, the inconvenience of having to deal with grapes at the same time as barley and oats proved too tiresome and Paynter gave up the vineyard.

Another early pioneer was George Freeth whose parents came from Bath and were among the first immigrants to arrive in Nelson. Freeth's first vintage at his Mount Pleasant winery, just south of Picton, was in 1880 and there are records of the Mount Pleasant Wine Vaults producing all kinds of fruit wines, including grapes, as well as raspberries, blackcurrants and gooseberries. In 1893, one case of fruit wine sold for fifteen shillings and sixpence, while 'a case of fruit wine, mostly grape, was sixteen shillings'. By 1940, the same style of wine cost 30 shillings a case. When George Freeth died in 1926 at the age of 80, his sons Albert and Richard continued production, and their wines became known throughout New Zealand. Their 'constancia', was especially popular, as well as their 'port', 'sherry' and 'Madeira'. The winery finally closed down in 1958, a year before the death of Richard Freeth. A bottle of Freeth's Port Wine is on display in the Picton museum.

Then there were two small wineries in the town of Blenheim itself, run by Mansoor Peters and Harry Patchett. Mansoor Peters had emigrated from the Lebanon around 1896 and had settled in Blenheim, going into business as a general-store keeper with his wife Josephine. He had a licence to make and sell wine, the grapes for which were grown behind the store and also bought at the local fruit market. His son Lou Peters remembered the primitive methods of winemaking, helping his father to extract juice from the grapes through muslin bags, then bringing the juice up to the boil and straining it to remove any sediment. The wine was fermented in wooden barrels and honey was added with boiling water to activate the yeast. Peters ceased production during the Depression of the 1930s when luxuries such as wine were hard to afford.

However, it was the Depression that turned Harry Patchett from grape grower to winemaker. When the grapes he grew for the table fetched only one shilling per pound, he felt that he would rather let them rot on the vines than sell them for such a derisory sum. Instead, he sent away to the Te Kauwhata Research Station for a recipe to make wine. He acquired some Scotch whisky barrels and thought up the novel way of extracting juice from the grapes by rubbing the bunches over an outsize sieve. The juice dripped into the cask until it was half full, then water and sugar were added and the contents given a good stir every few hours during the six-week-long fermentation. The wine was matured in whisky barrels for three years before selling for five shillings a bottle. Wild blackberries were sometimes added for additional colour. Patchett's vineyard survived until the 1960s and Harry Patchett himself lived until 1974, the year after Montana's first plantings in Marlborough.

There were two key figures behind the decision to plant vines in the untested land of the Wairau Plain. The first was the farsighted Frank Yukich who, with his brother Mate, had set Montana on an energetic course of expansion during the 1960s; the second was his young viticulturist Wayne Thomas. At the time, Montana were looking for vineyard land. They were considering Gisborne and Hawke's Bay, but there the prices reached $11,120 per hectare ($4,500 an acre). Thomas had graduated in horticulture from Lincoln College outside Christchurch and consequently was aware of the possibilities of the South Island. He knew that Marlborough had low rainfall, long sunshine hours and soil types that were suitable for viticulture. He told the story of how he and Frank Yukich were up in a light plane looking at potential vineyard sites on the North Island when he suggested that they took a look at Marlborough, which they did. And it looked good. Thomas then spent two months checking out climatic data, looking at the meteorological figures for the previous sixty years. Frost at ground level in some low-lying parts of the Wairau Plain seemed to be the only problem, but that was insignificant.

More problematic was the need to convince Seagrams, the new owners of Montana who had just taken control of the company, of the wisdom of planting vines in a completely untried and untested area. A company called Cloudy Bay Developments began buying land, paying about $400 to $500 per acre ($1,000 to $1,200 per hectare) for sheep-grazing land, and Yukich paid the 10 per cent non-recoverable deposit on 4,000 acres (just over 1,600 hectares) out of his own pocket, so convinced he was of the potential of the area. Speculation and rumour were rife, as illustrated by the headline '$1 million land deal near Blenheim possible'. But the decision was overturned by Seagrams at the next board meeting. Thomas then consulted various authorities at Davis in California, eminent professors of viticulture who upheld his theory of the suitability of Marlborough, considering sunshine hours, rainfall (especially during the period of harvest), freedom from unseasonable frosts and the characteristics of the soil, which is free draining and of medium fertility. In fact, Blenheim holds the record for maximum sunshine hours in the whole country and the average rainfall is less than 26 inches, with March being the driest month. At the next board meeting, the decision was reversed and planting in Marlborough began.

Thomas gives credit to Yukich's courage and vision, while Yukich rates Thomas's imagination and perception. The first vines were planted on the Brancott Estate at a ceremony on 24 August 1973. Thomas himself believes that the only mistake they made was not to buy cheaper land that was even more suitable for viticulture and cost a mere $70 per acre ($175 per hectare). It was particularly stony and it is that land which is now being planted as Marlborough expands. Today, bare land in Marlborough costs between $10,000 and $12,000 per acre ($25,000 and $30,000 per hectare) and on top of that you need another $6,000 per acre ($15,000 per hectare) for vines and an irrigation system. Montana's first plantings were done without the support of an irrigation system. Consequently, an enormous quantity of vines died during the first summer as there was a drought and with no irrigation the young plants simply could not survive in the exceedingly dry, stony conditions. Out of the initial planting of 1,000 acres (404 hectares), 750 acres (303 hectares) had to be replanted, but this setback was subsequently described as teething troubles. There are also stories about vines being planted upside-down by inexperienced planters!

Inevitably, Montana were deemed to be completely mad in some quarters and when they did lose a not insignificant amount of money through the demise of so many vines, people did not hesitate to say, 'I told you so.' However, the contract farmers were fairly easy to convince of the wisdom of turning over their land to vines. Instead of farming one sheep for every 9 acres (3 hectares) they could harvest 9 tonnes of grapes from every acre (22 tonnes per hectare), which seemed a much more rewarding exercise. Montana provided the finance to establish the vines, as well as a ten-year contract to take the grapes. There was a viticulturist on hand to teach the novice grape growers how to prune and trellis their vines and to advise on spray programmes, and so on. Many of the farmers welcomed the diversity, while inevitably others had reservations. Montana also took the far-sighted decision to concentrate on *vitis vinifera* varieties at a time when so many New Zealand vineyards were still planted with hybrids. It was Wayne Thomas who particularly favoured Sauvignon as he had worked on the mass propagation of virus-free stock under the auspices of the DSIR. And so Marlborough was born and in 1990 Frank Yukich was awarded the Marlborough Award by the Marlborough District Council in recognition of 'his vision, drive and enthusiasm to create a new industry in Marlborough'.

The growth of Marlborough has been steady ever since. Corbans quickly followed Montana's example and began contracting growers. The first small winery, Te Whare Ra, was set up by Allen and Joyce Hogan in 1982. They were soon followed by Hunter's, and Cloudy Bay, and now each year brings new wineries and new labels. The vision of Frank Yukich and Wayne Thomas has been fully vindicated, and the success of Marlborough with its own individual style of Sauvignon has created New Zealand's international reputation.

The first plantings in Marlborough were on the Brancott Estate, in the Fairhall River valley which flows into the Opawa River, which in turn joins the Wairau River just before the coast. This valley is now totally planted, as is much of the plain south of the Wairau River, between Renwick and Blenheim. Influenced by the shortage of land in the heart of Marlborough, people are now looking further afield for suitable vineyard land. There is one winery in the Awatere Valley which runs parallel to the Wairau Valley, with more vineyards planted by other wineries, and there is a growing interest in the Waihopai Valley further inland. This is the land that Wayne Thomas thought Montana should have bought, and it is only now that it is beginning to be developed for viticulture, notably by Corbans, but for the moment most of the valley is still very much sheep-grazing country. It is further from the coastal influence with a microclimate affected by the proximity of higher mountains in the Wether Hills, notably the highest peak Mount Horrible. There is a higher risk of frost as the lack of wind can create frost pockets, both in spring and autumn. The soil is of glacial origin. Plots of land are now being sold in small units of 20 acres for vineyard development, mainly to those termed as 'lifestylers'.

The free-draining gravel soils of Marlborough have proved eminently suitable for viticulture. Some vineyards, such as Corbans' Stoneleigh Vineyard, are very stony indeed. There you might be forgiven for thinking that you were in Châteauneuf-du-Pape, whereas others have fewer stones and more sandy loam, giving them a greater water-holding capacity. However, irrigation is usually necessary, especially to establish young vines as Montana found to its cost.

Blenheim is proud of its long hours of sunshine and, although there must have been some reason for Captain Cook naming Cloudy Bay as he did, there is a local saying that the sun always finds the hole in the cloud above the Wairau. Rainfall is usually low, with no one month being significantly wetter than another. However, as with any vineyard on the climatic margin for viticulture, rainfall can be unpredictable and cause considerable problems at the vintage – as it did in 1995, after a long, generally dry summer. Frosts are rare.

Montana

Montana is still very much a leading light in Marlborough today, with their Marlborough Sauvignon providing the benchmark for New Zealand Sauvignon and maintaining a growing position on the export market with keen pricing. Their very first Sauvignon harvest was 1979, with 1980 the first vintage of any significant size. They have on a couple of occasions hosted a vertical tasting of their Sauvignon, which in some years disprove the preconceived idea that Sauvignon does not age.

Marlborough is now the source of all their Sauvignon, some Chardonnay, some Cabernet Sauvignon, and the base wines for Cuvée Deutz. They are also producing a growing amount of Pinot Noir for table wine as well as sparkling wine, and some Merlot, Pinotage, and Muscat. Müller-Thurgau, which was initially important for bulk wine, especially in the contract vineyards, decreased significantly with the vine pull of the mid-1980s and is being replaced with varieties such as Chardonnay and Sauvignon.

Montana's winery is an enormous production plant, with a 20-million-litre capacity, including a forest of giant stainless-steel tanks. I was persuaded to test my agility by climbing into one of the largest that happened to be empty. For some reason it is less easy to climb out again, and my very undignified exit firmly convinced me that I was not cut out to be a cellarhand. Montana have expanded their barrel capacity enormously in recent years to some 1,800 barrels. New Zealand is called the shaky islands for a reason, and with the permanent risk of earthquakes barrels cannot be stacked one on top of the other. They rest on 80,000 dollars' worth of steel girders designed to withstand quakes. Similarly, all the vats are strengthened with enormous foundations which cost more money than the tanks themselves, and earthquake insurance is essential.

The showpiece wines are the estate wines from specific vineyards, such as Brancott Sauvignon and Renwick Chardonnay, as it is Montana's policy to own a large proportion of their own vineyards. In Marlborough they have a total of 632 hectares (1,540 acres), including the 259 hectares (640 acres) of Brancott and a newly planted block just by Hunter's. In addition, they control about 400 hectares (1,000 acres) under contract. However, the estate wines are just the tip of the production, followed by the three key Marlborough varietals of Sauvignon, Chardonnay and Cabernet Merlot. Bulk wine in boxes still represents one-third of their total sales.

Montana Winery, Main Road South, State Highway 1, Riverlands, (PO Box 331) Blenheim, telephone: (03) 578 2099, fax: (03) 578 0493

Stoneleigh Vineyard

Corbans is represented by Stoneleigh in Marlborough, and by one of the region's, indeed one of the country's, most talented winemakers, Alan McCorkindale. The creation of the vineyard goes back to the mid-1980s when Cooks, following their merger with Corbans, decided in a joint venture with Wolf Blass of Australia to develop their own vineyard and winery in Marlborough. Cooks had already planted about 40 hectares (100 acres) since 1980. McCorkindale at the time was working in Hawke's Bay, but was moved to Marlborough in 1988 and given the brief to design his own winery. It is essentially a large functional shed which can be easily extended as more facilities are required. On the rare occasions that McCorkindale is behind his desk rather than in the cellar, he looks down on his barrels from one side of his office and out at the vineyard from the other.

We wandered round the cellar, tasting from barrel to barrel, while McCorkindale talked about the strengths of Stoneleigh with his customary modesty. His particular enthusiasms are Chardonnay and Pinot Noir, and also Riesling. He particularly enjoys a challenge and when the pundits say that you cannot make good red wine on the South Island, he is one of those determined to prove them wrong. Marlborough so often equals Sauvignon, therefore he would rather make Chardonnay. He does so with a masterly touch as exemplified in his 1993 Cottage Block Chardonnay, which is very stylish, with an appealing toasted nose and a fine structured palate. At the other end of the Chardonnay range is the basic fruit-driven Stoneleigh Chardonnay, which is quite full and buttery. It spends about six months in wood, compared to a year of new oak for Cottage Block.

Pinot Noir is being gradually developed from an initial vintage in 1990. McCorkindale tries different techniques, so that part of it undergoes a traditional fermentation with some whole bunches, and part a variation on Accad's maceration principles. It is the blending of the different barrels that is all important and is more significant for the end result in the glass than the basic vinification process. He could never again make his Pinot Noir in just one way.

Stoneleigh Riesling has been made since 1986 and a vertical tasting demonstrated the staying power of this underrated variety and its potential success in Marlborough. The wines showed a wonderful capacity to develop, with peachy, slatey flavours combined with balancing acidity and a hint of well-integrated sweetness. McCorkindale is also responsible for Robard & Butler Amberley Riesling, for which the grapes are sent up from Waipara for vinification. A late harvest Riesling is another quest, but so far none has been produced in a commercial quantity. He tried in 1993, but the resulting 900 litres were blended back into the Stoneleigh Riesling. A sparkling wine will be another space to watch for the future.

In a funny sort of way, Stoneleigh does not appear to be part of a big company, even though it is. Instead it retains an air of independence under the more personal style of McCorkindale's management.

Corbans Winery, Jacksons Road, (RD 3) Blenheim, telephone: (03) 572 8198, fax: (03) 572 8199

Cloudy Bay

While Montana brought New Zealand to our notice at the cheaper end of the Sauvignon market, Cloudy Bay contributed international cachet with a brilliant marketing success story. It all began in Western Australia at Cape Mentelle, where since 1976 David Hohnen has been making successful red wines from Shiraz and Cabernet Sauvignon. He had planted Sauvignon and Sémillon too, but in the warm climate of the Margaret River they did not produce the elegance that he sought. It was a chance bottle left by a group of visiting New Zealand winemakers that led him to New Zealand in 1984, where he quickly identified Marlborough as the source of pithy, aromatic Sauvignon.

Land was bought in the Wairau Valley, while for the very first vintage of Cloudy Bay in 1985, Corbans agreed to supply some 40 tonnes of Sauvignon grapes which were vinified at their winery in Gisborne under the supervision of Cloudy Bay's newly appointed winemaker Kevin Judd. Judd is British born and Australian trained, a graduate of Roseworthy College who had already helped put Selaks on the New Zealand wine map and was considering returning to Australia when Hohnen offered him a job. Instead he moved to the South Island to supervise the building of a streamlined winery, which came into operation for the 1986 vintage.

Cloudy Bay Sauvignon, with its evocative label of the hills of the Richmond Ranges inspired by the view as you land at Blenheim's tiny airport, has captured the palates of the world, providing a benchmark for a certain style of New Zealand Sauvignon. It has more layers of flavour than Montana's overtly herbaceous wine and more subtlety, enhanced by the inclusion of a small amount of Sémillon. The amount depends on the vintage, between 2 and 15 per cent. The wine also spends a short time in oak, including a very small amount of new wood, which again adds yet another dimension. They also aim to pick the grapes over a range of ripeness, from 21.5° to 24° Brix, when conditions at the harvest permit, but that is not always possible.

The usual perceived wisdom is that Sauvignon does not age, but a vertical tasting of Cloudy Bay from 1994 back to 1986 disproved the preconception in the most satisfactory way. The 1994 had the ripe pungency that you would expect from young, fresh Sauvignon, while the 1991 had developed some very attractive herbal notes on both nose and palate, with some rich leafy fruit. It was a year in which everything came right. The 1988 had a more petrolly character, while the 1986 had a delightful, mature nutty nose and some ripe tropical fruit, which was quite unexpected in a wine that was nine years old and only intended to last a year or three.

Cloudy Bay also produces some very convincing Chardonnay that is barrel fermented and aged for about twelve months in wood. Good though it is, it has not acquired the same following as the Sauvignon. They also make some creditable Pinot Noir, though as yet without much depth as the vines are still very young. Their Cabernet Merlot blend is light and potentially charming in riper years, but will never have much weight.

Cloudy Bay's sparkling wine Pelorus is their other major venture. Although Veuve Clicquot has had a 70 per cent interest in Cloudy Bay since 1990, David Hohnen and Kevin Judd had already begun to develop a sparkling wine. They used the assistance of Californian Harold Osborne who assessed Marlborough's potential for sparkling wine based on his experience with Schramsberg and Champagne Deutz in California. And so Pelorus was created, with the first vintage in 1987, and the groundwork was laid on which Veuve Clicquot could build. The wine is named after Pelorus Jack, a friendly dolphin who for many years followed the boats in the Marlborough Sound. The wine is a blend of equal parts of Pinot Noir and Chardonnay. Some of the juice is fermented in small oak barrels, as well as in larger oak and in stainless-steel vats. The base wines are kept for nine months before blending and bottling, after which the wine spends another three years on the lees before disgorging. Riddling is carried out in the traditional *pupitres*. The wine has a ripe toasted character on the nose, and is full and rich in the mouth, with a light dosage.

Cloudy Bay is an attractive spot, with eucalyptus trees outside to recall its Australian connections. We sat drinking tea in their shade after the Sauvignon tasting and discussed the state of Marlborough while I was distracted by the winery cats, Roger and three-legged Spook.

Cloudy Bay Vineyards, Jacksons Road, (PO Box 376) Blenheim, telephone: (03) 572 8914, fax: (03) 572 8065

Cellier Le Brun

There are many people who believe that sparkling wine will be the next fashion in Marlborough, with growing interest from Jackson, Highfield, Johanneshof Cellars and others. Nautilus, the New Zealand arm of the Australian company Yalumba, make a successful example, as do Hunter's in association with Domaine Chandon of Australia. Meanwhile, Cellier Le Brun is the only winery in Marlborough to concentrate on sparkling wine as its main activity.

Daniel Le Brun is a *champenois* who learnt to make sparkling wine at the local oenology school of Avize. He then travelled the world looking for a suitable vineyard before settling on New Zealand. He had already dismissed California, South Africa and Australia, and arrived in Marlborough in 1980. He started from scratch, buying land and planting vineyards. His first wine was released in 1986, made from grapes from the 1983 and 1984 vintages. Marlborough has all the prerequisite conditions: dry summers, cool nights during the ripening period and cold winters. The soil is free draining and not too fertile and although it is not chalky, as in Champagne, you can add lime to it.

He has built a winery that is really an earth-covered culvert, which provides the naturally cool ambient temperature necessary for storing sparkling wine during the second fermentation and maturation on the lees. As you would expect, Le Brun's methods are traditionally *champenois*. He uses Chardonnay and Pinot Noir in varying proportions and, as yet unusually for New Zealand, a small amount of Pinot Meunier. His range comprises a non-vintage brut, a vintage wine, a *blanc de blancs* vintage, a rosé and a *tête de cuvée* named after his wife Adèle. He finds that the main difference between France and New Zealand is riper fruit. There is no need to chaptalize, and the harvest date is determined by the sugar and acidity content of the grapes. You have conditions in Marlborough that a *champenois* would see only in the very best years. However, the disadvantage may be that with lower acidity levels the wines develop much earlier. Usually his wines spend a couple of years on the lees and are riddled mechanically. As a style they tend to have quite rich, mouth-filling flavours.

Cellier Le Brun, Terrace Road, (PO Box 33) Renwick, telephone: (03) 572 8859, fax: (03) 572 8814

Hunter's

Jane Hunter is the personality behind Hunter's. The winery was created by her late husband Ernie, who apparently was one of the more colourful characters of the Marlborough wine scene until he was sadly killed in a car accident in 1987. Jane at the time was working as a viticulturist at Montana and on Ernie's death bravely took over the management of the winery. Ernie had first owned liquor stores in Christchurch. Then he planted vines as a contract grower for Penfolds and began producing wine, with his first vintage in 1982 made by Almuth Lorenz, who was later to create Merlen. A spectacular success with their Sauvignon at the Sunday Times Wine Festival in 1986 gave them enormous encouragement.

Jane Hunter is now one of Marlborough's, and indeed New Zealand's, most respected ambassadors of wine, for which she was awarded an OBE in December 1992. She has a winning smile when she is talking about New Zealand wine and is a friendly hostess at home, where you are also given a warm welcome by her large St Bernard dog Paddy, or in the attractive winery restaurant, where you barbecue your own steak to your taste. Hunter's winemaker is the amiable Australian Gary Duke who joined the company in 1991. They now have 16 hectares (40 acres) of their own vines, as well as nearly 48 hectares (about 120 acres) contracted across the Wairau Valley, and produce quite a wide range of different wines including a sparkling. They also provide the grapes for Domaine Chandon's New Zealand sparkling wine.

A tasting of the two provided an interesting comparison. Hunter's have inevitably benefited from advice from Tony Jordan, the highly qualified oenologist of Domaine Chandon in Australia, as well as from Richard Geoffroy, Moët's winemaker in Epernay. Hunter's are aiming for a more forward style than Domaine Chandon. Consequently their wine spends over three years on the lees, as opposed to just three for the Domaine Chandon wine, which also includes a slightly higher proportion of Pinot Noir.

As for table wines, there is a fresh Riesling dry, a textbook example of Sauvignon, as well as an oak-aged Sauvignon, of which about one-third is fermented in wood with good integration of oak. The oak adds an extra dimension and also allows for more ageing potential than plain Sauvignon. I also liked the 1992 Chardonnay, with quite a lean palate and a firm, oaky character. The Pinot Noir shows potential. Another star was made in just one vintage: Noble Hunter, a 1987 Chardonnay that was affected by botrytis as a result of some early rain, followed by a dry spell, and the grapes were picked at 39.5° Brix. The wine had a lovely roasted botrytis nose, was very wonderfully unctuous and smooth, and only 9.5° alcohol.

Hunter's Wines, Rapaura Road, (PO Box 839) RD3, Blenheim, telephone: (03) 572 8489, fax: (03) 572 8457

Vavasour

Vavasour for the moment sits in splendid isolation as the only winery in the remote Awatere Valley. It is a scenic drive from Blenheim, through the Dashwood Pass that provides a break in the Wither Hills. We saw a hawk taking off from a rock at the side of the road which at such close quarters was a dramatic sight. The winery is on the banks of Awatere River that runs vaguely parallel to the Wairau River. However, conditions are slightly different. The Awatere Valley tends to be windier and drier, but not necessarily warmer, just more exposed. A higher heat summation may make it more suitable for reds, resulting in riper flavours. The alluvial deposits are very similar to Wairau, and the soil is very stony, with good drainage. However, there is none of the underground water for the vines to tap that is found on the Wairau Plain. The harsher environment tends to result in lower yields.

Although Vavasour may be the only winery, their vineyards no longer stand alone and there are now about 24 hectares (60 acres) in the valley, of which 12 (30) are theirs. Other wineries have planted, or have encouraged contract growers to plant for them. Villa Maria, among others, are interested in the area. Vavasour planted their first vines in 1986 and their maiden vintage was in 1989. The key people in the enterprise are Peter Vavasour, whose family came out to New Zealand in the 1840s as sheep farmers. The gate posts have a stone cockerel on each post representing the Vavasour family crest. Richard Bowling is the viticulturist and Glenn Thomas, who was at Corbans before Alan McCorkindale, the winemaker.

On my last visit I tasted through the Vavasour range, as well as wines for their second label, Dashwood, named after the first surveyor of the valley. Fruit is bought in from Wairau for the Dashwood label, whereas Vavasour comes only from Awatere fruit. Dashwood Sauvignon may include some Sémillon, while Vavasour Sauvignon never does. However, Vavasour Reserve Sauvignon is partially fermented in barrel, providing some firm, subtle flavours. Glenn Thomas suggested that Awatere Sauvignon has a certain flintiness compared to the more tropical flavours of Wairau. The 1994 Vavasour Reserve Chardonnay is stylish and elegant, with a delicate degree of toastiness. As for their red wines based on Cabernet Sauvignon, under the Dashwood label they aim for fruit, whereas with the Vavasour range they would like a slower development. The best recent vintages for red wine, 1989 and 1991 (the 1994s were not ready to taste at the time of my visit), showed some excellent concentration of flavour and fruit, with good structure and potential for ageing. They have also planted a certain amount of Syrah, which showed some promise in the 1991 vintage, but Thomas admits that it is marginal here. Neither the 1992 nor 1993 ripened. Thomas and Bowling are also working on Pinot Noir and are attracted by the idea of a dry Riesling with ageing potential.

Thomas described himself as a minimalist in the winery, for 'if you have good grapes from your vineyard, the balance in the wine comes naturally'. Certainly, together with Richard Bowling as his talented viticulturist, who has an innate understanding of the vines, they make a good team.

Vavasour Wines, Redwood Pass, Awatere Valley, (PO Box 72,

Seddon) Marlborough, telephone: (03) 575 7481, fax: (03) 575 7240

Te Whare Ra

Te Whare Ra, which in Maori means 'the house in the sun', is the second oldest winery in Marlborough after Montana, and Allen Hogan has seen more vintages in the region than any other wine-maker in that 1982 was his first harvest. He was working as an air-traffic controller in Western Australia when he and his wife Joyce looked for land there, but without success. Instead they found their 4-hectare (10-acre) plot in the Brancott Valley when they returned to New Zealand for a holiday in 1977. Joyce explained how the bank refused to lend them money for a winery, but would consider a tractor shed. Allen had no winemaking quali-fications. He gained experience in some Australian wineries, and also with Montana and at Te Kauwhata, and Joyce admits ruefully that their first wines were not terribly good, but they have learnt. And indeed they have.

Most unusually for a Marlborough winery, they do not make Sauvignon. They did initially, but saw little point in doing exactly the same as everyone else. Instead, in 1985 they were the first winery in Marlborough to make a botrytized wine. This has earned them a reputation for sweet wines, something which they see as a mixed blessing because it is impossible to repeat each year. The cool nights at the end of the season result in heavy dews that the sun then burns off, which encourages the development of botrytis. In addition, Hogan avoids using botrytis sprays and also finds that there is quite a humid microclimate in the canopy. However, there are none of the dank autumnal mists that are essential in Sauternes and Barsac, and some years they have wasted rows of grapes by leaving them on the vines too long.

The development of botrytis also depends on the particular clones. The standard Riesling clone in New Zealand has very open bunches that do not encourage the formation of botrytis, whereas a new clone which is being introduced from South Australia is more susceptible. The 1991 Botrytis Berry Selection Riesling was ripe and unctuous, with some rich apricot fruit and great concen-tration of flavour, when I first tasted it in November 1993; some months later in February 1995, it had developed more marmalade notes, while retaining the same concentration.

The Hogans also make dry Riesling as well as a delicious Gewürztraminer which they sell under the Duke of Marlborough label. The 1994 Gewürztraminer has a delicate nose, with an elegantly spicy palate that was ripe, with balancing acidity, while the 1986, when it was nine years old, had developed that lovely mature, slightly nutty *pain d'épice* flavour of ageing Gewürztraminer, with some wonderfully rich toasted fruit. There is also a red wine, a Bordeaux blend of Cabernet Sauvignon with one-third Merlot and drop of Cabernet Franc, which is sold under the Sarah Jennings label to recall the Duchess of Marlborough and continue the historical theme.

Te Whare Ra Wines, Anglesea Street, Renwick, telephone/fax: (03) 572 8581

Grove Mill

Grove Mill was first set up in the original malthouse of an old brewery by a group of grape growers who were discontented at the widespread pulling up of vines instigated by the larger wineries in the mid-1980s. David Pearce, who first worked with Corbans, has been the winemaker since the maiden vintage, beginning with a 1988 Riesling. The winery was initially conceived as a small boutique winery, but has gradually expanded into something rather bigger. In September 1994 they opened a new winery building with a capacity of 1,000 tonnes, which represents a considerable leap in size from the 300 tonnes they squeezed into the old brewery. The new winery is a well-designed, spacious shed, methodically planned for easy use, functional but with the odd decorative touch. The steel girders are painted a brilliant blue and a large expanse of glass at one end provides good natural light and also allows visitors to look into the winery.

Although many of the shareholders of Grove Mill are grape growers, the winery does not automatically take all their fruit but remains selective in its sources. It takes grapes from different parts of Marlborough. These included the riverland area of Omaka, which, with its heavier soil, is good for Gewürztraminer; the stonier area of Rapaura; and Renwick, with its light, infertile soil. Their best wines, the Gold Label series, carry the names of the individual vineyards, such as Lansdowne Chardonnay, Blackbirch Cabernet and Drylands Sauvignon. They also have an experimental block of red varieties: Cabernet Sauvignon, Malbec, Syrah and Pinotage, as well as Pinot Noir, which they consider has good potential in Marlborough as the climate is quite similar to Martinborough. Gewürztraminer and, unusually, Pinot Gris, of which 1994 was the first vintage, complete the range.

I was treated to a fascinating vertical tasting of several varietals that demonstrated not only the annual fluctuations of the vintage, but also the variations of method. Three vintages of Sauvignon had different amounts of residual sugar, depending on the extract and alcohol in the wine. The proportion of malolactic fermentation could vary too, as well as the length of ageing on the lees. There were two versions of Chardonnay: a fruit-driven wine made from Marlborough fruit and Lansdowne Chardonnay from Gisborne fruit, which is made in a very Burgundian way with fermentation in barrel followed by several months of ageing on the lees. The 1991 was showing particularly well, with a fine nutty character.

The Riesling, too, showed interesting variations. The 1994 Dry Riesling was its first vintage. What Pearce really wants from Riesling is a Mosel Auslese, but with more body and alcohol. His 1991 was delicately honeyed, with a petrolly, peachy nose. It was a range of wines with considerable appeal and depth.

Grove Mill Wine Company, Waihopai Valley Road, (PO Box 67, Renwick) Marlborough, telephone: (03) 572 8200, fax: (03) 572 8211

Merlen

Almuth Lorenz is a young German who came out to New Zealand to explore the country after she had graduated from the Geisenheim Institute in 1981. She liked it so much that she tore up her return ticket. She worked for Ernie Hunter until 1986, when she set up Merlen with eleven other shareholders. She is the winemaker and majority shareholder.

With Lorenz's origins in the Rheinhessen, Merlen inevitably has a Germanic flavour, with Riesling, Müller-Thurgau, Gewürztraminer and even some Morio-Muscat which has been gradually replacing Müller-Thurgau since 1991. Apparently it grows like a weed, but the huge yield does not detract from its flavour, and its novelty value enhances its popularity. I found it much less overpowering than some I have tasted from the Rheinhessen, with some soft, slightly sweet fruit.

With Riesling, Lorenz aims for a wine with as little alcohol as possible and a minimum amount of skin contact to avoid any bitterness. Chaptalization can also upset the flavour balance. In 1994, the grapes were picked at a Kabinett level of ripeness and about 10 grams of residual sugar was left in the wine, which equates to a Halbtrocken. Lorenz's best Riesling vintages have been 1989 and 1991, when she also made the wine she calls Magic Merlen from fully botrytized grapes. She left seven rows of grapes in which some noble rot had already appeared and picked them in June. The wine was left to ferment in old oak barrels until the following January, when the fermentation simply ran out of steam, then the wine spent a further six months on its lees. Lorenz said modestly, 'It made itself,' then grinned, and less modestly and very enthusiastically exclaimed, 'I have never made such a nice wine!' And delicious it was too, with ripe honeyed apricots and hints of marmalade, and all wonderfully unctuous in the mouth.

Like other Marlborough wineries, Lorenz produces Chardonnay and Sauvignon and, more unusually, has just begun to make a pure Sémillon instead of adding it to her Sauvignon. As yet, it is still very much at the experimental stage.

Her latest venture is the installation of a still for making *eau de vie*. Distillation had formed part of her course at Geisenheim. She has imported a copper still from Germany and buys fruit from her neighbours. Her first year of production was 1992 and it is still very much at the learning stage, for she finds that you can create and destroy the flavours so easily. I liked the Poire William best among her range of fruit brandies. There is now another distillery in Marlborough which also produces fruit brandy, so with limited competition Lorenz is achieving a good following for her brandies and is now planning a calvados. Essentially, however, she sees it as a toy – she has christened the still Ethyl – but at least it is paying its way.

Merlen Wines, Vintage Lane, (PO Box 8) Renwick, telephone/ fax: (03) 572 9151

Highfield

Highfield winery is one of the new landmarks of Marlborough, an incongruous Italianate tower in the middle of the vineyards offering views of the surrounding area, with a functional cellar underneath. It was opened with some ceremony on a hot summer's day in February 1995. However, Highfield had an uncertain start. It was set up in 1990 by the Walsh family, who ran into financial difficulties after their first vintage, and is now owned by a unlikely group of three businessmen: a New Zealander, Neil Buchanan; a Japanese, Shin Yokoi; and a Sri Lankan, Tom Tenuwera, who is based in Britain. The winemaker is Roseworthy-trained Tony Hooper, who said he does everything except pay the bills.

Highfield's basic range consists of Chardonnay, Sauvignon, Riesling and some Merlot as an easy alternative to Cabernet Sauvignon. They were sound, but did not excite. Potentially more impressive is their project for sparkling wine, instigated by Shin Yokoi who is the agent for Drappier Champagne in Tokyo, which is how Michel Drappier came to be involved with sparkling wine in New Zealand. He acts as a consultant. He spent the 1993 vintage at Highfield, advising on the production of the first base wines. In turn, Hooper has spent time in Champagne and at Domaine Chandon in California. Samples are regularly exchanged and commented upon. They are using equal proportions of Chardonnay and Pinot Noir from just one vineyard, and the first wine, the 1993 vintage, will be released in 1997 after three years on the lees. However, we were given a preview at the opening of the winery, for a small quantity had been disgorged after only a few months which would have been inconceivable for a Champagne, with its much higher acidity. The wine promised well.

Highfield Estate, Brooby Road, RD 2, Blenheim, telephone: (03) 572 8592, fax: (03) 572 9257

Fromm Winery

One of the most recent entrants on the Marlborough wine scene is George Fromm, a serious and committed Swiss. He is the fourth generation of a winemaking family from the village of Malans close to the Liechtenstein border. As he said, he has had twenty-four years of making Pinot Noir in a cool climate, as well as

Gewürztraminer, Pinot Gris and Müller-Thurgau. He first came to New Zealand for a holiday and recognized the challenge presented in the vineyards. He is convinced that with appropriate vineyard management it is perfectly possible to make serious red wine in a marginal climate such as Marlborough. The first hurdle was to overcome the bureaucracy of the overseas investment committee, then he began buying land in 1991. He has been living in New Zealand since December 1993 and made some wine in 1994 at Grove Mill, while his own winery was built in time for the 1995 vintage. His winemaker is Hätsch Kalberer who made the wines at Matawhero during Denis Irwin's absences in Gisborne, Australia.

Even at this initial stage you feel that Fromm is a winery that is going to make its mark in a very positive way. The 1994 Sauvignon is quite unlike any other Sauvignon from New Zealand in that it is much more European in style and lacks the upfront fruit-driven flavours normally associated with Marlborough. However, although they produce not only Sauvignon but also Chardonnay, Fromm's avowed aim is quite simply to make the very best red wines on the South Island and to be known above all as a red wine winery. Both Fromm and Kalberer firmly believe that the key to their success lies with vineyard management. They have contracts with various growers who are prepared to follow their ideas about shoot thinning and leaf plucking to ensure sufficient sunlight in the canopy and that the vine is in balance. One is Mike Eaton, whose Clayvin vineyard is a rare hillside site. Isabel is another vineyard, as well as their own Lavinia vineyard which they have planted in much closer rows than is usual in New Zealand.

Fromm's first release of Pinot Noir has immense intensity of fruit, even without the support from oak ageing. Without oak the wine is packed with vibrant cherry fruit; with oak it takes on smoky overtones. They are also working on trial blocks of various red varieties such as Syrah, Sangiovese, Merlot (which is most promising), Cabernet Franc and Malbec, rather than Cabernet Sauvignon. Pinot Noir is what excites most of all.

Fromm Winery, Cnr Godfrey and Middle Renwick Roads, (Godfrey Road, RD 2) Blenheim, telephone: (03) 572 9355, fax: (03) 577 7697

Johanneshof Cellars

Johanneshof Cellars is the creation of Warwick Foley and his German wife Edeltraud, who comes from Rüdesheim in the Rheingau. Their winery is set apart from the rest of Marlborough in the hills to the north of the Wairau Valley off the road to Picton. However, most of their vineyards are in the Omaka Valley, apart from one small vineyard of Pinot Noir on the hill just by the winery. Here, the soil is sandstone packed with iron and the vineyard is unusual in having narrow spacing and no irrigation.

Sparkling wine is their main objective and they have been producing base wines since 1991. However, as yet nothing is ready for release. Instead, I tasted a range of still wines which showed an individuality indicative of Foley's personality. You feel that this is very much somebody who does not want to fit into a mould or conform to any usual preconceptions of Marlborough. Although he produces Chardonnay, mostly it is destined for sparkling wine, 'Every man and his dog has it' as a table wine. Riesling, too, is different in that it is matured in wood in keeping with his Geisenheim training. I enjoyed the 1992 Fumé Blanc Reserve, which is tightly knit with firm oaky undertones after two years' maturation in wood. The 1993 Sauvignon was also quite original as some of the grapes had botrytis, giving the wine some ripe honeyed fruit, with a distinctive leafy richness.

The other element of originality about Johanneshof Cellars is that they have created a cellar in the hillside – a major project that entailed the tunnelling of stone out of the hill. It makes a maturation cellar for the sparkling wine quite unlike anything I have seen anywhere in New Zealand. Not only is it the first hillside cellar in the country, but you could easily believe yourself in a centuries-old European wine cellar, with the wines quietly sleeping.

Johanneshof Cellars, State Highway 1, (RD 3) Koromiko, Blenheim, telephone: (03) 573 7035, fax: (03) 573 7034

Rapaura Vintners

The proliferation of new labels coming out of Marlborough has been prompted by the creation of Vintech, a winemaking facility that quite simply produces wines to specification. You provide the grapes, Vintech provide the equipment, you say how you would like your grapes vinified, and they do the work and present you with a bill at the end of the operation. The idea came from John Belsham, a highly qualified winemaker with a proven track record at Hunter's, while his partner Jeff Taylor provided the finance. Belsham saw the need for such a facility in Marlborough, for the large Auckland wineries had to truck their grapes north. They were at the mercy of the often inclement weather in the Cook Strait and one year a ferry strike caused severe disruptions in the transport schedules. Even when everything runs smoothly, the shortest journey time between Blenheim and Auckland is sixteen hours, which does little to enhance the quality of the fruit. Essentially, if your grapes are picked by machine, it means that the juice has sixteen hours of skin contact whether you like it or not.

Vintech came into operation in 1991 when just 1,300 tonnes were crushed. In 1995 they were expecting to handle 6,000 tonnes, but the harvest was even larger than anticipated, causing considerable logistical problems. The timetable planned before the start of the vintage broke down when the heavens opened in Marlborough and growers wanted their grapes crushed days earlier than scheduled. Even crushing through the night, Vintech ran out of vat space. Alternative facilities had to be found and Jackson Estate even managed to have vats built in record-breaking time. Vintech has now been purchased by a group of partners: Foxes Island Wines, important wholesalers Négociants NZ Ltd., Nautilus Estate, Shingle Peak Wines and Wairau River Wines. The new joint venture will be called Rapaura Vintners and will continue to service many but not all of Vintech's original customers.

It is a very functional winery. You can get an aerial view of a tank farm from the top of one of the many stainless-steel vats. Their objective is the efficient mechanical extraction of the juice using gentle bladder presses with minimal damage to the grape skins. The emphasis is on delicate handling. The client provides a specification and is given a daily report on the progress of fermentations and other treatments. Everything is highly computerized. Sauvignon, of course, lends itself to this sort of operation with its very straightforward fermentation and simple vinification process to produce a wine that is ready for early drinking.

For the 1995 vintage, Vintech had twenty-eight customers with what Belsham called fifteen core clients. Usually a minimum 100 tonnes of one variety is the most practical amount, with maybe two or three wines per company but, for historical reasons, they also included a couple of smaller operations, as well as Belsham's own Foxes Island. 1992 was the first vintage for a range comprising Chardonnay and Pinot Noir. The name originates from the site of the Vintech operation which is not in fact on an island, but a nearby river regularly floods and turns it into an island. The Foxe in question was William Foxe who surveyed for the New Zealand Company and went on to find gold in Arrowtown in Central Otago.

Foxes Island Wines, Rapaura Road, (RD 3) Blenheim, telephone: (03) 572 8299, fax: (03) 572 8399

Wairau River

Phil and Chris Rose, like many other of Vintech's original customers, were grape growers but, unlike the others, it is Belsham himself who determines the specification of their wines. The Roses began growing grapes for Montana back in 1977, a move which met with considerable opposition from the neighbouring arable and sheep farmers who feared that grape growing, with its different demands regarding treatments and sprays, would cause them problems. The Roses finally won their case in the Court of Appeal and, as they put it, the floodgates opened. The guys who objected have now planted vines themselves, or sold their land to people who have. Grape growing saved Marlborough from the worst effects of the last recession and land values have increased enormously.

Phil Rose is above all a farmer with an innate understanding of the soil and its effect on his vines. He has a total of 100 hectares (225 acres) of vines, of which about 40 hectares (100 acres) are Chardonnay and Sauvignon for the Wairau River label. In addition he grows Riesling, Pinot Noir, Pinot Meunier, Syrah, Cabernet Sauvignon, Merlot and Pinot Gris under contract for other wineries. Müller-Thurgau has now disappeared from his vineyards as he has undertaken a considerable replanting programme following the ravages of phylloxera.

Chris Rose has the marketing mind of the pair and runs the attractive restaurant across the road from Rapaura Vintners which provides a showcase for their wines. I like their Sauvignon with its zesty fruit. A second label may appear for a more forward style of

Sauvignon and they may consider a Riesling, and even a sparkling wine, all under the guidance of Belsham.

Wairau River Wines, Cnr Rapaura Road and SH 6, (Giffords Road, RD 3) Blenheim, telephone/fax: (03) 572 9800

Jackson Estate

Warwick and John Stichbury are the two brothers behind Jackson Estate. John is a viticulturist and Warwick a marketing expert. It was John's idea to plant vines in the first place as he was having a tough time growing vegetables in the mid-1980s. Warwick's reaction was that 8 hectares (20 acres) was too small, thought about economies of scale and made it 40 (100). Originally they thought to have their own winery, then Vintech opened and the convenience was too tempting. But now, after the problems with the 1995 vintage, they will invest in a winery. Martin Shaw of the South Australian winery Shaw & Smith, with an established reputation for one of Australia's finest Sauvignons as well as excellent Chardonnay, is their consultant. Why an Australian? He is one of the best Australian winemakers and any talented New Zealand winemaker was already gainfully employed. With his own vintage a month before Marlborough's, it is quite possible for Shaw to juggle the two, especially with close contact by fax. Then he comes over for the blending options.

Jackson Estate has an eye-catching label featuring the large gum tree planted by the Stichburys' great-grandmother at the end of the last century which still stands in the garden of the family house. The first Jackson, Adam, arrived in New Zealand in the early 1840s and acquired a 1,100 acre plot when Marlborough was being shared out by Edward Gibson Wakefield. It has since dwindled down to 110 acres (44 hectares), but has always remained in the family.

The initial range consisted of Sauvignon, Chardonnay and a Riesling which is labelled Marlborough Dry in deference to marketing exigencies and the current problems of selling anything exhibiting the word 'Riesling' on the British market. More recently the range was extended to include Pinot Noir, then a sparkling wine. A visit to the Stichburys is always a friendly occasion. The two brothers are quite different in character but spark off each other in a lively way. John is a man of the land; you feel he really understands his vineyard and is intent on learning more about his vines. He is content to remain in rural Marlborough, whereas Warwick is more a man of the world, preferring the brighter lights of Wellington and happily travels across the world to promote their wines.

The Jacksons have a weather station in the middle of their vines, a wooden tower providing a view over their land, equipped with a marine weather fax keyed into the American weather schedule which enables them to receive long-term weather patterns. They are building up an impressive record of weather patterns: ground and air temperatures, wind speed, rainfall, relative humidity, wind chill, as well as minimum and maximum temperatures. With this wealth of information they hope to remove some of the guesswork from their schedules in the vineyard and at the vintage. In the vineyard, John is working on different clones and rootstocks.

After a quick detour to check out Marlborough's newest pub the Cork and Keg before opening hours, which was doing its best to be at home in an English village, we sat down to taste round the large kitchen table in their turn-of-the-century weatherboard house. Marlborough Dry is delicate and fresh, with a floral character, and we heartily agreed that Riesling is due for a comeback. Sauvignon has rounded pithy fruit. In 1994 they made two Chardonnays: one that is ripe and mouth-filling, with obvious buttery fruit, and the reserve wine which comes from more mature vines, with tighter flavours and more structure. They have yet to master the intricacies of Pinot Noir, but 1994 shows some promise. Next came their first sparkling wine, from a 1992 base wine made from 60 per cent Pinot Noir and 40 per cent Chardonnay, with a delicately creamy nose and fuller mature biscuity fruit on the palate. A treat on which to finish was their 1991 Botrytis Riesling which has developed some lovely rich orange-marmalade fruit.

Jackson Estate, Jacksons Road, Blenheim (PO Box 30863, Lower Hutt.), telephone: (04) 569 6547, fax: (04) 569 7037

Allan Scott Wines

Allan Scott was brought up on a farm in north Canterbury and joined the wine industry in 1973, helping Montana with their first plantings in Marlborough. After working for Corbans, where he helped set up the Stoneleigh vineyard, in 1990 he decided to establish his own label. He had planted his own vineyards several years earlier, providing grapes under contract, and now has 24 hectares (60 acres) in production, as well as managing another 40 hectares (100 acres) for two growers who supply him and for Morton Estate's Stonecreek Vineyard.

His experience is very much that of a viticulturist. He has wondered whether to build a winery or maybe a barrel room so that he can conduct his own barrel fermentations, but for the moment has been using Vintech and his shop window is an attractive restaurant. We tasted in the garden, surrounded by flowering tree mallows. His 1994 Sauvignon has some tropical fruit flavours, with an extra dimension from a small amount of Sémillon. As for so many Marlborough wineries, Sauvignon is the mainstay of their business and all would echo Scott's sentiment, 'I hope it never goes out of fashion.'

Chardonnay is developing from his first vintage in 1991, about which he admits to being rather timid as he was uncertain of the style of wine he wanted. The 1991 turned out quite elegantly, but the 1992 was too oaky. In 1993 he tried all kinds of techniques, with a large proportion of barrel fermentation using more older barrels. He now has a greater variety of clones to add more complexity, which there certainly was in his 1994 Chardonnay. We finished with his 1994 Riesling, which was fresh and lemony with a little honey and perfect for a garden setting.

Allan Scott Wines and Estates, Jacksons Road, (RD 3) Blenheim, telephone: (03) 572 9054, fax: (03) 572 9053

Forrest Estate

John Forrest is a rugged-looking individual who got into wine by drinking it. Unfortunately we have never met, as he was on my side of the world when I was on his. However, his assistant Brigitte was able to give me a good overview of the activities of Forrest Estate. Forrest was a dairy-farmer's son and a biochemist by training who, after working in California and Australia, as well as in New Zealand, decided to settle at home and make wine. He now has a 6.5-hectare (16-acre) vineyard by Gibson's Creek in the Renwick area. Maybe there are long-term plans for a winery, but for the moment he has been Vintech's smallest customer. There is an attractive tasting room, and visitors are encouraged to bring a picnic and enjoy the gardens with the weeping willows by the creek.

The Sauvignon, which includes a small amount of Sémillon, is fresh and pithy. A medium Riesling is light and lemony, with quite a sweet honeyed palate. 1993 Gibson's Creek, a blend of Cabernet Sauvignon, Cabernet Franc and Merlot, is young and herbaceous, with some cassis fruit and a little tannin. Finally, there was a 1994 Late Harvest Chardonnay, picked on 4 June, which was surprisingly delicate and honeyed, with some acidity. It included the grapes from forty Muscat vines, which give just an extra hint of something else.

Forrest Estate, Blicks Road, Renwick, telephone/fax: (03) 572 9084

Hawkesbridge Wines

Michael Veal had a career in marketing and public relations in Wellington and, with his wife Judy, has caught the wine bug. We sat, chatted and tasted at their house, looking out on their 12 hectares (30-odd acres) of vines. Veal bought undeveloped land, except for a few acres of Müller-Thurgau in 1990, and has set himself the aim of growing the best possible grapes. He has done a viticultural course and is learning from reading, talking and common sense. He has planted a few acres each year, mainly Sauvignon and some Chardonnay. His first vintage, of 1994 Sauvignon, was made by Tony Hooper at Highfield, but from 1995 he will be using Tim Finn's facilities at Neudorf, with Chris Comerford acting as his consultant. We tasted his 1994: a typical Marlborough Sauvignon, with pithy fruit and fresh, clean flavours. Veal's enthusiasm, backed by his marketing expertise, should take him far.

Hawkesbridge Wines and Estates, Hawkesbury Road, (PO Box 9) Renwick, telephone: (03) 572 8024, fax: (03) 572 9489

Lake Chalice

Lake Chalice takes its name from a drowned lake in the Richmond Ranges on the north side of the Wairau Valley between Nelson and Marlborough. If the label is anything to go by, it is indeed a picturesque spot. There are three partners in the project: two of whom I met, Ron Wichman and viticulturist Phil Binnie, along with winemaker Chris Gambitsis. Wichman and Gambitsis ran a restaurant together which led on to this venture and the purchase of 28 acres of land in 1989. They began planting vines the following year and made their first wine in 1992, just a small amount of Chardonnay. Their vineyard now includes Sauvignon, Riesling, Sémillon, Cabernet Sauvignon, Cabernet Franc and Merlot, as well as Chardonnay.

For the moment, they are using contract winemaking facilities – first at Highfield and in 1995 at Whitehaven – but are planning their own winery for 1996. I tasted some of their white wines. A 1994 medium dry Riesling was light and fresh, with hints of peaches. In 1993 they made a drier, more austere Riesling, with some slatey acidity. Their 1994 Sauvignon was quite mouth-filling and in the same year they also made a pure Sémillon which was fermented and spent three months in American oak. It needs time to show its potential, as does the winery. For the moment, they are an example of the burgeoning wine scene of Marlborough which continues to grow at a breath-taking pace.

Lake Chalice Wines, Vintage Lane, (PO Box 66) Renwick, telephone/fax: (03) 572 9327

Cairnbrae Wines

Like many of the new entrants to the Marlborough wine scene, Daphne and Murray Brown have no winery, but a café and shop situated in the middle of their vineyards which provides a focal point to their activities and a place where visitors can taste their wine. That is what we did, and we talked about the changes they have seen in the fifteen years they have been in Marlborough. Murray Brown comes from Southland and was looking for a sheep and cattle property when he came to Marlborough, found nothing suitable and instead decided to buy land, plant a vineyard and involve himself in this exciting young industry. So they planted a 12-hectare (30-acre) block with Müller-Thurgau, Chenin Blanc and Riesling under contract to Corbans. However, hardly were their vines in production than Corbans announced the vine pull three days before Christmas in 1985. At the time it seemed devastating, but in fact they replaced their Chenin Blanc with Sauvignon and things began to look brighter with the new demand for the latter. They now have four varieties in their vineyard – Riesling, Sauvignon,

Chardonnay and Sémillon – and have used the facilities of Vintech, with Kim Crawford from Coopers Creek as their consultant wine-maker. Although they still continue to work to some extent with Corbans, they feel things are much more stable with the seemingly steady demand for Sauvignon and that the time has come for a new challenge. Life purely as a contract grower can be quite problematic if there is pressure on grape prices, but they doubt if they will ever build their own winery. Their 1994 Sauvignon is fresh and juicy, with good fruit and not too much acidity. The Sémillon is vinified without any oak and is quite lean with a firm, nutty taste. The Chardonnay is lightly oaked and the Riesling, which has a hint of residual sugar, is gentle, honeyed and understated. In other words, the wines bear the hallmark of Kim Crawford's talent.

Cairnbrae Wines, Jacksons Road, (RD 3) Blenheim, telephone/fax: (03) 572 8048

Saint Clair

Neal Ibbotson is yet another grape grower turned wine producer. He came north from Dunedin and, after working as a rural valuer and farm consultant, turned to viticulture, studying at Lincoln College and planting vines back in 1978. Until recently he was supplying Montana and Delegat's, but again the desire for his own label was a strong motivating force. Ibbotson now has 36 hectares (90 acres) of vines, including a new 16-hectare (40-acre) block of Chardonnay and Sauvignon in the Awatere Valley which will come into production in 1996. I tasted his first wines, which were made at Vintech, on the trade day of the Marlborough Wine and Food Festival. The 1994 Riesling was lightly flowery, but a little flat on the finish; the 1993 Chardonnay was quite firm and buttery, with some ageing potential.

Saint Clair Estate Wines, Rapaura Vintners, Rapaura Road, (739 New Renwick Road, RDO2) Blenheim, telephone/fax: (03) 578 8695

Lawson's Dry Hills

Ross Lawson's first vintage was 1992, even though he has been a hobby grape grower of Gewürztraminer since 1981. He has now sold his swimming-pool construction business to devote himself to wine, in partnership with other growers who supply him with grapes. His first wines were made at Vintech, but he is building his own winery and his winemaker is Roseworthy graduate Claire Allan.

The venture is very much in its infancy. They are planning a sparkling wine for which the first base wines were made in 1995, and they are planting Merlot and Pinot Noir to complement their white range of Sauvignon, Riesling, Chardonnay and Gewürztraminer. The 1994 Riesling is dry, with a hint of lemon meringue pie. The Chardonnay is quite oaky, with a good firm flavour, and I particularly liked the Gewürztraminer, which had some elegant spice that Allan described as green ginger.

Lawson's Dry Hills Wines, Alabama Road, (PO Box 4020) Blenheim, telephone/fax: (03) 578 7674

Conders Bend

In a way, Craig Gass bridges the gap between Nelson and Marlborough. Depending on your perspective, he was either my last visit in Nelson or my first in Marlborough, for he has been involved in both areas. We met at his house which boasts splendid views overlooking Nelson harbour. Gass is refreshingly opinionated, with a lively mind and an earthy sense of humour. Conders Bend is named after an area in Marlborough that was farmed by a Thomas Conder where there is a bend in the river. However, he had thought of slightly altering the name of his wine and coining the advertising slogan 'the wine for every conceivable occasion'! Gass explained how he set up one of the early Nelson wineries, Korepo, in 1975, then for various reasons sold the winery to David Moore in 1989, who renamed it Ruby Bay. Gass has had a varied career, first working at Villa Maria in the early 1970s, and after the sale of Korepo he went to Australia and worked with James Halliday and Tony Jordan. He was involved with Vintech at the start and that is where he made the first vintage of Conders Bend. Now he is involved with Rothbury's New Zealand venture and his allegiance lies firmly with Marlborough rather than Nelson.

Gass has neither a winery nor vineyards. His only assets are his barrels and accordingly he describes himself as an accountant's dream. For his grapes he has good contracts in good areas for Sauvignon, Riesling and Chardonnay. He maintains a close relationship with his growers, carefully following the growth of the grapes and advising on work in the vineyard. He is adamant that he will produce a wine only if the quality is right. For instance, he made no Riesling in 1994 as he did not think the grapes had enough flavour. In contrast, 1993 with its long, cool growing season made excellent Riesling. Gass is also planning a *blanc de blancs* sparkling wine for release in 1997.

In Sauvignon, he looks for ripe grapes with a tropical fruit flavour, and this was evident in his 1994, with its ripe nose, rounded green-pea flavours and tropical overtones. For Chardonnay, he wants something different. People accept that high acidity in Marlborough is a fact of life, but Gass does not. He wants to take what he called the lean acidic edge out of the middle palate by manipulating the canopy to obtain ripe fruit, and he is also experimenting with new yeasts. His 1994 Chardonnay was barrel fermented in new and one-year-old barrels which were all heavily toasted. He plays with solids, stirring the lees, and the wine spent nine months in oak. Although it has all undergone a malolactic fermentation, the lactic character in the wine is not overpowering. There was ripe fruit with some backbone and quite high alcohol at 13.5°, giving good mouthfeel.

Conders Bend Wines, Rapaura Road, (2/118 Princes Drive, Nelson) RD 3, Blenheim, telephone/fax: (03) 546 9322

Whitehaven

I met Simon Waghorn, who had previously been at Corbans in Gisborne, just before Whitehaven's first vintage. Greg and Sue White are the main shareholders in this new venture which will operate from the old Grove Mill winery. Greg White worked in banking but had tired of life in finance. After sailing round the world he decided to settle in Marlborough. Waghorn had also decided that the time was right to leave a large company and settle into something smaller. For their first vintage they were planning a dry Riesling, a Sauvignon Blanc and two Chardonnays, one very much modelled on a Burgundian style and a more accessible fruit-driven wine. Initially, they also plan to do some contract wine-making for some smaller growers such as Ponder Estate and Framingham. With Waghorn's proven expertise in Corbans' Gisborne wines, Whitehaven should be a name to watch.

Whitehaven Wine Company, 1 Dodson Street, Blenheim, telephone: (03) 577 8861, fax: (03) 577 8868

Gillan Estate

Gillan Estate came into the limelight by winning the Air New Zealand Sauvignon trophy in 1994 with their 1994 Sauvignon, which was their first example of the variety. It is absolutely typical of the fresh flavours of Marlborough, with good pungent, ripe fruit. Their first wines, made in 1992, were base wines from Chardonnay and Pinot Noir for a sparkling wine which will be their main objective. Their decision to concentrate on that is very much dictated by marketing considerations as they consider that the potential is enormous. As well as Sauvignon, there will also be Chardonnay produced by their winemaker Sam Weaver.

Terry Gillan has been involved with various local vineyards for some time. He was one of the original shareholders of Grove Mill and as an entrepreneurial builder has also been behind some of the new construction in the centre of Blenheim. Plans to build a full-scale winery met with objections so they have been curtailed to include a storage and disgorging area, and a sales point. Again, this is another space to watch in that Terry Gillan's energy will take him far, backed by his wife Toni.

Gillan Estate Wines, Rapaura Road, (PO Box 482) Blenheim, telephone: (03) 572 9979, fax: (03) 572 9980

There are several other emerging wineries in Marlborough, but considerations of time and space make it impossible to include them all. Harsh reality dictates that some may make only a fleeting appearance on the Marlborough wine scene, while others are here to stay. Only time will tell which are which. Meanwhile, Marlborough enjoys its annual Wine and Food Festival in early February. I was there for the trade day which provided a good opportunity to catch up with wineries I had not been able to visit. The festival takes place in a large paddock on Montana's Brancott Estate. Most of the Marlborough wineries participate and there are wines galore to taste and local food to sample. You can look down on the animated scene from the top of Rob's Nob, an artificial hill built for the Queen's visit in 1990.

16
Canterbury

====

The gracious city of Christchurch provides a focal point for the Canterbury vineyards. This is the most English of the New Zealand cities, with its own River Avon meandering through the centre. Willows line the banks and Japanese tourists attempt to master the art of punting. In spring the botanical gardens are a visual delight, a riot of exotic blooms and colours.

Christchurch prides itself on its civic sense. To be a bona fide part of the city, you must be able to trace your ancestry back to one of the families who arrived on the first four ships which landed here in 1850. Once Christchurch was established as a thriving community, the route to the west coast and the gold fields of Hokitika were opened up. This highly uncomfortable, not to say dangerous, journey took you over Arthur's Pass, named after a road prospector called Arthur Dobson, whose route, following an old Maori track, was finally chosen in 1864.

Wine came to the area a little earlier, thanks to French not British emigrants, when, in 1840, a group of French settlers landed at Akaroa. Today, it is a picturesque little town at the beginning of Banks Peninsula that still retains the vestiges of some French ambience. In *Winemakers of New Zealand*, Dick Scott describes the stalwart band of thirty French peasants, some shirtless, some even without trousers, who landed in New Zealand in 1840 carrying bundles of grape-vine cuttings, a few seeds and some fruit trees. With hand tools they confronted a rain forest, a tangle of trunks and undergrowth running out to the sea from all the hills ringing Akaroa Harbour. Most of the settlers were from wine districts, uprooted from their homes by deep agricultural depression. A typical example was Jean-Pierre Eteveneaux, a vigneron from the Jura. Three lean vintages in succession had driven him with his

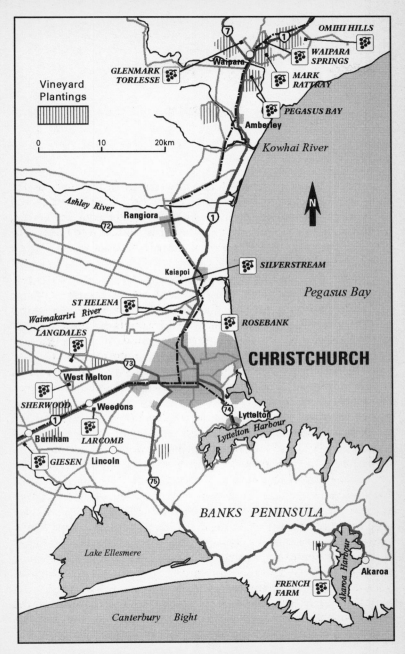

Canterbury and Waipara (South Island)

family to the seaport of Rochefort in search of a passage to Martinique. They had missed the ship across the Atlantic when their attention was caught by a newspaper advertisement announcing a settlement in New Zealand. They were tempted by the offers of free rations and free land on an island the other side of the world guaranteed to be under French sovereignty.

The settlers struggled to establish their hold on the land. The French naval commander Captain Lavaud recorded that every family had been able to work half an acre. 'They have sown some seeds and planted some potatoes but the south-west winds are violent and cold. Some of the vines are raising our hopes, but will they resist the wind and the cold?' Indeed they did, and wine was made.

In 1842, Captain Smith, Surveyor General to the New Zealand Company, wrote in a report: 'The French at once started to prepare their gardens and grow grapes, some of them developing their branch of horticulture to a high degree of efficiency making excellent wine therefrom.' But they were to suffer from lack of capital, misrepresentation by their sponsors the Nanto-Bordelaise company and sheer bad luck, for they had been promised that their land would be under the French flag, which it was not. However, they were allowed to fly the French flag and the British settlers largely ignored them. Many were disillusioned and returned to France. Nevertheless, there were reports of 'a very good red wine'.

Romeo Bragato provides the most detailed description some years later. He visited several vineyards at Akaroa and suggested that in their new home the settlers had established the industry which had doubtless been of interest to some of them in the land of their birth. The industry had prospered as long as its initiators remained at the helm, but as soon as they began to die off, the vineyards became neglected and consequently the vines died out too. It would seem that the pioneer French settlers of Akaroa failed to communicate to their offspring even a small percentage of their large measure of enthusiasm for the cultivation of the vines. Alternatively, Bragato suggests that the vines were attacked by oidium, thus causing the disappearance of vineyards which had been as a bit of the fatherland to their forebears.

However, he was presented with some ripe grapes of Chasselas, La Folle and Muscat Frontignan varieties by M. Le Lièvre, the oldest French settler in the district. They were all of very fine flavour and caused Bragato to think that 'if the settlers in this district would only enter upon the vine industry in a proper spirit, and upon an extensive scale, they would be able to produce a good light wine of similar character to that of the Rhine and Moselle'.

He confidently goes on to predict that Akaroa should in time become known as the 'Vineyard of Christchurch'.

The district is splendidly suited to the cultivation of the vine. If capitalists could be induced to invest some of their money, encouraged and assisted in their enterprise by the Government, they would undoubtedly be richly rewarded and Akaroa acquire world-wide fame. One of the first steps to be taken is to form an association of intending vine growers, so as to secure uniformity in the varieties planted, and afterwards to nurture and protect the interests of its members in every practical way.

Sadly, like other of Bragato's suggestions, this did not happen, and, as we shall see later in this chapter, Akaroa has had yet another false start in the acquisition of a viticultural reputation.

Viticulture in Canterbury subsided into oblivion, apart from a decade's fleeting presence when in 1940 W. H. Meyers built Villa Nova, a small winery in the Heathcote Valley not far from the city. Five years later he had a small vineyard of just over 2 acres planted with Verdelho, Pinot Gris, Muscat and other varieties. However, although some wine was made, the vines languished and were uprooted in about 1949.

Today, the vineyards of Canterbury are concentrated in two main areas: on the plains south-west of Christchurch and in Waipara to the north of the city, with a token presence on Banks Peninsula. The impetus for the current interest began in 1973 with research conducted at Lincoln College, the agricultural college outside Christchurch, under the direction of Dr David Jackson. He worked on trials to establish which varieties would ripen in the cool Canterbury climate. Generally, the temperatures are significantly cooler than Marlborough, with a high risk of spring and autumn frosts. Canterbury is also a region of strong winds – both hot, dry north-westerlies and cool easterly sea breezes. However, its saving grace is the low rainfall, with particularly long dry autumns, allowing the grapes to ripen slowly and maintain good levels of acidity. Late-ripening grapes do not fare so well, while current plantings prove the potential for Pinot Noir, Chardonnay and Riesling.

However, there is no doubt that Canterbury is a marginal area for viticulture, with enormous swings in quality and quantity from one year to the next.

St Helena

St Helena was the first new winery in Canterbury. It was set up under the auspices of Lincoln College, with the collaboration of David Jackson and Danny Schuster, who was the winemaker for a time and now has his own winery, Omihi Hills, of which more later. The land was provided by two brothers, Robin and Norman Mundy. They were horticulturists, growing potatoes which in 1976 they discovered were being attacked by nematodes in the soil, of a different variety to the species that is partial to vines, so they looked for an alternative crop for their land. They had seen the experimental vines at Lincoln College and had friends in Blenheim who had just started growing grapes for Montana, so they thought, 'Why not?' They already had blackcurrants and thought the black-currant harvester might suit the grapes too. So the potatoes were abandoned, vines were planted and a winery built in time for their first vintage in 1981.

Robin Mundy now runs the vineyards and winery with his wife Bernice, while his brother still owns a small share of the 20-hectare (50-acre) vineyard on Coutts Island in the middle of Waimakariri River, just to the north of Christchurch, and well before you reach the hills of Waipara. The island was once called St Helena Island, hence the winery name. Viticulture is now Mundy's forte. He is concentrating on improving the vineyard, changing the trellising systems over to Sylvoz and Scott Henry, and looking at new clones, while the winemaking is now in the hands of Petter Evans, a Roseworthy graduate like so many New Zealand winemakers, who has also worked in Australia and Germany, as well as at Pleasant Valley outside Auckland.

St Helena made its mark with its Pinot Noir. The 1982 vintage won all kinds of accolades, proving a turning point in the reputation of Canterbury as a wine region. It led them to concentrate on that variety and one-third of their vineyard is devoted to it. They also have some Chardonnay, Pinot Gris, Pinot Blanc and Riesling, as well as Bacchus and Müller-Thurgau – a range with which they are satisfied within the climatic limitations of the region.

Müller-Thurgau is their biggest seller, providing necessary cash flow, and in years when the crop is affected by frost they do not hesitate to buy in grapes from Marlborough. The 1994 Marlborough Müller-Thurgau was fresh and fragrant, with some floral fruit and a little residual sugar.

They find Pinot Blanc a consistent variety and as yet are one of the very few wineries to produce it. Evans has experimented with vinification techniques. The 1990 was very ripe, resulting in a wine that was almost sweet, with extract and richness and a leafy character. In 1991, he played with a little wood, making a wine that was much drier with higher acidity and an almost Chablis-like quality. In 1994, the wine was aged in old barrels for six months and included a small amount of barrel fermentation, which for my tastebuds masked the delicate fruit of the grape. In 1995, he is making a wine without any oak at all.

Pinot Gris is another more original flavour, but has proved problematic in the vineyard so that none was made between 1991 and 1995. This is a shame as the 1991 does have some appealing mushroomy spice and makes a refreshing change from Chardonnay.

Since their unexpected initial success with the 1982 Pinot Noir, the ensuing vintages have been somewhat chequered. The best vintages have been 1984, 1988 and 1991, while 1995 is promising well. Frost problems made 1992 and 1993 particularly difficult years. Tasted in February 1995, the 1991 had some sweet fruit and a backbone of tannin, while a cask sample of the 1994 was still tight and closed, but promised some good fruit as well as elegance. Our tasting concluded with a conversation about the hazards of being invited to judge home-made wines, of which there is a band of enthusiastic winemakers in Canterbury. Thistle, spinach and parsley featured among the most popular flavours, as well as feijoa, a New Zealand fruit that I have yet to encounter and which Evans suggested bore a faint resemblance to Chenin Blanc.

St Helena Wine Estate, Coutts Island Road, (PO Box 1, Belfast) Christchurch, telephone: (03) 323 8202, fax: (03) 323 8252

Giesen Wine Estate

The other big winery on the Canterbury Plains is Giesen, which lies to the south-west of the city at Burnham on the road out towards Dunedin. This was the very first Canterbury winery I visited, back in February 1991, and I was immediately bowled over by the quality of their late harvest Rieslings. They were a complete revelation as to the quality and potential of Riesling in New Zealand. The three Giesen brothers, Marcel, Alex and Theo, came to New Zealand in 1979 to work in the family marble and granite business. Winemaking was far from their thoughts, although they had grown up in the Rheinpfalz at Neustadt an der Rhein, and their father had 2 acres of vines as a hobby, making wine for home consumption. When they found that they could not buy any decent wine and that the considerable selection of Müller-Thurgau was mostly labelled Riesling, they decided to plant their own vineyard and make their own wine.

Although they looked in Hawke's Bay and Marlborough, they decided on Canterbury as they believe that the cooler climate of the region is more suitable for Riesling. The further south you go, the more character Riesling retains. Acidity can fade very quickly in a hot climate. And what they are aiming for with their Riesling is wines in the dry style of Alsace, as well as some late harvest or botrytized wines, as and when the unpredictable Canterbury climate allows.

The Giesens' winery has grown in the four years between my two visits. Now they have about 26 hectares (65 acres) in production in the Canterbury area and intend to concentrate on Chardonnay, Pinot Noir and Riesling for fine flavours, and Müller-Thurgau for cash flow. They have planted another 20 hectares (50 acres) and also use contract growers in Canterbury. In addition, they have bought a 9-hectare (20-acre) vineyard in Marlborough which will be planted entirely with Sauvignon. There are now two winemakers: Marcel Giesen and an Austrian, Rudi Bauer, who until 1993 was making the wine at Rippon Vineyard in Central Otago. This makes Giesen the largest winery in Canterbury, representing some significant growth from their first plantings in 1981 and their first vintage in 1984.

On the Burnham Plains the soil is silty loam over free-running river gravel, making for good drainage and low water retention. Their main problem is the climate. Frost is a distinct hazard which they try to combat by using helicopters to churn up the freezing air. Normally, the summers are long and dry, with a little rain coming with the north-west winds.

Their dry Riesling shows enormous potential, with some good slatey fruit, especially when, like the 1991, it has matured for a few years and developed some appealing mineral notes. They very much want their Rieslings to age and give them a couple of years of bottle age before they leave the winery. This is quite contrary to most New Zealand Rieslings which are sold six months after the vintage and drunk within the year. As for Chardonnay, they consider that their techniques are becoming more Burgundian in style, with whole-bunch pressing, barrel fermentation, a full malolactic fermentation and twelve months on the lees, making a wine that is rich and full bodied.

Pinot Noir is a relatively new venture and this is where Bauer's experience at Rippon comes into play. We tasted cask samples of the 1994 – in the company of a cream-coloured cat who answered to the name of Merlot – which illustrated different techniques and clones, some cold maceration, different percentages of whole-bunch pressing and different fermentation lengths. The flavours showed potential, with some sweetness and spice. This will be a wine to watch for, as maybe a sparkling wine. Several people said during my days in Canterbury that the area had potential for sparkling wine, but so far the Giesens are the only ones to take up the challenge and, even then, only with some experimental base wines in the last two vintages.

Giesen Wine Estate, Burnham School Road, No. 5 RD, (PO Box 11066) Christchurch, telephone/fax: (03) 347 6729

Sherwood Estate

Just up the road from the Giesens is Sherwood Estate in West Melton. In some ways this is very typical of the newer Canterbury wineries. Jill and Dayne Sherwood are both Cantabrians. The family property, like most land on the Canterbury Plains, had been used for sheep farming, but this young couple wanted their own business and an end product to sell. Dayne attended courses at Lincoln University and worked for Hunter's in Marlborough in order to gain some practical experience. They planted their first vines in 1986, just 2.5 hectares (6 acres) initially, which they have now increased to 5.6 (14). Their first harvest came in 1990 and the compact weatherboard winery was ready for the 1991 vintage. It is a neat, functional shed, with a small wine bar and restaurant attached. This is the way that several of the Canterbury wineries operate, with a small café or restaurant which attracts visitors in the first place and accounts for a significant proportion of their sales. Larcomb is another, as are Rosebank and Langdale's, of which more later.

The Sherwoods first planted Pinot Noir and Chardonnay, then extended their range to include Riesling and Müller-Thurgau. Dayne admits to the climatic problems of growing grapes in Canterbury. As well as taking grapes from contract growers in the region, he also buys grapes from Marlborough to make up for the deficiencies of the local crop, emphasizing however that it is a problem of quantity not quality. His Pinot Noir is a blend of the two regions and says so clearly on the label. Frost and cool weather are the principal factors affecting quantity, while the cool climate can make for less than ideally ripe grapes. Hail can also play its part in reducing the crop. The resulting high levels of acidity mean that the wines take longer to show their fruit and they benefit from some months of ageing in bottle.

Pinot Noir is Sherwood's favourite wine to make, although he admits to finding it difficult and, since his first harvest in 1991, is still trying to work out a style. His 1993 is quite firm and tannic, with some acidity, too, and understated fruit. In 1994, he made two different wines: a reserve wine from the best fruit, which had an attractive spicy, oaky nose when it was a year old, as well as some concentration of flavour; the basic wine, containing a higher proportion of Canterbury fruit, was lighter and a little green. Sherwood is still finding his way with this temperamental variety.

He also makes two qualities of Chardonnay: one that spends only about three months in oak and is light and easy to drink, and a more serious reserve wine that is fermented in new Burgundian barrels and given several months ageing on the lees, resulting in some attractive toasted flavours and a good integration of oak and fruit. It promises well for the future.

Sherwood Estate Wines, Weedons Ross Road, (RD 5) Christchurch, telephone: (03) 347 9060, fax: (03) 347 8225

Rosebank Estate

Rosebank is another new establishment. I cannot really call it a winery as there are no winemaking facilities. They use mostly

Marlborough fruit, which has been vinified for them at Vintech, as well as a small amount of Canterbury fruit, for which they use the facilities at French Farm. Mark Rattray, of whom more later, is their winemaking consultant. However, Brian Shackel, whose brainchild Rosebank is, is adamant that he is as involved in the industry as any other winemaker. He does not have his own facilities for the simple reason that those at Vintech are so much better than anything he can afford himself. However, he is very concerned about his wines, spending the vintage at Vintech selecting his own barrels, deciding on which cooper and what degree of toasting, as well as maturation times, and so on. His expertise is really in marketing, a skill he rightly considers that many winemakers lack. His enthusiasm for wine came from an interest in food and a career in the meat business. When he first bought his property in 1987, he had intended to set up a winery. Indeed the building was constructed, but instead is used as a restaurant, which Shackel considers a much better decision.

It certainly is a pleasant place to visit, with an attractive airy restaurant, an agreeable tasting and sales room, and a garden of roses which are an absolute delight, a riot of delicate blooms and colour. There is also just 1 acre of vines planted with Chardonnay, Pinot Noir and Bacchus, with delicate white Iceberg roses at the end of every row. The vineyard is more for show than for any practical purpose. As for the wine, the Marlborough Riesling was fresh and floral, with good acidity; the Müller-Thurgau, also from Marlborough, soft and easy. The 1994 Marlborough Chardonnay should develop well, with a toasted nose and a firm palate. Much less successful were the two red wines, both blends of New Zealand and Australian fruit, or more precisely Marlborough and the Barossa Valley. One was a Cabernet Shiraz blend and the other Pinot Noir. With the Cabernet Shiraz, Shackel said that he wanted a New Zealand red with some Australian character. In fact, the herbaceous notes of unripe New Zealand Cabernet dominated the Barossa Shiraz, which was fermented in Australia, then shipped and blended. The label clearly states the origins of the wine, but the practice seems more acceptable for wine that is served from a cask rather than a bottle. However, there is no doubt that Rosebank has a successful professional polish that some other wineries lack.

Rosebank Estate Winery, Cnr Johns Road & Groynes Drive,

Belfast, (PO Box 2829) Christchurch, telephone: (03) 323 7353, fax: (03) 323 8538

Silverstream Vineyard

Just across the river from St Helena is the small winery of Silverstream which was set up by Peter and Zeke Todd. She is Dutch but was brought up in New Zealand, and he is an Anglo-Italian. They planted their first hectare (couple of acres) of vines in 1988 and now have 4 hectares (10 acres), concentrating on Chardonnay and Pinot Noir. Unlike most of the other Canterbury producers, they make wine only from their own grapes in the small winery adjoining the vineyard. It is a neat little shed, with tanks outside and barrels inside. Apparently, they are planning something grander for the 1996 vintage.

The vineyard is protected by wind shelters of willow and poplar trees that help not only against the wind, but also the frost. Although there were severe frosts in 1994, 1993 and 1992, their vineyard was not too badly affected. They do not allow any weeds between the rows, using herbicides to remove them, which also helps prevent frost as the hard clay surface radiates any warmth. Autumn frost can also be a problem and for that reason few people in Canterbury actually made Pinot Noir in 1992 and 1993. Drip irrigation has proved essential for establishing the young vines, especially as they lost 80 per cent of their first plantings in 1989 through drought in a particularly hot summer. Most of the rain comes in the winter.

Todd has a degree in microbiology and finds the process of winemaking a very logical one. He has helped elsewhere with the harvest and has sought advice from other winemakers in the area. From the 1995 vintage they have had a Roseworthy-trained winemaker, Sally, so it will be interesting to follow the progress of this small winery. Their 1992 and 1993 Pinot Noir certainly showed promise, with some varietal character. Unlike some, they are very aware of the financial constraints of making wine and have no great ambitions to expand. As Todd put it, 'We want to be here in twenty years' time, and be able survive a bad vintage in the meantime.'

Silverstream Vineyard, Giles Road, Clarkville, (RD 2) Kaiapoi, telephone: (03) 327 5231, fax: (03) 327 5678

Larcomb

There are a handful of other wineries on the Canterbury Plains on the outskirts of Christchurch. Larcomb runs an attractive wine bar restaurant during the summer months – I have never seen such a spectacular display of blue hydrangeas – and the kitchen doubles up as a fermentation room during the winter. John Thorn grew up on a sheep and cattle station in Hawke's Bay and trained as a vet. He remembered his parents buying flagons of 'sherry' and '*crème de menthe*' from the old Te Mata Vineyard. New Zealanders drank beer or sparkling Cold Duck, so it was overseas trips to America and Europe that converted him to wine, and a hobby became his work. He makes a selection of wines that are ideal for the wine bar: a light Sauvignon, a delicate Pinot Gris, an easy Breidecker, a Riesling and an accessible Pinot Noir. But the time has come to move on as, with a young family, he finds the winery much too demanding.

Larcomb Road, Christchurch, telephone (03) 347 8909

Langdale's

Langdale's is typical of a trend in the Canterbury wine scene: a winery café that had opened just the week before my visit. The vines were planted in 1989 and the wine made in somebody else's winery for the express purpose of providing wine for the café. A winery is planned in due course, but the assumption is that the café will sell the wine. However, you need to be a pretty determined drinker as Langdale's is not easy to find and requires a bumpy drive along a dusty dirt track.

Langdale Wine Estate, Langdales Road, West Melton, Christchurch, telephone/fax: (03) 342 6266

French Farm

However, as the wine industry of Canterbury becomes more established, the perceived wisdom is that Waipara is the up-and-coming area with the greatest potential. But first we will detour to French Farm on Banks Peninsula for a story that illustrates some of the intrinsic problems of the New Zealand wine industry and, the most fundamental one of all, the lack of profit in a highly capital-intensive industry. When I was in Christchurch in November 1992, everyone was talking about French Farm, an exciting new winery which had just opened near Akaroa and the site of the first French settlers. Banks Peninsula is a dramatic volcanic outcrop, named after Joseph Banks, the talented botanist who accompanied Captain Cook on the *Endeavour*.

I spent an afternoon with the winemaker Tony Bish, who enthused about the potential of the site for hillside vineyards, which are fairly unusual in New Zealand. The undulating land of the peninsula would provide a vineyard with a good aspect and excellent drainage in an appropriate microclimate. It is a very sheltered area and would be protected from frost, with an old volcanic crater providing a heat trap which would help ripen the grapes. Pinot Noir and Chardonnay were planted and the 100-tonne winery was opened just in time for the 1991 vintage, for which fruit was bought from Canterbury and Marlborough. No expense was spared on the winery facilities, with stainless-steel tanks, heating and cooling facilities, and everything else that a winemaker might require, all in one large shed. There was a café to attract the visitors, who were indeed flocking. As for the wines, they did not immediately excite but they showed potential, with only two vintages to date, and none of their own vines yet in production. But two years later, the aspirations of the winery had failed. The winemaker has left and the remaining partners have converted the winery into a large-scale restaurant, relegating the tanks to the backyard, and the vineyard, which is now in production, is leased. It was a case of accountants who had false expectations of the profitability of a winery, then discovered it was the restaurant and not the winery that was making money. Hopefully by the time this book is published, French Farm may be under new ownership and making wine again from a vineyard of fine potential.

French Farm, French Farm Valley Road, (RD 2) Akaroa, telephone: (03) 304 5784, fax: (03) 304 5785

WAIPARA

The name Waipara means 'muddy water' in Maori. A cluster of homesteads give their name to a larger area and a river. Waipara forms quite a distinct, separate area from the Canterbury Plains.

Driving north out of Christchurch, you follow the road over open plains until you reach more undulating terrain at Amberley. Essentially, Waipara is a basin, a valley with the Waipara River flowing through it narrowing into a gorge surrounded by hills which protect the area from the easterly winds that come in from the sea.

The climate is distinctly warmer than in Christchurch and on the plains. On the February morning that I was there, it was drizzling and grey in the city; as we approached Amberley, the clouds cleared. There were fine views of the foothills of the Southern Alps to the west and by lunch-time, sitting outside it was scorchingly hot. Here, degree days average 1,100°, compared to a mere 750° at Lincoln College outside the city. However, within Waipara there are distinct microclimates influenced by the wind patterns and the gaps in the hills that allow cold air to come down off the Southern Alps. As a result, some areas are distinctly more prone to frost than others. The prevailing winds are north-westerlies which, to quote John McCaskey from Glenmark, 'beat hell out of the vines'. They control the vigour and reduce humidity in the vineyard considerably. In his opinion, wind shelters only create frost traps. As yet, phylloxera has not reached Canterbury and so all the plantings are still on ungrafted vines.

As regards soil, Waipara is of particular interest to the viticulturists as limestone forms the basis, interspersed with layers of silt loam. The suitability of limestone for Chardonnay and Pinot Noir, which is proven in the old world, excites the enthusiasm of New Zealand winemakers. Now the whole area of Waipara is flourishing, for the interest in wine has brought a revival in its fortunes when not so many years ago it was desolate. Drought brought devastation to farming in the early 1970s, resulting in the development of the Glenmark Irrigation Scheme. Although only five of the ten proposed dams were actually built, at least water became available as never before and the farmers of the area were able to diversify from sheep farming to consider kiwi fruit and vines.

John McCaskey of Glenmark was the first to plant vines in Waipara over twenty years ago, but they were hybrids which were washed away in a flood a couple of years later. He eventually replanted in the mid-1980s, this time with *vitis vinifera* vines. McCaskey explained how the original farms in the area were vast tracts of pastureland. Between 1860 and 1917 Glenmark itself was a 73,000-hectare (180,000-acre) sheep farm. The gate lodge and stables remain, but the old homestead burnt down in about 1890, then in 1917 the property was subdivided into 400-hectare (1,000-acre) lots. McCaskey's father arrived in Waipara from Marlborough in 1935 and acquired land. Now there are further subdivisions and diversifications, with 40-hectare (100-acre) blocks available, advertised by a large billboard: 'Grape Growing Premium Blocks for Sale'. The area is coming to life again with a wave of vineyard plantings, maybe as much as 200 hectares (500 acres) in 1994, including a large American investment of 80 hectares (200 acres) on some limestone hillsides. The view from the top of Mount Cass provides a splendid panorama of the area, looking over the limestone hills to the snow-capped Southern Alps and the new plantings of vines which are, with a few exceptions, on the flat valley floor.

Waipara West

Impressive for the spread of planting is Vicky Tutton's 18-hectare (45-acre) vineyard. She and her partner Lindsey Hill are planning a winery, to be called Waipara West, for the 1996 vintage. For the moment, they sell most of their grapes to Waipara Springs and to Mark Rattray. Their very first wine, the 1995 Sauvignon, shows good promise with some ripe, pungent fruit. Most of the vineyard was planted in 1989. They had been looking for vineyard land, located this site as suitable and discovered that it was indeed being advertised for sale in the local newspaper. It then transpired that a great-great-uncle had once owned the property. Chardonnay and Sauvignon are the two main varietals, but there are also Riesling and Pinot Noir, as well as Cabernet Sauvignon, Cabernet Franc and Merlot, all on various different sites for there are terraces at different levels in the river valley with a variety of soil types. Their vineyards are at the western end of the valley in the foothills, which means that they do not suffer from frost as the cold air is pushed through the gap at the beginning of the valley then fanned out. They are also in the rainshadow of Mount Brown, making irrigation essential. The terraces ensure that the heat is radiated off the stony banks, creating a really hot site for Cabernet Sauvignon that might otherwise be difficult to ripen. However, when Waipara West is in operation they intend to concentrate on producing their own Chardonnay, Sauvignon and Pinot Noir.

376 Ram Paddock Road, Amberley RD2, North Canterbury, telephone (03) 314 8330

Glenmark and Torlesse

Glenmark has joined forces with another operation, Torlesse, to share both a winery and a winemaker, Kym Rayner. Glenmark have Riesling, Müller-Thurgau, Cabernet Sauvignon, Gewürztraminer and Chardonnay, to produce wines which are mainly sold through the Wine Garden restaurant. Riesling is the most successful, with some ageing potential, as demonstrated by the 1990 Riesling Dry which had a lovely mature nose, with good slatey acidity and honeyed undertones.

Torlesse, which was originally at West Melton outside Christchurch, has had a rather chequered history. It was set up by a group of ten grape growers in 1987, but they lacked cohesion, with the result that the accountant among them, Andrew Tomlin, put the company into receivership, then bought it. There are vines planted in Waipara, as well as on the plains, and they also buy in grapes from Marlborough and produce a varied range of wines which I tasted at Annie's Kitchen, a wine bar in the old arts university building that boasts the best range of local wines in Christchurch. The Waipara Riesling was delicate and limey; a Canterbury Gewürztraminer lightly spicy, but with no great intensity; the Marlborough Chardonnay was still very young, with ripe bananas and oak; the Marlborough Cabernet Franc light, with fresh cherry fruit. I have a feeling that they have not yet found their true direction after the various changes.

Glenmark Wines, 'Weka Plains', Mackenzies Road, (No. 3 RD, Amberley) Waipara, telephone/fax: (03) 314 6828

Torlesse Wines, Ferguson Ave, (PO Box 8237) Waipara, telephone/fax: (03) 377 1595

Mark Rattray

One of the key players in Waipara, and indeed in Canterbury, is Mark Rattray. Initially he seems very reserved, but he has a perceptive appreciation of the Canterbury wine scene which he has been involved with since 1986. He does not see the wine industry through rose-coloured spectacles, but with harsh objectivity and realism. He trained at the Geisenheim Institute and has worked for Montana and Penfolds, before making the wine at St Helena from 1986 to 1990. From there he went briefly to Waipara Springs, before concentrating on his own winery, Mark Rattray Vineyards, for which his first vintage was 1992. Rattray has 4 hectares (10 acres) of his own on the valley floor of Waipara, and buys grapes from other growers including Vicky Tutton. His small winery is across the highway from Waipara Springs.

We sat in his garden and tasted Sauvignon, Chardonnay and Pinot Noir. Rattray's 1990 Pinot Noir from Waipara Springs was one of the wines that first captured my enthusiasm for New Zealand Pinot Noir; successive vintages have been no less exciting. His 1990 Pinot Noir was rich and voluptuous, and his 1993 is equally rich and chocolatey, with the spicy nose of new oak and some ripe vegetal fruit. As Rattray says, good Pinot Noir tastes great the year it is made and it gets better and better. This will last a decade. Maybe his wines do not have the tannic structure of some, but they have everything else that Pinot Noir should in the way of fruit, flavour and a silky texture.

Rattray's 1994 Sauvignon is quite refined and subtle (if that is possible for New Zealand Sauvignon), while his Chardonnay has good structure, with a balance of fruit and acidity. Not modest by nature, Rattray confidently described his 1993 Chardonnay as 'the best wine I've ever made', and certainly it was elegantly toasted on the nose, with finesse, flavour and very good mouthfeel. When I quizzed him as to how he had achieved such delicious results, he said dismissively, 'It's immaterial how I did it.' This is unusual for a New Zealand winemaker for most are willing to divulge the most intimate details of their winemaking.

Mark Rattray Vineyards, 418 Omihi Road, (PO Box 1) Waipara, telephone/fax: (03) 314 6710

Waipara Springs

Across the road at Waipara Springs I encountered Kym Rayner again, who has been making the wine since Rattray's departure in 1993. The Grant family, represented by young Andrew Grant, are the major shareholders in the estate. They have 20 hectares (50 acres) of vines, including Chardonnay, Pinot Noir, Riesling, Sauvignon and Cabernet Sauvignon. It is Chardonnay that has really made the reputation of Waipara Springs, with some fine mouth-filling flavours, good acidity and balancing fruit.

The winery is neat and contained, with stainless-steel fermentation tanks and rows of barrels. We tasted some barrel samples of the 1994 Pinot Noir that showed plenty of potential, with some young sweet fruit, good tannin and acidity. It had more structure than the 1993, which none the less had some attractive liquorice notes and spicy oak. They like to think that Waipara is giving Martinborough a run for its money with Pinot Noir, and indeed it is.

Waipara Springs Wines, SH 1, (PO Box 17) Waipara, telephone/fax: (03) 314 6777

Omihi Hills

Danny Schuster at Omihi Hills is another Pinot Noir enthusiast. He has had a varied career, travelling the world, and has a more European outlook on life than many of his colleagues. For a start, he was born in Prague of an Austrian mother and German father, and studied French and German before becoming fascinated by red wine. Even now he speaks English with what sounds more like an Italian lilt in his voice, with Mediterranean charm to accompany it. From Bordeaux and Burgundy, he went to Australia where he worked for Seppelts, then on to Nederburg in South Africa, via New Zealand, when he met David Jackson from Lincoln College. This led to a proposal to spend five years helping to develop the vineyard at St Helena, then the idea of planting his own vineyard. He looked for limestone hillsides, rather than the usual gravel of so many New Zealand vineyards, and found Omihi Hills on the eastern side of the Waipara Valley. Gravel may be good for Cabernet Sauvignon, but Pinot Noir grown on gravel lacks density. Meanwhile, he continues to consult for Ornellaia in Tuscany and Stags Leap in the Napa Valley.

His is one of the few hillside vineyards of the area. It is an enchanting spot. You could almost think you were in Tuscany, with tall sombre pine rather than cypress trees, and yellow slopes of dried grass in the distance. Adjoining the vineyard is a neat winery shed. This is very much off the beaten track, with no offers of tastings let alone the usual winery café that is popular with so many Christchurch wineries. A notice in the winery, 'No machine can replace me until it learns to drink', summed up the attitude of the man.

Schuster criticizes New Zealanders for their tendency to produce wines that make a statement, when we need wines we can actually drink, and his wines do have a European subtlety about them. They may not have the upfront appeal of some New Zealand wines, but have an old-world charm that may not be immediately accessible. The upfront fruit is part of the New Zealand character, but Schuster also uses techniques that do not overdevelop the fruitiness, and thereby gives structure, harmony and balance to the wine. Essentially, he believes in keeping the winemaking as simple as possible. A Pinot Blanc made from Hawke's Bay fruit was described as 'poor man's Chardonnay' and was for a few months in wood with lees contact to give it length and elegance. The Chenin Blanc had some grassy, honeyed fruit and delicate oak, with good acidity. As for Chardonnay, he last made it in 1988 and has given it up because everyone else makes it.

With his Pinot Noir, he is producing some interesting flavours with more tannin and structure than some of his colleagues. I liked his 1992 Reserve which had some elegant fruit and structure. Schuster says that he goes along with the grapes and sees what happens. Each year he learns from the vineyard and alters the handling to suit the grapes. The vines are on slopes some 300 metres above the valley floor, allowing for good air movement, and the roots go deep into the porous limestone. Schuster does not keep the roots up near the surface, which is one of the adverse effects of irrigation.

Omihi Hills Vineyard, Reeces Road, Omihi Valley, Waipara (5 Paulus Tce, Christchurch 2), telephone: (03) 337 1763, fax: (03) 379 8638

Pegasus Bay

My final visit in Waipara was to Pegasus Bay, the result of Professor Ivan Donaldson's love affair with wine. His wife Christine is also involved, while their son Matthew is the winemaker, as befits a Roseworthy graduate. The Donaldsons planted their first wines at the western end of the valley in 1986 and their first wine was made in 1991 in Ivan's garage in the centre of Christchurch. For a year it was a registered winery, until the winery at Pegasus Bay was built for the 1992 vintage. It is a large shed, with a smart tasting room and an outdoor restaurant. Ivan's rather mouth-watering empties line the winery wall.

Essentially, they make five wines produced from their own vineyards: Riesling, Chardonnay, Pinot Noir, a Bordeaux blend of Cabernet Sauvignon, Cabernet Franc and Merlot, and a blend of Sémillon and Sauvignon, for they are the only Canterbury winery to grow Sémillon. Sadly, they have suffered badly from frost damage so they have had to buy in grapes from Marlborough in order to produce sufficient wine.

Matthew Donaldson is particularly excited by his Pinot Noir. I tried two different clones of the 1994 vintage, of which the 10/5 was particularly satisfying, with some ripe spicy fruit, while the 1993, drunk later over dinner, had some weight and a smoky flavour. The Sauvignon Sémillon blend includes some new-oak fermentation and lees ageing which rounds out the herbaceous notes. The 1991 demonstrated how well it developed in bottle, with firm green-pea fruit. The Chardonnay promises well with good structure and mouthfeel. The Riesling is fresh and fruity and easy to drink.

The burgeoning wine industry of Canterbury is not without its problems. The climatic conditions particularly, accentuated by frost problems, can make yields very erratic. Even the 1994 vintage, which was good in quality, was described by John McCaskey in his forthright way as 'the pits' because it was so small in quantity. Quite simply, if you have a winery, you need the grapes to make it work.

Pegasus Bay, Stockgrove Road, (RD 2) Amberley, telephone/fax: (03) 314 6869

The wineries of the Canterbury Plains are still finding their way, while the growers of Waipara have a more positive sense of direction in the challenge of Pinot Noir and Chardonnay. It may be, as was suggested by Mark Rattray and others, that sparkling wine will be the future for the region, but that theory is as yet unproven.

17
Central Otago

The very first New Zealand winery that I visited was Gibbston Valley, which lies on the 45th parallel south – in other words, just about as far south as you can go in winemaking terms, and significantly closer to the South Pole than any vineyard in South America. In terms of the northern hemisphere, the 45th parallel runs through the southern Rhône, with numerous vineyard areas well to the north; and on the other side of the Atlantic it crosses the Willamette Valley in Oregon. The significant difference between the two hemispheres is one of land mass, in that there is very little between Central Otago and the massive icepacks of Antarctica, other than the sheep farms of Southland.

The recent pioneers of the area were ridiculed and the suggestion that vines could survive so far south was scorned, yet the first vines were planted in the area well over a hundred years ago, long before Marlborough was even dreamt of. Central Otago was opened up in the 1860s when gold was discovered there in 1862. The subsequent gold rush brought a considerable increase in population, and the development of gold-mining towns like Alexandra and Clyde. The Chinese came from the gold-mining fields of Victoria, but once the first flush of enthusiasm had died down by the end of the decade, fruit farming took over in importance. Queenstown, which lies at the heart of Central Otago, was settled in the 1860s and acquired its name in 1863 when someone commented that its fine position on Lake Wakatipu was fit for a queen. Today it is a bustling tourist town, the gateway to the fjords and glaciers of the west coast and the way to the scenic delights of Milford Sound. In winter it is an important ski resort and in summer much frequented by Japanese tourists.

Landing at Queenstown airport is dramatic enough. The plane

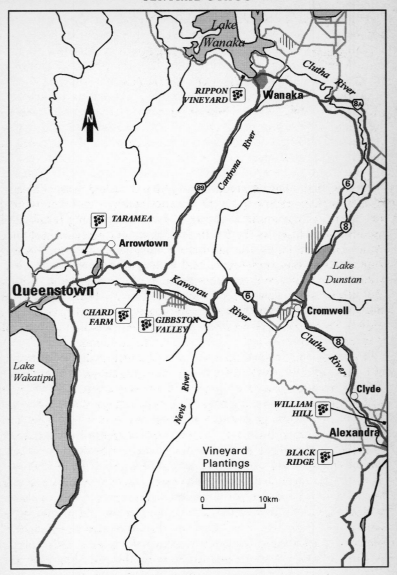

Central Otago (South Island)

flies up the Cardrona Valley, with the rough hillsides closing in around you. It is easy to see why Queenstown airport is frequently closed. With low cloud cover, not to mention unsophisticated aircraft (Mount Cook Airlines still proudly use their Hawker Siddeley aircraft, of uncertain vintage), navigation becomes impossible, yet on a clear day the views are spectacular, but with scenery that looks more like Scotland than any vineyard region. Just outside the airport is a group of signposts pointing to London and many of the other capitals of the world, telling me that I was 18,939 kilometres away from home.

Otago was in the main occupied by Anglo-Saxon settlers whose interest in alcoholic beverages centred more on beer and whisky, and Dunedin does indeed boast a whisky distillery. However, the first vines were planted there by a Frenchman, some say from Bordeaux, called Jean Désiré Feraud. He sounds a colourful character who arrived at the Dunstan goldfields with his partner Bladier some time in 1863, soon after the discovery of gold in the district. They staked a claim to what is called Frenchman's Point on the Clutha River, just south of Alexandra, and successfully mined gold until 1865. However, once they had struck rich they began to develop other interests, in horticulture rather than pastoral farming.

In the spring of 1864, one or both of them went to Australia and returned with a wide variety of plants, including several thousand vine cuttings, as well as fruit trees and bushes. Record is made of a visit in 1865 to Bladier's farm 'for the purpose of seeing two bunches of grapes growing from vines planted in this season ... The vines upon which grapes so unexpectedly appeared are two of the Paris Chasselas sort.' The two men were also pioneers in methods of irrigation which was essential for successful fruit farming in the area. Bladier, a rather shadowy figure, apart from being described as a 'vigneron of considerable experience' disappeared without trace, while Feraud continued to grow grapes and ultimately to make wine. It is he rather than Bladier who takes the credit for developing viticulture and winemaking in Central Otago.

He went on to become mayor of Clyde, then became involved in local disputes about water rights for irrigation. Another plan was to build canals to make the Clutha River navigable to the coast as an alternative to the railway. Meanwhile, his wines won prizes in the Australian shows in Sydney and Melbourne in 1879,

1880 and 1881, for strange descriptions like 'aniseed liquor' and 'Constantia wine'. However, there was also a Burgundy wine. In 1882 he moved from Clyde to Dunedin, where he set up a cordial-manufacturing business and imported grapes from Australia for the purpose. Then, like his partner Bladier, he disappeared from view. There is no record of his death in Dunedin. All that remains are two of his wine bottles, 'large, deep blue and translucent', in the museum in Clyde, and the old stone winery still stands as one of the solid grey buildings in Clyde's main street.

Winemaking continued until the turn of the century. Bragato first tasted wine from Central Otago on his fact-finding visit of 1895. 'At Arrowtown I was presented with my first glass of New Zealand wine. My acceptance of this was invited by Mrs Hutchison, and although made after the most primitive fashion, it reflected great credit upon the producer, and need not be despised by any one.' No clue is given as to the grape variety, or even the colour of the wine.

However. Bragato travelled extensively in Central Otago. Of Queenstown he writes

this being the most elevated part of the Central Otago district, registers a low temperature throughout the year, still it does not descend to such a degree of coldness as to entirely preclude the cultivation of the vine. Judgement needs to be exercised as to where vines are planted and which varieties, and the cultivation and pruning must be adapted to the requirements of colder vine-growing zones.

Looking at orchards, he marvelled at the quality of the fruit and how heavily laden the trees were. At Cromwell and Bannockburn he comments that these districts are 'pre-eminently suitable to the cultivation of the vine, both of winemaking and table varieties and that greater results would be achieved if there was some form of irrigation'. At Clyde on 25 February, he found grapes that although of a late variety were almost ripe. Earnscleugh was also deemed suitable for viticulture, as well as other areas that are not yet developed today.

Viticulture disappeared from Central Otago around the turn of the century and was not revived until 1976 when Rolfe Mills planted vines at Rippon on the shores of Lake Wanaka, and in 1981 Alan Brady followed at Gibbston Valley. Brady remembers how the sceptics said it was 'too cold, too high, too far south and, in any case, what did an Irish journalist know about making wine?' His answer to the last question was, 'Absolutely nothing,' but he had done his homework. He had first bought his land in 1976 for weekend breaks, then the following year decided to give up city life and do something with his land. He conducted a serious study of the weather patterns.

Central Otago has very dry summers and cold, dry winters, with an average rainfall of 20 inches per year. Summer temperatures can reach about 35°C, but drop to 12° or 15°C at night, providing a desirable diurnal difference. He found similarities with the Rhine, but the heat summation can be better, with an average of 1,100–1,200°, which may drop to 950° in a very cool year or reach 1,300° in a hot one. The lack of humidity means less disease, while irrigation is generally necessary, especially as the soil is not water retentive. It is gravel over thin, silty loam, with schist from glacial valleys. Frost can be a problem, so vineyard sites must be carefully selected. However, at Gibbston Valley the river provides an air current to carry the cold air away.

At Wanaka, too, everyone said, 'It's not hot enough and you will have problems with frost.' Yet again, the heat summation can vary significantly. In 1990 it was 1,350°, which is similar to Auckland, while 950° is the lowest dip, and an average of 1,100° usual. As for frost, it tends to roll down the vineyard slopes straight into the lake. The summer days are long, with great intensity of light. Really, Central Otago is about as continental a climate as is possible in New Zealand, and is the only region not to have easy access to the coast. Dunedin is 276 kilometres away, and Invercargill 248. The vineyards themselves form a triangle of Queenstown, with Cromwell, Clyde and Alexandra at the base, and Wanaka at the apex, making three distinct areas.

In the four years since my first visit to Central Otago in 1991, the vineyard area increased significantly, while for the moment there are still just five wineries: Gibbston Valley and Chard Farm outside Queenstown, Rippon Vineyards at Wanaka, and Black Ridge and William Hill at Alexandra. However, membership of the Central Otago Grape Growers' and Winemakers' Association has grown significantly from about twenty-five members in 1990 to eighty in 1995 as more people have planted vines. There are now 180 hectares (444 acres) of vines, representing thirty-one individually owned vineyards and marking a dramatic growth from around 20 hectares (50 acres) in 1990.

When Brady first bought his land in 1976, he was the first newcomer to the area for at least thirty or forty years, and the valley between Bannockburn and Queenstown was farmed by just five families, but that has all changed. The huge sheep farms of several thousand acres have been divided up and sold off in smaller plots. The land was not considered good enough for anything but sheep, for the free-draining rocky schist is some of the most infertile land in New Zealand. Brady had once said, tongue in cheek, that the Gibbston Valley, stretching between the dramatic outcrop of Nevus Bluff and the bridge of the Kawarau Gorge which is popular with bungee jumpers, would be covered with vines. At the time it seemed a crazy dream and an unfounded fantasy, but today, as more and more vines are planted, it is not so far from reality.

Some of those planting vines see it as the first step towards their own winery, while others are committed viticulturists and want to grow grapes to sell under contract to an existing winery. There are now about ten growers in the Gibbston Valley, with some 80 hectares (200 acres) of vines, not all of which are yet in production. Some of the growers are local; one has come from New Caledonia. Then there is a project on the shores of Lake Hayes, in association with Chard Farm, with the possible long-term plan to produce sparkling wine.

A little further east at Bannockburn, Robin Dicey has been a powerful influence. He is a South African by birth who trained at Stellenbosch and has lived in New Zealand for a couple of decades or more working in the wine industry. Not only does he have his own vineyard and lecture for the new viticulture course at the local Otago polytechnic, but he also acts as a consultant for several other growers. He has provided a strong element of professionalism in a field where lifestyle amateurs have tended to dominate.

Around Alexandra there is a growing band of small growers, selling their grapes mainly to William Hill or Black Ridge, or else making their own wine more as a hobby than as a commercial exercise. For the moment, there is no phylloxera in Central Otago and there is a strict protocol about bringing vine cuttings into the area in an attempt to keep it away. Vines have to be dipped with some disinfecting chemical when they leave the nursery, then dipped again on arrival before planting. When I was there in

February 1995, several growers were suffering from the fact that some recently planted vines were dying in the vineyards, through no fault of their own but as a result of a overdose of the necessary chemical. Despite this setback, there is no doubt that the enthusiasm for grape growing is there, with a buoyant interest in viticulture in Central Otago.

The other viticultural hazard in Central Otago is rabbits and all the new vineyards are completely surrounded by net fences against them. Extra protection is provided by plastic guards to protect the young vines, whose succulent shoots the rabbits find particularly appetizing.

Gibbston Valley

Alan Brady at Gibbston Valley, as befits a former television journalist, is one of the most articulate exponents of the problems and thrills of producing wine on the 45th parallel. He is a friendly bearded Ulsterman who came to wine more by accident than by design, but, once involved, has tackled it in a very professional way. He quickly realized the tourist appeal of visiting a winery and, with his prime spot on the main road out of Queenstown, has set up an attractive restaurant where visitors can eat as well as taste, opportunely attracting the passing trade as well as the odd coachload of Japanese.

The Gibbston Valley winery is compact and neat, a well-designed shed intended to vinify 100 tonnes. In 1994, Brady actually crushed 101 tonnes and realized that the time had come for expansion, which he has now done, excavating into the hillside behind, so that he now has 76 metres of tunnels opening out into a large cavern, providing space for about 500 barrels and many more bottles, all stored at a constant temperature. This is particularly significant, given the extremes of temperatures which occur in Central Otago.

Gibbston Valley has only just over 3 hectares (8 acres) of its own vines, including a new steeply sloping plot of Riesling, of which Brady has high hopes for a late Harvest Riesling. Many of the original vines were experimental to see what would grow well, which was far from obvious back in 1981. Now that he has a better idea of what is suitable, Brady prefers to encourage other people to grow the grapes for him. In years of short crops, notably

1993 and 1994, they have bought in grapes from Canterbury and, more significantly, from Marlborough. Brady admits that in buying fruit from other regions, he is treading the knife edge of credibility. However, his winery has been designed for a specific tonnage, at which it needs to run in order to be economically viable. Several of the Auckland wineries buy fruit from areas where they do not own vineyards and the labelling is perfectly clear as to the provenance of the grapes. It is all a question of balance and, with the much more prolific and successful 1995 vintage, it will swing firmly back into Central Otago's favour.

Brady's winemaker is Grant Taylor. He is a New Zealander who studied agriculture at Lincoln College, went on to Davis and worked in California for several years, including at Domaine Napa and Pine Ridge, before coming back to New Zealand for a holiday in 1994, whereupon he tore up his air ticket back to San Francisco.

I have tasted a range of Gibbston Valley wines on three or four occasions over the last four years and have been fascinated to see their evolution. In 1991, Brady said that the future lay with Pinot Noir and Chardonnay, and that is certainly true of Pinot Noir. The cooler climate of Central Otago really does seem to suit that temperamental grape variety, whereas any other red varieties are wellnigh impossible to ripen. I tasted Gibbston Valley's 1990 Pinot Noir, the best of recent vintages, when it had just been bottled in February 1991. It had full, sweet raspberry fruit with some tannin and the characteristic sweetness of the grape variety. Two years later it had become richer and more mouth-filling, with chocolatey overtones; by February 1995 it was redolent of ripe fruit, standing up superbly to chorizo sausage and a tournedos of cervina, which the New Zealanders call farm venison. However, delicious though 1990 was, the 1994 Pinot Noir showed a considerable advance in subtlety and complexity on this first vintage. Even as a cask sample, there were layers of flavours with good grip and balance. As more clones come into production and new techniques are mastered, the flavours will improve yet more.

Gibbston Valley make their Central Otago Sauvignon in quite a different style from their Marlborough Sauvignon. A third of the blend is aged in wood and undergoes a malolactic fermentation so that the wine has a firm green-pea character and well-integrated oak, while the Marlborough Sauvignon is fresh and juicy, with a hint of residual sugar on the finish. More intriguing was the 1990

Central Otago Sauvignon which, when tasted in February 1995, had developed leafy, honeyed characters, with some wonderful mature flavours. It was beautifully distinctive and still full of life.

Brady admits to an affection for Pinot Gris. Here, the example set by Dry River in Martinborough provides the benchmark for the style. His 1994 has some delicate spicy fruit, with a little residual sugar. In the vineyard it is undemanding to grow, while Riesling is proving more problematic as it is a late-ripening grape and Central Otago does not always have the long autumns that Riesling requires to ripen fully. Brady admits that they have not yet cracked how to make it. However, his 1994 Riesling was quite closed, with lean stony fruit and acidity.

Gibbston Valley Wines, Main Queenstown–Cromwell Highway, (SH 6) Gibbston, RD 1, Queenstown, telephone: (03) 442 6910, fax: (03) 442 6909

Chard Farm

Chard Farm is the neighbouring estate. In the 1870s the land was used for market gardening for the gold miners; it was run by the Chard family who had come out from the eponymous Somerset village and had owned the land for about a hundred years. The winery was started in 1987 by the Hay brothers: Rob the winemaker and Greg the viticulturist. Rob had been working in Germany and on his return to New Zealand chanced to see a programme about the 45th parallel featuring Alan Brady and Gibbston Valley. This fired his imagination and, as it happened, Brady needed a winemaker while Rob needed somewhere to make his wine, until their own winery was built in time for the 1990 vintage.

The dirt track to the Chard Farm winery demands strong nerves, especially after a tasting, for it is narrow and winding, with several sharp corners and a steep drop into the Kawarau River below. The two craggy hills known locally as the Judge and Jury dominate the skyline. Use your imagination and you can see the judge towering over the rather hunched-up jury.

Chard Farm has a couple of hectares (nearly 5 acres) of vineyards, including a block that nestles on north-facing slopes amid scenery which resembles the Scottish highlands more than any other European vineyard. There is a block of Chardonnay, mainly of the Mendoza clone, a block of Pinot Noir with a mixture of clones 10/5, 2/10, and the Davis clones 6 and 13, then there is a smaller plot of Pinot Gris, as well as some Sauvignon, Gewürztraminer and Riesling. In addition, they also manage another 6.5 hectares (16 acres), including the large project on the shores of Lake Hayes in association with several local businessmen.

Like Gibbston Valley, they also buy some Marlborough fruit which sells under the Southern Lakes label. Our tasting concentrated on Chardonnay, beginning with the 1993 Southern Lakes which includes a proportion of barrel-fermented wine, but not too much, so that the oak is well integrated into the fruit. A vertical tasting of their best Chardonnay label, Judge and Jury, showed the evolution in style and technique since 1990. In 1990, they used older barrels, along with a small proportion of new barrels; it was a ripe year and the wine had a broad toffee nose and palate, with some nutty fruit. It is always barrel fermented, with varying degrees of malolactic fermentation, depending very much on the characteristics of the vintage. Acidity levels are high here and a full malolactic fermentation will convert a considerable amount of acidity – very much more, say, than in Hawke's Bay. The 1991 is quite lean in style. The 1992 is quite perfumed and peachy, and Hay considered it successful for the year. He did not chaptalize, but preferred to deacidify and have a full malolactic fermentation, so that both malic and tartaric acid were removed. The 1993 was even more problematic for the wine refused to go through a malolactic fermentation after deacidification, despite three attempts at inoculation. As a result, it has a somewhat curious balance, but still with some buttery fruit. In 1994, Hay made two Chardonnays: Closeburn, after a nearby creek, as well as the Judge and Jury, for which he chose the best fruit, checking the barrels by blind tasting six months later. The emphasis is on fruit in the Closeburn Chardonnay, while the Judge and Jury has some complexity, with a tighter structure and backbone.

Pinot Noir also shows good potential. A reserve wine benefits from a limited amount of new oak, generally about 20 per cent, while the best *cuvée* Bragato enjoys as much as 40 per cent, which will probably increase in forthcoming vintages. It has to be said that Central Otago winemakers suffer from a lack of finance. They cannot always afford to buy the barrels they would like. With the 1993 Bragato, Hay conceded that this was the first time that they could afford to hold some wine back and bottle age it themselves, instead of selling it at the earliest possible moment. There was some good sweet, smoky fruit, with youthful tannins.

In 1992 they made not only their first, but New Zealand's very first ice wine from naturally frozen Riesling grapes harvested in the snow on 22 June. This may be another potential direction for Central Otago. Again, there is a strong sense this is a winery that is building the future of the region.

Chard Farm, Chard Road, (RD 1) Queenstown, telephone/fax: (03) 442 6110

Taramea

While we are still in the Queenstown area, there is one other participant in the industry who deserves a mention, namely Anne Pinkney from Taramea. She was one of the early pioneers of the region, planting her vines in 1982. Her 2-hectare (5-acre) vineyard in the Coronet Valley close to Lake Hayes has had a slightly chequered history, as Pinkney has not been able to devote herself entirely to wine. Although she comes from Southland rather than Otago, she admits that she always had an idea of making wine in Otago. In fact, it was almost an obsession. As a schoolgirl, she made wine in her tuck-box from tamarillos, or tree tomatoes. Then she went to Germany in the mid-1970s and worked there, as well as in Alsace and Australia. It is no surprise, therefore, that Riesling and Gewürztraminer are her two particular enthusiasms. Although she has not made any wine in the last few vintages, for personal as much as for climatic reasons, her 1989 Gewürztraminer drunk in February 1995 had some wonderfully subtle spicy fruit, a gentle, understated and very successful style, with a delicate note of maturity sustained by good acidity.

Speargrass Road, RD1 Queenstown, telephone (03) 442 1453

Rippon Vineyard

If you are driving from Queenstown to Wanaka, you have a choice of roads. The longer, but probably the faster, takes you on a well-tarmacked and cambered road almost to Cromwell, then north to Wanaka. The alternative, which is more exciting for its dramatic scenery and the ruins of an old gold-mining village, takes you in a straighter line over the hills. However, for most of the way it is a bumpy dirt track and is certainly not kind to your car's suspension. Yet Wanaka and Rippon Vineyard are well worth the journey. Rippon must feature in anyone's list of the top ten most spectacular vineyard sites in the world. The vineyards stretch down almost to the shores of Lake Wanaka. On a clear summer's day the lake is a dazzling blue, the water broken up by a small tree-covered island a few hundred yards from the shore. In the background are the mountains of Mount Aspiring National Park which form part of the Southern Alps. When I was there one November, there was still snow on the slopes and in brilliant sunshine the effect was almost too beautiful to be real. It was the picture you expect to see on a Swiss chocolate box.

Rolfe and Lois Mills, who created Rippon Vineyard, are immediately welcoming and hospitable. Their family already owned land there and Rolfe decided to do something with a golden handshake from a previous career. He began by measuring heat summation to see if grapes would actually ripen in Wanaka and set about learning about winemaking. He also took his family to spend nine months in France, not in an obvious choice of location, but in the little backwater village of Sigoulès in the heart of Bergerac. We found ourselves reminiscing about meals in the village café.

Lake Wanaka has a significant effect on the microclimate of the vineyard, for the cold air rolls off the hills straight into the lake so that they have never suffered from frost, even in the coolest years. The vineyards lie at about 1,000 feet in a high basin surrounded by mountains. The days are long. You can still play tennis at ten o'clock on a midsummer's evening, so those long sunshine hours help to ripen the grapes, as indeed does the intensity and clarity of the light. Rainfall tends to be a little higher than in the rest of Central Otago.

Underneath the topsoil there are 8 or 9 feet of gravel of glacial origins which provide very good drainage while retaining a little moisture. The vineyard has gradually expanded over the years so that there are now 12.8 hectares (32 acres), with some newer plantings right on the lakeside. Rolfe and Lois had grand plans for building a winery that would be operated by gravity. Although they seemed to have changed their minds about this, there is no doubt that they need to enlarge the small shed in which their winemaker juggles with as many as nine different wines. Rolfe's enthusiasm led him to plant all sorts of different varieties, some which may not really be suited to the cooler conditions of Otago. There is Syrah, because Rolfe likes it; Cabernet Sauvignon and Merlot, which in recent vintages have tended to be rather green; Osteiner, a grape variety that I had never heard of before which is a Geisenheim cross with some Riesling characteristics; as well as Riesling, Gewürztraminer, Chardonnay, Chenin Blanc, Sémillon and Müller-Thurgau. However, it is Pinot Noir that excites above all the others.

On my first visit they had Austrian winemaker, Rudi Bauer, who set them on the right path in search of the Holy Grail of Pinot Noir. He has now joined the Giesen brothers in Canterbury and for the last three vintages Rippon has benefited from the expertise of talented young French winemaker, Clothilde Chauvet, whose father has vineyards in Champagne. She trained in Montpellier and recognized that she needed to expand her horizons beyond the classic vineyards of Europe. She worked the 1991 vintage with Larry McKenna in Martinborough and visited other wineries while she was in New Zealand, including Rippon, then heard that they were looking for a winemaker.

Her 1993 Pinot Noir is generally considered to be one of the best wines of that vintage, with fruit and structure and layers of complexity. It was drinking deliciously in February 1995, but also had plenty of ageing potential. The 1991, made by Rudi Bauer, was softer in comparison. Chauvet attributes this to the main difference in their winemaking: she has introduced a significant percentage of whole bunches into the fermentation, enhancing the structure of the wine.

Other wines include a Sauvignon that is fermented in old oak barrels and given a substantial percentage of malolactic fermentation. The oak softens some of the acidity on the palate. A Gewürztraminer is delicately spicy and a Riesling lightly slatey with firm acidity. Chardonnay is quite firm and lean, as you will never obtain rich buttery flavours in Central Otago, although a full malolactic fermentation gives more body. We tried different barrel samples from the 1994 vintage, from various coopers: François Frères, Taransaud and Seguin Moreau.

Rippon White is a fruit salad of a wine – Müller-Thurgau, Breidecker, Pinot Gris, Chenin Blanc and Sémillon – with some fresh fruit and high acidity. Chauvet enjoys the flexibility of winemaking in New Zealand, admitting that in France there are so many rules, whereas here you can do just what you like and play with any grape variety you choose. Sadly for Rippon Vineyard, she is returning to France after the 1995 vintage and the Mills are looking for another winemaker.

Rippon Vineyard, Mount Aspiring Road, (PO Box 175) Wanaka, telephone/fax: (03) 443 8084

Black Ridge

I reluctantly left the tranquillity of the lake to head to Black Ridge at Alexandra, where the scenery is much more arid and rugged, with such scraggy hillsides it seems surprising that even vines can survive, but they do. This part of Central Otago is significantly warmer than either Queenstown or Wanaka, a quite distinct area separated from the other two with greater extremes of temperatures, both in summer and winter. It has much less rainfall, an average of 6 inches per year, as opposed to 20 or so at Gibbston Valley.

Verdun Burgess and Sue Edwards are the people behind Black Ridge. Burgess is a carpenter by training, an enthusiastic, extrovert and immediately likeable character whose feet are kept firmly on the ground by Edwards. He is gradually building their winery which has been operational since the 1992 vintage. He also built their house, with its wonderful landscape windows that allow you to enjoy dramatic views of the Otago hillsides while you taste their wines. Although the first vines were planted in 1981, their first vintage was not until 1988 as their young vines suffered badly from frost in the first few years. They now have 6.5 hectares (16 acres) well established with five varietals: Riesling, Gewürztraminer, Chardonnay and Pinot Noir, as well as some Breidecker for cash flow. Gewürztraminer seems to do particularly well here. The 1993 has a dry, elegantly spicy nose, and with good mouthfeel and acidity, without too much weight. The 1994 again shows the same elegant, understated potential. Riesling also performs well, but for a dry style rather than a late harvest wine as the season is not quite long enough. However, they would like to try their hand at making an ice wine.

Pinot Noir has shown a significant improvement in the two years since my first visit and their winemaker Mike Wolter admits to benefiting enormously from the annual New Zealand Pinot Noir conference. Although he is still handicapped by the fact that the vineyards at Black Ridge for the moment only consist of the Bachtobel clone, in 1994 he produced a very appealing peppery, liquorice-flavoured wine that certainly belied the usual reputation of the clone.

Black Ridge Winery, Conroys Road, (PO Box 54) Alexandra, telephone/fax: (03) 449 2059

William Hill

The final winery of any note in Central Otago is William Hill, run by Bill and Jill Grant, or, to give Bill his full name, William Hill Grant. For various reasons, I have never been able to visit them. Apparently they produce Riesling, Gewürztraminer, Chardonnay, Sauvignon Blanc and Pinot Noir. It has grown from just two rows of vines planted as a hobby in 1973, to a fully fledged winery in 1994. Mike Wolter makes their wine, as well as that of Black Ridge, but a tasting opportunity has always escaped me.

William Hill, Dunstan Road, RD 1, Alexandra, telephone: (03) 448 8436, fax: (03) 448 8434

Others are planting vines too, such as John and Judy Currie at Briervale Estate, just outside Alexandra. Their 1.6 hectares (4 acres) of vineyard constitute a veritable hotchpotch of varieties with all manner of vines – Riesling, Pinot Noir, Muscat, Pinot Blanc, Malbec, Merlot, Cabernet Sauvignon, and others – in an attempt to see what will grow. They admit to suffering badly from frost and in 1993 made just 100 litres of Riesling and 15 litres of Pinot Noir. The Riesling had some appealing slatey flavours. They are not alone in their enthusiasm. There are numerous other small growers planting a few acres, maybe as little as one. With the proliferation of planting in the region and lack of wineries, there may be an opportunity for an operation similar to Vintech in Marlborough to accommodate the numerous growers.

There is no doubt, despite the scorn poured upon the early plantings in Central Otago, that the wine is there to stay and with each vintage it becomes increasingly well established. It is not easy, for production costs are high. Alan Brady refused to tell me how much he would pay for grapes, but the price is so much higher than that of contract growers further north and the yields per acre are low. Some vineyards are affected by frost, which means that site selection is a prime consideration for success. With high costs, the price of the wine in the bottle is inevitably expensive. The better wines of Central Otago are presented in an elegant tapered bottle which is highly distinctive and eye-catching, but a nightmare in practice for it does not fit a standard bottling line, or an average wine carton, and when binned in a cellar it wobbles precariously.

One thing that immediately strikes you is the camaraderie in this pioneering region. Clothilde Chauvet, who is used to the rather more closed approach of the average French winemaking community, commented enthusiastically on the way the four professional winemakers in Central Otago meet regularly to taste each other's wines, as well as wines from other regions. This would rarely happen in France, nor would her colleagues be so ready to help out with a problem. There is a great spirit of adventure in these southernmost vineyards of the world. They may never be part of the mainstream of the New Zealand wine industry, but their potential is developing, certainly for Pinot Noir, probably for aromatic white varieties, and maybe for ice wine, given their climatic extremes. There is also a view, as yet unproven, that sparkling wine may provide the *raison d'être* of many of the new vineyards. Certainly, the future expansion will not be without its problems, but there are also encouraging successes, epitomized by Rippon's 1993 Pinot Noir, with others following closely on its heels.

18

An Overview of Recent Vintages:
1991–95

New Zealand is a long country and climatic conditions in the different regions can vary quite considerably. A good vintage in Marlborough does not necessarily mean a successful vintage in Hawke's Bay, or vice versa.

1995 This was a difficult vintage, but despite the problems some good wines have been made, and also some bad ones.

The most successful area was Central Otago, where they enjoyed a dry summer, with long hours of sunshine and not a drop of rain from *véraison* right through to the end of the harvest, making it their best vintage for several years. Canterbury also had a fine summer, resulting in some good wines, while Marlborough and Nelson suffered badly from rain during the harvest. In Marlborough, it was a season of extremes, with a very dry October and December and a wet November, followed by more rain in January, February and March. The combination of humidity and warmth inevitably caused problems with rot, resulting in a huge variation in quality. People who had worked well in the vineyard achieved better results in the cellars. Nelson, lying closer to the west coast, was even wetter, with Riesling and Sauvignon the prime casualties. Pinot Noir and Chardonnay are more successful.

Martinborough had a difficult harvest, with six weeks' picking condensed into three. There were some problems with rot, but the red wines have turned out better than initially expected, with good fruit and colour, though maybe slightly lacking in concentration.

In Hawke's Bay they had severe drought conditions from December right through to March. Most of the Chardonnay was picked before the rain, which came as the red grapes were being harvested. However, it did not do too much damage and those who worked well have made successful reds in 1995. One view is that the flavours for red wine are determined by the weather in January and December, which was warm, making for grapes that essentially were ripe. Montana consider their Church Road reds to be better than the 1994s and the better wineries are very happy with the results. It is very much a question of those who are conscientious and talented making fine wines, in contrast with those who are not.

Generally, Gisborne, with more earlier ripening varieties, fared the best of the North Island regions, producing good Chardonnay and also Gewürztraminer.

Auckland and the Waikato suffered with rain after a fine summer. Waiheke had its hopes for its best vintage ever dashed by rain. It was hot and dry until two weeks before the harvest, but none the less the reds have good fruit, though may slightly lack concentration.

David Hoskins in Matakana described 1995 as his poorest vintage since he began in 1991. The rain started in mid-January and continued intermittently throughout the season, causing problems with fungal disease. He picked no Cabernet Sauvignon at all.

To sum up, generalizations are impossible and it all depends on the individual producers. I have tasted some delicious 1995 Sauvignons with good fruit, while others were distinctly European in style – that is to say, dilute.

1994 New Zealand felt that it had finally shaken off the lingering effects of the eruption of Mount Pinatubo in the Philippines. After a cool spring, the summer temperatures were distinctly warmer than the previous two years throughout the country, with fine weather at flowering having a beneficial effect on yields. There is much more uniformity between the various regions than in 1995.

Auckland experienced drought conditions, resulting in ripe grapes and fine wines. Waiheke produced good ripe fruit, and Northland was hot and dry. In Gisborne, the summer was warm and sunny with the odd patch of rain, but nothing to cause problems. Hawke's Bay enjoyed baking-hot days in January which benefited the red grapes. There was a drop of rain in March and good ripe grapes in the vineyards. Martinborough produced some of the best wine since 1991.

In Marlborough, the summer came after a cool spring and was

followed by a long dry, sunny autumn, which produced wonderful ripe fruit. Nelson enjoyed similar conditions, while Canterbury was still cooler than average, with more rain in the spring and summer, but none the less produced some good wines. Central Otago had a difficult year, with a cool summer and more than average rainfall, but everything came right in the end with the long autumn.

1993 In 1993, Auckland was the success story of the country, enjoying a wonderful warm summer. Spring came late and the summer was relatively dry and followed by a warm, dry autumn. Waiheke also enjoyed warm conditions, while Northland, in contrast, was cool and dry.

In Gisborne, the spring and early summer were cool and wet, and after a fine, warm January, rainfall in February was the highest since 1936. However, some good white wines were made.

In Hawke's Bay, everything was late, from budburst to the flowering and then the harvest. The summer was one of the coolest on record, resulting in variable reds but some good whites.

Martinborough had its latest ever harvest, following a late cool summer. The early-ripening Pinot Noir and Chardonnay developed relatively well, while the later ripening varieties enjoyed an Indian summer throughout most of May.

Marlborough suffered from the late season, with cool weather delaying budburst and cloudy weather at flowering. The harvest, although late, took place in good weather. In Nelson, too, everything was late, with a cooler summer than average and some rain in February, followed by a warm spell which ripened the grapes satisfactorily.

In Canterbury and Central Otago, too, everything was affected by the much cooler than average season.

1992 In 1992, New Zealand suffered from the effects of the eruption of Mount Pinatubo in the Philippines which created a shading layer of volcanic ash in the upper atmosphere, reducing light intensity and temperatures. In addition, the weather was affected by the wind pattern known as El Nino and the combination of the two resulted in a cool season, beginning with spring frosts and rain. Cool weather at flowering reduced the yield and resulted in a later than average harvest.

Auckland had a cool growing season, so did Waiheke and Northland. Gisborne produced some good wines, with a warmer February and March, and low rainfall.

Hawke's Bay had a damp, cool spring and a slightly cooler than average summer, followed by a long dry autumn, which produced some good white wines. The reds benefited from the low crop. Martinborough was cooler and wetter than usual, and affected by early and late frosts.

Nelson had a late cool spring, with some rain at flowering. The early summer was cooler and wetter than usual, but late summer was warm and dry. Although the harvest was late, the grapes were ripe.

Marlborough had the third coolest season since 1948. It was windy but dry and the reduced crop ripened satisfactorily. Canterbury suffered spring frosts, and cold weather at flowering reduced yields, but the warm and dry late summer and autumn produced good fruit. Central Otago suffered lower temperatures and a difficult vintage.

1991 1991 was generally a later harvest than usual, but with a good overall quality. Auckland, Waiheke and Northland enjoyed good conditions, with a dry spring, as well as a dry late summer and autumn. Gisborne and Hawke's Bay both had a windy and cool spring, some rain in January and February, and a fine late summer, making for good ripe fruit. Martinborough produced some fine reds.

Marlborough had a hot, dry spring with an early flowering, followed by a long hot summer. Good wines were made in Nelson, too, as well as in Canterbury and Central Otago.

Appendices

APPENDIX 1 Summary – New Zealand Wine Industry Statistics (1985–95)

	1985	1986	1987	1988	1989	1990	1991	1992	1993	1994	*1995
Total Vine Area (hectares)	6,000	4,500	n/a	4,880	5,440	5,800	5,980	6,100	6,100	6,680	7,500
Producing Area (hectares)	5,900	4,300	4,300	4,300	4,370	4,880	5,440	5,800	5,980	6,110	6,110
Average Yield (tonnes per hectare)	13.2	12.7	11.6	12.0	13.8	14.4	12.1	9.3	7.1	8.8	12.2
Tonnes Crushed	78,000	54,694	49,727	51,509	60,335	70,265	65,708	55,500	42,621	54,000	74,500

*Estimate

APPENDIX 2 National Vineyard Areas by Variety
As at 30 June 1995, ranked by total area, showing % change from
1994

Variety	Producing		% Change	Total		% Change
	1994	1995		1994	1995	
Chardonnay	1,307	1,385	6	1,439	1,917	25
Sauvignon Blanc	852	936	9	1,062	1,472	28
Müller-Thurgau	1,014	885	−15	1,058	992	−7
Cabernet Sauvignon	549	526	−4	626	753	17
Pinot Noir	428	415	−3	447	569	21
Merlot	229	282	19	272	435	37
Riesling	285	289	2	288	427	33
Sémillon	175	183	5	188	231	19
Dr Hogg Muscat	222	204	−9	222	228	3
Chenin Blanc	177	145	−22	209	186	−12
Unknown	19	70	73	1,359	156	−774
Gewürtztraminer	134	124	−8	136	138	1
Others	103	90	−14	105	121	13
Cabernet Franc	82	80	−3	89	113	22
Reichensteiner	98	98	0	98	98	0
Golden Chasselas	95	87	−10	96	90	−6
Pinotage	77	66	−16	77	73	−6
Palamino	84	72	−16	84	72	−16
Pinot Gris	19	23	16	19	38	50
Shiraz	16	14	−14	20	38	47
Breidecker	26	26	2	26	27	4
Sylvaner	35	25	−40	35	25	−40
Flora	27	23	−16	27	23	−16
Albany Surprise	12	19	37	12	21	43
Blauberger	17	18	7	18	18	2
Malbec	14	11	−27	16	17	8
Pinot Blanc	6	4	−50	6	6	−5
Chambourcin	3	5	34	3	5	34
Gamay	2	1	−81	2	2	−25
Total	6,107	6,108	0	8,039	8,293	3

*NOTE: includes vines planted but not in full production and vines planted winter
1995

Appendix 3A New Zealand Vintages (1986–95)

By Grape Variety (Tonnes)

	1986	1987	1988	1989	1990	1991	1992	1993	1994	1995
Müller-Thurgau	20,740	19,458	19,411	21,438	25,767	21,992	17,491	10,229	13,687	15,387
Chardonnay	2,594	2,777	2,722	4,472	6,026	6,422	6,172	5,301	8,786	12,346
Sauvignon Blanc	2,096	1,837	1,993	2,911	4,659	5,554	6,137	5,705	5,083	11,015
Chenin Blanc	4,718	3,128	3,402	3,624	3,652	3,172	2,446	1,401	2,112	2,428
Gewürztraminer	1,345	786	979	2,043	1,716	1,643	592	429	732	985
Palomino	3,103	2,422	2,485	2,132	2,446	1,900	1,988	1,224	1,197	1,487
Riesling	1,885	2,546	2,765	3,248	3,658	3,178	3,144	2,204	2,699	2,949
Muscat Varieties	3,210	3,203	4,484	5,918	6,881	6,053	4,350	3,274	4,181	5,036
Sémillon	n/a	923	1,081	1,185	1,443	1,431	1,317	1,125	1,385	2,528
Chasselas	n/a	1,163	1,592	1,292	1,401	1,654	1,210	719	779	1,126
Sylvaner	n/a	n/a	877	1,034	932	762	621	305	381	313
Reichensteiner	n/a	n/a	983	1,248	1,599	1,500	1,335	1,055	1,324	1,867
Other White Varieties	7,563	2,888	802	1,093	1,122	1,080	819	683	813	928
Cabernet Sauvignon	2,591	2,586	3,143	3,306	3,148	3,238	2,596	2,091	2,689	4,360
Pinot Noir	1,216	980	729	1,088	1,425	2,054	1,597	1,880	2,593	4,480
Pinotage	725	583	941	964	860	940	615	596	832	1,097
Merlot	362	286	562	722	1,062	1,018	803	711	1,237	2,660
Cabernet Franc	n/a	n/a	n/a	n/a	326	307	252	309	373	637
Other Black Varieties	187	182	262	336	262	281	275	266	330	354
All White Hybrids	475	119	147	245	251	97	101	122	141	204
All Black Hybrids	268	142	114	258	246	205	81	160	137	339
Total	53,078	46,009	49,474	58,557	68,882	64,481	53,942	39,789	51,491	72,526
Industry TOTAL	54,694	49,727	51,509	60,335	70,265	65,708	55,500	42,621	54,000	74,500

APPENDIX 3B By Region (tonnes)

	1986	1987	1988	1989	1990	1991	1992	1993	1994	1995
Auckland	n/a	n/a	2,070	1,981	1,818	1,788	1,150	1,585	1,185	1,874
Waikato/BOP	n/a	n/a	875	746	681	616	430	449	505	617
Gisborne	n/a	n/a	13,420	21,884	24,255	23,185	19,502	13,169	17,555	22,289
Hawke's Bay	n/a	n/a	16,678	17,155	20,302	18,601	14,244	8,431	15,116	20,632
Wellington	n/a	n/a	n/a	n/a	n/a	371	280	372	501	933
Marlborough	n/a	n/a	16,265	16,425	21,385	19,122	17,735	15,115	18,851	24,509
Nelson	n/a	n/a	n/a	n/a	n/a	359	248	376	366	683
Canterbury	n/a	n/a	n/a	n/a	n/a	343	234	235	197	756
Otago	n/a	n/a	n/a	n/a	n/a	56	71	56	125	168
Other	n/a	n/a	167	366	441	40	49	0	90	64
Total	53,078	46,009	49,475	58,557	68,882	64,481	53,943	39,788	51,491	72,526
Industry TOTAL	54,694	49,727	51,509	60,335	70,265	65,708	55,500	42,621	54,000	*74,500

*NOTE: The data shown are the results from the Institute's Annual Vintage Surveys, whereas 'Industry Total' represents the tonnes crushed by the total wine industry. The difference between 'Total' and 'Industry Total' is data from wine companies who did not respond to the Vintage Survey.

SOURCE: Wine Institute Annual Vintage Surveys.

APPENDICES

APPENDIX 4 National Vineyard Areas by Region
as at 30 June 1995, ranked by total area in hectares, showing % change from 1994

Variety	Producing		% Change	Total		% Change
	1994	1995		1994	1995	
Marlborough	2,095	2,123	1	3,000	3,233	7
Hawke's Bay	1,642	1,776	8	2,268	2,276	0
Gisborne	1,427	1,356	−5	1,464	1,514	3
Canterbury	208	216	4	260	325	20
Wellington-Wairarapa	188	189	0	275	271	−1
Auckland	248	215	−15	272	248	−9
Otago	48	47	−3	237	152	−56
Nelson	92	70	−32	102	137	25
Te Kauwhata	159	118	−35	161	137	−18
Total	6,107	6,108	0%	8,039	8,293	3%

*NOTE: includes vines planted but not yet in full production and vines planted winter 1995

Bibliography

Tim Atkin, *Chardonnay*, Viking, 1992

Andrew Barr, *Pinot Noir*, Viking, 1992

Stephen Brook, *Sauvignon Blanc and Sémillon*, Viking, 1992

C. Brooks, *Marlborough Wines and Vines*, 1982

Michael Cooper, *The Wines and Vineyards of New Zealand*, 3rd ed., 1988, 4th ed., 1993, Hodder & Stoughton

Len Evans and Frank Thorpy, *Australia and New Zealand Complete Book of Wine*, 1974

James Halliday, *Wine Atlas of Australia and New Zealand*, 1991, HarperCollins

Richard Hough, *Captain James Cook: A Biography*, Hodder & Stoughton, 1994

Stuart Piggot, *Riesling*, Viking, 1992

Jancis Robinson, *Vines, Grapes and Wines*, London, Mitchell Beazley, 1989

Dick Scott, *Winemakers of New Zealand*, Southern Cross, 1964

Dick Scott, *A Stake in the Country, A. A. Corban and Family, 1892–1977*, Southern Cross, 1977

P. Shaw and P. Hallett, *Art Deco Napier*, Craig Potton Publishing, New Zealand, 1987

André Simon, *A New Zealand Holiday*, Wine & Food, Autumn 1964

Richard Smart, *Sunlight into Wine*, Wine Titles, Adelaide, 1991

Frank Thorpy, *Wine in New Zealand*, Collins Bros, New Zealand, 1971

Romea Bragato, *Report on the Prospects of Viticulture in New Zealand 1895*

Wine Institute Wine Annual Reports

New Zealand Wine Annuals, Cuisine Publications

Index

INDEX

Chan, Nick, 119
Chan, Stanley, 149
Chard Farm, 67, 298–300
Chardonnay grapes, 5, 6, 34, 54,
59–65, 94
Chasselas grapes, 22, 74
Château Pétrus, 82, 117
Chauvet, Clothilde, 76, 86, 302–3, 305
Chenin Blanc grapes, 75–6
Chifney, Stan, 32, 75, 208, 215–16
Chifney Wines, 215–16
Chignell, Michelle, 102
Christchurch, 270
Church Road Winery, 81, 186–8
Cinsaut grapes, 89, 90
Clark, Rice Owen, 117
Clarke, Allan, 42, 47, 54, 59, 92
Clearview Estate Winery, 180–1
Clos de Ste-Anne, 163
Closeburn Chardonnay, 299
Cloudy Bay Vineyards, 2, 30, 46, 49,
57, 95, 242, 246–8
sparkling wine (Pelorus), 93, 95–6,
247–8
Coleraine, 196
Collard, Brian, 109, 110
Collard, Bruce, 109, 110
Collard, Geoffrey, 109, 110
Collard, John, 109
Collard, Lionel, 75, 109–10
Collard Brothers, 75, 109–10
Compton, Mark, 145, 146
Conders Bend Wines, 267–8
Coney, John, 152
Continental, 103
contract grape growers, 25, 33–4
Cook, Captain James, 155, 170, 237
Cooks, 29, 112–13, 186–7, 245
Cooper, Jane, 229
Coopers Creek Vineyard, 64, 110–11
Corban, Alex, 21, 71, 101, 112
Corban, Alwyn, 112, 190–1
Corban, Assid Abraham, 17, 112
Corban, Joe, 45–6, 47, 71, 112
Corbans Wines, 26, 71, 90, 132
Auckland region, 15, 16, 112–13
Cooks, 29, 112–13, 186–7, 245
Gisborne region, 158, 168–9
Hawke's Bay region, 113, 181–2,
186–7
history of, 15, 16, 21, 23, 112–13
Marlborough region (Stoneleigh),
67, 87, 113, 242, 243, 245–6
sparkling wine, 96, 182

Cordier, 81, 187
Cork and Bottle, 1
Corporate Investments, 132
Cortese grapes, 92
Cottage Block, 113, 168, 181–2, 245
Covell, Bob, 154
Covell, Desarei, 154
Covell Estate, 154
Cowley, Peter, 195
Craighill Estate, 211, 212
Craike, J. O., 16, 173
Crawford, Kim, 111, 266
Creech, Wyatt, 218
Cresta Doré, 23, 28, 72, 176
Crone, Keith, 201–2
Crossroads Wine Company, 182–3
Culley, Neil, 107
Currie, John, 304
Currie, Judy, 304
Cyprien, Brother, 171

d'Abbans, Count Alexandre, 171
Dagaud & Jaegle, 61, 63
Dartmoor Vineyard, 200–1
Darwin, Charles, 9
Dashwood Sauvignon, 251
DB Group, 113
De Redcliffe, 24, 145–6
Delegat, Jim, 20, 114
Delegat, Nikola, 114
Delegat, Rose, 20, 114
Delegat, Vida, 20
Delegat's Wine Estate, 24, 29, 60, 61,
114–15
Demptos Frères, 61, 167
Deutz Champagne, 94, 188
Deutz Cuvée Marlborough, 93, 94–5
Dicey, Robin, 295
Dixon Vineyard, 124
Dobson, Arthur, 270
Dolcetto grapes, 91
Domaine Chandon, 24, 97, 249–50
Domett, Alfred, 170
Donaldson, Christine, 288
Donaldson, Ivan, 79–80, 81, 288
Donaldson, Matthew, 67, 288, 289
Dr Hogg Muscat grapes, 73
Draper, Robin, 217
Draper, Tom, 217
Drappier, Michel, 96, 256
Dry River Wines, 68, 69, 78, 211–13
Drylands Vineyard, 128, 254
du Fresne, Viggo, 227–8
Dubordieu, Denis, 57, 58, 200